The Spice and Spirit of Kosher ~ Jewish Cooking

ב"ה

Lubavitch Women's Organization — Junior Division

Distributed by BLOCH PUBLISHING COMPANY INC. NEW YORK, N.Y.

Published and Copyright © 1977
by Lubavitch Women's Organization: Junior Division
Brooklyn, New York

Library of Congress Catalog Card Number: 77-72116

ISBN: 0-930178-01-7

For Information write to:

Cookbook
Lubavitch Women's Organization
770 Eastern Parkway
Brooklyn, N.Y. 11213 U.S.A.

Printed in the United States of America

A Message from the Lubavitcher Rebbe שליט"א

Rabbi Menachem M. Schneerson

The Role of the Jewish Home –
Primarily Entrusted to the Woman

. . . In a Jewish household, the wife and mother, the <u>akeres habayis</u>, largely determines the set-up and atmosphere of the entire home.

G-d demands that the Jewish home—every Jewish home—be quite different from a non-Jewish home, not only on <u>Shabbos</u> and <u>Yom Tov</u>, but also on the ordinary weekdays and in "weekday" matters. It must be a <u>Jewish</u> home in every respect.

What makes a Jewish household different from a non-Jewish household is that it is conducted in all its details according to the directives of the <u>Torah</u>, <u>Toras Chayim</u>—meaning that it is the Jew's Guide in daily life—given by G-d. Hence the home becomes an abode for G-d's Presence, a home for G-dliness, one of which G-d says: "Make Me a sanctuary, and I shall dwell among them." (Exod. 25:5).

It is a home where G-d's Presence is felt not only on <u>Shabbos</u> and <u>Yom Tov</u>, but on every day of the week; and not only when <u>davenning</u> and learning <u>Torah</u>, but also when engaged in very ordinary things, such as eating and <u>drinking</u>, etc., in accordance with the directive, "Know Him in all your ways".

It is a home where mealtime is not a time for indulging in ordinary and natural "eating habits" but a hallowed service to G-d, where the table is an "altar" to G-d, sanctified by the washing of the hands before the meal, reciting the blessings over the food, and Grace after the meal, with every item of food and beverage brought into the home being strictly <u>kosher</u>.

It is a home where the mutual relationship between husband and wife is sanctified by the meticulous observance of the laws and regulations of <u>Taharas Hamishpocho</u>, and permeated with awareness of the active third "Partner"—G-d—in creating new life, in fulfilment of the Divine commandment: "Be fruitful and multiply". This also ensures that Jewish children are born in purity and holiness, with pure hearts and minds that will enable them to resist temptation and avoid the pitfalls of the environment when they grow up. Moreover, the strict observance of <u>Taharas Hamishpocho</u> is a basic factor in the preservation of peace and harmony (<u>Sholom Bayis</u>) in the home, which is vitally strengthened and fortified thereby—obviously, a basic factor in the preservation of the family as a unit.

It is a home where the parents know that their first obligation is to instill into their offspring from their most tender age on, the love of G-d and also the fear of G-d, permeating them with the joy of performing <u>mitzvos</u>. With all their desire to provide their children with all the good things in life, the Jewish parent must know that the greatest, indeed the only real and eternal, legacy they can bequeath to their children is to make the <u>Torah</u> and <u>mitzvos</u> and traditions their life-source and guide in daily life.

In all that has been said above, the Jewish wife and mother—the <u>akeres habayis</u>—has a primary role, second to none.

It is largely—and in many respects exclusively—her great task and privilege to give her home its truly Jewish atmosphere. She has been entrusted with, and is completely in charge of, the <u>kashrus</u> of the foods and beverages that come into her kitchen and on the dining table.

She has been given the privilege of ushering in the holy <u>Shabbos</u> by lighting the candles on Friday, in ample time before sunset. Thus she actually and symbolically brightens up her home with peace and harmony and with the light of <u>Torah</u> and <u>mitzvos</u>. It is largely in her merits that G-d bestows the blessing of true happiness on her husband and children and the entire household.

In addition to such <u>mitzvos</u> as candle-lighting, <u>challah</u> and others which the <u>Torah</u> entrusted primarily to Jewish daughters, there are matters which, in the natural order of things, lie in the woman's domain. The reason for this being so in the natural order is that it stems from the supra-natural order of holiness, which is the source and origin of the good in the physical world. We refer, of course, to the observance of <u>Taharas Hamishpocho</u> which, in the nature of it, is in the hands of the Jewish women. The husband is required to encourage and facilitate this mutual observance; certainly not hinder it in any way, G-d forbid. But the main responsibility—and privilege—is the wife's.

This is the great task and mission which G-d gave to Jewish women—to observe and disseminate the observance of <u>Taharas Hamishpocho</u>, and of the other vital institutions of Jewish family life. For besides being the fundamental <u>mitzvos</u> and the cornerstone of the sanctity of Jewish family life, as well as relating to the wellbeing of the children in body and soul—these pervade and extend through all Jewish generations to eternity.

Finally, it is to be remembered that the Creator has provided each and every Jewish woman with the capacity to carry them out in daily life in the fullest measure, for otherwise, it would not be logical or fair of G-d to give obligations and duties which are impossible to fulfill.

The points mentioned above—all too briefly in relation to their vital importance for our people Israel, individually and collectively, especially in the present day and age, as discussed at greater length elsewhere—should be the objects of intensive and widespread activity by Jewish women everywhere. There is a crying need to bring them to the attention, and within living experience, of the widest possible Jewish circles. There can be no danger of overemphasizing these vital aspects of Jewish life, nor of overpublishing on these subjects. Every additional volume is to be heartily welcomed . . .

Table of Contents

• • •

Agudas N'shei Ubonos Chabad

The Chabad Movement

There is scarcely a corner of the world that has not felt the warming touch of the *Lubavitch* movement. Lubavitch, often known as *Chabad*, was founded over two centuries ago by the saintly Rabbi Schneur Zalman of Liadi. The movement is based on the *Chassidic* philosophy revealed two generations earlier by the Baal Shem Tov. This philosophy places particular emphasis on *Ahavas Yisroel*-the love for, and preciousness of each and every Jew, and also on serving G-d with our heart and soul filled with love and happiness in performing His Divine mitzvos.

CHaBaD Chassidus derives its name from the three intellectual faculties, *Chochmah* (wisdom), *Binah* (understanding), and *Da'as* (knowledge), which are at the basis of its philosophy. These faculties add depth and meaning to the Baal Shem Tov's work by paving a way which combines intellectual understanding of G-d and the Torah with the unquestioning faith and love commanded of each Jew. One without the other can only create a void. Knowledge of Torah without true feeling for it leaves the heart out, in service to G-d. On the other hand, a person cannot just feel or desire a closeness with the A-mighty. In order to attain that closeness he must learn and understand what G-d wants him to do on earth. Only with both the desire and the knowledge can one's service to G-d be complete.

The Chabad movement later became known as Lubavitch, the name of the city where it was situated for several generations. Lubavitch means "city of brotherly love," a most fitting name for the movement.

As high and lofty as Chabad ideals are, they cannot and do not remain in the realm of theory. Everything must be transmitted into action. These ideals must be incorporated into our daily lives, for ourselves and also for every Jew whom we meet. Indeed, under the inspiring leadership of our revered Lubavitcher Rebbe *Shlita*, Rabbi M.M. Schneersohn, the Chabad movement, always loved and admired in past generations, has now become a major influence for the good of all world Jewry.

Although its main headquarters are in Brooklyn, N.Y., Chabad now has centers in all parts of the globe. Chabad houses, centers and schools can be found in nearly every state in the United States, and in such places as South America, Africa, Europe, Australia, and Canada. Chabad is also extremely active in Israel with several settlements, centers, and yeshivohs throughout the land.

Agudas N'shei Ubonos Chabad

What about the women and girls of Chabad?

Indeed when we refer to the movement we mean the women as well as the men, for Torah recognizes the greatness of women, and *Chassidus* develops this to its fullest. The women's and girl's organization, known as *Agudas N'shei Ubnos Chabad*, is guided and inspired in their work by the Rebbe *Shlita*, who often directs his message to the great potential of women, citing instances where their influence was and is greater than those of men and boys.

Agudas N'shei Ubnos Chabad, actually involves each and every woman and girl in Lubavitch. Members of the organization bear its name proudly, contributing to its many projects and functions. Because of its wide variety of activities, every woman and girl is able to find a means of bringing out her individual talents. Agudas N'shei Ubnos Chabad is involved with informing and teaching, learning groups, speaking at lectures, and opening their homes to a variety of guests. The objective of these women is not merely to tell others what Judaism is about, but rather to inspire them by showing them the practices and values of a Torah woman, especially through the warmth and closeness found in a Chassidic home.

The Agudas N'shei Ubnos Chabad places special emphasis on bringing the message of Torah to the Jewish woman, and particularly to the main mitzvos entrusted to her. These involve the observance of a warm and meaningful Shabbos and Yom Tov, ushered in by the lighting of candles; the kashrus of the home; and the maintenance of the Divine Laws of family purity, laws which give birth to a nation healthy in body and soul. The strength and influence of the woman in raising the family is of great magnitude. She is known in Jewish teachings as the *Akeres Habayis*—the pillar of the home. It is through the mother that the religion of a child is determined at birth, and she continues to be the strongest influence on him. This is not to say that all the activities of Agudas N'shei Ubnos Chabad are directed only at the above mitzvos, for indeed Jewish women are involved in all aspects of Torah life.

The girls, the Bnos Chabad are not merely functioning under the mother shadow—but are an extremely active group on their own. In addition to energetically being involved in many Chabad functions, they also have a great variety of activities—outings, crafts, classes, and meeting with other girls their own age, showing them the warmth of Lubavitch, and inspiring them to a meaningful fulfillment of Torah and mitzvos. The energy and enthusiasm of Bnos Chabad shows how G-d's Will is beautiful and relevant to every teenage Jewish girl, even in current times.

Highlights of the organization's activities include the two conventions held every year—one in the headquarters in Brooklyn, and the other hosted by a sister group in another city. Chabad women and girls from all over the country meet together, and are often priviledged to be addressed by newly arrived Russian immigrants, or by Lubavitch women from other continents, who come to share their experiences and ideas, and to take the experiences and ideas of others back to their own N'shei Ubnos groups.

The time and talents which the women contribute are nearly always on a voluntary basis. Many assume leadership of large projects which might be tantamount to a full time job. This book too is the result of a voluntary community effort by the women and girls of Chabad under the guidance of the Junior Division of the women's organization. Motivated by the needs of world Jewry today, many have been able to work tirelessly on this and many other projects.

In these ways the women and girls of Chabad are ever widening their activities and scope of influence, with the gratifying knowledge that each action of theirs, coupled with each action of every Jew everywhere, brings added physical and spiritual light to the world. With increasing speed we come ever closer to the true hope and ideal of every Jew— the coming of Messiah speedily in our days, when "all the world will be filled with the knowledge of G-d."

In Gratitude

Words cannot adequately express our appreciation to the many people who generously granted so much of their time and their talent to aid in the development of this book. Their valuable advice and encouragement supported us throughout. We cannot repay our debt to you all. May the fruits that the book bears be as our payment.

To our whole community and to the many other friends of Chabad who helped make this a true communal effort we, the editors, extend our heartfelt thanks; to mention you all by name would require another section. You inspired us toward a much fuller realization of the potential found in our original seed of an idea. You helped us see the extent of the need for such a book and its importance to the Jewish public. You offered constructive criticism and allowed us to make use of your skills and creativity. As Rabbis you shared your knowledge and expertise with us to improve all aspects of the book. Without all of you *The Spice and Spirit of Kosher Jewish Cooking* would not have been possible.

To our mothers, our deepest gratitude for so patiently teaching us our culinary arts, combined with the inspiration of its relevance to the Jewish home in general, the Shabbos, Holidays and special occasions; for giving us an understanding and appreciation of all the dietary laws;—and above all on raising us to be fulfilled Jewish women.

We offer our thanks, most of all, to the One Who with an unseen and yet increasingly evident hand guided all the events leading to the production of this book: to G-d A-mighty, Who makes all things possible.

Many thanks to all of the following without whose dedication and invaluable help this book could not have been produced.

Contributors
S. Avtzon
Mr. M. Friedman
Rabbi Goldshmid
Fayge Jacobson
Sara Leiberman
Sara Pinson
Rochel Rubin
Rabbi Zurkind

Recipe Consultants
Rochel Duchman
Yachet Eichorn
Malka Simon
Ray Schildkraut

Production Staff
Devorah Layeh Avtzon
Bina Tirzah Berman
Adela Bernstein
Dinah Borenstein
Mindy Borenstein
Chasha Brownstein
Yetta Chrin
Brina Doman
Nechama Eichorn
Judy Lawrence
Dobra Levitt
Menucha Moser
Chaya Perman

Malka Podrizki
Avi Popack
Nechama Pruss
Pesha Fraida Rasnick
Fayge Rubenfeld
Fayge Seewald
Bronya Shaffer
Fayge Silberman
Leah Silberman
Tamar Strauss
Chaya Sudolsky
Gittel Susskind
Alessa Wircberg

Recipe Contributors

Esther Abehsera
Yehudis Abrams
Fraida Andrusier
Devorah Antecol
Mrs. B. Avtzon
Devorah Barnett
Chaya Leah Berger
Adela Bernstein
Itka Brill
Mrs. H. Blau
Esther Blau
Mrs. Chaitovsky
Freeda Cohen
Mrs. Cukier
Bina Cunin
Meryl Dalven
Bonnie Deitsch
Cyrel Deitsch
Mrs. M. Deitsch
Mrs. J. Dubrowsky
Mrs. Rochel Duchman
Mrs. Edelman
Mrs. Eichenthal
Yachet Eichorn
Mrs. Toby Epstein
Mrs. Fried
Mimi Furst
Mrs. Garfinkel
Mrs. R. Geisinsky
Mrs. Adela Gittelman
Rochel Gluck
Leah Goldberg

Malka Goldberg
Raizelle Goldberg
Leah Goldberger
Mrs. Goldstein
Seema Goldstein
Mrs. Yehudis Gottlieb
Rochel Gottlieb
Mindel Halberstam
Esther Horowitz
Miriam Hurwitz
Fayge Jacobson
Edie Jaffe
Chaya Fraida Kahan
Mrs. N. Kaplinsky
Chaya Rivkah Kaplinsky
Sara Karasik
Zysie Klein
Chanie Kovacs
Zahava Krevsky
Mrs. Ruth Krinsky
Henia Laine
Hinda Langer
Mrs. Tziporah Lapa
Michla Laufer
Mrs. Gloria Lauterbach
Mrs. Martha Lauterbach
Judy Lawrence
Mrs. M. Levertov
Freeda Levertow
Chavie Levine
Chanie Levitin
Susan Levitin
Chana Levitt

Rosie Melamud
Sandy Newman
Chaya Ohana
Chaya Perman
Avi Popack
Mrs. Rosenfeld
Gertrude Rosenfeld
Mrs. H. Rosenfeld
Marilyn Rosenfeld
Faigy Rubenfeld
Sylvia Rubenfeld
Rochel Sandman
Frida Schapiro
Mrs. Schneid
Mrs. Ann Schildkraut
Mrs. Ray Schildkraut
Chaya Sara Silberberg
Leah Silverstein
Mrs. Malka Simon
Mrs. J. Spira
Martha Stock
Shterna Tenenbaum
Mrs. Ella Tilles
Shulamit Tilles
Chana Tornek
Cherry Uhlman
Sari Veshlizer
Mrs. Weiss
Mrs. R. Wilschanski
Mrs. Lottie Winnetz
Ella Zeiler
Mrs. S. Zuber
Mrs. Zurkind

Preface

THE SPICE AND SPIRIT OF KOSHER JEWISH COOKING is, as its name implies, a unique blend of many concepts. Many Jewish cookbooks are available today, but few provide extensive information on the dietary laws which are the focal point of the Jewish kitchen, and none presents as rich and authoritative a foundation in Jewish lore as we have attempted to provide within these pages.

The recipes, representing "spice," are from the kitchens of women who excel in culinary arts. This book has been a community project, and the recipe variety is indicative of the wide range of lifestyle and taste found in a cross-section of our community. You will find recipes for whole-grain challah as well as homemade wine and gefilte fish, chicken soup, and tempting cakes and traditional Jewish foods for every Jewish occasion — and the year is bursting with Jewish occasions, as you will discover as you read the book through. The essays on Kashrus, Shabbos, Jewish Holidays and "Yiddishe Simchas" represent the "spirit" in Jewish cooking and living that we want to share with our readers. These various aspects of the book are inevitably intertwined, especially in connection with food, and it has been difficult to separate one section from another. Cross references have been made wherever they were deemed most helpful.

To derive the most benefit from this book we recommend reading through the book at least once for both pleasure and general information. Later you can refer back to those sections most relevant to the occasion or time of year. Below is an overview of the book's contents.

The Recipes

The recipes in *The Spice and Spirit of Kosher Jewish Cooking* are presented in menu order: beginning with challah or bread and ending with dessert, with a choice of meals based on dairy (Section 5), fish (Section 7) or meat and poultry (Sections 8-9). All other recipes are *pareve* (neither meat nor dairy) unless otherwise indicated.

Each section begins with a complete listing of the recipes in that section. Before planning a menu you can thus choose with a glance the right dish for any occasion. The recipes within each section are listed alphabetically for easy reference.

The recipes were selected to provide a variety of foods for all occasions—simple lunch, family dinner, Holiday meal or special event—and to satisfy varying tastes. Included are several different recipes for all the traditional staples of the Jewish table. Special notations indicate the traditional foods for Shabbos and Holiday meals, with cross-references to more complete descriptive information.

The Halacha

Halacha means Jewish Law; throughout the book you will find information about both *halacha*, the Law, and *minhag*, or custom—practices hallowed through tradition so that they have become equivalent to Law ("a custom of Israel is Torah").

Most of the halachic material deals, naturally, with Kashrus, and the practices of the kosher kitchen. This is found primarily in the sections entitled THE KOSHER KITCHEN and A GUIDE TO OBSERVANCE, while some of the laws of kashrus are mentioned in the various recipe sections. For example, diagrams of kosher meat are found in the meat section, and a discussion of kosher fish types is at the beginning of the fish section.

THE KOSHER KITCHEN includes an introduction to kashrus and a basic guide to its observance, while A GUIDE TO OBSERVANCE outlines in greater detail the laws of setting up a kosher kitchen, including sections on the *koshering* of meat and chicken etc., and other practical and specific instructions for fulfilling the mitzvohs related to food and its preparation. Included also is an outline of some of the major laws for preparing the house for Pesach and knowing which foods are allowed for Pesach use. At the end of the section is a Glossary of Terms related to the observance of kashrus, Shabbos and Holidays.

The kashrus and other laws have been carefully reviewed by esteemed Rabbis. However, it has not been possible for us to do justice to all laws pertaining to the observance of kashrus. Omission of some laws or a brief presentation of others in no way implies that they are not important. All of the sections dealing with *halacha* are meant to serve as a basic informative guide. It is important to read the footnotes wherever they appear. It is also important to have a *Rav,* a competent Rabbi, with whom to discuss Jewish observance, or to clarify further the laws presented here. When questions arise, the Rabbi's word should be taken as authoritative. The selection of a Rabbi should be based on his piety and his scholarly knowledge of the Torah and Jewish Law.

Jewish Life

The rest of the book is devoted to a description of the rich life that unfolds within the Jewish home. For how could we write about *cholent* and not burst into songs of praise for the glories of Shabbos; how could we write about the meal of a *chassanah* (wedding) and not talk about the Jewish marriage, the spiritual concepts behind it, the idea of *shalom bayis* (peace of the home), the sanctity created through the many mitzvohs observed in the home—not to mention the chassunah itself, replete with symbolism and mystical overtones. Similarly with each of the Holidays, the stages in the life of a child, and the unique and important responsibilities of the Jewish woman.

We hope *The Spice and Spirit of Kosher Jewish Cooking* will be a source of both pleasure and knowledge as an introduction to, or affirmation of, the beauty of the Jewish home and its value as manifested in the kosher kitchen.

The Kosher Home

The Kosher Home

The Kosher Home

Enter with us into the world of the Jewish kitchen. Step in, if you will, to the special atmosphere of delicious aromas combined with the hallowed sense of refinement and discrimination evident in every detail. Witness the bustling Thursday night preparations for a coming Shabbos of peace and renewal, taste the kosher wine of sanctification, smell the freshly-baked challah, enjoy the unforgettable and unique customs and foods associated with each Jewish Holiday.

For the Jewish kitchen, the kosher kitchen, is more than a physical place devoted to the storage, preparation and cooking of food. It is a spiritual center of the home, a place where the woman, reigning supreme, has the opportunity to create a firm foundation in the service of G-d. The very physical act of eating carries with it so much potential for holiness and is connected with so many *mitzvohs* that of the 613 commandments which G-d gave to Israel, at least fifty can be traced to observance at the table. Through agricultural laws, the taking of *challah*, and the saying of blessings, a single grain of wheat may become the vehicle for a *mitzvah* through the entire cycle of its existence. Maintaining a kosher kitchen and eating only kosher food is one of the ways in which all our everyday actions become sanctified. We become aware of each action and attuned to the potential revelation of G-dliness each mundane action can effect. It is written: "In all your ways, acknowledge Him" (Proverbs 3). This ideal becomes a practical reality when we observe the commandments given in the Torah; only when we put them into actual practice can we begin to perceive the quality of holiness that they convey.

The following pages present a brief outline of some of the commandments observed in the kosher kitchen. Other laws pertaining to specific types of food are explained in their appropriate recipe sections, while more detailed laws of keeping kosher are discussed at length in Section XVII—A Guide to Observance. This book should in no way be considered a substitute for the *Shulchan Aruch* (Code of Jewish Law) and in all cases where a question arises, a *Rav* (Rabbi competent to judge in matters of Jewish law) should be consulted.

What is Kashrus?

Kashrus is the word commonly used to refer to the observance of the Jewish dietary laws. The word *kosher* literally means fit or proper, and describes those types of foods which Torah Law declares fit for us to eat as well as the way in which these permissible foods are to be prepared.

Kashrus belongs to the category of *mitzvohs* for which no rational explanation is given in the Torah. Although various health and other physical benefits definitely accrue from their observance, this is in no way the reason we observe the laws of kashrus. We observe them because they are the will of G-d and were given to us for all time at Mt. Sinai. New reasons for observing kashrus may be "discovered" by each generation, but the basic laws concerning the foods proper for a Jew to eat have not changed any more than has the basic need to eat. Thus kashrus is not a set of hygiene or other laws which can become outdated with modern methods of sanitation or food inspection or production.

Our Sages teach us that each Jewish home is like a "small Sanctuary," a dwelling place for the Divine Presence, and the table is likened to the altar in the Sanctuary. In the Sanctuary utmost care had to be taken that only that which according to Jewish Law was perfectly fit for the altar was offered upon it. Likewise should we be extremely careful that only what is absolutely fit according to the dietary laws is brought to our table—the miniature altar—in order to ensure a home blessed with the Divine Presence and truly serving as a small Sanctuary.

Kashrus: A Key to Holiness

"For I am the L-rd your G-d; sanctify yourselves therefore and be holy; for I am holy."
(Leviticus 11:44)

The mitzvah of kashrus, together with all the commandments received at Mt. Sinai, was given to us so that we can be partners in the world's Creation, elevating and sanctifying all our mundane acts, serving G-d in all we do and at the same time refining and disciplining ourselves.

Eating, one of the most fundamental physical necessities common to all mankind as well as all creatures, becomes within the framework of Jewish law a hallowed act. The passage in Leviticus quoted above mentions holiness and sanctification—surely spiritual concepts. Yet it is found in the section of the Torah dealing specifically with the kashrus of animals, a rather precise outline of the foods which are prohibited to us and those which are permitted.

To understand how holiness or sanctification can be related to such physical activities as eating we must realize that the purpose of the Jew—given at Sinai—is to effect a transformation in this physical world itself, to purify it and make of it a place where G-dliness is revealed. This is why so many of the commandments involve physical objects and physical actions: *tefillin,* Shabbos candles, *mezuzah,* kashrus.

"Matter" and "spirit" are thus intertwined and interdependent, and everything we do affects and is affected by both. We know that food has a broad-ranging effect on us. Modern nutritionists recognize what the Torah has always taught, that mental and emotional states, the behavior and entire life of a person, can be affected by excesses or inadequacies in diet. In other words, "you are what you eat."

In becoming part of the flesh and blood of the body, which is connected to the soul, the food a person eats has a direct effect upon his character and his personal refinement and development. Therefore it is important that children, whose character is just beginning to be formed, be given kosher food, on the highest standard, to eat. Foods must be good for the soul as well as for the body.

The body, to fulfill its higher purpose and not merely satisfy those needs which it shares with all animals, must be an appropriate vessel. The Torah tells the Jew how to eat so that his body will be an instrument of the soul. By exercising control and discrimination (and not by rejecting the physical through asceticism), we strengthen the bond between ourselves and G-d—Who created both our bodies and our souls and gave us the Torah to teach us how to use them. When a Jew eats kosher food exclusively he ensures that his body will be a more perfect vessel to receive the G-dly flow of life that is his inheritance as part of the totality of the Jewish people, and he ensures his own sensitivity to that G-dly flow.

Keeping Kosher Today

It is not difficult to keep kosher. Even if it were difficult to observe kashrus, it should, of course, not deter a Jew from observing it, since it is G-d's commandment.

Today, we are fortunate in that we can shop in nearly any supermarket and find a wide variety of foods with a certified *hechsher*—seal of kashrus—and can buy fresh or frozen meat and poultry from reputable kosher butchers.

A *hechsher* is an insignia or statement on the label of a product certifying that its contents and manufacture have been supervised by a competent Rabbi and are kosher according to that Rabbi's standards. We should check labels carefully for such a hechsher and to check whether a food is "meat," "dairy," or "pareve".

Many restaurants and caterers also carry a certification of kashrus supervision. One should take the same care in choosing such establishments as one takes in choosing products to bring into one's home (see pages 332-334). The unfortunate practice of maintaining a double standard regarding kashrus outside the home ignores the fact that everything we eat, at home or away from home, must be kosher, and the effects of kashrus as explained above are constant at all times and in all places. Inconsistency in this area affects our entire orientation to Judaism adversely and is damaging to the firm Jewish foundation we want to give our children.

It is not difficult to change to a completely kosher kitchen. Many Rabbis will be glad to advise and help.

Asking A Rabbi

In any kosher kitchen, it is only natural that questions will arise. What happens if you stir the chicken soup with a dairy spoon? Can you *kasher* a particular type of pot, and if so, how must it be done? Whether one has just begun to keep kosher or has been doing so for years, it is important to ask a *sha'alah* (question in *halacha,* or Jewish law) every time a situation in kashrus or any other area of Jewish life needs to be clarified.

It is best to secure the name and telephone number of a *Rav*, or Rabbi who is competent in *halachic* matters, and to abide by his ruling in all cases. A Rav will be very happy to answer your questions. You will find that the wisdom of Jewish Law allows for every type of situation and decrees that two similar cases are not always alike. For if a Rabbi is asked a legal question and five minutes later is asked the same question about a second matter, he must again return to his sources to look up the answer. Jewish Law deals not with abstractions but with actual problems and their solution. It includes all aspects of life and one's relations with others, so you may find to your delight that talking to a knowledgeable Rabbi will shed light on many things that are on your mind.

Meat, Dairy and Pareve

All foods in the kosher kitchen are included in one of the following three classifications: MEAT, DAIRY, or PAREVE.

Meat

Any food made with meat or fowl, or meat and fowl products like bones, soup or gravy is considered *fleishig* (meaty). All meat ingredients in any product (including liver pills), must meet *all* requirements for kosher meat:

1. It must come from an animal that chews its cud and has split hooves.
2. It must be slaughtered according to the dietary laws by a *shochet*, a skilled and carefully trained kosher slaughterer.
3. The permissable parts of the animal must be *salted* before cooking.

There are many laws concerning the kashrus of the meat we eat. These laws are further explained in the meat recipe section, pages 163–167. For details on how to kosher your own meat, refer to pages 335–340.

Dairy

Any food derived from milk is considered *milchig*, and can only be served in or on dairy utensils. The term "dairy" refers to all types of milk, butter and yogurt, and every variety of cheese, whether hard, soft, or cream. Even the smallest amount of dairy in a food causes the food to be considered dairy. Many different kinds of candy and cereal contain milk products, as do some low-calorie sweeteners. Many milk derivatives (like sodium caseinate and lactose) are not immediately recognizable by their names—so be careful.

Dairy foods also require a certification of kashrus, verifying that the milk and cheeses:

1. are from a kosher animal.
2. have no meat-fats, or any kind of meat substances mixed into them.
3. contain no non-kosher substances.

6

Cholov Yisroel

The *halacha* states that to ensure that only milk from a kosher animal is used, a Jew must be present during the processing. Despite the fact that today government inspection allows us to be reasonably certain that milk products are pure, we do not change the *halacha*. Conditions may always change according to time and place, and deeper reasons exist for the performance of the mitzvohs, not dependent upon immediate circumstances. Milk and milk products supervised by a Jew from the time of milking through their complete processing are known as *Cholov Yisroel* (products from milk supervised by a Jew).

Jewish mystical tradition, especially, stresses the importance of using *Cholov Yisroel* products exclusively. Even when *Cholov Yisroel* is very difficult to obtain, many people go out of their way to acquire these products, visiting local dairy farms themselves where possible and having products shipped from other cities. Certainly one should not be lenient in this matter where *Cholov Yisroel* products are available and should inquire about their availability in one's area. There are cases in which a *Rav* might advise leniency, as where questions of health or the welfare of children are involved, but there is no all-inclusive allowance for the use of non-*Cholov Yisroel* products. *Cholov Yisroel* products have written on their containers the words חלב ישראל

Imitation Dairy Products

A number of non-dairy products with properties similar to milk are now available. These are used in place of butter, milk, or cream. If these foods are certified as kosher and pareve, they may be used during meat meals, or in cakes and other foods. However, when serving a product such as margarine or "coffee lightener" at a meat meal, it should be served in its original container so as not to be mistaken for genuine dairy. One should be aware of the fact that many margarines and some coffee lighteners are *not* pareve.

Pareve

Foods that are not meat or dairy, or derivatives of them, are considered pareve. A list of main types of pareve foods will be found on the following page.

Pareve foods can generally be served with either meat or dairy meals, can be prepared in meat or dairy pots, and may be served on meat or dairy dishes. However, once a pareve food has been cooked in a meat pot, even if the pot was completely clean, it may be served only on meat dishes. The same applies to pareve foods cooked in dairy pots; they may be served only in dairy dishes. If no meat or dairy products were mixed into the pareve foods, no waiting period is necessary as between meat and dairy, see page 9.

Of course, any pareve food cooked or mixed together with any meat or dairy product is considered as a meat or dairy product respectively. The waiting periods of such foods is the same as after meat and milk products. If the pareve food has only *touched* the milk or meat food, then washing is sufficient to keep it pareve, if the two items are cold (room temperature), and neither was a pungent, sharp food (mixed with onions, lemon, pickle, etc.).

It is not necessary to have a completely separate set of dishes for pareve foods. But it is common to set aside serving trays and especially baking ware as pareve. These are always washed separately from meat and dairy dishes. One should also have separate dish sponges, dish towels, draining boards, etc. A pareve knife is also recommended. Pareve foods with a sharp taste such as onion, garlic and pickles, when cut with a meat or dairy knife, are considered as a meat or dairy dish respectively; even if they are not cooked in a meat or dairy pot, they may not be used with foods of the opposite type.

Below are some laws pertaining to specific pareve food types.

Fish

All kosher type fish must have both *fins* and *scales*. A list of basic kosher and non-kosher fish types, and also some dietary laws concerning fish, is included in the fish section, page 133.

Our Sages have warned us that the combination of fish with other food may be damaging to our health, see page 133 for details.

Eggs

Eggs must be opened and examined. A blood spot in an egg, whether raw, cooked, or fried, renders that egg unkosher. Each egg should be opened into a glass and examined before being cooked or mixed with other eggs. If a blood spot is detected, the whole egg should be poured out and the vessel into which the egg was opened rinsed out very well in cold water. For *halachic* reasons, it is customary to cook at least 3 eggs at a time.

Leafy Vegetables and Grains

Green leafy vegetables and certain grains and fruits which could contain worms and insects must be inspected before they can be used. It is necessary to examine these foods thoroughly and sometimes even immerse them in water in order to remove any worms or insects, since these are not kosher and may not be eaten. An insect found in food does not, however, render the food or utensils non-kosher; it is sufficient to remove it.

It is also common to find worms in packages of noodles, grains, etc., especially if they have been stored for a long time.

Oil

In recipes where oil or shortening is required, only a *pure* vegetable shortening made under Rabbinic supervision may be used. Shortening and oils are basic ingredients in many processed foods and therefore these foods require strict kashrus supervision.

Basic Pareve Foods

Following is a list of some pareve foods. They are pareve as long as they are not mixed with any meat or dairy products.

Products that have been processed in any way should be bought only if there is a reliable hechsher on it. A list of ingredients alone on a label is not sufficient as there are many ingredients (especially when used in small quantities) that are not required by law to be listed on the label. In other situations the ingredients of a product may have been slightly changed, yet the manufacturer may be allowed to continue using their previous wrappings until new ones are printed.

Breads*	Soft drinks	Juices
Some cakes	Eggs	Noodles
Some hard candy	All types of kosher fish	All vegetables
Cereals*	All fruits	
Cookies*	All grains	

*Commercial brands often contain milk or milk derivatives; check label to make sure it states that the product is pareve. If it is not pareve, various problems are involved which make it necessary to consult a Rav.

Separation of Meat and Dairy

The separation of meat and dairy foods, dishes, kitchenware, etc., is perhaps the most obvious feature of the kosher kitchen. The prohibition against the combination of meat and dairy foods is mentioned in the Torah, elaborated upon in the oral law taught to Moses by G-d on Mt. Sinai, and passed down through generations of Prophets and Rabbis. It teaches us that this prohibition applies to three different ways we should not utilize a mixture of meat and milk.

A. Eating: Not to eat any meat and dairy foods or their derivatives together.
B. Cooking: Not to cook any meat and dairy food together even for a purpose other than their being eaten by a Jew. (An example might be in a non-Jewish cooking class.) The term cooking also refers to baking, frying, roasting, and so forth.
C. Having Benefit: Not to have any benefit from meat and dairy foods cooked together, such as selling them or doing any business with such foods.

In order not to transgress the above prohibitions of mixing our meat and dairy foods, our Rabbis have taught us how to set up a kosher kitchen. For further laws, see *Setting Up the Kosher Kitchen,* pages 327-330.

The Waiting Time Between Meat and Dairy

Meat and dairy foods may not be eaten in the same meal—even if they are in separate dishes and even if the waiting time elapses.

After eating dairy food, it is necessary to rinse the mouth, and to eat something pareve, before eating any meat or meat products. A minimum of one-half hour must pass before eating meat or meat products; others have the custom of waiting one complete hour. Certain hard cheeses (Swiss, Muenster, etc.) require a *six-hour waiting period* before meat may be eaten.

After eating meat foods it is necessary to rinse one's mouth and to wait *six full hours* before eating dairy foods. If one finds a small piece of meat between one's teeth even after six hours it is necessary to remove it and only then can one eat dairy—it is not necessary to wait another six hours. For people on special dairy diets and for children under nine years old, a Rav should be consulted. If there are no special problems involved, it is advisable to train children at an earlier age in the practice of waiting between meat and dairy foods.

The six-hour waiting period is standard for all Jews, except those groups which have *halachically* established other customs.

If, when tasting, one does not chew or swallow the food, but eliminates it immediately from the mouth, the waiting period is not necessary. One should still rinse the mouth well. If even the smallest amount of food is chewed or swallowed, the full waiting period becomes necessary.

If pareve foods (excluding sharp or spiced foods) were cooked or prepared alone in meat or dairy utensils, the above waiting periods are not necessary, even though that pareve item may have technically become *fleishig* or *milchig* and may not be eaten with the opposite type foods or on the improper dishes.

Kashrus on Pesach

"In the first month, on the fourteenth day of the month at even, you shall eat matzohs. . . . There shall be no leaven found in your houses: for whoever eats that which leavens, that soul shall be cut off from the congregation of Israel. . . . You shall eat nothing that leavens; in all your dwellings you shall eat matzohs." (Exodus 12:18–20).

All dietary laws observed throughout the year apply to Pesach as well. In addition, no *chometz* may be eaten or owned. This is one of the most stringent prohibitions of the entire year and is compared to the prohibition against eating on Yom Kippur. *Chometz* is a mixture of flour and water that has been allowed to rise, either naturally or through a leavening agent. Bread and challah are chometz, as are noodles, cake, cookies and pastries made of flour. This prohibition recalls the unleavened dough our forefathers ate when G-d brought them out of Egypt hurriedly, before their dough had time to rise.

No vessels in which leavened products have been used during the year may be used on Pesach unless *kashered* properly for Passover (see *Laws of Kashering*, page 330). Therefore, extra sets of meat and dairy pots, dinnerware, flatware and kitchen accessories are kept, stored away carefully for Pesach, and used from year to year.

Concerning the meticulous observance of the laws of kashrus on Pesach, our Rabbis say "the more one does, the more praiseworthy one is."

For by having even one particle of chometz left in our house, any food that might come in contact with it would likewise become chometz!

Our tradition explains the great personal lesson to be learned from the laws of chometz on Pesach. Dough that is leavened rises and becomes puffed up. It is compared to a person who is "puffed up" with his own self-image. Such a person cannot see his own faults and wrong actions, and rationalizes them away if he does see them. Matzoh, being thin and flat, suggests the idea of humility. Pesach teaches us that chometz—arrogance—is the antithesis of the ideal of Torah.

The Holiday of our miraculous redemption is thus a time of renewed spiritual salvation and elevation. Every year it should find each Jew with an unleavened, that is, humble spirit before G-d. It is a time for much soul-searching where we should make all efforts to rid our character of any empty traits—blown out of proportion by the leavening of pride and arrogance.

Besides not eating any chometz, one may not possess or have benefit from chometz. More detailed laws are outlined in *Pesach Preparation and Laws*, pages 350–356. The traditions and customs of Pesach are explained at length in the Yomin Tovim Section.

Blessings Over Food

The earth's abundance fills us with awe: ripe grapes bursting forth from the vine, crisp apples, golden wheat, fragrant spices. To partake of this goodness without at least a brief word of acknowledgement to the Creator of all things would be tantamount to stealing, for it is written: "The Earth is the L-rd's and all its fullness" (Proverbs).

How do we take possession of the food we eat and other necessities? By making a *brocha . . .* A brocha is a short prayer said before and after partaking of food of all kinds. It invariably begins with the words, "Blessed art Thou, L-rd our G-d, King of the Universe," and ends with a reference to the category of food eaten (see pages 345-350). Our ancestor, Abraham, the first Jew, was also the first to spread and encourage the practice of thanking G-d for the food we eat. For Abraham's tent in the wilderness was open to all and together with Sarah his wife, Abraham was host to innumerable desert travelers. Each one he would serve personally. When the guest began to thank him for his hospitality, Abraham would tell him that gratitude was due not to him but to G-d, the Provider of all sustenance.

In reciting these blessings with the proper intention we acknowledge the purposeful and intricate pattern G-d has set up in the world and also help break down the tempting delusion that we live and prosper only through our own efforts. The feeling of gratitude thus nurtured is one which begins at an early age, as the Jewish child begins to say his or her first brochos, and which permeates each day's activities.

One aspect of the Jew's mission in this world is to elevate physical matter in the service of G-d. This is done by using physical objects (or by refraining from using them if they are not permitted) in the performance of G-d's commandments. When we make a brocha over the food we eat, the food becomes sanctified and its function is elevated to this service of G-d.

We further elevate and sanctify the food we eat when it becomes part of our bodies. We serve our Creator with every fiber of our bodies—the hand gives charity, the lips pray, the heart loves. In being incorporated into the substance of the body instead of returning to earth, the plant or animal eaten as food has the opportunity to rise further to G-dliness. Of course only permitted, kosher food is thus elevated, and only when a brocha is recited.

Eating, then, to the Jew, becomes a sacred and cherished means of serving G-d. By eating kosher food and saying brochos, we help carry out our aim of making this physical world "a dwelling place for G-d, may He be blessed."

11

A further and more detailed discussion of the following laws are discussed in Section XVII, A Guide to Observance, pages 325 to 362.

Setting Up the Kosher Kitchen
    Separation of Meat and Dairy
    Kashering Utensils
    Food Products Brought into Your Home
Eating Out
Laws of Koshering Meat, Fowl and Liver
Laws of Separating Challah
Blessings Over Food
    The Different Brochos and When to Say Them
    Laws Concerning Saying Brochos
Pesach Preparation and Laws
    The Prohibitions Concerning Chometz on Pesach
    Laws and Customs Concerning Foods Eaten on Pesach
Glossary of Terms; for the Kosher Kitchen, Shabbos and Holidays
Mitzvohs - An Everlasting Link

For further clarification of these laws or any topic in Jewish law consult a Rav.

Shabbos and Yom Tov

SECTION 2

Shabbos and Yom Tov

Shabbos and Yom Tov

Rich in tradition and beautiful in observance, the Shabbos and Yom Tov testify strongly to our faith in and love of G-d. They provide the highlights of our Jewish experience throughout the year.

The observance of Shabbos and Yom Tov are similar in many ways: candle-lighting, the festive Kiddush meal, and special prayers. We also hear the Torah read in shul, wear festive clothing, and mark the transition back to ordinary "weekday" time with the prayer of "separation" called *Havdalah*. We have therefore combined Shabbos and Yom Tov in one section in which we deal with the significance and importance of the Shabbos as well as the many customs and observances common to both.

Nevertheless, basic differences underlie our celebration of Shabbos and Yom Tov, both in meaning and in laws of observance. (Within the following chapters distinctions are noted wherever relevant.)

The Shabbos stands as a sign between us and our Creator. By observing Shabbos we openly show the world our strong belief in G-d as Creator of the world. "In six days He created the heaven and the earth and on the seventh day He rested."

While Shabbos proclaims our belief in G-d as the Creator of the whole world and everything in it, the Jewish festivals (Yomim Tovim) emphasize the bond between G-d and the Jewish people. He redeemed us from Egypt (Pesach), gave us the Torah (Shavuos), forgave us for the Golden Calf (Yom Kippur), protected us as we wandered the desert (Succos). All these provide opportunities for us to rejoice in being G-d's own people—"Happy is the man whose G-d is the L-rd." (Psalm 145)

An important difference between Shabbos and Yom Tov is in the types of activities permitted on each. The thirty-nine *melachos* or forms of creative work (see Glossary) prohibited on Shabbos are mostly prohibited on Yom Tov, with the exception of activities necessary for the preparation of food for that day of Yom Tov. This includes cooking, baking, etc., but even these activities are governed by certain conditions (see page 31).

We have tried to evoke something of the spirit and atmosphere of these special days and to emphasize the ways in which the physical setting—from festive meals to clothing and song—serves to enhance the spiritual content.

Note: The Shabbos begins on Friday, 18 minutes **before** sunset and ends the following evening after dark when three stars can be seen (approximately 25 hours later).

The Holidays also begin 18 minutes before sunset and end after dark on the last day of Yom Tov.

When determining the day of a date on the Jewish calendar, it must be kept in mind that the Hebrew date begins at sunset and ends the following night. Thus a Holiday which is on Thursday, for example, really begins on Wednesday night.

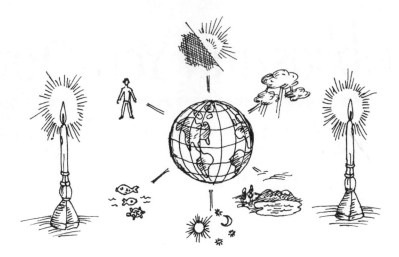

The Shabbos Queen (A Weekly Visitor)

And G-d Rested on the Seventh Day . . . and He Blessed it and Made it Holy

(Genesis 2:2-3.)

Another busy week is drawing to a close as the family eagerly prepares for Shabbos. The last-minute rush to be ready comes to an end; all shopping, cooking, and personal preparations are complete. All thoughts of the week are put aside. Physical objects too seem to have an air of anticipation, from the specially-set stove keeping food for Shabbos meals warm, to the shining candlesticks waiting to be lit. Shortly before sunset Friday evening, the women and girls of the house will light the candles ushering in the holy day of Shabbos.

An atmosphere of tranquility and family unity descends upon the house. Shabbos is indeed a day of rest—physically, mentally and emotionally. It is a time to relax with family and friends and, indeed, with ourselves.

Shabbos stands as a constant sign for the Jew, as every week we reaffirm our strong belief in G-d as the Creator of the world. In six days G-d completed all Creation, making "something from nothing," *ex nihilo*, and on the seventh day He rested.

To observe the Shabbos was one of the first commandments given to us by G-d at Mt. Sinai. There we were chosen by G-d to perpetuate His teachings throughout the centuries wherever we might be. By keeping the Shabbos, we stand as an open testimony to the world, teaching that it is G-d Who created the world and everything in it, from the smallest inanimate object to the crown of creation—man. We also affirm our belief that G-d truly provides for our livelihood, and that the sustenance alotted us is not decreased when we do not work on Shabbos.

By keeping Shabbos we are thus also reaffirming the mission of our lives given to us at Mt. Sinai—to be as a priestly kingdom for the nations of the world.

Shabbos is a day of renewal, a time to stop and think, to reflect on the marvels of G-d's world and meditate on His greatness. On Shabbos the Jew halts his preoccupation with, and participation in mundane affairs. It is "a day unto G-d" Who is the source of all sustenance and blessings we receive during the week. All the good of the past week is elevated on Shabbos and simultaneously Shabbos is the source of all the blessings of the week to come.

Zochor V'Shomor

Many activities are forbidden on this day, not necessarily corresponding to the common definition of "work." It is forbidden, for example, to carry the smallest item into the street—but permissible to carry even heavy objects inside the house. "Work" in the *halachic* or Jewish legal sense refers to the thirty-nine general categories of creative activity (*melacha*) which were employed in the building of the *Mishkan* (portable Sanctuary which the Jews carried with them during the forty years of wandering in the desert). These *melachos* are processes by which man changes and/or controls the natural world. By ceasing to do such "creative work" one day a week, we relinquish our control over our environment and remind ourselves that G-d is the Creator of the universe and its true Master.

Thanks to the laws of Shabbos, we are free from the pressures of the world. Time stretches on Shabbos and sometimes it even seems to disappear. The Shabbos and Yom Tov meals are always relaxed and can go on and on for as long as everybody likes.

Shabbos is enriched not only with rest but with activity. This is alluded to in the two expressions *Zochor*—Remember the Shabbos to sanctify it (Exodus 20:8) and *Shomor*—Guard the Shabbos to sanctify it (Duet. 5:12). *Shomor* refers to guarding oneself from doing any forbidden work, while *Zochor* refers to all the beautiful observances of Shabbos: the lighting of the candles, reciting the Kiddush, dining on a festive meal, dressing well, praying, hearing the Torah reading in shul, learning and discussing portions of the Torah. By observing all these, we experience a day of true spiritual elevation.

Each Jew also receives an additional soul on Shabbos. This "Shabbos Soul" bestows an extra measure of light, understanding and peace, and of energy, strength and appetite. No wonder we can pray and learn Torah with such zest. Our "Shabbos Soul" gives us extra strength and extra power to reveal through the mitzvohs performed on this day the Divine energy that is latent in the world.

And so it is with eager anticipation as well as joy that the women light the candles on Friday evening and the congregation chants "Welcome Bride, Welcome Shabbos Queen."

By The Light of the Candles

Illuminating the Home

To usher in the Shabbos and Yom Tov with the peaceful glow of candlelight is one of the special mitzvohs given to the woman. The mitzvah of lighting Shabbos and Yom Tov candles is known as *Bentching Licht*. *Licht* means "light" or "candle," and *Bentch* means "to bless." Through the mitzvah of Bentching Licht, the kindling of Shabbos and Yom Tov candles, we as Jewish women bring light and blessings into the world, and particularly into the home, in a very real way.

We know that Shabbos candles were lit from the very earliest days of our history. The Torah relates how Sarah, the first Jewish Matriarch, lit the candles every week before Shabbos. Her reward was very great: the tent of Abraham and Sarah was illuminated from Shabbos to Shabbos, a whole week through. When Sarah died, the light departed. Three years later when Rivkah (Rebecca), the wife of Isaac, began to light the Shabbos candles, this special light, one of warmth, happiness and peace, returned and lit up the home once again throughout the week.

What is the power of this light? We know that one small action in the physical world—a button pressed, a switch turned on—can accomplish a great deal. One small candle in a dark room dispels all the darkness, gloom and obscurity of the entire room. The mitzvah of candle-lighting, performed in a few moments before the onset of Shabbos each week with just a pair of candlesticks and two candles, brings the illuminating message of warmth, happiness and peace into Jewish homes and spreads this message outward to dispel darkness in the entire surrounding world.

The message of light—a universal symbol of vision, clarity, knowledge, truth—and the message of the Shabbos are intertwined. The very first Shabbos brought to the world an air of tranquility and holiness. This unique atmosphere reappears in the world, and to each individual each week at the moment of candle-lighting, when the woman brings Shabbos into her home.

We usher in the Shabbos with a minimum of two lights, corresponding to the two expressions with which the Torah commands us to observe the Shabbos: "remember" and "guard," (Exodus 20:8 and Deuteronomy 5:12).

A Message of Peace

Our Sages have said, "Great is the mitzvah of candle-lighting as it brings peace into the world." The light of the Shabbos candles brings peace by illuminating the house so that people do not stumble in the dark or bump into each other. In a deeper sense, Chassidus teaches, the Shabbos candles light up the house and every member of the family with the light of Torah, to walk safely through the path of life which is full of dangerous pitfalls.

How can the physical light of a pair of Shabbos or Yom Tov candles illuminate our lives spiritually?

The quality of a flame is that it always reaches upwards and that even the "smallest light can dispel an abundance of darkness." If such are its characteristics in the physical world, so too are its characteristics in the parent cosmos, the spiritual world. In fact, it is because of its existence in the spiritual world that it has a corresponding nature in the physical.

Every mitzvah of the Torah is likened to a candle: *Ki Ner-Mitzvah, v'Torah-Or* (a mitzvah is a candle and the Torah is light). Each mitzvah that a person does effects a physical and spiritual illumination. Each mitzvah—each light, reaching upwards—tunes us in more closely to the spirituality latent in this world. Each mitzvah, although its action may be small, illuminates a world overcast in darkness—the darkness of ignorance, moral and ethical confusion, spiritual malaise. If such is the power of every mitzvah, how much more so, our Sages conclude, is it so with a mitzvah that is done with light itself—the mitzvah of kindling the Shabbos and Yom Tov candles!

A Special Prayer

Candle-lighting time has always been a special and auspicious moment, one of meditation and quiet prayer. As a woman stands before the kindled flames with eyes covered, she prays that all the qualities of light become manifest, and for much more.

At this moment, when the family is gathered together, she has traditionally offered a silent or verbal prayer on behalf of her husband and children—a prayer that they be granted health and happiness, a prayer that she have much *yiddishe nachas* from them—that they should be "living lighthouses" by their shining examples to the world.

How correct was their intuition in linking this personal prayer to the moment of lighting candles. The great Kabbalist and Torah scholar, Rabbi Isaac Luria, known as the Holy Ari, writes that in fact a woman's prayer on behalf of her husband and family is especially received by G-d at this moment.

Again we understand why righteous women throughout the ages have not only given the preparation of Shabbos special attention but have regarded this time as special. Their candlesticks were more precious than jewelry, and a woman would often put aside precious savings to buy beautiful *leichter*. She would be sure to allow time to prepare herself in advance for candlelighting—house already immaculate, the food tastefully prepared, the table set, the family clothed in special Shabbos garments, each of these contributing to the glow of Shabbos.

This glow, stretching from Shabbos to Shabbos and from Yom Tov to Yom Tov across the years, like the light in Sarah's tent, continues to light our path and to remind us of the hope for future redemption as expressed in the words of our Rabbis: "If you will observe the kindling of the Shabbos lights, you will merit to see the light of the redemption of the Jewish people."

Candle-Lighting by Our Daughters

Anxious for the day when they can light their own candles, our daughters look on with special pride as the candles are being lit. Just as our matriarch Rivkah, at the tender age of three, understood the great powers of these flickering flames, so, too, do our young daughters sense a certain warmth and inner happiness brought on by the Shabbos candles and look forward to the time when they too will have their own candlesticks.

In past generations, a widespread custom, especially among great Rabbinic families, was to grant their daughters the privilege of candle-lighting from a very young age. The sense of participation in mitzvohs from an early age is an important part of Torah education. By lighting their own candles, a little girl feels that she is personally helping to usher in the Holy Shabbos.

When times grew difficult for the Jew in Europe, especially in the past two generations, it was often only with great difficulty that a woman managed to obtain a few candles. It often became necessary to light only the minimum of two candles in honor of the Shabbos. Sadly, a woman had to relinquish—temporarily she hoped—the comforting sight of the additional candles lit in honor of the birth of each child; and reluctantly unmarried girls forewent their own candle-lighting.

Today, this precious custom of a Jewish girl's childhood is being widely revived. In a relatively short time, this custom has spread to include tens of thousands of young girls, many of whom testify to a deeper understanding and appreciation of the Shabbos and their Jewishness—ascribing it proudly to the glow of their very own candlesticks.

In a world so painfully lacking in sense, peace, wholeness, and tranquility, has there ever been a greater need for this added light?

Laws and Customs of Candle-Lighting

Time for Candle-lighting

Every woman should light the candles every Friday evening, no later than eighteen minutes before sunset. It is strictly forbidden to light the candles after sunset (check time on a Jewish calendar or in local newspaper). Candle-lighting time varies from city to city.

For the time of lighting candles for Yom Tov see below.

Number of Candles to be Lit

A minimum of two candles should be lit corresponding to the two passages in the Torah regarding the observance of Shabbos:
1. Remember the day of the Sabbath to sanctify it (Ex. 20:8).
2. Guard the day of Sabbath to sanctify it (Deut. 5:12).

Another custom, accepted by many women, is to add an additional light with the birth of each child, and to continue lighting it throughout the years. Thus a woman with three children lights five candles.

A girl lighting her own candle lights one candle.

Giving Charity Before Candle-lighting

It is customary to put some coins in a container designated for a Jewish charity before lighting the candles. This is a most important and beneficial activity, and should not be neglected.

Procedure for Candle-lighting

The procedure for lighting the candles is as follows:
- light the candles
- wave hands over flames toward oneself to usher in the Shabbos, and then cover eyes
- recite the blessing
- say a private prayer
- uncover eyes and gaze at light of candles . . . enjoy the light and say "Good Shabbos" (or *Shabbat Shalom*) to any family or guests.

The Blessings Said Over Candle-lighting for Shabbos

Bo-ruch A-toh A-do-noi* E-lo-hai-nu* Melech Ha-olom A-sher Kid-sho-nu B'mitz-vo-sov, Vi-tzi-vo-nu Le-had-lik Ner Shel Shabbos Ko-desh.

*Note: The real name of G-d has been used in this text. When practicing the blessing, say *Hashem Elo-kai-nu* instead of the third and fourth words, so as not to say G-d's name in vain. One may say the actual Name, however, when teaching a child under *Bar* or *Bas Mitzvah* age how to say the brocha.

A Private Prayer

It is customary to offer a private prayer for the welfare of loved ones while the eyes are still covered, and especially that G-d bless them with "sons who will shine with Torah," as this is a most auspicious time. Some also say a prayer beseeching the redemption of Zion. Many women will say "Good Shabbos" upon uncovering their eyes as if to announce that the Shabbos peace has now descended on their homes.

Who Lights the Candles

The obligation to light candles is on the woman of the house. However, if a man lives alone, or if his wife or daughter over *Bas-Mitzvah* (12 years old) is not at home, then he should light the Shabbos candles in the same customary manner and say the proper blessing over them.

It is also important that girls age three and up be taught to light the Shabbos candles every week. Each daughter should light one candle all her own. The custom of giving charity should also be imparted to them. Mothers should make a habit of lighting candles after their daughters so as to be available to give any necessary assistance, which would not be permitted had she lit the candles first.

Candle-lighting for Yom Tov

It is also necessary to light candles for each Biblical Yom Tov (Rosh Hashanah, Yom Kippur, Succos, Shemini Atzeres, Pesach, and Shavuos). Outside the land of Israel, where Yom Tov is two days, candles are lit on both days. During *Chol Hamoed*, the intermediate days of Pesach and Succos (see Glossary), candles are not lit, but only on the first and last two days of Pesach and Succos, unless Chol Hamoed occurs on Shabbos.

All the above laws and customs related to lighting the Shabbos candles apply on Yom Tov as well, except that different blessings are said.

The Two Blessings—Said Over Lighting the Candles on Yom Tov.

1. Bo-ruch A-toh A-do-noi* E-lo-hai-nu* Melech Ha-olam A-sher Ki-d-sho-nu B'mitz-vo-sov Vi-tzi-vo-nu Le-had-lik Ner Shel Yom Tov

2. Boruch A-toh A-do-noi* E-lo-hai-nu* Melech Ha-olam She-he-chi-yo-nu Vi-ki-ye-mo-nu Ve-hi-gi-o-nu Lē-zman Ha-zeh.

On the last two days of Pesach, only the first blessing is said.

When Shabbos and Yom Tov occur on the same day the first blessing is said in this way:
Bo-ruch A-toh A-do-noi* E-lo-hai-nu* Melech Ho-olam A-sher Ki-de-sha-nu Bi-mitz-vo-sov Vi-tzi-vo-nu Le-had-lik Ner Shel Sha-bos Vi-shel Yom Tov.

On Rosh Hashanah, instead of "Yom Tov" say "Yom Hazikaron," and for Yom Kippur, instead of "Yom Tov" say "Yom Ha-ki-pu-rim."

*See *Note*, page 21.

Time for Lighting Candles for Yom Tov

The first day of Yom Tov, the candles should be lit as for Shabbos: 18 minutes before sunset, except of course, when the first day of Yom Tov falls on Sunday, in which case candles must be lit after Shabbos is over on Saturday night. On Yom Tov only, one may, if necessary, light the candles after sunset. When doing so, care must be taken to light candles only from a pre-existing flame. (See Note below.)

When Yom Tov is two days, candles should be lit on the second evening after nightfall. Some prefer to wait until the family has assembled for the meal after the evening prayers before lighting the candles on the table.

Note: In any case, since one may not strike a match on Yom Tov, when lighting candles on the second night of Yom Tov (or at the end of the day if it is Friday and Shabbos immediately follows Yom Tov) one should light the candles from a pre-existing flame. For example, light one candle from an already-kindled flame on the stove or from the pilot light, and light the remaining candles from that first one.

Around the Table

The Set Table

Family and guests are finally gathered; those who have attended services have returned with hearty greetings of "Good Shabbos" (*Shabbat Shalom*) or "Good Yom Tov" (*Chag Sameach*). The flickering radiant light of the candles adds a warmth to the good feeling everyone has at being together in the special atmosphere of *shalom*.

The whole house radiates a festive mood. The table is transformed by a fresh, white table-cloth. On it, covered, are the twin loaves of challah and all the items needed for the holiday meal. The set table shows that a special guest is coming, one who must be treated with great honor. This is the time for our finest dishes and silverware and all our most beautiful accessories. Candlesticks, Kiddush cup, wine decanter, bread knife, salt dish—all may be simple or elaborate according to one's personal style, but all reflect our desire to greet "Our Queen Shabbos and Our Holy Yom Tov" with all the beauty and dignity befitting a royal guest.

Some Special Ingredients

Torah—The Shabbos and Yom Tov meals differ from weekday meals in that they are more leisurely and joyful, imbued as they are with a sense of the spiritual and historic significance of the day, often expressed, more so than during the less leisurely week, in a lively discussion of the Torah Reading for the week or for the Festival, the laws and customs of the day, and other relevant topics. This is an important element of the meal and shows that the Shabbos meal is a source of both physical and spiritual enjoyment.

". . . if three have eaten at a table and have conversed in Torah, they are as though they have eaten from the table of G-d" (Ethics of the Fathers, 3:4)

Song—Melody is said to be "the pen of the soul." Some of the songs, or *zmiros*, sung at Shabbos and Yom Tov meals are from the prayer book and some are from the Psalms and other Holy Writings. Some, *nigunim*, are wordless . . . revelations beyond the power of words to express. The melodies may be complex or simple, fast or slow. Each is full of the feelings of faith and joy that overwhelm us on these days.

Guests—Hospitality has always been a strong Jewish tradition and performing the great mitzvah of inviting fellow Jews into one's home has been a wonderful way to enhance the Shabbos and Yom Tov table. The benefits are plentiful—for you as well as the guest; good feelings are heightened and conversation enlivened. It is a natural process—no special talents are necessary—just a good Jewish heart. It can be especially rewarding and exciting if you have a "spiritually poor" guest who has never experienced these high points of his or her tradition and whose wonder and questions can add depth to your own experience.

"Let your house be wide open; treat the poor as members of your own family . . ." (Ethics of the Fathers, 1:15)

The Shabbos and Yom Tov Meals

On Shabbos and Yom Tov it is a mitzvah to eat two festive meals, one in the evening and the other on the following day. (With Yom Tov on two consecutive days, the evening and afternoon meals are eaten on both days.) The Shabbos and Yom Tov meals are basically the same and follow a pattern within which the spiritual and symbolic aspects of the occasion unfold. The head of the household makes Kiddush over wine, all wash in the ritual manner and break bread with the traditional blessing of thanks to G-d Who "brings forth bread from the earth." The meal is then served, and concluded with the Blessings-After-A-Meal.

However, the main difference between the Shabbos and Yom Tov meals, is in the preparation of food for the meals. On Shabbos no food whatsoever may be cooked or baked, while cooking is allowed on Yom Tov for *that day only*. (See Laws of Cooking for Yom Tov, page 31.) This allows for the serving of warm food at all meals. Yom Tov is also an opportunity to serve really festive meals, and prepare a variety of side dishes and special desserts which will be appreciated by all.

In addition, on Shabbos it is a mitzvah to eat a third meal, which is called *Shalosh Seudos* (see page 27).

The Kiddush

The Shabbos and Holiday meals begin with the Kiddush, recited by the head of the household or any male member over thirteen. Many people have the custom that *all* male members at the table over the age of thirteen recite the Kiddush. The Kiddush is said over a cup of wine. Usually a silver cup holding a minimum of approximately four ounces is reserved for this purpose. The one who recites the Kiddush drinks at least two ounces and the rest is distributed among all those who are included in his Kiddush. Some have the custom that members of the family and guests stand while the Kiddush is being recited. Everyone answers *Amen* at the end of the brochos.

The Friday night Kiddush testifies that G-d, the Creator of the world, rested on the seventh day, declared it holy, and gave us, the Jews, this holy day to observe. The Afternoon Kiddush speaks about observing the Shabbos, a sign forever between us and G-d.

"Hamotzi" (Blessing over Bread)

After Kiddush, everyone washes hands by pouring water from a vessel (two times or three according to custom) on one hand and then on the other. The appropriate blessing is then said (see below) and the hands dried. This is a blessing for purification, not for cleaning; the hands should be clean before beginning.

The head of the household then recites the blessing *Hamotzi* over the two challahs and everyone responds *Amen*. Just before saying the blessing, he lightly draws the knife across the challah to indicate the place for cutting, then raises the challahs and recites the blessing. He cuts a piece of challah for himself and dips it in salt and eats it so that there is no unnecessary lapse in time between the blessing and the act of eating. Then he distributes challah to all those present and each one eats of it before resuming conversation. A popular custom is to place two small whole loaves of challah in front of all other male participants so that each may make his own blessing.

See also *Laws of Blessings,* pages 345-350.

The Meal

It enhances the mitzvah of Shabbos enjoyment to have wine, fish and meat or chicken on the Shabbos and Yom Tov table, and so our meal is usually planned around these three basic foods.

Many of the Holidays have special symbolic foods and dishes to help glorify the occasion. Gefilte fish, kugel, chicken soup and cholent are among the many traditional dishes that have always spelled "Shabbos" or "Yom Tov." The main ingredient, however, is food that you will have pleasure in eating. Types of food, method of preparation, and accompanying side dishes will vary according to taste.

Bentching: (Blessings After the Meal)

These blessings comprise one of the oldest prayers we have. "When you have eaten and are satisfied you shall bless G-d your G-d" (Deuteronomy 8:10). The Talmud records that the first blessing comes from Moshe (Moses), the second from Yehoshua (Joshua) and the third from Kings David and Shlomo (Solomon), with the rest being Rabbinical additions.

See also *Laws of Blessings,* pages 345-350.

The Shabbos and Yom Tov Menus

Below are the standard menus for the Friday night and Shabbos afternoon meals, followed by some brief notes on some of the traditional foods. The Holiday meals follow a similar pattern. All necessary cooking for the Shabbos meals must be done before the Shabbos begins. (See *Laws of Cooking for Shabbos*, page 30.)

Friday Night
Wine for Kiddush
Challah
Fish (and Salad)
Soup
Chicken
Side Dishes, such as:
   Tzimmes, Coleslaw, Potato Salad or Kugel.
Dessert
Soda or Juice*

Shabbos Afternoon
Wine for Kiddush
Challah
Fish (and Salad)
(Chopped Liver and Eggs)
Cholent
Meat and/or Chicken
Side Dishes such as:
   Lokshen or Potato Kugel, Coleslaw
Dessert
Soda or Juice*

*Serve between fish and meat (see page 133).

Challah

These are the traditional loaves of bread with which we begin the meal, saying the blessing of *Hamotzi*. For the significance of challah, its connection to Shabbos, how to shape them and for many recipes see Section IV.

Fish

The type of fish usually served is gefilte fish—a cooked ground fish mixture. The origin of its preparation as well as instructions and recipes for how to prepare it are all included in Section VII.

Soup and Cholent

On Friday night, hot chicken soup is the standard favorite, served with thin noodles, rice, or fluffy matzoh balls (*knaidlach*).

During the second meal, it is a hallowed custom to eat *cholent* instead of soup. Cholent is a type of heavy soup or stew made of potatoes, beans and meat in varying proportions. Before Shabbos, the Shabbos stove or *blech* is set up in order to keep the cholent warm until serving time. Soup and Cholent Recipes, as well as an interesting story related in the Talmud (page 30) about cholent, are included in Section VI. On Yom Tov, cholent is not served.

Chicken and Meat

On Shabbos we usually have meat or chicken. As chicken is a little easier to digest, it is usually reserved for the evening meal, and cold sliced meat, or warm meat from the cholent is served by day. Recipes are included in Sections VIII and IX.

Kugel

Kugel is a popular baked dish made of boiled noodles or potatoes mixed with eggs, seasoning and other ingredients. It is served as a side dish with meat or chicken. Recipes are included in Section XI.

Shalosh Seudos

The third meal of Shabbos is called either *Shalosh Seudos* or *Seuda Shelishit.* It says in the Talmud (Shabbos 118A) that a person who fulfills the obligation of three meals on Shabbos will have a good judgment in the world to come.

Depending on local custom Shalosh Seudos may or may not be a complete meal. If one is satiated and doesn't want bread, it is best to have some cake or cookies or lokshen kugel so as to be able to make the special after-blessing.

As with the other Shabbos meal, the Shalosh Seudos is also accompanied by *zmiros* or Shabbos songs. The Shalosh Seudos must begin before sunset, and if it is a complete meal in which *Hamotzi* is said, may continue until after it is already dark. If after Shabbos is over (check calendar for correct time), and one is still in the middle of the Shalosh Seudos, it is still Shabbos for all those participating in the Shalosh Suedos, and one should only begin the evening services and say the *Havdalah* after completing the Blessings-After-A-Meal.

Havdalah

When Shabbos first entered on Friday evening, we received her with much honor. For approximately twenty-five hours we were bestowed with an additional Shabbos soul and the unique uplift of Shabbos; now that it is time for her to leave we cannot let her go unnoticed. Her departure, like her entrance, must be announced with wine and blessings.

After Shabbos ends, the *Havdalah* is said to mark the distinction between "the holy and the profane," between the Shabbos that has ended and the ordinary days of the week that have begun. Included is a petition that the week to come be one of happiness and deliverance from exile. Food may not be eaten and if possible one should also refrain from doing work until after Havdalah is said. Work may only be performed before Havdalah if one first declares the separation between the Shabbos and weekday in the evening services, or by saying the words "*Boruch Hamavdil Bain Kodesh L'chol.*" The Havdalah should then be said as soon as possible afterwards.

The Havdalah prayer is said over a cup of wine, and so the blessing for wine is also said. However, beverages such as grape juice or beer may also be used instead of wine.

In addition, two other blessings are also recited. The first blessing is said over the smelling of spices. Sweet smelling spices have the ability to revive broken spirits, and now that Shabbos is over and our added spiritual soul has departed, our mood needs to be uplifted and revived.

The second is a blessing for fire, said over the light of a Havdalah candle (a special candle made by combining several wicks or by joining the flames of two candles). One reason this blessing is said is as a remembrance of the "light" (fire) which Adam made by rubbing two stones together when he first experienced darkness, which was on Saturday night. After the blessing, we hold our nails to the light to see the difference between light and dark reflected on our hands.

The order of these four blessings is: wine, spices, fire, *havdalah* ("Blessed art Thou, L-rd our G-d, King of the Universe, who makes a distinction between the holy and the ordinary").

If one forgot to say the Havdalah he may make it up anytime until Tuesday sunset, whenever he remembers, by reciting the Havdalah with blessings on wine but without the blessings on spices and fire. The sooner this is done, the better.

Havdalah for Yom Tov

The Havdalah prayer is also said at the end of Yom Tov. However, if Yom Tov ends in the middle of the week, the blessings over fire and spices are not said.

If Yom Tov ends on Friday night when Shabbos begins, no Havdalah is said, since the holiness of Shabbos is even greater than that of Yom Tov.

If Yom Tov starts at the end of Shabbos (on Saturday night), a separate Havdalah prayer is not made. However, a few additional sentences are added to the Yom Tov Evening Kiddush and the Havdalah blessing is recited—but with the last word changed. "Blessed art Thou who makes a distinction between the holy and the *holy*." The blessing for fire is made on the light of the Yom Tov candles, but the spices need not be smelled since the holiness and joy of Yom Tov is certainly adequate compensation for the departure of our Shabbos soul.

Melava Malka

As the Shabbos Queen departs, we escort her royally and do our best to retain her presence by setting the table, and sitting down to another meal. By having the *Melave Malka* feast, we prolong the benefits and uplifted spirits that were ours on Shabbos. The Talmud relates many rewards and benefits we receive from partaking of a Melave Malka meal on Saturday night. It also explains that food eaten for Melave Malka is the primary source of nourishment for the *luz* bone, the small bone at the top of the spine which never decays and thus will be the physical basis of resurrection in the days after the Messiah comes.

Some people make a point of serving a meal that includes washing the hands with a blessing and eating bread. If everyone is too full, or if no bread is available, then some cake or cookies will be sufficient. If even this is not possible, at least have a little fruit. Whatever is eaten, it should be done with the idea in mind that it is for the sake of the mitzvah of Melave Malka.

It is a common practice to mention the name of Eliyahu HaNavi (Elijah the Prophet) on Saturday nights, since his coming will signal the advent of Messiah, and also because he is the one responsible for recording the fact that we kept the mitzvah of Shabbos. As always, it is fitting that matters of Torah be discussed.

In addition, Chassidim have always had the custom to tell stories at Melave Malka about the Baal Shem Tov (the founder of Chassidus 1698-1760) or other great Rabbis and *Tzaddikim* (saintly people) up to and including our time. It is said these stories and the faith they invoke and strengthen in us are an antidote to the chaos of the present day,

Often, a simcha such as a Bar Mitzvah, engagement, or *Upsherenish* will be celebrated on Saturday night in conjunction with a Melave Malka. On such occasions, more elaborate food than usual will be served.

Among Chassidim, traditional food for Melave Malka, besides challah and bread, is herring or some other kind of smoked fish, whole cooked potatoes and some hot tea. Usually the meal is pareve, although there may be some leftovers from the Shabbos meat meal. If dairy products are desired, remember it is necessary to wait six hours from the time of the last Shabbos meal, if it was a meat meal.

For menu suggestions for Melave Malka, see page 303.

Laws of Cooking for Shabbos

1. All food preparations for Shabbos must be completed before Shabbos begins.

2. **If a food is cooked before Shabbos (or at least ⅓ cooked before Shabbos begins) and one wants to eat it warm on Shabbos, one may place it on a covered flame before Shabbos begins and remove it from the covered flame right before serving.** *Cholent* is a classic Jewish dish that is always prepared and served according to this principle.

The covered flame or Shabbos stove is prepared by using what is called in Yiddish a *blech*. A blech is an aluminum or asbestos sheet shaped to cover both the burners and handles of a stove. Before Shabbos it is put over a gas or electric fire which will burn the entire Shabbos. The blech remains covering the stove top until the end of Shabbos and serves to keep food placed on it warm, even though the flame is very low.

Note: A gas flame will automatically become higher under the blech, so set it a little lower than desired and check it once the blech is set up.

3. Returning food to the blech on Shabbos is permissable *only* if all of the following conditions are met:

   a. The pot was lifted from the blech with the conscious intention of returning it directly.

   b. The food is fully cooked.

   c. The food is still slightly warm.

   d. The contents were not transferred to a different pot.

   e. The pot was not put down (on table, chair or the like).

Note: One should keep all the above in mind when temporarily lifting off a tea kettle from the blech, intending to put it back.

4. If on Shabbos it is noticed that the cholent or some other food is drying out, it is not permitted to add more water to it (since that water will become cooked on Shabbos). If the water is taken from a boiling kettle on the blech, some authorities permit it. But it is preferable to move the pot to a place on the blech which is not directly over the fire (providing the food is completely cooked).

5. One may not serve any food directly from a pot on the blech. It must first be lifted off.

6. Preparing a salad on Shabbos.

   a. If slicing vegetables thinly, do it close to mealtime.

   b. When preparing the dressing, first add the oil and vinegar and then the salt.

Important Note: There are more laws pertaining to the preparation of food *on* Shabbos, which would require a more intensive study of the laws of Shabbos.

Laws of Cooking for Yom Tov

1. The Torah specifies that all *melachos* (work) (see page 358) are forbidden on Yom Tov, except for such work which is related to the preparation of food for the Yom Tov (Exodus 12:16). (Whereas on Shabbos no form of work at all is allowed.) This includes such actions as kneading, baking and cooking. These are permitted on Yom Tov because with freshly-cooked food, the happiness of the holiday is enhanced. If a food would taste equally good if prepared before Yom Tov, it should be done before.

Some actions such as grinding and selecting certain items and cutting and mashing vegetables, may be done in a modified way on Yom Tov, slightly different from the regular way they are done. (However, no actions may be done with electric appliances or other type of machinery.) To have a fuller understanding of which actions are permitted and which are not on Yom Tov, it would be necessary to study in great detail the 39 Principle Categories of Work (*melachos*) which may not be done on Shabbos, and how they apply to Yom Tov.

2. Any form of work which is forbidden on Shabbos yet is permitted on Yom Tov, is allowed only in connection with the preparation of food needed for *that day only.* Food may not be prepared on the first day of Yom Tov for the second day of Yom Tov.

The only exception is when the second day of Yom Tov or the day immediately following Yom Tov is Shabbos, in which case the food must be prepared on Yom Tov for Shabbos, since it cannot be done on the Shabbos itself. Even so, this can only be done by making an *Eruv Tavshilin* before Yom Tov begins.

Eruv Tavshilin means the mixing of cooking. In order that the preparation of food for Shabbos may be allowed on Yom Tov (when Shabbos immediately follows Yom Tov or else coincides with the second day of Yom Tov), the Eruv Tavshilin is prepared in the afternoon before Yom Tov begins. This is done by saying the special blessing over two whole foods, one cooked and one baked, such as challah or matzoh (at least two ounces), with a piece of gefilte fish or a hard-boiled egg (at least slightly more than an ounce). These are then put aside and eaten on Shabbos day. This makes it permissible to continue preparing for Shabbos during the day of Yom Tov that precedes Shabbos, but not on the first day of Yom Tov, if the first day would fall out on a Thursday.

3. One may not create a new flame on Yom Tov. Striking a match is prohibited. But one may make a new flame from an already existing flame—from a stove, a candle, or a lit pilot.

4. A flame that will be used for baking or cooking on Yom Tov should be made before Yom Tov. It is permissible to light a very small fire, and then make it higher on Yom Tov in the

process of cooking. It is best to keep two flames burning on Yom Tov—one low and one high. Some halachic authorities allow that if the only available flame is the high one, it may be lowered, if necessary for cooking, but it is better to start a new small one from an already existing flame, than to lower an existing one. Raising the heat on an electric range is only permissible if it does not involve a separate coil becoming heated.

5. Although carrying is a labor that is forbidden on Shabbos, it is allowed for the sake of preparing food for Yom Tov and also for other actions necessary for the sake of Yom Tov. Example: Carrying one's prayer book to shul, carrying a handkerchief, carrying or strolling little children to shul, or for visiting. It is important not to take liberties with this allowance and to carry only when it is necessary for the benefit of Yom Tov.

The Yomim Tovim

The Yomim Tovim

The Yomim Tovim

Each Jewish Holiday is eagerly awaited, and when it comes is royally greeted in the most festive manner. Many of our most cherished memories are connected to these Yomim Tovim. The Seder together with grandparents and other family members, the solemn prayers in shul on the High Holidays, the sound of our singing filling the streets as we enjoy the Kiddush meal outside in the Succah, and the dancing lights of the Menorah all awaken in us a very special feeling of Jewishness.

The Yomim Tovim bring to mind our very rich heritage, the history of our ancestors and G-d's special love toward the Jews throughout the generations. Yet they are not only reminders of the past to be "traditionally" observed today, but also indicate the reoccurance of the special Divine Powers which were manifest at certain times in the past which are renewed every year at the same time. (See *Year by Year,* page 36.)

We celebrate different types of Holidays throughout the year. Those set for us by the Torah are known as Biblical Holidays. Rosh Hashanah and Yom Kippur, the High Holy Days, are the days which G-d revealed to us as being most opportune for beseeching Him and requesting of Him a good and healthy year for ourselves and our families. Pesach, Shavuos and Succos all remind us of G-d's special involvement with the fate of the Jewish people in miraculously taking them out of Egypt, then giving them His most treasured gift, the Torah, and then protecting them constantly throughout their forty years in the desert.

Then there are the Holidays of Chanukah and Purim, known as Rabbinical Holidays. They were established for all generations by our Sages as very festive holidays reminding us of great miracles performed for us by G-d. They stand out as a sign of G-d's everlasting and continuous protection of the Jews. Rabbinical Holidays are not governed by the same laws as are Biblical holidays, but are marked with special prayers, laws, and customs of their own.

Each Holiday and special occasion is marked with its own unique observances. To the housewife, the coming of each Jewish Holiday also brings to mind the various traditional foods to serve especially on that occasion in addition to the regular Kiddush meal. The significance and history of each of the Holidays, its special laws and customs, and the foods traditionally served are described in the following pages. The Holiday meals follow the Shabbos pattern, but can be freshly cooked, enhancing the spirit of the festive meal and allowing for more variety. The laws concerning preparing food for Yom Tov are found on pages 31-32. All of the Holidays and special occasions are presented in the order in which they occur throughout the year.

At the end of this section you will find a chapter on the Jewish calendar, which is based upon the movements of the moon. This chapter explains the significance of the lunar calendar system, the meaning of Rosh Chodesh, why we have leap years and how they are determined, and why the Holidays have an added day outside the land of Israel.

We hope that the insights and information contained in the following pages will enrich and deepen your experience of the Jewish Holidays throughout the years to come.

Year by Year

A year in Jewish life takes us through a full cycle of feelings, moods, and attitudes. Weeks and months are punctuated with timeless remembrances that color and enrich our lives. Each Holiday is more than a token remembrance of the past, and much more than the occasion for a sumptuous meal. When received properly, each event in the Jewish calendar presents us with a unique opportunity, one which is offered anew each year in its time.

As there is a beginning and end to each week, so, too, there is a beginning to our year, and a time toward the end to take stock of all our deeds. Each Shabbos, each Yom Tov and each mitzvah opens special "channels" through which we can bind ourselves to the Divine gifts that were first presented at these times and are intrinsically bound up with those times of the year.

Thus it is that the tenth day of the month of Tishrei has the quality of being able to elicit Divine forgiveness for all Jews. On this day, after Moshe's forty days and nights on the mountain, G-d forgave the Jewish people for their sin of making a Golden Calf to worship. Yom Kippur was then established by G-d forever as a day of pardon, and new beginning with a clean slate.

Similarly, the month of Nissan, in which the exodus from Egypt took place, is a month of redemption and liberation, not only in the past but for all generations. "In the month of Nissan we were redeemed and in the month of Nissan we are destined to be redeemed." Shavuos, on the sixth of Sivan, is "the time of the giving of our Torah." It is the most propitious time for Torah to flow into each Jew. It is the time when each Jew is most able to receive the Torah and attach himself to it.

And so from year to year and month to month we grow, making each Holiday, its ideas, impressions and special mitzvohs a part of ourselves. With each Shabbos and each Holiday comes a regeneration of strength and inspiration with which to overcome any obstacle which may arise during the week and during the year.

Candle-lighting

The following Yomim Tovim are ushered in with candle-lighting: Rosh Hashanah (both days), Yom Kippur, Succos (both days), Shemini Atzeres, Simchas Torah, Pesach (first two and last two days) and Shavuos. For the appropriate blessings and correct time for candle-lighting on these days see page 22.

These Holidays are also marked with the prohibition of doing any form of *melocha*, creative work, except for some work which is necessary for the cooking for that day of Yom Tov only. (See Cooking for Yom Tov, page 31.) On Yom Kippur, however, no *melochos* whatsoever may be performed.

The Month of Elul
Preparing for the New Year

A King in the Field

Rabbi Schneur Zalman, the founder of Chabad Chassidism, liked to use this parable in describing our preparation during Elul for the High Holy Days to follow in the month of Tishrei: A king resided in his palace all year. Those who wished to gain an audience with him traveled great distances to the palace and even then were faced with difficulties in gaining an audience with the king. But once a year the king would leave his palace and go out into the fields and towns to receive everyone graciously—even the simplest people—and give them a chance to speak to him or request something of him. G-d—the King of Kings, is also "in the field" once a year, during the month of Elul. He is eager to listen to us during this time and we are grateful to avail ourselves of this opportunity to return to Him and beseech His aid.

Repentence, Prayer, Charity

Three key activities in Elul have the power to nullify any harsh judgment and enable us to receive the verdict during Tishrei for a year of good: Through *teshuvah* (repentance or return), we return to our inherent good selves, since a Jew by his very nature is good and desires no evil. Through *tefillah,* (prayer), we cleave to the Creator, Who is the source of our soul and for Whom our soul is always yearning. By giving *tzedokah* (charity), we are performing a deed which is really only just (*tzedek* means justice), for we are merely the guardians of the wealth extended to us by G-d and are His messengers for distributing it to those in need. It is not so much kindness we practice by giving of our wealth to others, as justice, for in truth, we are not the real owners.

During Elul we listen to the *shofar,* a call to repentance, every day after morning services (except on Shabbos and on the day before Rosh Hashanah). We add Psalm 27, with its allusions to the holidays of Tishrei, to our daily prayers. In the final days of Elul, in the very early hours of the morning, we highlight our preparation for the new year with the *selichos,* heartfelt prayers for forgiveness.

Hatoras Nedorim is recited preferably on Erev Rosh Hashana to nullify one's vows except those made to one's fellows, such as a promise to repay a debt. It is said in shul before at least three men but preferably ten men, and includes such personal vows as a resolution to increase in one's performance of a particular mitzvah.

And so Rosh Hashana will find us well prepared, as we enter the month of Tishrei with joy in our hearts and confidence that G-d, in His mercy, will grant us a truly good and blessed year.

Rosh Hashanah

The Head of the Year

Our New Year's Day is a day for deep soul-searching and resolution. Yet, as its very name indicates, Rosh Hashanah—Head of the Year—is not just the beginning of another cycle; it is the head of these days. Just as the brain is the chief of the organs, directing and integrating all of a person's functions and behavior, so, in the same way, this day of Rosh Hashanah directs the course of the ensuing new year. Through it the life force, blessing and sustenance for the days that follow are provided. On Rosh Hashanah, the anniversary of the creation of man in the world, the inhabitants of the world are judged anew.

The main themes of Rosh Hashanah, as expressed in our prayers, are a) coronation: we accept G-d's kingship over us anew each year; and b) that we ask G-d to grant us a year of life, health and happiness. Although Rosh Hashanah is an awesome day, and obviouly a time for solemn reflection and self-evaluation, it is not a day of sadness. We have faith in G-d's mercy and are confident that He loves us despite our many faults. We approach Rosh Hashanah with happiness because it is the day for ensuring a new year better than the one before; we cannot be sad.

"This day is holy to G-d, your G-d; do not mourn and do not weep . . . for the joy of G-d is your strength." (Nechemiah 8:9–10)

The Shofar

The special mitzvah of Rosh Hashanah is hearing the blowing of the *Shofar* (ram's horn) which symbolizes the coronation of G-d as King of the universe and brings to mind several great events which involved a ram's horn—among them the Giving of the Torah at Mt. Sinai and the Binding of Isaac on the altar on Mt. Moriah. It will also herald the coming of the Messiah. The sounding of the shofar is a call to look into one's soul and improve one's ways, saying, as expressed by Maimonides: "Awake you sleepers from your sleep, and you slumberers, arise from your slumber—examine your deeds, repent and remember your Creator" (Hilchos Teshuvah, Chapter 3).

Women, too, have taken upon themselves this mitzvah, even though it is bound to time—the factor which serves in most cases to exempt women from being obligated in a mitzvah.

The Shofar is the oldest of wind instruments. So simple and so primitive and so much a part of Jewish history, its piercing sounds penetrate our beings and bring us close to G-d and the observance of His commandments. As the prophet affirms, "Shall the Shofar be blown in a city and people not tremble?" (Amos 3:6)

Special Foods and Customs

Rosh Hashanah has numerous special customs, and many of them are connected with the Holiday meal.

• On the first night of Rosh Hashanah, we dip our challah into honey instead of salt. (This custom may go on until Hoshanah Rabbah, depending on family custom.) Right after the blessing over bread, a sweet apple is dipped into honey and a special prayer is said asking G-d for a sweet year.

• The head of a fish is usually eaten, signifying our hope to be the "head," outstanding in righteousness and an example for all. A popular way to prepare the head is to stuff it with the same mixture used for gefilte fish and then cook it like regular gefilte fish.

• On the second night, a new fruit which was not yet eaten this season is put on the table, preferably at the time of candle-lighting. When the blessing *shehechiyonu* ("Who has kept alive and bought us to this season") is made (by the women at candle-lighting and by the men during Kiddush) this fruit is kept in mind. It is also good to have in mind a new garment one is wearing. This new fruit is eaten right after Kiddush and is often a pomegranate, because this is one of the fruits for which the Land of Israel is praised in the Torah, and also because it is said to contain 613 seeds, equal to the number of our commandments.

• *Tzimmes* is a sweet carrot dish generally eaten on Rosh Hashanah and throughout the month of Tishrei. The Yiddish word for carrots is *meren*, which also means increase. Tzimmes thus symbolizes the desire to have our merits increase above our shortcomings.

• Honey cake has always been a traditional and popular dessert during this time.

• Many people use round challahs on Rosh Hashanah, and also round farfel for soup, to express the hope that the new year will likewise be rounded out and perfect and bring the best of everything to everyone. In addition, the word *farfallen* represents the hope for a falling away of our misdeeds of the past year.

• There is a custom *not* to eat nuts because of the similar numerical equivalent of the letters in the word for nut (*egoz*) and the word for sin (*chet*). A very practical reason not to eat nuts is in order to keep the throat clear for the long prayer services of the Yom Tov.

On the first day of Rosh Hashanah, after the afternoon services, we customarily "throw" our sins into a body of fresh water which has in it live fish. This custom is known as *tashlich,* from the statement (Michah 7:19): "And you shall cast away (*tashlich*) all your sins. . . ." If the first day of Rosh Hashanah falls on Shabbos, Tashlich is said the second day.

Since Rosh Hashanah is the Head of the Year, it sets the pattern for each of the days to come. For this reason we should try to be extra careful in everything we do and think and say on this all-important day. Whether praying or serving food, making blessings, eating, or conversing at the table, we try to keep in mind at all times that this is Rosh Hashanah, and as this day goes, so will the rest of the year. It is customary not to nap during the day so that we should be up and alert when receiving our verdict for a good year.

After the service on Rosh Hashanah we all greet one another with the good wishes of

L'shona Tova Tikosaivu V'saichosaimu

May you be inscribed and sealed for a good year.

Ten Days of Repentance and Return

A Significant Week

Rosh Hashanah, Yom Kippur, and the days in between are known as the Ten Days of Teshuvah (repentance or return).

During these days we are especially careful in all the mitzvohs we perform. As in the month of Elul, special attention is given to the three mitzvohs of *teshuvah, tefillah* and *tzedakah* (see Elul).

The seven days between Rosh Hashanah and Yom Kippur are highly significant and should be filled with Torah and mitzvohs to the fullest measure. Not only is this the last week before Yom Kippur, it is also the first complete weekly cycle of the new year and serves as an atonement for all the Sundays, Mondays, etc. of the past year.

The third of the ten days, the day after Rosh Hashanah, is the Fast of Gedalia (see Fast Days).

The Shabbos between Rosh Hashanah and Yom Kippur has a special distinction. It is known as *Shabbos Shuva* (Shabbos of Return) because of the beginning words of the Haftorah of this Shabbos: "Return Israel unto G-d your G-d." (Hosea 4). It is customary for Rabbis to speak to their congregants on this day on the importance of *teshuvah,* repentance and returning to G-d's ways.

Special Customs

An interesting custom symbolic of forgiveness is *Kaparos* (atonement). Men and women each take a rooster or hen, respectively, and say a short prayer while holding and circling it above their heads. It is hoped that the realization that this animal is going to die, a fate which we ourselves might be deserving, will bring us to a total repentance.

It is preferable to observe this custom early in the morning before Yom Kippur. (Some women practice this custom during the week between Rosh Hashanah and Yom Kippur.) The chicken or the equivalent value of the chicken is then given to charity—for charity brings forgiveness and averts harsh decrees.

Kaparos can also be observed with money instead of a live chicken. The money is also waved aloft and the prayer said, substituting, "This money will go to charity" for "This fowl will go to its death." Afterwards, the money is given to charity.

During all ten days of repentance, additional sentences are inserted in different parts of the daily prayer, emphasizing the fact that we are now amidst these awesome days. Many Jews have the custom of continuing the *Selichos* (Prayers for Forgiveness) during the weekdays between Rosh Hashanah and Yom Kippur.

Yom Kippur

The Day Before Yom Kippur

Among the many preparations for the awesome day of Yom Kippur, and perhaps one of the most important, is the seeking of forgiveness from friends, relatives and acquaintances—for actual wrongs done or to soothe bad feelings that may have arisen during the year. This is one aspect of our behavior that cannot be forgiven by G-d unless forgiveness is first sought from those we have wronged. Another custom practiced on Erev Yom Kippur is that of going to the *mikvah* (See *Glossary*) and immersing ourselves in it so that we become pure in preparation for Yom Kippur. It is customary too, during that day, for parents to bless their children. The afternoon service, *Minchah,* is said early in the afternoon. The *Viduy* (confession) prayer is included in the *Amidah* (standing prayer). It is a mitzvah to eat two full festive meals on Erev Yom Kippur. The meal before the fast is eaten in the late afternoon and is finished no later than an hour before sunset. So important is it to eat well before Yom Kippur that we are told that this mitzvah is equal to the mitzvah of fasting on Yom Kippur itself. To ease our fast, the food we serve at this meal should not be salty or spicy. Partaking of a festival meal at this time demonstrates our faith in G-d's abundant mercy and our confidence in being forgiven and sealed for a good year.

It is traditional to eat *kreplach* at this meal. *Kreplach* are pieces of dough filled with ground meat or chicken, then cooked or baked and served with soup. Only chicken kreplach are served on Erev Yom Kippur because no meat is eaten on this day. This special traditional dish alludes to our hope that kindness will "cover" any strict judgment we may deserve.

Forgiveness—an Eternal Gift

"I have forgiven" are the eternal words spoken by G-d on the tenth of Tishrei, after Moses prayed to G-d and fasted for forty days on behalf of the Jewish people. This day became Yom Hakippurim, the Day of Atonement, for all generations. Any time a Jew sincerely repents he is forgiven, but this day has a special power because of the forgiveness granted to the Jews on the original Yom Kippur.

Yom Kippur and all the laws pertaining to it start before sunset, as do all the holidays, with candle-lighting by the women of the house. A twenty-four hour candle is also lit in the house in honor of the holiday, as we cannot honor it with festive meals. The light also reminds us of the Second Tablets that were given to the Jews on this day, for light symbolizes Torah. This candle is an addition to any *yahrzeit* candles.

On Yom Kippur, no *melachos* (work—see Glossary) may be done. The *machzor* (Holiday

Prayer Book) should be brought to shul before sunset. Since women begin the holiday when they light candles and may not carry afterwards, they should be sure to get their *machzors* to shul earlier in the day. Indeed, Yom Kippur is refered to in the Torah as Shabbos Shabbason, a total rest day just like Shabbos. In fact the doubled wording teaches us that even if Yom Kippur comes out on Shabbos, the laws of Yom Kippur are observed on that day and are not postponed, unlike other fast days when they occur on Shabbos.

On Yom Kippur five activities are specifically prohibited: eating and drinking, anointing oneself with perfumes or oils, and washing (for pleasure), wearing leather shoes, and marital relations.

Men go to shul in their white garments called *kittels*, and women often dress in light colors or white, which symbolizes purity.

Special Prayers

The evening service begins with the chanting of *Kol Nidrei*. During each main prayer we say the *Viduy* (confession), beating the heart with the right hand at each phrase as we enumerate all the sins we may have committed and ask G-d for forgiveness. The Viduy is phrased in the plural ("We have sinned"), for all Jews are considered as one body, and we are all responsible for one another.

One of the unique prayers of Yom Kippur is the *Avodah* section in the *Musaf Prayer*, which describes in detail the great and awesome service performed on Yom Kippur by the Priests in the Holy Temple. This Service was highlighted by the entry of the High Priest into the Holy of Holies, the place where the original tablets of the Ten Commandments were kept. Only on this one day a year, and only after much preparation, was the High Priest allowed to enter. Described are his preparation, the Service, and the exciting conclusion: when the red string at the window of the Temple turned white, the Jews knew they were granted forgiveness. The High Priest then emerged safely from the Holy of Holies. If his concentration or purity of thought had wavered but an instant, he would not have been able to withstand the intense revelation of G-dliness within the Holy of Holies.

The fifth and final prayer of Yom Kippur day is the *Neilah* prayer said after the *Minchah* (afternoon) services. A fifth prayer service is unique to Yom Kippur Day. *Neilah* (locking) is the closing time of our prayers, when G-d's inscription for us for the coming year is sealed. We muster together all our remaining strength to say this prayer with real devotion. Everyone recites out loud the "Shema Yisroel" and the sentences which follow it, and the prayer culminates with the final blowing of the Shofar.

The evening services are then said, quietly but in a mood of triumph and confidence in having been sealed for a good and healthy year. Afterwards, if it is a clear night, the "Sanctification of the New Moon" blessing should be said for the month of Tishrei (if it has not yet been said).

As at the conclusion of every Yom Tov, the Havdalah is said, but with the distinction that after Yom Kippur the blessing over light is included, since during Yom Kippur we were prohibited from using fire. (Fire is not included in the Havdalah of the other Holidays because it is permitted for cooking on those days.) Care should be taken that the Havdalah light be kindled from a pre-existing flame, lit before Yom Kippur. The fast is not broken until the Havdalah is said.

Everyone goes home to break the fast. That night or early the next morning we are already involved in building the *Succah*, so that no time should elapse between all the good resolutions for the coming year and the actual doing of the mitzvohs.

Succos

The Season of our Rejoicing.

The "Ten Days of Awe and Repentance" are followed by "the Season of our Rejoicing." This is one of the names given to the holiday of Succos, for the Torah commandment to "rejoice" is mentioned more often in connection with the holiday of Succos than for any other Yom Tov.

Succos is indeed a time of rejoicing. Following closely after Yom Kippur, the day of forgiveness, it is a time of starting the new year fresh. Succos begins on the fifteenth day of Tishrei, at the time of the ingathering of the crops—a further cause for rejoicing, as one looks with a sense of pride and accomplishment upon the fruits of one's labor of the previous months.

The seven-day holiday of Succos is one of the *Sholosh Regolim,* the three Festivals when all Jewish males over age thirteen were commanded to come celebrate the Yom Tov in the proximity of the Holy Temple. (The other two Sholosh Regolim are Pesach and Shavuos.) Women and children joined these pilgrimages whenever possible.

The Temple celebration during Succos was highlighted by the ceremony of water-drawing for the Holiday offerings. This ceremony was unique in that all year the libations on the Altar were performed with wine, but on Succos *plain water* was used. Yet it was said that "whoever has not seen the joy at the place of the water-drawing has never seen true joy in his life!" (Succah 51) The joy expressed in this ceremony was the joy of a simple and pure acceptance of G-d's will, as symbolized by clear water, as opposed to the acceptance that is based on understanding, symbolized by wine.

The Succah—A Symbol of G-d's Protection

The dominant mitzvah is, of course, the Succah. The Succah is built before the holiday begins. Almost anything can be used for the walls, but the roof covering must be *schach,* which is plant-life material meeting to certain specifications. Evergreen branches, corn-stalks or bamboo are popularly used. During the entire festival we live in these temporary dwellings as much as possible.

The Succah is symbolic of the clouds of glory which protected the Jews during their forty years in the wilderness. These clouds of glory, serving as a shade and a shield were an ever-present reminder of G-d's kindness and love for His children. As we sit in the Succah, we too are aware of and grateful for G-d's protection.

All meals must take place only in the Succah unless it rains. Care is taken on Shabbos to carry food between the house and the Succah only if an *Eruv* (see Glossary) has been put up before Shabbos, if needed. The most appealing meals are prepared for the Succah and the fanciest dishes and accessories are brought out to dress the Succah table. Many observe the custom of decorating the Succah beautifully. The Succah is a place of rejoicing and festivity for the whole family.

It is considered very desirable to have poor people as guests in one's Succah for each of the festive meals, corresponding to the heavenly guests who are said to visit every Succah. The mitzvah of dwelling in a Succah is unique in that the person's whole body participates in it. We fulfill the mitzvah by entering and having something to eat as long as it is with the *awareness* that this mitzvah was given to us in remembrance of our Deliverance from Egypt. On the first two nights of Succos one makes the blessing ". . . to dwell in the Succah" if he eats a *k'zayis* (one ounce) or more of bread. Thereafter he makes this blessing if he eats bread, cake or other food made of the five grains which is more than two ounces.

The Four Kinds

A most beautiful and meaningful mitzvah of Succos is the "taking of the four kinds." The four plants enumerated in the Torah are the *Esrog* (citron), *Lulav* (palm branch), *Hadassim* (myrtles) and *Aravos* (willows). Much energy and money is expended in acquiring the most beautiful ones possible. This mitzvah is performed every day of Succos except on Shabbos. It should be done early in the day but is permissible until sunset. The Lulav, Haddasim and Aravos are taken in the right hand in a specified manner and the blessing is recited. The Esrog is then taken in the left hand and held to the other three species. All are swayed together, in accordance with various customs. The resulting sight is quite beautiful and memorable to behold.

A left-handed person takes the Lulav in the left hand and the Esrog and the other species in the right hand. While women are not obligated in this mitzvah, they have generally taken upon themselves to perform it throughout Succos. When "taking the four kinds" one should be careful to have the hands free of gloves, rings, etc.

This mitzvah can penetrate very deeply and has extraordinary relevance to our lives today. In our oral tradition, it is explained that each of these four kinds corresponds to a different type of person, from the Esrog which has both refreshing taste (constant Torah learning) and delightful fragrance (good deeds) to the Aravah, which has neither of these qualities. Despite their differences, the Torah instructs us to take these four and bind them together, for they complement one another. So too does one Jew complement another, and only when there is true harmony among all the Jewish people can we hope for an ideal existence. May it happen soon!

Yom Tov and the Intermediate Days

Outside Israel, Succos is celebrated an additional (eighth) day, (see *Calendar,* pages 70-72). The first two days are Yom Tov, to which all the laws of Yom Tov apply. The third through seventh days of the Holiday are called *Chol Hamoed.* These days are not highlighted with candlelighting or Kiddush meals, but only very necessary work may be done.

The seventh day is called Hoshana Rabbah. It is the last day of shaking the Lulav and Esrog. The Holiday culminates in Shemini Atzeres, which is Yom Tov once again.

Hoshanna Rabbah

The Great Hoshanna—Special Prayers

Hoshanna Rabbah is the name of the seventh day of Succos, and is almost a Holiday in itself. It is the final day of Chol Hamoed Succos (the Intermediate Days) and is the last day on which we can make the blessing on the Waving of the Four Kinds. Special prayers, called Hoshannas, are said towards the end of the morning services. These prayers are accompanied by the beautiful ceremony in which everyone circles the *Bimah* (platform) seven times, Lulav and Esrog in hand.

Hoshanna Rabbah is the final day on which G-d might change our inscription for a good year. Although the gates of heaven have officially been closed at the conclusion of the Yom Kippur service, it is still possible for G-d to open them this one last time on Hoshanna Rabbah, as we ask Him to do in our prayers on this day. It is for this reason that we beat the Hoshannos (willow branches) on the floor during our prayers, driving away any harsh judgments. It is also customary to stay awake the night of Hoshanna Rabbah to learn portions of the Torah, and recite Psalms.

Holiday Meal and Kreplach

A special festive meal is eaten in the afternoon of this day, for this is the final occasion of the year on which to make the blessing "to dwell in the succah."

The traditional dish for Hoshanna Rabbah is *kreplach*—small triangular pieces of dough filled with ground, seasoned meat or chicken. They may be fried or cooked. They are usually served in chicken soup. These *kreplach* suggest the covering up of G-d's stringency with loving-kindness, for on this day, as on Yom Kippur, G-d may finalize a verdict for a good year for all his people. Kreplach are also traditionally eaten on Erev Yom Kippur and on Purim, for the same reason.

Shemini Atzeres

A Special Day of Celebration

Shemini Atzeres corresponds to the eighth day of the holiday of Succos, but is a separate and a complete Yom Tov in its own right.

Rashi, one of our greatest commentators on the Torah, likened Shemini Atzeres to the special feast of a king for his beloved son. For a full week the king celebrated with all his kingdom. After this week of festivities, the king said to his son: "It is difficult for me to part with you. Please stay another day to celebrate." For seven days of Succos we brought seventy sacrifices to the Holy Temple on behalf of all the nations. ("If the nations of the world would have known the value of the Temple for them, they would have surrounded it with fortresses in order to protect it." Midrash Raba) G-d set aside an eighth day of celebration on which only one holiday sacrifice was offered, this one on behalf of the Jewish nation, and it became a day of unique celebration between G-d and His loyal children, the Jews.

The above parable can be linked to the name of the holiday itself. *Atzeres* means holding back, referring to the king who held back his son from leaving with the rest of the celebrants.

Outside the land of Israel, a final meal is eaten in the Succah on Shemini Atzeres. Some go into the Succah only for Kiddush in the morning. In any case, the blessing for "dwelling in the Succah" is not said.

Simchas Torah

Rejoicing with the Torah

Outside the Land of Israel, Simchas Torah is celebrated the day after Shemini Atzeres, making a total of nine consecutive days of festivities. "Simcha" denotes joy and great rejoicing. That is certainly the case on Simchas Torah; all the Torah scrolls are brought out from the Ark, and everyone, scholars and laymen alike, dance around the shul, proudly taking turns clutching the holy Torah scrolls to their hearts. Everyone present becomes passionately involved in the *hakafos,* as these dances are called, for part of every Jew's inheritance is a love for the holy Torah which G-d gave us.

Even those not privileged to express this feeling adequately during the year through study of the Torah can rejoice with all on Simchas Torah, for this is the time of singing and dancing, of joy without limitations and beyond understanding—a greater joy than is achieved through intellectual study alone.

In the Land of Israel, Shemini Atzeres and Simchas Torah are celebrated on the same day. Accordingly, Chassidim here have the custom to take out the Torah Scrolls for *hakafos* on the night of Shemini Atzeres as well.

On Simchas Torah all males over Bar Mitzvah age are called up to the Torah, and this one time a year even young boys get to have a special *aliyah* called *Kol N'arim,* in which they are all called up together.

During the morning of Simchas Torah, the reading of the final portion of the Torah is completed and the scroll is immediately rolled back for the reading once again of *Bereshis bara . . .* The cycle continues! The joy increases as the reader chants the first chapter of Genesis. For in truth one never finishes the learning of Torah. Its wisdom is Infinite, and it is the eternal force that has connected the Jews to G-d for over 3,000 years.

Chanukah

The Miracle: Many into the Hands of a Few

Whenever we sit and look into the flickering Chanukah lights we recall the miracle that occurred over 2,000 years ago when a handful of valiant Jews stood victorious in battle over the hordes of their enemies. Whenever righteousness conquers evil despite overwhelming odds, it is an occasion for thanksgiving and rejoicing, a miracle worthy of being commemorated forever. Still, this is not the primary message of the dancing Chanukah lights, for the major miracle of Chanukah was the very existence of those flames. After the Jews were victorious over their Greek oppressors, they wished to re-kindle the Menorah in the Holy Temple and to rededicate the Temple which had been spoiled by the enemy. But it would have taken eight days to prepare acceptably pure olive oil to burn, because all the available vessels of oil had been defiled by the Greeks. Before despair could fasten its grip, G-d demonstrated His everlasting kindness and the Jews discovered a single small jar of olive oil, buried beneath the ruins, with the seal of the High Priest still intact upon its lid, clearly untouched by Greek hands. Although this provided only enough oil to burn for one day, they decided to light the Menorah anyway, and behold, they had light from this oil for the entire eight days of the dedication.

The miracle of the discovery of a small amount of pure oil and its burning for eight days is the focus of the Chanukah celebration. It is therefore necessary to understand why it was so important for the Jews to find olive oil that was yet untouched by Greek hands. And why, since events were already in the realm of the miraculous, was an amount of oil sufficient for eight days not provided by G-d? The answer is clear when we consider the nature of the Greek exile of that time.

A Spiritual Victory

The Greeks were not trying to kill all the Jews, as was Haman (in the story of Purim) or later tyrants. Nor were they against Jewish culture or against Jews studying the wisdom of the To-

48

rah. They had in mind a broader sense of destruction; they aimed to stamp out the Jews' belief and faith in G-d by eliminating their study and observance of those of His commandments, like circumcision and Shabbos, that were not based on human understanding but on faith. With Judaism reduced to a rational structure, the Jews and their Torah would easily be assimilated into the dominant Greek culture and approach to life. This resistance to being stamped "Greek" at the cost of their traditional Jewishness is the reason why it was so important to find *pure*, untouched oil. With a small quantity of oil they could begin lighting the Menorah, because from this the light was sure to increase. This is a message for all of us as we watch the Chanukah flames increase in number and intensity night after night. The irreducible, uncompromisable faith of the tiny band of Maccabees which is then miraculously rewarded by G-d represents for us one of the secrets of Chanukah that have come down through the generations to illuminate and guide us today.

The Name of Chanukah

The name Chanukah suggests several possible meanings. The Hebrew letters that spell the words—Ches, Nun, Vav, Chaf, Hai can be interpreted to mean:
• Rest on the 25th (Chanukah starts on the 25th of Kislev)
• Dedication—of the Temple which had been defiled by the Greeks but was now once again in Jewish hands.
• Education—a time to educate our youth in the purity of Torah which provides the strength to resist the pressures of assimilation.

In fact, all three explanations together outline the story of Chanukah. From the third explanation was also born the custom of Chanukah *gelt*. Gelt, which means money, should be intended as a reward (or an inducement) for studying Torah.

The Menorah

The Menorah should have a place for eight flames, in an even row, plus a place for the *shamas* (ministering) flame which usually stands a little higher (or lower) than the others. The first night, one flame is kindled, and each night another one is added until finally, on the eighth night, all eight are burning brightly. The Chanukah flames are not lit directly, but rather from the flame of the *shamas.* If no Menorah is available, small metal caps or small glass cups may be used.

On the first night, one lights the flame on the extreme right of the Menorah. The following night, we add one immediately to the left and light it first. Then we kindle the light of the previous night. This pattern is followed nightly, adding lights from right to left, but kindling them from left to right.

Some people place their Menorah in a window facing a public thoroughfare; others place it in the doorway, opposite the mezuzah.

It is best to burn oil in commemoration of the actual miracles. Candles may be used instead, but certainly not electric lights or bulbs.

The flames are kindled with the appropriate blessing at either twilight or dark, depending on family custom. In either case, they must burn for a half hour after nightfall.

On Friday night, Chanukah lights must be lit before the Shabbos candles. We are extremely careful about this, since it is forbidden to light any candles once Shabbos has begun and one must make sure that the light will continue burning until after dark, by filling cups with much more oil than usual or by using larger candles. On Saturday night the Chanukah lights are lit after Havdalah.

The man of the house lights for the household. If he does not light, the woman does. Children are permitted to light their own Menorahs.

The Dreidel

Since no work is permitted while the Chanukah lights are burning (and since they now have some Chanukah gelt!) the children are sure to seize the opportunity to play *dreidel*. The dreidel is a small spinning toy with four sides. Each side has one letter, either a *nun, gimmel, hai,* or *shin,* standing for the words *Nes Gadol Haya Sham*—A Great Miracle Happened There. In Israel, the words are A Great Miracle Happened *Here,* with a *pay* for *poh* (here) replacing the shin for *sham.* The dreidel-playing reminds us of those days when Greek decrees forbade Torah study, and the children would play dreidel to disguise their Torah study whenever the Greek soldiers appeared.

Latkes and Dairy

Because of the great significance of oil in the history of Chanukah, it is customary to eat *latkes* (fritters fried in oil) during this holiday. There is also a custom to eat dairy on Chanukah to commemorate its association with the way in which a clever woman, Yehudis, daughter of the High Priest, brought about the downfall of a cruel Greek general and thus saved many lives.

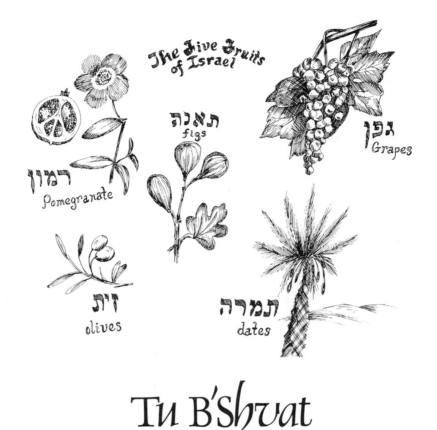

The Five Fruits of Israel

רמון
Pomegranate

תאנה
figs

גפן
Grapes

זית
olives

תמרה
dates

Tu B'Shvat

A New Year for Trees

The fifteenth day of the Hebrew month of Shvat is also a New Year's Day for it is the Rosh Hashanah for trees. The day marks the beginning of the season in the Land of Israel when the trees begin to sprout and are judged as to their future. It is a time of rejuvenation and blossoming. It is also a time for man to relearn an important moral lesson.

"For man is a tree of the field," the Torah tells us (Deuteronomy 20:19) and so, like a tree, man too must produce fruit. The fruits of mankind are Torah and good deeds. Just as a tree must bear fruit to stay healthy, so too, must man engage in giving to others and in furthering goodness in the world.

On Tu B'Shvat it is customary to eat a lot of fruit. Some even have the custom of serving fifteen kinds of fruit, corresponding to the date of the month, and to the fifteen "Songs of Elevation" (Psalms 120–134). The most desirable fruits are specifically those fruits for which the Land of Israel is praised, namely: olives, dates, grapes, figs, pomegranates. A new seasonal fruit should also be eaten on this day for the first time in the year and the blessing *shehechiyonu* ("Who has kept us alive and brought us to this season") pronounced over it, in addition to the usual blessing for fruit. (For further details, see *Blessing Over Foods,* pages 345-350.) *Bokser* (carob) is a fruit traditionally associated with this day.

Purim

A Day of Joy and Elevation

Purim is fun. It is also a time of elevation to wonderful heights. This is not despite all the wild merrymaking that goes on during this day, but because of it. In general, there is a sort of topsy-turvy quality about Purim. Its history begins with the worst of all possibilities: a decree of death for all Jews. Suddenly each disaster turns into its opposite, and behold, the Jews stand supreme and with all others wishing to join them. For on Purim, all the Jews again took upon themselves the yoke of Torah and thus Haman's wicked decree was abolished, the Jews elevated and the enemies conquered. "For the Jews there was light and joy, gladness and grace." (Book of Esther 8:16)

Purim commemorates the miracle that happened in Persia in the years between the First and Second Temples. It is not a holiday commanded by the Torah from the time of Moshe but one ordained by Rabbinical Law. It is thus not ushered in by the lighting of candles and work is not forbidden. However, one should avoid any unnecessary work in order to enjoy the festivities of the day.

Special Mitzvohs of the Day

The various mitzvohs of Purim express the joy of the moment when the Jews were delivered from their enemies. They serve to perpetuate both the miraculous victory that occurred and the faith that it inspired for all generations. There are four main mitzvohs:

• *Reading of the Megillah*—All men over the age of thirteen and women over the age of twelve are obligated to hear the reading of the Megillah of Esther, the scroll in which the story of Purim is recorded. It is advisable, as with many mitzvohs, to start the education of a child as early as possible, so we should encourage a young child to listen to the reading of the Megillah too. The children stamp their feet or wave special noisemakers (*gragers*) whenever wicked Haman's name is mentioned.

Our Rabbis stress that in order to fulfill one's obligation of hearing the Megillah, one must hear every word. Nor may the Megillah be read backwards; the reader may not go back and reread missed parts.

The Baal Shem Tov, founder of the Chassidic movement, deepens our understanding of this saying by explaining that anyone who reads the Megillah backwards—as a story that happened many years ago—and doesn't realize that the story of Purim, the story of constant Divine Providence guiding the "natural" events of the world, happens constantly as well—has not fulfilled his obligation to hear the Megillah.

The name of G-d is not mentioned once in the Megillah. Yet in reviewing the entire story it becomes clear that the unseen hand of Divine Providence shaped the events of Purim from beginning to end. The teaching for us today is that even when no *open* miracles take place before our eyes, miracles are happening constantly through G-d's Providence as it is concealed in the natural world.

It is compulsory for everyone to listen to the reading of *Parshas Zochor,* the Torah reading for the Shabbos before Purim. This is a special portion which tells us to remember what Amalek, from whom Haman descended, did to the Jews when he attacked them without cause after the exodus from Egypt.

• *Mishloach Manos*—Everyone sends a gift of a minimum of two types of immediately edible food to at least one friend. (Women send *mishloach manos* to women; men, to men.) More, and larger, *mishloach manos* can be sent. Often these foods are presented in fancy boxes, or decorated in other ways but this is not necessary. The minimum amounts required are one ounce of solid foods and at least 3½ ounces of liquid. Children should also participate in this mitzvah and they have a wonderful time doing it.

• *Matanos L'Evyonim*—Everyone gives charity—at least one penny each to two poor people. As we enjoy the holiday of Purim, it is certainly befitting that we remember the poor, so they too can enjoy the happiness of the day.

• *Seudas Purim*—a festive holiday meal in the late afternoon on Purim day, and before noon if Purim is on Friday.

• *Mach'tzis Hashekel*—Coins in any half-denomination amount (e.g. a half-dollar or the equivalent) are given in shul on the day before Purim (the Fast of Esther) or during the Morning Service on Purim.

The Purim Feast and Traditional Foods

The Purim feast is one of the happiest events of the year. The whole family gathers together, candles are lit (no blessing), and the blessing *Hamotzi* is made on a sweet challah. The Purim meal is quite unusual and is celebrated with much merriment. This is one holiday when drinking is encouraged; many valiant souls even try to attain the exalted level mentioned in the Talmud of drinking until "no longer able to tell the difference between 'blessed be Mordechai' and 'cursed be Haman.'" This refers to a level that is higher than rationality—the true, inner self of the Jew which accepts the Torah and its commandments totally and with unlimited joy. This is expressed on Purim.

Hamantashen are the three-cornered pastries stuffed with all kinds of delicious things that are eaten throughout the entire day (see Section XIII). Many times the challah for the Purim Feast is also shaped as a *hamantash.* The name probably alludes to the three-pointed hats worn in the days of the story of Purim. The original *hamantashen* were filled with poppy seeds in memory of Queen Esther who led a three-day fast, during which she prayed to G-d to repeal the horrible decree against the Jews. She and her maidservants subsisted on seeds between the days of the fast. Today, many different fillings are used. The pastry with its filling hidden inside reminds us of the miracle of Purim. This was a hidden miracle, because it came in a seemingly natural way and not through an obviously supernatural turn of events as happened in the case of Chanukah.

(For Fast of Esther, the day before Purim, see Fast Days.)

As on Erev Yom Kippur and Hoshanna Rabbah, *kreplach* (see Section VI) are eaten during the Purim feast. For Purim and Yom Kippur (Yom Hakipurim—day that is like Purim) are quite similar in essence, even though the practices of Yom Kippur are reversed on Purim! All the heavenly blessings and bounty a Jew can draw for himself with the solemnities of Yom Kippur can be brought down and manifested through the service of utter joy on Purim.

The end of Purim is a signal that we have only thirty days until Pesach. Those who wisely plan ahead begin now to prepare the home for that momentous holiday.

Pesach

The Festival of Our Liberation

"Pesach is coming!"

This awareness always stirs a sense of excitement in every Jew as spring approaches. Replete with tradition and symbolism, Pesach portrays the ideal of freedom that is so vital to all mankind. The importance of Pesach is such that the story of our going out of Egypt is written in the same sentence as the First Commandment, "I am the L-rd, your G-d, Who brought you out of the land of Egypt."

Pesach is one of the *Sholosh Regolim,* the three pilgrimages when it was a mitzvah for all males to celebrate the Holiday in Jerusalem. Pesach lasts for eight days. The first two and last two days are considered Yom Tov, and are ushered in with candle-lighting. The middle days are known as *Chol Hamoed* (see *Glossary,* page 357).

It is now more than 3,000 years since our ancestors were freed from their bondage of slavery in Egypt, yet every year at the Seder table we are careful to tell the story in exquisite detail and with great enthusiasm. What is more, we are told, "remember the day of your leaving Egypt each of the days of your life." (Deuteronomy 16:3). Why? What meaning can this possibly have for us today? What is it about our Festival of Matzos that makes it so special to us? Matzoh, *charoses* and the other traditional foods of this day are all vivid in our minds, yet certainly Pesach means more to each of us than just the food we eat.

Pesach is often referred to as *z'man cheiruseinu,* the season of our freedom. The Hebrew word for Egypt is *Mitzrayim,* meaning "limitations." Perhaps the most imprisoning slavery of all, the cruelest limitation, is the bondage of those who do not even know that they are bound, and thus have no desire at all to escape from their limitations.

It says in the Passover Hagaddah (just before the second cup of wine), that each of us, in every generation, must see ourselves as if we personally were taken out of Egypt. Each day we must experience this redemption from *Mitzrayim* (limitations). As individuals, we must seek to extricate ourselves from enslavement to the pettiness of mundane lives based only on satisfying physical pleasures and material desires. We must elevate ourselves to a life of meaning and growth and G-dliness—to fulfill the needs of our Jewish souls.

54

The Day Before Pesach

At night, the search for *chometz,* foods containing leavened flour, is carried out and in the morning all chometz is removed from the house. This important mitzvah is usually possible only after a few weeks of extensive housecleaning. On Erev Pesach, the day preceding Pesach, no chometz should be eaten from approximately 9:30 A.M. (depending upon location; check Hebrew calendar for exact time) and none should be in one's possession after about an hour later. If these deadlines are inadvertently missed, a Rav should be consulted immediately. These important laws of removing and selling of all chometz before Pesach are explained more fully in *Laws of Pesach* (pages 350–356).

After noon, neither matzoh nor any of the other mandatory foods of the Seder plate may be eaten. Apples and nuts, which are ingredients of *charoses* are also customarily not eaten on Erev Pesach.

First-born males are obligated to fast on this day in memory of the tenth plague that befell the Egyptians when their first-born died, while the Jewish first-born were spared.

The afternoon of Erev Pesach is the traditional time for baking matzoh, but matzoh baked earlier may be used.

Only after the kitchen is completely Kosher for Pesach—which usually doesn't happen until the night of Erev Pesach immediately before the search for chometz—may Pesach food be brought into the kitchen or placed in the refrigerator. Erev Pesach is usually a whirlwind of activity for the woman of the house and her helpers; all the Pesach dishes and utensils must be hauled out of storage and rinsed, and all the Pesach supplies brought in. Hopefully all the matzoh, wine, fish, meat, vegetables, aluminum foil, and so forth were obtained earlier in the week; however, the morning of Erev Pesach often sees a lot of last-minute shopping.

Of course, the main concern of Erev Pesach is preparing the Seder meal. Erev Pesach is one of the busiest and most exciting days of the year. Its outcome—the Seder night—makes the bustle well worth while.

The Seder

"Why is this night different. . . ." With these words we begin once again our recital of the wonderful and miraculous story of our liberation from Egypt long ago. The Pesach Seder, the traditional Holiday meal of the first and second nights of the festival, has throughout the ages been a unique opportunity for all members of the family—grandparents, uncles, aunts and, of course, all the children—to join together in thanksgiving to G-d for His miraculous redemption of the Jewish people.

As we recall the many miracles G-d performed for our ancestors from the time of Abraham to the going out of Egypt, and afterwards, we again live through those times and are inspired by the wondrous ways of G-d. We recall the Ten Plagues, the Crossing of the Red Sea, the Manna from Heaven that G-d fed us each day in the Wilderness, and the eager anticipation with which the Jews awaited the giving of the Torah—the ultimate purpose of their deliverance from Egypt.

Our Sages explain that when these times are remembered, the same Divine influences that brought about the miraculous events of old are stirred again by the process of recollection and remembrance. The singular atmosphere that surrounded the original events of the festival, with all its soul-stirring aspects, becomes re-awakened and actually re-occurs as we remember them each year with the advent of Pesach.

The Torah commands us to ". . . tell your children the story of Pesach." Indeed, the children (and those young in Torah knowledge) play a major role in the Seder. Many of the unique practices of the Seder table—eating matzoh, dipping the *moror* in *charoses*, sitting in a reclined position, are designed to stimulate the child's curiosity, which is expressed formally in the Four Questions, beginning with *Ma Nishtanah* of the Hagadah—"Why is this night different from all other nights?"

The Hagadah is a special book setting forth the pattern of the Seder. The Seder gets its name from the Hebrew word for "order" and refers to the pattern, established by the Sages, which begins with Kiddush and continues through the telling of the story, the eating of matzoh and *moror,* the meal and culminating with the Praise of G-d (Hallel). We end with the words "Next year in Jerusalem," looking forward to the future redemption, speedily in our days, to which G-d will bring us as He redeemed our ancestors in the past.

The word Hagadah comes from the word for "telling." It recounts all the events and miracles of the liberation from Egypt and directs us in the course of the Seder: when to drink each of the four cups of wine, when to eat the Matzoh, and so on. It is available in all languages.

Using the Hagadah should not limit us in our discussion of the story of Pesach but should rather serve as a stimulus for further inquiry and discussion. The Haggadah itself recounts how five of our greatest Sages sat a whole night in discussion of the story of the going out of Egypt, until daylight signaled the time of the Morning Prayers. The story is concluded with the words. "Whoever increases in the telling of the going out of Egypt—behold this is praiseworthy."

The Four Cups of Wine

In addition to the festive Holiday meal itself, the matzoh, and the items on the Seder plate, we drink four special cups of wine during the Seder, for wine is symbolic of freedom and happiness.

The four cups of wine correspond to the four expressions which refer to the stages of G-d's deliverance of the Jews: *And I brought out—And I delivered—And I redeemed—and I took.* The four cups are drunk in turn at Kiddush, before the meal, immediately following Blessings-After-A-Meal, and at the very end of the Seder.

The Cup of Elijah

There is a fifth expression of redemption used in the Torah: *And I brought*. This is represented by the Cup of Elijah, usually set in the center of the table and filled at the end of the meal. A beautiful and large wine cup is usually reserved as the Cup of Elijah. After the cup is filled we go to the door to greet the Prophet Elijah, who is known to visit every Seder.

The honor of announcing the coming of Messiah has been reserved for the Prophet Elijah. Every year as we open the door for Elijah after telling the inspiring story of our ancestors' deliverance from the Exile in Egypt, we hope that we too will merit to hear from Elijah about the coming deliverance from our current exile—speedily in our days.

The Afikoman

At the end of the meal a small piece of matzoh is eaten, known as the *afikoman*, which means dessert. The afikoman reminds us of the Pesach Sacrifice which was eaten at the conclusion, of the Pesach meal. Today, the person conducting the Seder breaks the middle one of the three matzohs of the seder plate into two unequal parts and places the larger part between the pillows of his reclining seat or another safe place. This is then eaten before the saying of the Blessings-After-A-Meal.

The Seder Plate: Its Foods and Preparations

Just as establishing the atmosphere of the Shabbos and Holidays is largely due to the preparations made by the woman of the house, so too will the smooth order in which the Seder is conducted largely depend on her.

In particular, all preparations for the Seder plate and the Seder meal should be completed in advance, so that the Seder can begin as soon as everyone returns from the Holiday Evening Service. Remember that the Seder is largely directed to the children, so all efforts should be made to start as early as possible.

Preparing the Seder plate requires several hours of work. It is advisable to get other members of the house to help so that the work will be completed before the Seder begins. It is best to prepare all the seder foods before Yom Tov in order to avoid *halachic* questions. (Foods prepared on Yom Tov may not be used the second seder night or the following day. See Laws of Cooking for Yom Tov, and details below concerning individual foods for the seder plate.)

The special foods we eat on Pesach are also food for thought. Every item on the Seder plate abounds in meaning and allusion. The Seder plate has six items on it, arranged in a special order. The plate is placed on top of the covering of the three matzohs and is placed in front of the head of the household. Some also have the custom of setting a separate Seder plate for each male member of age thirteen and over.

The foods of the Seder plate are listed below, with the reason each is included, the method of preparing it, and its role in the Seder meal.

Zeroah. A piece of roasted meat represents the lamb that was the special Pesach Sacrifice on the eve of the exodus from Egypt. The Pesach sacrifice was brought in the afternoon before Pesach in the time of the Holy Temple.

Preparation: Remove meat from neck of chicken and roast neck on all sides over an open fire on the stove. This should be done before Yom Tov; if cooked during Yom Tov it must be eaten on that day of Yom Tov, but not at night because roasted foods may not be eaten at the seder due to their similarity to the Pesach Sacrifice.

Role in the Seder: The Zeroah is not eaten. After the meal it is refrigerated and used a second time on the Seder plate the following night.

Betza. A hard-boiled egg represents the Holiday Offering in the days of the Holy Temple. The meat of this animal constituted the main part of the Pesach meal.

Preparation: Boil one egg per Seder plate and possibly more for use during the meal.

Role in the Seder: Place one egg on each plate. As soon as the actual meal is about to begin, remove the egg from the Seder plate and use during the meal.

A popular way of using these eggs is to chop and mix them with the salt water which was set on the table. Salt water should be prepared on Erev Shabbos if the first night of Pesach falls on Friday night. If one forgot, an amount just enough for use on that night may be prepared. The eggs prepared this way are then served as an appetizer before the fish.

Maror. Bitter herbs remind us of the bitterness of the slavery of our forefathers in Egypt. Fresh horseradish, romaine lettuce and endive are the most common choices. The greens must be washed extremely well before Yom Tov begins and care must be taken to check for insects. Afterwards, they are dried very well.

Preparation: This *must* be done before Yom Tov begins. Peel the raw horseradish roots and rinse them off well. (Dry them very carefully, since they will be eaten with the matzoh later on for the "matzoh and maror sandwich" and not even a drop of water should be left on the horseradish.)

Next, grate the horseradish with a hand grater or electric grinder. (A word of warning: Whoever gets this job will begin to shed copious tears or cough a lot. Covering the face with a cloth from the eyes downwards helps prevent inhalation of the strong, bitter odor.) The maror is placed on the Seder plate on top of a few cleaned, dried leaves of romaine lettuce (which is also maror).

Role in the Seder: After the recital of most of the Hagadah comes the ritual hand-washing. Then a *k'zayis* of matzoh is eaten followed by some maror folded in one or two romaine lettuce leaves, followed in turn by a sandwich of matzoh, maror, and romaine lettuce leaves.

Charoses. A mixture of apples, nuts and wine resembles the mortar and brick made by the Jews when they toiled for Pharaoh.

Preparation: Peel walnuts and apples and chop finely. Mix together and add a small amount of wine. It is best to prepare charoses before Yom Tov. If preparing on Yom Tov, however, one must make sure not to *grind* any of the ingredients but rather mash them in an unusual manner (see *Laws of Cooking on Yom Tov*). If the first night falls on Shabbos, one must also combine the ingredients in an unconventional manner such as adding apples to wine instead of vice versa.

Role in the Seder: This is used as a type of relish into which the maror is dipped (and then shaken off) before eating.

Karpas.   A non-bitter root vegetable alludes to the back-breaking work of the Jews as slaves. The Hebrew letters of *karpas* can be arranged to spell "*Perach-Samech*". Perach means back-breaking work and Samech is numerically equivalent to 60, referring to the 60 myriads (10,000), equalling 600,000, which was the number of Jewish males over 20 years of age who were enslaved in Egypt.

Preparation: Peel an onion or boiled potato. Cut off a slice and place on Seder plate. On the table, next to the Seder plate, place a small bowl of salted water.

Role in the Seder: After recital of Kiddush, the family goes to the sink and ritually washes hands, but without saying the usual blessing. Then the head of the household cuts a small piece of the root vegetable used, dips it in salt water, and gives each person at the table a very small piece over which they say the appropriate blessing. Care should be taken that each person eats less than 17 grams (½ ounce).

Chazeres.   Usually Romaine lettuce—more bitter herbs. Romaine lettuce too symbolizes the bitter enslavement of our fathers in Egypt. The leaves of Romaine lettuce are not bitter, but the stem, when left to grow in the ground, turns hard and bitter. So it was with our enslavement in Egypt. At first the deceitful approach of Pharoah was soft and sensible and the work was done voluntarily and even for pay. Gradually, it evolved into forced and cruel labor.

Preparation: Romaine lettuce is often very sandy. Start well before Yom Tov. Wash each of the leaves separately, checking very carefully for insects. (Pat gently with a towel and let sit until completely dry, so that there will be no moisture to come in contact with the matzoh.) Depending on how much romaine lettuce is needed, it can take several hours to prepare. This task should be completed before candlelighting time on the first night. Prepare enough leaves for both nights and store in the refrigerator. Soaking of the Romaine leaves may not be done on Yom Tov.

Role in the Seder: Chazeres is used in conjunction with horseradish. It is used when eating the maror and when eating the matzoh and maror sandwich.

Place the leaves in two piles on the Seder plate, one under the maror and one separately at the bottom.

Keep a stack of extra cleaned leaves handy in the refrigerator in case additional leaves are needed.

Matzohs—Unleavened Bread

All of the Seder plate items are placed on top of the three covered matzohs, for the lesson of matzoh is the foundation of the entire Pesach Seder. Matzoh, a flat, humble bread, is contrasted to yeasted bread which is inflated, attractive and tasty. All leavened food is chometz and we are forbidden to eat or even possess chometz throughout the holiday of Pesach.

The lightness and attractive tastiness of chometz-type food is a result of the leaven which fills it with air. In the same way, when we search for the chometz in ourselves, we see how the chometz-like qualitites of self-love, vanity and arrogance are also essentially empty.

Once the leavening process in baking is completed, the dough can rise no more. When matzoh is being made, however, stringent precautions are taken that the dough not be left unattended for a second too long, lest it begin to rise.

When the Jews left Egypt, they did not have time to let their dough rise; they baked it immediately and it became matzoh. Therefore it is a special mitzvah for every person to eat at least a small piece, a *k'zayis*, of matzoh on Pesach seder nights—at least ½ of a handbaked matzoh (equivalent to one whole machine-baked matzoh), which is approximately one ounce.

Shmura Matzoh: Matzoh is made from flour and water which is prepared and baked very quickly. In order to make sure that it has no chance to ferment, several precautions are taken months before the baking process. Matzoh so protected is called Shmura-Matzoh—guarded matzoh.

There are different types of Shmura-Matzoh. Some are made by hand. With some the flour is guarded from the time the grain is cut, with others only from the time the grain is ground. At least for the mandatory k'zayis that is eaten at the Seder, every effort should be made to have hand-made Shmura-Matzoh made from flour which was guarded from the time the grain was cut. These matzohs are round.

Combining Baked Matzoh with Liquids: There are various customs that allow the combining of *already* baked matzoh or matzoh meal with a liquid, to form such treats as matzoh balls. This custom is known as eating *g'broks*—dipping in.

However, there are many who do not do this because if even the minutest particle of flour in the matzoh or matzoh meal remained unbaked and came into contact with water or other liquid, it would become actual chometz. (See pages 355-356.)

It is said that on Pesach all stringent measures are to be respected and applied; thus this practice of not eating *g'broks* is highly recommended. However, even those who do not eat *g'broks* make an exception on the 8th day Pesach, which is observed as a Rabbinic ordinance outside Israel.

Recipes specifically for Pesach are not included in this book because of the many differences in existing practice, regarding the foods eaten on Pesach (see pages 354–356).

Pesach Sheni

A Second Opportunity

A "second Pesach," *Pesach Sheni*, comes on the fourteenth day of the month of Iyar. The first Pesach Sheni occurred soon after the Jews left Egypt, when those Jews who had been unable to participate in the Pesach offering one month earlier, because they had been impure at that time, came to Moses to ask how they too could be included in the mitzvah. G-d was pleased with their request, and a second day for bringing the Paschal Lamb Sacrifice was set aside for them.

Pesach Sheni demonstrates the Jew's love for doing mitzvohs. A person's eagerness to do a deed can often be measured by his reaction when not given the chance to fulfill it. It also teaches us that for a Jew it is never too late. We must never lose hope; G-d always provides another chance.

Though Pesach Sheni is not observed as a Yom Tov, it is still a special day. It is customary to eat matzohs, and many of the people who eat the special round, hand-made, shmura-matzoh put some away at the end of Pesach to eat on this day. There is no prohibition against chometz so bread and all other foods of the year are permissible.

Lag B'Omer

The Counting of the Omer

Fifty days separated the going out of Egypt from the giving of the Torah. Each day from the second night on was counted by the Jews, and each day's higher number reflected a progress from the previous day in the preparation to receive the Torah. We too are commanded to count each day from the second night of Pesach until Shavuos, the festival marking the giving of the Torah. We use this time to prepare ourselves, each day more than the day before, to be ready to receive the Torah anew.

The counting of these forty-nine days, which is done with a blessing every night after the evening prayers, is called "The Counting of the Omer." These days are given the name Omer, from the offering which was brought to the Holy Temple on the second day of Pesach, the night of which the counting begins. The Omer offering is a certain measurement of grain from the new crop offered to G-d. Only after this offering was brought were the rest of the grains from the new crop permitted to be used. An offering of barley was brought on Pesach, while on Shavuos, two loaves of bread baked from wheat of the new crop were presented.

The Students of Rabbi Akiba

These days have yet another meaning for us—in connection with the students of the great Rabbi Akiba, who lived almost 2,000 years ago. It was during the Omer period that many of Rabbi Akiba's students died during an epidemic. Our Sages then declared that these days should be commemorated as partial mourning days for all times, for this was indeed a loss for the Jews. Thus, during this time (or part of this time, according to different customs), rejoicing is curtailed and there are no weddings, no dancing, no haircuts.

On the thirty-third day of the Omer, the epidemic stopped. This day is called Lag B'Omer (the numerical value of the Hebrew letters comprising the word LAG–Lamed, Gimmel—is 33). This is a day of great rejoicing. Weddings and other celebrations are permitted. Also, boys who have reached the age of three during the first thirty-two days of the Omer now receive their ceremonial haircutting, the *Upsherenish* (see page 310), on this day.

Rabbi Shimon Bar Yochai

There is yet another reason for the celebration of the thirty-third day of the Omer. It is the *yahrzeit* (the anniversary of the passing on) of our holy Sage, Rabbi Shimon Bar Yochai. The *yahrzeit* of a great person is often marked with celebrating, since on this day every year, the person's soul ascends to greater heights in the eternal world. Because of Rabbi Shimon Bar Yochai's uncompromising determination to teach Torah publicly, his death was decreed by the Romans. Forced to flee from his home, he hid in a cave with his son for thirteen years. During this entire time, he and his son ate from a carob tree which G-d miraculously made grow right outside their cave. There they also learned the deepest inner meanings of the Torah. Rabbi Shimon Bar Yochai is also the author of the *Zohar*, one of the earliest and most important written sources of Kabbalah and Jewish mysticism.

It is written about Rabbi Shimon Bar Yochai that during his lifetime no rainbow appeared in the sky. The rainbow, as G-d told Noah after the Flood, is a sign that even if G-d is angry with the world, He will never again destroy it with a flood. Rabbi Shimon Bar Yochai was so great that while he was alive, not only he, but all other Jews (so great was his influence) did not need the reminder and guarantee of the rainbow.

To remember the greatness of Rabbi Shimon Bar Yochai, it has become a custom that on Lag B'Omer children are often taken on outings in the parks or woods. Some also have the custom to play with bows and arrows in the park, a reminder of the absence of the rainbow.

Shavuos

The Giving of the Torah

Coming after forty-nine days of counting the Omer, the impatiently awaited Yom Tov of Shavuos heralds the giving of the Torah at Mt. Sinai, when the Jewish people became a real nation and their identity was established with their acceptance of the Torah with the words, *"Na'aseh V'nishmah,"* We will do and we will hear." *First* we accept upon ourselves to do as G-d commands, *then* we apply our intelligence to learning and understanding the Torah. The entire Jewish nation witnessed an unparalleled revelation of G-dliness at Mt. Sinai and pledged themselves for all generations to fulfill the task of being "a kingdom of priests and a holy nation." We can see the connection of the two Holidays of Pesach and Shavuos, for the spiritual preparation that takes place during the counting of the Omer shows that the purpose and completion of the exodus from Egypt is our receiving of the Torah and reaching, through it, a spiritual freedom even greater than the physical freedom we had already achieved.

It is the Torah that has been the preservation and motivating force of the Jewish people's existence throughout the ages. Cultures, diets, languages and countries of residence all change; yet Torah remains constant because it is founded on an unconditional truth, the only kind of truth that can continue to insure the unique existence of the Jewish people despite all odds. And only the truth of Torah is unconditional, for it was given by G-d to the Jewish people to keep and guard for all generations, wherever they may be.

An interesting detail of the Shavuos story is related in the Midrash. Just prior to the giving of the Torah, G-d asked the Jewish people, "Who will guarantee the Torah? How can I be assured that the Torah would be cherished and observed throughout the generations?" The Jewish people offered many possible guarantors, from the patriarchs to the prophets and great men as yet unborn, but G-d was not satisfied. Only when the little children were suggested did G-d accept. It is only in the merit of children that the Torah was given to us, and it is due only to their merit that we have this guide to live by. Giving our children as our guarantors for the keeping of the Torah is a sign of our pure committment to the Torah, and the transmission of it from generation to generation.

Shavuos Customs

Shavuos is the Yom Tov of our accepting the Torah itself as a whole. It is one of the *Shalosh Regolim* (Pilgrimage Festivals). Many interesting customs are observed on this day.

On the eve of Shavuos it is customary for all men over 13 to stay up all night absorbed in the study of Torah, to show our eagerness to receive the Torah. The Torah reading on Shavuos is about the giving of the Ten Commandments at Mount Sinai. When the reader comes to the actual Ten Commandments, all congregants stand up. On the first day of the Yom Tov it is customary to eat a dairy meal. (Many people complement the dairy dishes with a complete Yom Tov meat meal, after a one-hour interval. If the meat meal is eaten first, one must be careful to observe the six-hour waiting period before eating dairy.) Cheese dishes, particularly blintzes, are traditionally served. Many reasons have been put forth for this, one being that on Shavuos the Jews had just received the Torah which contain the laws of what one may and may not eat and as they were not yet well-versed in the laws of *shechita* (kosher slaughtering), they refrained from eating meat.

Shavuos is also the festival of fruits. On this day, the first fruits were brought to the Holy Temple in beautifully arranged baskets, and offered with great pageantry and an inspiring ceremony. For this reason, some people also have the custom on Shavuos of eating for the first time that year one kind of fresh summer fruit and saying the blessing *shehechiyonu* (see *Blessings over Foods*, pages 345–350).

Many people observe the custom of decorating their homes with fresh flowers on Shavuos in memory of Mount Sinai, a once barren spot which came into full bloom when the Torah was given on its summit. (Of course the flowers are cut before Shavuos.)

Shavuos is also the anniversary of the passing away of King David, who descended from Ruth. Ruth was a modest, righteous woman who, because of her true love for Torah and mitzvohs, accepted this Torah despite many difficulties and converted to Judaism. It was because of her honest convictions and humble conduct that she had the merit to become the mother of the kings of Israel. From this line of great kings our righteous Messiah will be born and will redeem us from exile. Like Ruth, we, the people of Israel, accepted the whole Torah and all its mitzvohs whole-heartedly and in complete faith. For these reasons, Megillas Ruth (the Story of Ruth) is read in shul on the second day of Shavuos in many communities.

Fast Days

The Holy Temple

While there are many Jewish celebrations marking happy occasions, unfortunately there have been several tragedies which also must be commemorated in an appropriate way. Thus, our Sages have ordained certain days of mourning to help us remember properly the destruction of the Holy Temple. On these days we fast, pray and learn about the history of the Temple.

At the time when the Holy Temple stood (First Temple 2928–3338, Second Temple 3408–3828, according to the Jewish calendar), it was the central force and inspiration for all Jews. There the *Kohanim* (priests) led the nation in the service of G-d, and there all Jews gathered three times a year for the Holidays of Pesach, Shavuos and Succos. Nearby was the place where the Sages sat and taught from the ever-flowing wellsprings of Torah.

The destruction of Jerusalem and the Holy Temple was a tragic loss for the Jews and endangered their physical and spiritual existence. Judaism has nonetheless continued to survive and even flourish in almost all places where Jews have been scattered in exile. This is due to the power of Torah, the vital key to Jewish existence, giving strength to all those who observe it even now, long after the destruction of the Temple. Yet when we reflect upon our greatness and our good fortune in the time of the Temple, we begin to realize the extent of our exile. By contrast, in our days, Truth and the Torah are hidden "within multiple veils," and we pray from our depths for the time of Messiah when all of mankind will perceive and acknowledge G-d's omnipresence, when all Jews will be able to freely and unashamedly fulfill all the laws of Torah, and express their love for Torah, and when Jews will be honored and respected as the priestly nation of G-d.

Throughout the nearly 2,000 years of exile, Jews have never forgotten the days of the Holy Temple, and with each year we are confident that we are coming ever closer to the time of Messiah when all of the above will be fulfilled and the days of mourning will be changed to days of rejoicing.

Meriting the Redemption

Our Sages teach us: "All those who mourn the destruction of Jerusalem will merit to see it rebuilt."

After the destruction of both Temples, the prophets prophesied to us in the name of G-d, that when Jews will repent and return whole-heartedly to G-d, they will be forgiven all their sins, the Exile will end, and the Holy Temple will be rebuilt. This third Holy Temple will remain permanently with us, never to be destroyed as were its two predecessors. All the beauty and glory of two Temples and the miracles witnessed within them will return, together with all the services which may only be performed at the Temple and were therefore not practiced during this exile of nearly 2,000 years.

What is the connection between mourning the previous destruction and witnessing the rebuilding of the Temple? One explanation is that when we mourn the destruction—when we actually feel the loss of the Temple—G-d sees that we feel the pains, both physical and spiritual, of the exile and that in our hearts we wish to be able to serve Him completely. He sees that we yearn for the time when all of the world will see and understand the greatness of G-d, and His infinite wisdom as revealed through our timeless Torah. Our mourning shows our true appreciation of the Temple, through which we will merit to see it rebuilt speedily in our days, with the coming of Messiah!

The Four Fast Days

There are four days of fasting and mourning for the destruction of both Holy Temples. Following are the Hebrew dates of these fast days and a brief statement of the historical significance of each.

Tenth of Teves—The king of Babylonia laid siege to the city of Jerusalem in the time of the First Temple.

Seventeenth of Tammuz—The walls of Jerusalem were breached at the time of the Second Temple. (During the destruction of the First Temple, the walls were breached on the ninth, and this too, is an aspect of the fast of the seventeenth, as the Rabbis didn't want to declare two fast days within eight days. The seventeenth of Tammuz was fixed to commemorate both destructions.)

Ninth of Av—Actual destruction of both the First and Second Temples, known as *Tisha B'Av* and is a major fast/day.

Third of Tishrei—(The Fast of Gedaliah) After the First Temple was destroyed, a remnant of Jews remained in Israel under the leadership of Gedaliah. When he was murdered, all final hopes for the Jews in the Land of Israel were lost.

The Three Weeks

There are exactly three weeks from the seventeenth of Tammuz until the ninth of Av, the two most serious fast days related to the destructon of the Temple.

These three weeks are marked with partial signs of mourning; listening to music, taking haircuts, and buying new things are prohibited. The last nine days (between Rosh Chodesh Av and the ninth of Av) have additional signs of mourning; for example, eating of meat (except on Shabbos) is not allowed.

The ninth of Av the only Torah learning permitted is that dealing with the destruction of the Holy Temple and also the laws pertaining to its construction, which will be applicable in the time of the Third Holy Temple—may we see it rebuilt in our days.

Other Fast Days

Tenth of Tishrei—Yom Kippur, Day of Atonement designated by the Torah.

Thirteenth of Adar—The Fast of Esther, the day before Purim. It commemorates Esther's fast for three days before appealing to King Ahashveros to abolish Haman's wicked decree against the Jews. It is through the merit of this fast and the unrelenting prayers of thousands of little children Mordechai gathered, that G-d's mercy was shown and the Jews were victorious over their enemies.

Fourteenth of Nissan—The Fast of the First-Born, the day before Pesach.

On the day before G-d took the Jews out of Egypt, the first-born Egyptian males were killed in a plague. Since no Jewish families were affected by the plague, this day has become a fast day for all Jewish first-born males, to humbly thank G-d for His special protection over them on this day.

If a first-born boy is under the age of thirteen, his father should fast for him.

However, it is customary for the first-born to become exempt from this fast by participating in a *siyum*. If one finishes a tractate of the Talmud (Mishna or Gemorra), and celebrates the siyum (completion) in shul by offering food and refreshments, then the first-born males among those present may break his fast and participate in the celebration of this great event.

Laws of Fast Days

Eating and drinking are prohibited on a fast day from daybreak until nightfall, except on Tisha B'Av and Yom Kippur which are full day fasts, from before sunset to the following night. On these two days, wearing leather shoes, washing for pleasure, using perfumes, and having marital relations, are also not permitted.

Fasting is required for all Jewish males over age thirteen and all Jewish females over the age of twelve. Under certain conditions involving health, a *Rav* may advise leniency concerning these fast days—especially for pregnant and nursing women and people requiring special medical care. Each situation must be judged according to the various halachic guidelines involved, and the *Rav* should be consulted before the fast begins. The laws concerning Yom Kippur and Tisha B'av are more stringent than those for the other fast days. If one feels ill or weak during these fasts, a *Rav* should be consulted at that time. Even in the case when one is permitted to eat on a fast day, one should eat only what is necessary and not indulge in food.

Boys under age thirteen and girls under age twelve are not required to fast, but on Tisha B'Av and Yom Kippur, young children who are able to understand the importance of the fasts should not eat from sundown until the following morning, while older children, if they are able, are encouraged to fast until mid-day, at least. Even young children who are not fasting should be made aware of the importance of the day by relinquishing treats or desserts.

Food Before and After the Fast

Before: Eating good meals on the day before a fast is very advisable. Even if one isn't too hungry, one should eat a complete meal a few hours before the fast begins to provide strength for the following day. In fact, on the day before Yom Kippur, not only is it advisable to eat a good meal before the fast, it is also a mitzvah.

Salty foods in general should be avoided, and a glass of tea at the end of the meal helps reduce thirst.

After: Work is permitted on these days (except Yom Kippur), so you can be sure your family will expect a nice meal as soon as it is permissible to eat. Fast-breaking foods should be light and easily digestible. Fillet of fish, simply prepared, is a popular main dish. Hot vegetable soup is also a good idea for the beginning of a fast-breaking meal. Before sitting down to a complete meal after the fast, it is best to first have a light snack and some milk, juice or tea. Then continue with the regular meal about one hour later, as it is difficult to digest a complete meal immediately after a fast.

Special for Tisha B'Av,

Before the Fast: On Tisha B'Av two meals are eaten in the afternoon before the onset of the fast; a regular meal and a special final one called "meal of separation" eaten shortly before sunset.

During this final meal it is customary to have a piece of bread and a hard-boiled egg dipped in ashes. Other food, uncooked, may also be eaten.

Breaking the Fast: Although work is discouraged on Tisha B'Av (especially in the evening and morning), it is not forbidden as on Yom Kippur. Preparing food during the latter part of the afternoon is permissible (if you have the strength!). However, do not prepare a meat meal as meat may not be eaten until the afternoon of the next day, since much of the destruction of the Temple also took place on that day, the tenth of Av.

Weeks of Consolation

The three weeks of mourning, culminating in *Tisha B'Av*, the ninth of Av, are followed by seven weeks of consolation in which the Prophetic passages in the *Haftorah* read each of these weeks reflect the theme of rejoicing over the hope for the coming of Messiah and the rebuilding of the Holy Temple.

The Fifteenth of Av, coming in this period is also a day of festivity, serving as a memorial for a number of events which brought rejoicing to the Jewish people at various times. It was in earlier generations a day of forgiveness from sin similar to Yom Kippur, yet marked with festivity and dancing.

The Jewish Calendar

The Moon: A Message of Hope, Renewal and Trust

The Jewish calendar is a lunar one, as opposed to the solar or Gregorian calendar used by most of the world. The fact that we reckon our time and set the rhythms of our life according to the moon is significant in several ways.

Our Sages have often compared the Jewish People to the moon and have read a clear message in the sight of the moon when it is new.

To us, the new moon is a sign of hope. At times the moon casts a very faint light and sometimes may even seem to disappear. But in essence, it is always complete, although only a part of it may be seen. Moreover, it is at the very darkest of these moments, when all seems lost, that the moon suddenly begins to appear larger and brighter with each day. So it is with the Jewish people: although its fortunes may wax and wane, it can never be completely obliterated. Like the moon, we are always perfect in essence, and always ready to grow stronger and brighter, having a perpetual capacity for renewal.

Rosh Chodesh

Declaring the New Moon

The first commandment G-d gave the Jews after they left Egypt was to recognize and proclaim the new moon. *Rosh Chodesh* is the day of the appearance of the new moon and thus the first day of the Jewish month. The days of the festivals are determined on the basis of this proclamation of the lunar month. In the times of the Sanhedrin (Great Court), the new month was proclaimed only when two reliable eye-witnesses reported that they had seen the new moon. While this date was also calculated mathematically by the Sages according to the methods handed down traditionally since the revelation at Mt. Sinai, the month did not become official until proclaimed by witnesses. In this way, the Jewish calendar was made dependent upon the activities of man rather than solely on celestial movements. This is highly significant in that the holidays were determined by this proclamation of the new moon. Pesach, occurring on the fifteenth day of Nissan, was observed fifteen days after the new moon was observed by *man*.

Rosh Chodesh, once like a holiday for the Jews, is still recognized as different from other days. Special prayers are said accordingly. On the Shabbos preceding the new moon we say a special blessing for the new month. And one night during the first half of the month, when the sky is clear and before the moon is full, you may see a group of Jewish men standing outside and gazing up at the moon, reciting *Kiddush L'vanah*. This is the blessing on the new moon which we are commanded to recognize—the moon which appears larger and larger with each successive day.

Rosh Chodesh is regarded as a special day for women, a partial holiday said to be a reward for their not taking part in the sin of worshipping the Golden Calf. On this day women traditionally do no sewing, laundry, or heavy domestic work.

Extra Days of Yom Tov Outside the Land of Israel

One result of the ancient practice of declaring the beginning of a month on the basis of eye-witness reports (see *Rosh Chodesh*, above) is that the holidays of the first and seventh days of Pesach, the first and eighth days of Succos, and the one day of Shavuos, are each extended an extra day outside the Land of Israel.

The moon takes approximately 29½ days to circle the earth; therefore the lunar months were set to consist of either twenty-nine or 30 days. Rosh Chodesh could have fallen on either one of two days and the other days of the month would be calculated accordingly. The festivals, then, could also fall on either of two days. When the new moon was declared in Jerusalem, messengers were sent to outlying areas and it was on the basis of their reports that the proper days for the festivals were made known. In places outside of Israel, where the information sometimes did not reach the people until after two weeks of the month had already gone by, the holiday was kept on both possible days so that the exact date would not be missed.

This Rabbinical law of observing an extra day of Yom Tov outside the Land of Israel is as strongly observed now, even though we no longer wait for witnesses but rely on the fixed calculations of the oral tradition. It reminds us that Man is the most important factor and not the movements of stars and planets. It is a sign of G-d's love for us that He leaves it to us to determine when to celebrate the Holidays.

The Leap Year: An Extra Month

There are twelve months of twenty-nine and a half days each in the lunar year, or a total of 354 days—eleven days shorter than the solar year which controls the seasons. Thus, if the lunar and solar calendar year begin at the same time, the lunar year would progressively fall short every year by eleven days, and after nine years, Pesach would occur in the winter.

However, the Torah tells us to take care that Nissan, the month of Pesach, should also always occur in *Aviv*, Spring. This indicates that the lunar calendar should always be kept aligned with the solar. This was made possible by proclaiming a leap year, adding a complete month to the calendar seven times every nineteen years.

The Calendar at a Glance

Hebrew Month	Holiday	Fast Day	Date	Corresponding English Month(s)
Tishrei	*Rosh Hashanah		1-2	September-October
		Fast of Gedaliah	3	
	*Yom Kippur	Yom Kippur	10	
	Succos¹		15–22	
	*Yom Tov		15-16	
	Chol Hamoed		17-20	
	Hoshannah Rabbah		21	
	*Shemini Atzeres		22	
	*Simchas Torah		23	
Cheshvan				October-November
Kislev	Chanukah		25-30	November-December
Teves	Chanukah		1-2	December-January
		Tenth of Teves	10	
Shvat	Tu B'Shvat		15	January-February
Adar²		Fast of Esther	13	February-March
	Purim		14	
	Shushan Purim		15	
Nissan		Fast of the First-born	14	March-April
	Pesach¹		15-22	
	*Yom Tov		15-16	
	Chol Hamoed		17-20	
	*Yom Tov		21-22	
Iyar	Pesach Sheni		14	April-May
	Lag B'Omer		18	
Sivan	*Shavuos¹		6-7	May-June
Tammuz		Seventeenth of Tammuz	17	June-July
Av		Ninth of Av	9	July-August
Elul	Preparation for the New Year			August-September

*Each day of these holidays are ushered in with candle-lighting.

¹Succos, Pesach, and Shavuos are celebrated an additional day outside the Land of Israel, and the additional day and date are indicated in this chart.

²In a Jewish leap year, Purim is celebrated in the second Adar.

Challah
and
Bread

Challah and Bread

Challah and Bread

Bread has always been a mainstay of the Jewish table. Many times in the Torah the word "bread" is used meaning "food." Today, no Shabbos or Festival meal can possibly begin without two loaves of fresh-baked challah on the table (except, of course, on Pesach!). On Fridays we bake our indispensable challahs, while many other varieties of bread may be baked during the week. Included in this chapter are delicious challah recipes, the bread of our celebrations, replete with instruction for its braiding, blessing and baking, and insights into its historical and symbolic significance for Jewish people today, followed by a selection of breads and muffins, and many useful bread making hints.

The Story of Challah

"Challah" is the name of the special loaves of braided bread which are served at the Shabbos and Holiday meals (except for Pesach, when matzoh is served), and at many festive celebrations. They are made in all sizes and shapes from small, roll-sized ones approximately 2-3 ounces, to big two-pounders, or even larger. Challah on the table is a sign of festivity.

On Shabbos and the Holidays it is a mitzvah to eat festive meals, which begin with the Kiddush and the traditional washing over bread. To give honor to the occasion we say the blessing over whole loaves of bread. Two whole loaves are used to remind us of the double portion of *Manna* which the Jews received in the desert every Friday, so that they would not have to gather this "bread from Heaven" on Shabbos. Thus we remind ourselves that G-d provides for all our needs, for those of Shabbos as well as those for the week, even though we do not work on Shabbos. The whole loaves are shaped in a number of interesting ways, many of which recall yet another miracle, that of the twelve showbreads in the *Mishkan* and Holy Temple.

The Daily Manna

When the Jews were in the desert after leaving Egypt, they had no food since their small suppy of matzoh was used up, and they did not have any means of procuring food for themselves. Instead G-d Himself sent each family a daily portion of "manna," which was a food from heaven. It is said that the manna contained within it whatever taste the person eating it would imagine or desire. How fortunate were our ancestors to receive a fresh reminder each day that, in truth, man is dependent on the grace of G-d for his daily food.

On Friday the Jews received a double portion of manna, since on Shabbos they would not be allowed to carry the manna from the fields to their homes. In commemoration, instead of beginning the meals on Friday night and Shabbos afternoon with regular bread, we say the blessing over two whole loaves of challah, to remind ourselves of the double portion of manna that fell on Friday, for Friday and Shabbos.

When the manna fell on the ground it remained fresh, for it was lined by a layer of dew beneath and above it. This is one of the reasons that we place a plate or board under the challah and a special cover (or table napkin) over it.

From the Biblical description of manna it seems that it looked like whitish poppy seeds. Thus many people sprinkle the tops of the challah with poppy seeds.

The 12 Loaves of Bread (Lechem Hapanim)

The portable *Mishkan* (Tabernacle) in the desert, and later the Holy Temple in the land of Israel, was the House of Worship for G-d. Different vessels were kept inside, representing different types of services. There was the Ark which held the Ten Commandments, the Menorah-oil lamp which was lit every day representing the light of the Torah, the two Altars used for the bringing of incense and animal sacrifices, and then there was the Table representing our physical needs (as for food) for which we are also dependent on the will and grace of G-d.

The Table had 12 small open shelves on top. Each shelf represented one of the twelve tribes of Israel. Every Friday the *Kohanim,* the priests in charge of the sacrificial service, baked 12 loaves of bread, and on Shabbos exchanged these loaves for the ones baked the previous week. The loaves taken off were still fresh, and were eaten by the Kohanim on Shabbos.

Every week a miracle occurred with these 12 loaves of bread. Despite the fact that these loaves had been kept on open shelves for a week, every Shabbos when the Kohanim removed them, they were as fresh and as warm as when they had been placed on the shelves a week ago. This miracle is another connection between challah and the Shabbos.

Our challah on the Shabbos reminds us of both of these miracles. The miracle of the manna is recalled in the blessing for bread on the Shabbos being said over *two* loaves, while the intricate shapes and number of braids of the challah bring to mind the miracle of the breads in the Temple.

The Mitzvah of Separating "Challah"

When preparing bread using a certain amount of flour, it is necessary to remove a small piece of dough prior to baking. The small piece which is separated is called *challah.* In the time of the Temple, this piece was given to the Kohanim. Today challah is also the name by which the special Shabbos loaves are called. *Separating Challah* is one of the three special commandments which are primarily the woman's privilege and obligation to fulfill.

Today we are no longer able to give the *challah* portion to the Kohanim. Nevertheless, we must still observe this mitzvah of *separating* the challah. This is done by removing a piece of the dough before baking, and burning it. The reason for burning it is that even though we do not actually present it to the Kohanim, this priestly portion is no longer ours and we have no right to any personal benefit from it.

When a woman takes *challah* and makes the appropriate blessing, she spiritually "elevates" the dough. Through this act she testifies to her complete trust in G-d. For by taking off a portion of dough, she acknowledges that all the bread (i.e. all the physical sustenance) in her home comes only as a gift from G-d and she is ready to give up part of it, according to His will. Since the woman is so involved in

76

the daily upkeep of the home, it is her spiritual service and obligation to elevate all things in the home by utilizing them in the service of G-d.

Since taking *challah* is one of the three special mitzvahs for women, and since the deeper meanings of this mitzvah are so inherently bound up with women, many women are careful to maintain the custom of baking their own loaves at home for Shabbos and Yom Tov so that they may fulfill this precious mitzvah. It is especially significant to separate *challah* on Erev Shabbos (Friday).

For the three special mitzvohs, see pages 361-362.

Guide for Separating Challah

It is necessary to take *challah* from a dough when several requirements are met, related to the type and amount of flour used and the liquid content of the dough. The precise laws related to this mitzvah are to be found on pages 341-344.

The Art of Making Challah

Challah loaves are a most welcome sight at the Shabbos table. Try making your own for this coming Shabbos, Holiday, or special occasion. It's easier than you think and your house will be filled with a special *Shabbosdik* aroma as your challah is baking.

Preparing the Dough
1. Dissolve yeast in small amount of lukewarm water (+ 1 tablespoon sugar) for 8-10 minutes.
2. Add remaining ingredients according to recipe.
3. Knead mixture well until it has a stiff and smooth consistency (15-20 minutes). If too soft add a little flour; if too firm, add a little water. Continue kneading for a short while (5-7 minutes).

4. Put dough into large, oiled bowl. Turn over so that top can be oiled also (the dough rises nicely when oiled on all sides).
5. Place in warm place and cover.
6. Let rise until double in size (1-2 hours).
7. Punch down so that there are no air pockets.
8. Let rise again ½ hour, but only if called for in recipe.
9. Take *challah,* making the blessing when appropriate (see *Laws of Separating Challah,* pages 341–344).
10. Grease pans (enabling the challah to come out easily and the bottom to brown nicely).
11. Divide dough into pieces and shape into individual challahs or loaves smaller than the size of the pan.
12. Let rise again in pan approximately ½ hour or until double in size.
13. Pre-heat the oven to 350° for 10 minutes.

Glazing the Challah

14. Glaze the tops and sides of the challah a few minutes before putting it in the oven (doing it earlier could hamper the growth of the challah in the oven). Use a small egg brush. Some different mixtures are:
    1. 1 egg yolk
    2. 1 egg yolk + 1 teaspoon sugar
    3. 1 egg yolk + a few drops of water
    4. 1 whole egg
    5. 1 whole egg + 1½ teaspoon sugar

    In all the above mixtures, beat the egg well before spreading. One egg can glaze quite a few challahs, so use your eggs sparingly.
15. After glazing, poppy seeds, reminding us of the *manna* of the desert, may be sprinkled on the challah. Sesame seeds are a fine alternative.

Baking the Challah

16. Bake according to the recipe.
17. When the challah is done it should look browned but not too dark on all sides. Test to see if it is done by knocking on the bottom. It should sound hollow. Or check it with a cake tester. It should be able to go in very smoothly and come out dry and clean. (If you like your challah very brown and with harder crusts, you can leave it in a few minutes longer. Very small challahs take less time to bake and must be taken out of the oven before they get too dark, or the inside will be too hard.)
18. Take the challah out of the baking pans right after they come out of the oven or the bottom will become soggy. If baked properly challah should not stick too much to the sides of the pan.
19. Place hot challah on a cooling rack for at least 15 minutes or until completely cooled.

Shaping the Challahs

To keep fresh in our minds the miracle of the 12 loaves (see Story of Challah) there is a popular custom to make the two loaves of challah out of twelve pieces of dough. Over the years, Jewish women have originated many types of designs and methods for shaping and braiding the challah, as well as various ways of combining the pieces of dough to total the number 12.

A. Choose From The Following Combinations for Shabbos Challah Symbolizing Twelve Loaves
1. 3-braided challah—2 at each meal at 2 meals = 12 pieces per Shabbos.
2. 3-braided challah, topped with small braids, 2 at each meal = 12 pieces per meal.
3. 6-braided challah, 2 at each meal = 12 pieces per meal.
4. Challah loaves made out of 3 or 6 sections = 12 pieces per meal or 12 pieces per two meals.
5. Oval shapes with 5 additional small balls on top of it, 2 at each meal = 12 pieces per meal.

Regardless of what shape you are going to make the challah, here are a few guidelines you should be familiar with before you start.

B. Cutting the Dough

When your dough has risen to its proper size according to the recipe you choose, begin cutting off pieces and shaping them into challahs. (Don't forget to first separate a piece for the mitzvah of taking *challah*.)

C. How Much Dough to Use

The amount of dough needed to shape an individual challah depends on the size pan you are going to use. The amount of dough should be only about ½ the final size you want the challah to be after it is baked, for the dough will expand in width and rise a good deal—both before it is baked and also during the time it is in the oven. Since the challah grows a lot in the baking process, don't let the shaped, raw challah touch all the sides of the pan.

D. Determining What Size Pan to Use

1. Keep in mind the size of the challah you want to make.
2. Oval-shaped challah and braided challah look their best in individual oval-shaped pans. However, if you do not have these size pans you can place them in square pans or on a large cookie sheet spaced well apart to allow for growth. The number of challahs you will place on a sheet will of course depend on the desired size of the challah and the size of the cookie sheet.
3. Round challah come out best in round, shallow cake pans.
4. Three-, four- and six-sectioned loaves come out best in standard loaf pans. For six sections use larger loaf pans.
5. In making small challahs (bun-size) use large cookie sheets. Space challahs well apart so they will have room to expand. For nice size little challahs place 8-10 on a standard cookie sheet.

E. Other Shapes of Challah

1. Round challah is customarily baked for Rosh Hashana and Yom Kippur to symbolize continuity where there is no beginning or end. This is the auspicious time of year when we pray to G-d for continuity of life.
2. Ladders and hands—Another custom, although not so widespread, is the shaping of the challah like a ladder or a hand, to serve at the meal eaten before Yom Kippur. The ladder symbolizes that we ascend great heights during the year; and the hand that we may be inscribed for a good year.
3. Triangular challah (*hamantashen*)— On Purim it is a mitzvah to eat a complete meal during the day. This festive meal is usually started over challah, although regular bread may be used instead. Women who bake their own challahs sometimes shape them like full triangles, similar to the shape of the *hamantashen* and *kreplach* eaten on that day.

Illustrated Directions for Shaping Your Challahs

Here is a simple suggestion to help avoid confusion when braiding challahs the first few times (especially when making the six-braided challah): PRACTICE WITH STRINGS FIRST.

1. Take some string, cut off 6 strips approximately 9″ each. (Use only 3 strips for the basic braided challah).
2. Take Scotch tape and connect all the pieces at the very top.
3. Take small pieces of paper and number the pieces 1-6.
4. Again with Scotch tape attach a number to each string, according to the illustrations on the next few pages.
5. Practice the procedure over and over again until you have it correct throughout the whole process.

Note: It is best to do the practicing during the day or on an evening when you are not baking so that you won't be pressured for time.

A. THREE-BRAIDED CHALLAH:

This is a very simple procedure, identical to any braiding procedure.

1. Roll out three long, thin pieces (Fig. 1). The pieces should be a bit longer than the size of the pan in which the challah will be placed, for once it is braided it will be smaller than the pan.
2. Pinch the tops of all three pieces together (Fig. 2).
3. Take the one on the outer right (#1), cross it over #2 and bring it into the middle (Fig. 3).
4. Now take the one on the outer left (#3), cross it over the middle strip (#1) and let it rest in the middle (Fig. 4).
5. Repeat this procedure until the end, alternating bringing the one on the outer right to the middle, and then bringing the one on the outer left to the middle, until you have completed shaping the challah (Fig. 5).
6. Some women also make a thin braid over the large braided challah (Fig. 6), so that the challah is made with a total of six pieces, and together with the second challah on the table, there will be a total of twelve.

B. SIX-BRAIDED CHALLAH:

1. Roll dough into six equal strips approximately ten inches each.
2. Lay out strips evenly and pinch them together at the top. (Place a knife on top of the pinched section to keep it down and make it easier to maneuver the strips.)
3. Push the three strips on the right further to the right and the remaining three, more to the left (Figure 7.)

   Now you are ready to braid.
4. With right hand, take #6 and with left hand take #1 (left hand is crossed *over* right hand) moving right and left hands simultaneously. Cross #1 *over* #6 inside the center (thus uncrossing your hands. Figure 8).
5. Swing #6 over the pinched section and rest it upon the pinch and beyond. Bring #1 down to the right side group, placing on the left side of #3 (making #1 the innermost strip of the right side group and #2 the outermost strip.)

   Now the strips are in this position. (Figure 9).

   From now on the right and left sides will have two or three strips alternately, while there will always be one strip above and on top of the others.
6. Now to have three strips on the left side do the following: With your left hand, take the outermost strip, #2, from the side that already has three strips (the right side) and with your right hand take the uppermost strip, #6 (crossing the right hand *over* the left). Simultaneously, bring #2 under #6 and place it on top and beyond the pinch (replacing #6) and bring #6 to rest in the left side group, on the right side of #4. (Figure 10.)

   All the steps thereafter take on the same pattern, merely alternating between right and left

Fig. 1   Fig. 2   Fig. 3   Fig. 4

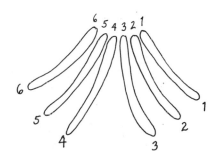

Fig. 5   Fig. 6   Figure 7

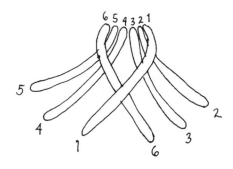

Figure 8   Figure 9   Figure 10

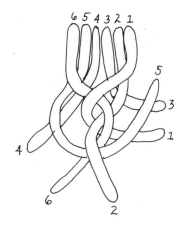

Figure 11   Figure 12   Figure 13

sides—making the right side group have three strips while the left has two and then the left side group have three strips while the right has two. The outermost strip of the three-strip side is always placed on top of and beyond the pinch, while the strip which is on top of the pinch and beyond it is always brought to the innermost place of the two-strip side, thus making it a three-strip side.

To illustrate further: (Figures 11-13, on page 81.)

7. Take #5 with right hand and #2 with left hand (left hand *over* right), moving #5 and #2 simultaneously. Bring #5 under #2 and swing it (#5) around, placing it on top of the pinch and beyond (so that it takes the place of #2) while bringing #2 down to the right side group and placing it on the left-hand side of #1. Now the right side group has three strips—#2 is the innermost strip and #3 the outermost. (Figure 11.)

8. Take #3 with left hand and #5 with right hand (right *over* left) and simultaneously bring #3 under #5. Place #3 on top of pinch and beyond, while bringing #5 to the left side group, to the right of #6. (Figure 12.)

9. Place #4 on top of pinch and beyond and bring #3 to right side group, making it the innermost strip. (Figure 13.)

Continue until strips are too short to work with. Then pinch all the ends together—and you have a six-braided loaf!

C. OVAL SHAPED CHALLAHS WITH FIVE BALLS:

1. Take a large piece of dough.
2. Smooth it with your hands until it takes on an oval shape, narrower at the two ends and fuller and higher in the middle (Fig. 14.)
3. Take five very small pieces of dough. Shape them into small balls.
4. Make a thin slit with a knife on the top of the oval loaf (approximately 4″ long and ½″ wide).
5. Place five small balls slightly apart into slit. (Fig. 15.)

D. SECTIONAL CHALLAHS:

Keeping in mind the size pan you will use, take six equal pieces of dough. Shape them into thick oval or rectangular strips nearly as long as the width of the pan. Each piece should be about 2″ wide and about 3″ high.

Place them into a loaf pan, nearly touching one another. (Fig. 16.)

E. SMALL CHALLAHS:

Small challahs are very popular. They are made in order to be able to place a challah in front of each person making *Kiddush* at the Shabbos table, or in front of each individual when setting up a meal for a *simcha*. (Section XVI.) They are made into various shapes, usually weighing about 2–3 ounces.

1. *SMALL BRAIDS*
   1. Take three small, thin strips of dough about 4″-6″ long. Twist according to directions for three-braided challah (#A, Figures 1-4, and 17).

2. *QUICK-TWISTS*
   a. Take a piece of dough and form into a long strip, approximately 8″ long × 1″ wide (Fig. 18).
   b. Cross one side over the other. You are left with a small hole in the middle (Fig. 19).
   c. Take the tip (about 2″) of the higher half, bend it under the lower half, filling in the middle hole and sticking up a little bit at the top (Fig. 20).

3. *ROUND*
   Take a piece of dough about 3″ long and thick. Round it out with your hands shaping it into a ball flattened at the bottom and rounded on the top (Fig. 21).

   Note: Place small challahs well spaced on a cookie sheet. Approximately 8–10 challahs can fit on one sheet (Fig. 22).

Fig. 14

Fig. 15

Fig. 16

Fig. 17

Fig. 18

Fig. 19

Fig. 20

Fig. 21

Fig. 22

F. HOLIDAY SHAPES:

1. *ROUND*

   There are two ways of making round challah.

   a. Take a large thick piece of dough. Smooth it on all sides until it looks like a smooth circle. Smooth it also around the top making it a little higher on the top. Place it in a round shallow cake pan (Fig. 23).

   b. Take a large piece of dough. Roll out into a long thick strip (about 18″ long and 2″-3″ wide). One end should be slightly thicker than the other (Fig. 24).

   Take the thicker end, place it in the middle of a round pan, and wind the rest of the strip around it 2-3 times (Fig. 25).

2. *LADDER*

   Take six small pieces of dough. Roll out into 2 long, thick pieces to fill bottom of loaf pan. Then roll out four thin strips to place across the lower 2 strips—as if to make four rungs on the ladder (Fig. 26).

3. *HAND*

   a. Take a large piece of dough. Roll it out to about 12″ in length and 3″ in width, or make it smaller if you wish.

   b. Fold one side over the other and leave only a small hole in the middle.

   c. On one end make three one inch slits into the dough, and slightly separate the pieces. This is to give it the semblance of fingers (Fig. 27).

   Because we are alluding to our hope that G-d inscribe us for a good year, we are careful not to shape five fingers, so as not to compare G-d's hands with ours.

4. *TRIANGLES*

   a. Roll out a piece of dough. The size and thickness of the dough will depend on the size you want the *hamantashen* challah to be.

   b. Fill the middle with the desired prune or poppy-seed filling.

   c. Lift up side 1-2 and side 1-3 and let them meet in the middle (over the filling). Pinch the ends together (Fig. 28).

   d. Fold over the top side (3,4,2) to the middle, and pinch it together to the other open ends of the *hamantashen* (Fig. 29).

Fig. 23

Fig. 24

Fig. 25

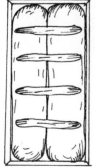

Fig. 26

Fig. 27

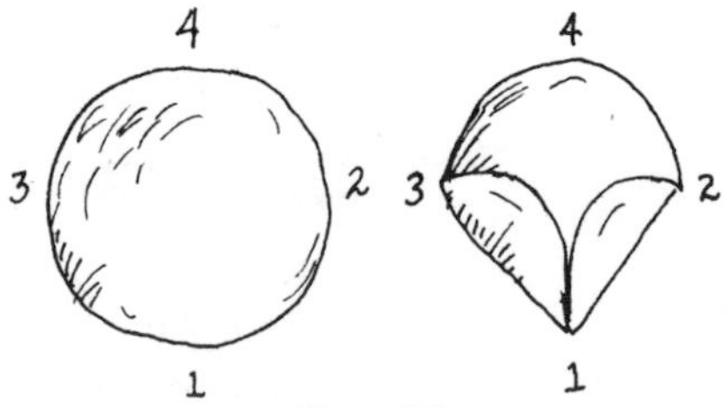

Fig. 28

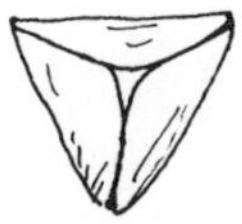

Fig. 29

Challah

To know when to separate *challah*, and whether it should be separated with or without a *brocho*, refer to Laws of Separating Challah, pages 341–4. One may never intentionally avoid taking *challah* through using a smaller quantity of flour.

When eating challah, as when eating all bread, it is necessary first to wash hands ritually with a *brocho*, and to say the *brochos* of *Hamotzi* ("Who brings forth bread . . . ") and the Blessings-After-A-Meal. (See Laws of Blessings, pages 345–349.

One should not include any dairy ingredients when making challah or bread, since most people take for granted that they are pareve and may want to use them at a meat meal. If one does make a dairy loaf, it should be made in a unique shape to differentiate it clearly from a pareve loaf, unless it will all be eaten immediately.

FAMOUS CHALLAH

We placed this recipe first, out of alphabetical sequence, because of its great popularity.

13-14 cups flour	1 cup oil
2 ounces fresh yeast	2 tablespoons salt
or	1 cup sugar
4 packages dry yeast	4 cups warm water
2 eggs, beaten	

Dissolve yeast in water. Water temperature should be 80°-90° when using fresh yeast, 95°-105° for dry yeast. When dissolved, add sugar, salt, and half the flour. Mix well. Add eggs and oil, then slowly stir in most of the remaining flour. Dough will become quite thick. (Until kneading stage, dough can be mixed in Mixmaster.)

When dough pulls away from sides of the bowl, turn onto floured board and knead for approximately 10 minutes. Add only enough additional flour to make dough manageable. Knead until dough has acquired a "life of its own"; it should be smooth and elastic, springing back when pressed lightly with fingertip.

Place dough into a large, oiled bowl. Turn it over so that the top will be oiled as well. Cover with a damp towel and let rise in a warm place for two hours, punching down in four or five places every 20 minutes.

Separate *challah*. Shape loaves and place into well-greased bread pans or onto greased cookie sheet. Allow to rise again until doubled in bulk. Brush tops with beaten egg and sprinkle with poppy or sesame seeds. Bake at 375° for approximately 20 minutes, or until nicely browned.

BIG CHALLAH RECIPE

5 pounds flour	¾ cup oil
4 ounces fresh yeast	2 tablespoons salt
4 cups water	1½ cups sugar
6 eggs	

Sift flour into large pan. In another bowl, dissolve yeast in ½ cup lukewarm water and 1 teaspoon sugar. Form a well in flour and add yeast mixture. Mix in enough of the flour to form a paste. Let stand for 5 minutes or until yeast paste rises and little bubbles form.

Meanwhile, in a glass bowl, beat eggs and add oil, salt and sugar. Mix. Slowly add the remaining water, then gradually stir the liquid mixture into flour. Use a wooden spoon. Knead for 25 minutes adding flour if necessary. Cover and let rise until double in bulk. Take a piece for *challah*. Shape challahs and bake in preheated oven at 300° for 50 minutes.

CLASSIC CHALLAH

1½-2 ounces yeast	¼ cup oil
1¼ cups lukewarm water	4 eggs, beaten
1 tablespoon salt	9 cups flour
½ cup sugar	

Dissolve yeast in water for 10 minutes. Add salt, sugar, oil and eggs. Mix. Add 3 cups of flour at a time and mix after each addition. (Make sure all 9 cups of flour are in.) If you need more flour to work the dough, add it in.

Knead the dough until smooth, then knead for an additional 7 minutes. Place in a large greased bowl and leave in a warm place (perhaps near stove) for 1½ hours or until it has risen to double its original size.

Punch down completely so there are no airpockets. Take off a piece for *challah*. Divide dough, braid and shape as desired. Place onto greased cookie sheets. Let challah rise again until double in size. Brush with egg yolk and water mixture and bake at 350° for ½ hour.

HI-GLUTEN CHALLAH

1¼ cups boiling water	1¼ cups very warm water
3 tablespoons oil	1¼ ounces fresh yeast
¼ cup sugar	1 egg, slightly beaten
2 teaspoons salt	7 cups hi-gluten flour

Place first 4 ingredients into a small container and set aside. Put the 1¼ cups warm (not hot) water into a large mixing bowl. Crumble in fresh yeast and stir. While stirring add the slightly beaten egg, and then add the hot water mixture from the other bowl. Mix together. Add 7 cups flour and knead thoroughly. Add more flour gradually if necessary to achieve a stiff, smooth consistency.

Cover dough and let rise in a warm place for approximately 1 hour or until double in bulk. Punch down and let rise again until double in bulk (about another ½ hour).

Take off *challah.* Shape into 3 medium-sized loaves and place into greased pans. Let rise 1½ hours uncovered. Glaze with well-beaten whole egg. Bake at 350° for 35-60 minutes or until firm and rich brown in color.

Note: If you can't obtain hi-gluten flour, use 9 cups of regular flour. For information on hi-gluten flour, see *Helpful Hints.*

"KITCHEN-AID" TESTED CHALLAH

4¼ cups warm water	1 cup sugar
2 ounces yeast	4-5 eggs
1 tablespoon sugar	2 tablespoons salt
1 cup oil	5 pounds flour

Dissolve yeast in water with a little sugar. Combine all the other ingredients together and mix in Kitchen-Aid (mixer). Let the dough rise until double in size. Separate *challah* with a blessing. Shape. Bake at 450° for 15-25 minutes, then at 350° for another 20 minutes.

NO-KNEAD CHALLAH

2½ packages dry yeast	10 tablespoons oil
2½ cups lukewarm water	2 tablespoons salt
10 cups flour	6 eggs
10 tablespoons sugar	

Mix water and yeast in a small bowl. Put aside. In a large metal bowl, combine flour, sugar, oil, salt and eggs. Add the yeast and water. Mix together with a wooden spoon. When it gets difficult use your hands, but do not knead. Sprinkle a little flour on top of dough, cover with towel, and let rise in a warm place for about 3 hours. Flour bottom of 2 large pans, do not grease. Take off *challah.* Braid challahs and brush egg on top. Let rise in pan for 20-30 minutes. Bake at 325° for 50-60 minutes.

RAISIN CHALLAH

4 packages dry yeast	2½ teaspoons salt
or	1 whole egg
3½ ounces fresh yeast	4 egg yolks
1 teaspoon honey	1½-2 cups raisins
1 cup lukewarm water	2½-2¾ cups hot water
½ cup oil	5 pounds flour

Mix yeast and honey in lukewarm water. Add oil, salt and eggs. Pour hot water over raisins, drain them, and add to mixture. Mix together well. Next, add all the flour.

Knead dough. Brush all sides with small amount of oil. Let rise until double in size. Take *challah.* Shape challahs. Bake at 375° for 30 minutes until double

Note: Challahs can be glazed with remaining egg whites.

SWEET VANILLA CHALLAH

2 ounces yeast	4 eggs
1 teaspoon sugar	1 cup oil
½ cup warm water	2 teaspoons vanilla
12 cups flour	½ teaspoon salt
1 cup sugar	2 cups lukewarm water

Glaze:

2 egg yolks	½ teaspoon sugar
1 teaspoon vanilla	

Dissolve yeast in water with a little sugar. Put flour in a large bowl or pot, form a small well and pour in the yeast mixture. Cover and set aside.

Blend eggs, sugar, oil, vanilla and salt. Pour mixture into pot with flour and add the lukewarm water. Knead dough approximately 3-5 minutes until flour is no longer visible. If mixture is too soft add a little flour, if too firm a little water. Cover and put in unheated oven for 1-1½ hours.

Flour a small working area. Separate *challah*. Shape challahs and grease baking pans. Size of dough in pans should be slightly smaller than pan. Pre-heat oven to 250-300°. (Pans may be pre-heated by setting them on stove for 15-25 minutes.) Blend vanilla glaze and brush on each challah. Bake approximately 30 minutes for medium-sized challahs.

Whole Wheat Challah

There is a tremendous difference between unprocessed whole wheat flour and white flour, even if the latter is "enriched." Whole wheat flour still has the *bran* and the *germ* in it. For our readers who would rather bake with only whole wheat or natural flours, and for those who would like to try their wholesome, hearty taste for the first time, here are a few excellent challah recipes.

ROUND WHOLE WHEAT CHALLAH

⅓ cup hot tap water, cooled down	1 cup oil
1 tablespoon honey	½-1 cup honey
2 packages yeast	5 cups warm water
5 pounds whole wheat flour (approximately 20 cups)	2 egg yolks or oil caraway, poppy or sesame
3 tablespoons salt	seeds

In a small bowl, mix yeast in small amount of water with a little honey. Leave in a warm place. Allow yeast to rise (approximately 10 minutes).

In a different bowl combine salt and flour. Add yeast mixture. Then add the oil, then the honey and water. Mix with a wooden spoon, then knead with hands 5-8 minutes.

Form dough into a ball. Cover bowl with a towel and place in a warm place away from draft. (If necessary a small amount of extra water or flour can be added to the dough to improve texture.) Let rise for 45-50 minutes until double in bulk. Punch down. Knead another few minutes. Take *challah*. Shape into round loaves then place on a greased and lightly floured aluminum or metal tin. Let rise ½ hour—45 minutes in pan.

Cover with egg yolk or oil and sprinkle with seeds. Bake for 1-1¼ hours. Start at 325° and raise temperature 25° every 20 minutes. When finished, place on rack and knock bottom to see if it sounds hollow.

WHEAT AND HONEY CHALLAH

1½	ounces fresh yeast	2-3	tablespoons salt
2½-3	cups hot water	4	cups whole wheat flour
¼	cup oil	1	cup whole wheat pastry flour
¼	cup honey	4	cups unbleached white flour
4	eggs	1	cup rice flour

Dissolve yeast in water. Add oil, honey, eggs, and salt. Mix with wooden spoon. Add all the flour. Knead well. Let dough rise for 2 hours. Punch down and knead again for a few minutes. Separate *challah,* then shape into loaves. Bake at 375° for approximately 35-40 minutes.

Variations: 1. Substitute ½ cup soy flour for ½ cup of white flour. Soy flour will add a sweet, cake-like taste.

      2. Whole wheat pastry flour, if not available, can be substituted by regular whole wheat flour.

HEALTHY WHOLE WHEAT CHALLAH

5	pounds whole wheat flour	2	tablespoons honey
2	tablespoons salt	1	teaspoon dry yeast
2	tablespoons oil	4	cups lukewarm water

Sift bran from whole wheat flour (and save for muffins). Add salt, then oil. Work oil into flour.

Dilute honey in 2 cups lukewarm water. Add the yeast to water and honey and let it foam. Add yeast-honey mixture to flour mixture and then add the remaining water. Knead for 10 minutes. Let rise overnight, covered with a wet cloth. In the morning, punch down.

Take *challah.* Bake for ½ hour at 250° and ½ at 300°.

Bread

BASIC BREAD

12 cups white flour	6 cups water
4 cups whole wheat flour	½ cup sugar
2 ounces yeast	2½ tablespoons salt
or	½ cup honey
4 packages dry yeast	¾ cup oil

Make a well in the flour and add yeast, water, sugar, salt, honey and oil. Gradually knead in all the flour. Let rise in warm place until double in bulk. Punch down, place in pans, and let rise again. Separate *challah,* shape and then bake at 375° until done.

FRENCH BREAD

1 package dry yeast	1 tablespoon sugar
¼ cup warm water	¾ cup cold water
1 cup boiling water	1 egg white
1 tablespoon shortening or oil	6 cups flour
2 teaspoons salt	

Sprinkle yeast on warm water. Let stand a few minutes, then stir until dissolved. Pour boiling water over the shortening, salt and sugar in large mixing bowl. Add ¾ cup cold water and cool to lukewarm. Add yeast and gradually beat in enough flour to form a stiff dough. Turn out on floured pastry cloth or board and knead until smooth and satiny. Put in greased bowl, turn once, cover and let rise 1-1½ hours, or until doubled.

Shape in 2 oblong loaves about 14″ long. Put on greased baking sheets. Let rise 1 hour, or until doubled. Brush with beaten egg white and make 3 slashes across the top with a knife. Bake in preheated 425° oven for 30 minutes. Reduce heat to 350° and bake 20 minutes more.

REAL RYE BREAD

This is a very good rye bread. It is a little heavier than the rye bread you buy in the store, but is really much more like the way rye bread used to be. Also, you will notice that much less yeast than usual is used in this recipe; this is compensated for by the extra rising time.

3	cups rye flour	⅓ teaspoon yeast diluted in ½ cup
2	cups whole wheat flour	warm water
1	cup unbleached white flour	2 cups water
1½	teaspoons salt	1 egg yolk, beaten
3	tablespoons oil	1 tablespoon caraway seeds

Prepare dough in the evening.

Mix the flours and the salt in a large bowl. Add the oil and rub it in well with your hands to break up lumps. Add yeast diluted in water and mix well. Add water slowly and mix it in by hand. Knead for approximately five minutes until dough is stiff enough not to stick to sides of bowl. Then place dough on a floured surface and knead for five minutes more. Place in a well-oiled bowl, and cover with a wet towel. Let stand overnight.

In the morning, knead for 5 more minutes. Allow bread to stand on an oiled baking sheet for another two hours, covered with a damp cloth. Divide dough into loaves. Brush top of bread with a beaten egg yolk and sprinkle with caraway seeds. Bake at 375° for approxomately 50 minutes, or until done. You will love it.

WHOLE-WHEAT BREADS

Use recipes for whole wheat challahs, and shape into loaves.

Bagels and Muffins

MIZONOS BAGELS

3	ounces yeast	1½ cups oil
1	tablespoon salt	1½ cups raisin or rice water, warm
1	dozen eggs	5 pounds flour
3	ounces sugar	

Dissolve yeast in water. Combine all ingredients. Knead well. Let rise until double. Punch down and let rise again. Separate *challah*. Shape into bagels or knots. Boil water with salt to taste, in a large pot. Drop in bagels several at a time and let boil for 3 minutes. Lift with slotted spoon into ungreased tin and bake at 400° for 15-18 minutes.

Note: To make raisin water, boil ½-¾ cup raisins in water.

GOLDEN CORN MUFFINS (Dairy)*

1¼	cup flour	1 teaspoon salt
¾	cups yellow corn meal	⅔ cup milk
3	tablespoons sugar	⅓ cup oil
4½	teaspoons baking powder	1 egg

Mix dry ingredients together until well-blended. Beat the milk, egg and oil together and add to flour mixture. Stir until blended. Mixture will be lumpy. Fill lined cup cake tins ⅔ full. Bake at 425° for 25-30 minutes or until brown.

*Separate dairy utensils are required and a separate, portable dairy oven is recommended for baking dairy foods. (page 329)

WHOLE WHEAT MUFFINS (Dairy)*

1 cup whole wheat flour	1 egg, beaten
1 cup white flour	1 cup milk
3 teaspoons baking powder	1 teaspoon vanilla
¼ cup sugar or honey	½ cup raisins
¼ cup oil	

Combine and mix all ingredients. Grease or line 12 muffin tins. Fill cups about ⅔ full using all the batter for the 12 cups. Sprinkle top with cinnamon and sugar. Bake at 375° for 15-20 minutes.

MEXICAN FLOUR TORTILLAS

2 cups flour	1 teaspoon salt
¼ cup shortening	½ cup lukewarm water

Put flour and salt into bowl and mix together. Then cut in five pieces of shortening. Mix. Then add water slowly. Toss with fork and make a stiff dough.

Form into a ball and knead until smooth. Flour surface of dough lightly. Divide dough into 8 pieces and roll out as thin as possible.

Drop onto hot ungreased griddle. Bake about 20-30 seconds and turn over. Serve with butter.

Leftover Bread—Matzoh Brei

There are a lot of things that can be done with leftover bread. Use it in kugels, stuffings, French toast or make into bread crumbs for cooking and frying. Here are a few suggestions.

LEFTOVER BREAD AND APPLE PUDDING

4 hardened rolls	4 tablespoons sugar
4 eggs	1 teaspoon lemon juice
4 apples	

In one bowl mix 4 egg yolks with 4 tablespoons sugar and 1 teaspoon lemon juice. Then add hardened rolls, cut into pieces.

In another bowl whip up 4 egg whites with a drop of sugar. Fold into roll mixture. Then peel and slice 4 apples in a separate dish. Grease pan. Pour one half of bread batter on bottom. Then add apple slices, and remaining half of mixture on top. Bake at 350° for approximately 1 hour.

SWEET APPLE BREAD KUGEL

¾ pound challah	3-4 tablespoons oil
boiled water	⅓ cup raisins
2 eggs	2 teaspoons cinnamon
2 apples, peeled and sliced	½ teaspoon salt
⅓ cup sugar	

*Separate dairy utensils are required and a separate, portable dairy oven is recommended for baking dairy foods. (page 329)

Put challah into colander. Pour boiling water over it. Squeeze out excess water.

Add the remaining ingredients. Bake in loaf pan at 350° for 45-50 minutes. Crust should be hard when done.

CHALLAH LATKES

1 large challah	1 large onion, grated
water	salt
3 eggs, beaten	pepper

Put challah into pot with water to cover. Soak briefly, then remove challah crust and drain water. Add eggs, onion, and salt and pepper to taste. Heat oil in frying pan, then drop mixture by large spoonfuls into the hot oil, frying until golden brown on both sides.

MATZOH BREI

2 whole pieces matzoh	salt and pepper to taste
water	oil for frying
1 egg	

Soak matzoh in enough water to cover for 2-3 minutes. Drain and squeeze out water very well. Mash matzoh. Add egg and seasoning and mix well.

Heat oil in frying pan. Then add matzoh mixture and fry on both sides until crispy.

MATZOH MEAL PANCAKES

½ cup matzoh meal	1 teaspoon salt
3 eggs	¾ cup water
1 tablespoon sugar	oil or margarine for frying

Beat eggs thoroughly. Mix matzoh meal, sugar and salt and combine with eggs. Add water.

Drop mixture on greased frying pan or griddle tablespoon by tablespoon. Brown on both sides.

Yields 12-16 pancakes depending on thickness. Serve with applesauce or jam.

Helpful Hints

Freezing Bread: Yeasted breads freeze very well. If you don't need to use all your challah or bread immediately, freeze it when still very fresh (preferably the same day as the baking), making sure it has completely cooled. If you don't use a lot of bread at a time, first divide it into a few separate sections. Freeze in separate plastics and remove in individual packets as needed.

Glazing: It is best to freeze breads without glazing them. Before using, after defrosting, heat it up in the oven; they can then be glazed.

Defrosting: Large challahs take approximately 4-6 hours to defrost. Small challahs take approximately 2 hours.

Hi-Gluten Flour: Hi-gluten flour can be bought at your local bakery or at wholesale flour warehouses. It will make your challah lighter. When using hi-gluten flour in the regular recipes included in this book, reduce amount of flour by approximately ⅙.

To Refreshen Bread and Rolls: Place in a paper bag. Twist top of bag closed. Warm in oven for approximately 10-15 minutes. Use immediately, since breads that have been warmed up in this way have a tendency to harden faster, once they are taken out of the bag.

Storing Bread: Always keep challah and bread secured in tightly tied plastic bags to retain freshness. To avoid molding, keep in refrigerator. However, this might cause it to lose its fresh taste more quickly.

Storing Yeasted Dough: Prepare your whole dough at one time, but it's not necessary to bake it all on the same day. Keep leftover dough in the refrigerator in the following way: grease top of dough very well, cover with wax paper, and then with a damp cloth. If dough remains in refrigerator for a few days, make sure the cloth is always kept damp. Bake the dough as you need it during the next few days. Storage time: about 3 days.

KOSHER CHEESE

Milk חלב ישראל

Dairy and Eggs

Dairy and Eggs

DAIRY
Cheese Blintzes
Cheese Fondue
Cheese Latkes
Cottage Cheese and Raisin Latkes
Farmer Cheese Latkes
Sweet Cheese Latkes
Corn Stuffed Onions
Creamy Blender Coleslaw
Eggplant and Cheese Pancakes
Eggplant Parmesan
Macaroni and Cheese Casserole
Mushroom Macaroni and Cheese
Potted Macaroni and Cheese
Creamy Noodle Kugel
Noodle Pudding
Plain Pancakes
Sweet Fruit Pancakes
Pizza
Poppy Cheese Loaf
Creamy Potato Salad
Potato Varenikes
Rice Pudding
Quick Rice Pudding
Spring Salad
Diet Squash Mash
Dairy Vegetable Loaf
Breakfast Cereals
Indian Corn Meal
Basic Kasha
Kasha and Oatmeal Club
Brown Rice Cream

EGGS
Perfect Boiled eggs
Deviled Eggs
French Toast plus Variation
Exotic Breakfast Omelets
Gourmet Poached Eggs
Scrambled Eggs and Cheese
Sunny Side Up
Vegetable Omelet

Helpful Hints
Mix 'n' Match Lunches

Dairy and Eggs

Dairy

Dairy as defined by the dietary laws means milk, or any food containing milk derivatives. They are prepared, cooked and served in dairy utensils. After eating dairy foods it is necessary to wait at least one-half hour and to rinse the mouth before eating meat products. Many Jews, however, have the custom of waiting a minimum of one full hour between dairy and meat. After eating certain hard cheeses, a six-hour waiting period is necessary before eating meat foods.

When preparing baked or toasted dairy dishes, the use of a separate, portable oven is recommended (see page 329).

For other dairy laws and the importance and meaning of using only such dairy products that were supervised by a Jew, from the time of milking, see pages 6-7.

Substitutions: In any of the recipes in this section that call for milk, you may replace the milk with an equal quantity of a non-dairy creamer, or half non-dairy creamer and half water. Make sure that non-dairy creamer has a certification of kashrus, and that the label states that it is pareve. Your dish is then pareve as long as no other dairy products are included.

NOTE:

A dairy meal can be accompanied with pareve foods cooked in dairy or pareve dishes. However, meat products may not be included in a dairy meal even if the required waiting period has passed.

CHEESE BLINTZES

Blintzes are a popular dish made of thin square-shaped dough rolled with many possible fillings. Cheese blintzes are a special favorite on Shavuos when it is customary to eat a dairy dish. They are served hot, with sour cream or applesauce.

Batter:

4 eggs	1 cup milk or water
1 cup flour	oil for frying
1 teaspoon salt	

Filling:

1½ pounds dry cottage cheese	sugar and cinnamon to taste
2 egg yolks	

Beat eggs and salt, add flour alternately with milk. Heat oil in frying pan. Pour only enough batter into pan to make a very thin pancake, tipping pan in all directions so that batter covers pan. Fry on one side until it blisters. Shake out onto waxed paper.

Combine filling ingredients and place one tablespoon of mixture on browned side of each pancake. Fold in sides to form square. Brown in frying pan or broiler. Serve hot with sour cream or applesauce.

CHEESE FONDUE

1 egg	½ cup milk
1 cup cheese	seasoning
1 slice bread	

Beat egg. Cut cheese and bread into cubes. Add liquid and seasoning and mix well. Bake at 350° for ½ hour.

Variation: RED FONDUE—Use tomato juice instead of milk.

CHEESE LATKES

1 pound cottage cheese	salt
3 eggs	pepper
½ cup flour	oil for frying
3 tablespoons milk	

Mix all the pancake ingredients together. Heat oil in frying pan. Drop tablespoonfuls into hot oil and fry until golden brown on both sides.

COTTAGE CHEESE AND RAISIN LATKES

2 eggs, separated	1 pound cottage cheese
¼ cup water	¾ cup flour
2 tablespoons sugar	½ cup raisins
1 teaspoon salt	oil for frying

Mix together egg yolks, water, sugar and salt. Add cottage cheese and flour and mix until well blended. Add raisins. Beat egg whites until stiff and add. Mix everything together.

Heat oil in skillet. Add large spoonfuls of mixture and fry on both sides until golden brown.

FARMER CHEESE LATKES

4 eggs	3 tablespoons oil (or margarine)
8 ounces farmer cheese	dash of salt
3 tablespoons sugar	½ cup matzoh meal
1 teaspoon vanilla	oil for frying

Beat eggs and mix in farmer cheese. Mix together the sugar, vanilla, shortening and salt. Add matzoh meal and mix well. Fry in heated oil until brown.

SWEET CHEESE LATKES

1 pound cottage cheese	1 cup farina
2 teaspoons vanilla sugar	2 eggs
½ cup sugar	oil for frying

Mix cottage cheese, vanilla sugar, sugar, farina and eggs. Heat oil in frying pan. Pour tablespoonfuls of mixture into oil and fry on both sides until golden brown.

CORN STUFFED ONIONS

6 medium onions	dash of pepper
1 12-ounce can corn, drained	1 cup milk
2 tablespoons water	2 tablespoons chopped pimentos
2 tablespoons butter	4 ounces processed American
2 tablespoons flour	cheese, shredded
½ tablespoon salt	

Hollow the onions. Chop removed centers to make one cup. Fill onions with corn. Set aside remaining corn and chopped onions. Place onions in 9″ × 9″ × 2″ baking pan. Add water to bottom of pan and cover. Bake at 400° for one hour. Cook chopped onion in butter. Stir in flour, salt, and pepper. Add milk or water. Cook and stir until thickened. Add reserved corn and pimento. Return to bubbling. Stir in cheese until melted.

Place onions in serving dish and spoon sauce over them. Makes 6 servings. *Note:* To make this recipe pareve, use mayonnaise instead of the shredded cheese, margarine instead of butter, and water instead of milk.

CREAMY BLENDER COLESLAW

1 small head cabbage	2 tablespoons lemon juice
2 large carrots	2 teaspoons sugar
1 small green pepper	1½ teaspoons salt
1 cup mayonnaise	¼ teaspoon pepper
1 cup sour cream	

Coarsely chop the cabbage, thickly slice the carrots, and cut the green pepper in chunks. Fill blender container about half full with water, and add in about ⅓ of the vegetables. Cover blender and blend at high speed until vegetables are finely chopped. Pour mixture into colander and drain well. Repeat two more times until all vegetables are chopped.

In a large bowl, mix the other ingredients well. Add the vegetables to the mayonnaise mixture and stir until well mixed. Cover and refrigerate about 1 hour or until well chilled. Serves approximately 12.

Variation: See Vegetables, Section X, for non-dairy coleslaw recipes.

EGGPLANT AND CHEESE PANCAKES

1 eggplant	dash of garlic powder
2 eggs	2-3 slices hard cheese
1½ cups matzoh meal	4 ounces tomato sauce
1½ teaspoon salt	oil for frying
dash of pepper	

Peel eggplant and slice across width into 8-10 slices. Dip each slice into eggs, and then into matzoh meal seasoned with salt, pepper and garlic powder. Fry on both sides until golden brown and tender. Then place sliced cheese between eggplant slices, forming 4-5 sandwiches. Replace in frying pan, add tomato sauce and heat over low flame for a few minutes until cheese begins to melt and sauce to bubble. Remove with spatula, and serve warm.

EGGPLANT PARMESAN

1 large eggplant	½ cup hard cheese (grated)
2 eggs, beaten	2 teaspoons dried oregano
1 cup bread crumbs	3 8-ounce cans tomato sauce
¾ cup salad oil	½ cup cottage cheese (optional)

Peel eggplant and cut into ¼" slices. Dip each slice into egg and then into bread crumbs. Sauté in hot oil until golden brown, drain and let dry. Place a layer of eggplant in 2-quart casserole. Sprinkle with cheese and oregano. Cover well with tomato sauce. Top last layer with cheese. Bake, uncovered, at 350° for ½ hour or until sauce is bubbly and cheese is melted.

MACARONI AND CHEESE CASSEROLE

8 ounces macaroni, cooked and drained	1 teaspoon salt
	1 teaspoon dry mustard
2 tablespoons butter or margarine	1½ cups milk
	2 cups shredded cheese
1 tablespoon minced onion (optional)	¼ cup buttered bread crumbs or 1 sliced tomato
2 tablespoons flour	paprika

Cook macaroni and drain in a colander. In saucepan melt butter (with onion), and remove from heat. Add flour, salt and mustard. Mix well. Add milk and stir over low flame until sauce is smooth and thick. Add 1¼ cup cheese. Heat until melted, stirring occasionally. Combine macaroni and sauce in 2-quart greased casserole dish. Top with remaining cheese, bread crumbs and paprika. Bake at 375° for 20-25 minutes or until lightly browned.

MUSHROOM MACARONI AND CHEESE

8 ounces macaroni	1 tablespoon butter
1 can mushroom soup	2 eggs, beaten
2 slices American cheese, grated	1 teaspoon salt

Cook macaroni and drain. Combine with rest of ingredients in a casserole dish. Mix well. Bake in greased casserole dish at 300° for one hour. Serves 4.

POTTED MACARONI AND CHEESE

1 cup macaroni	1 tablespoon oil
2 cups water	3 slices hard cheese
1 teaspoon salt	

Heat water, salt, and oil over a high flame. When water comes to a boil, add the macaroni. Boil for 6-7 minutes, add cheese slices, and boil another 2 minutes so that cheese melts. Stir, and serve immediately.

CREAMY NOODLE KUGEL

12 ounce broad noodles	4 ounces sour cream
½ cup butter	salt
1 pound large curd cottage cheese	2 eggs

Cook noodles and drain. Stir in butter until melted. Add cottage cheese, sour cream, and salt to taste, then add the eggs and mix well. Bake in a greased, 9″ glass pan at 350° for 2 hours.

Variations: For plain and sweet *pareve* noodle kugels, see Noodles, Section XI.

NOODLE PUDDING:

1 pound broad noodles	1 teaspoon vanilla
1 stick margarine	1 quart milk
4 ounces sour cream	6 eggs, beaten
½ cup sugar or honey	1 package frozen strawberries, thawed.
8 ounces cottage cheese	
4 ounces cream cheese	

Boil noodles 12 minutes and drain. Add margarine, sour cream, sugar, vanilla and cheeses. Warm the milk and add eggs. Stir slowly into noodle mixture. Pour into two 9″ × 12″ greased pans. Bake for 1½-2 hours at 325°. Serve warm. Add strawberries.

PLAIN PANCAKES

1¾ cups milk	1 teaspoon salt
2 eggs	3 tablespoons sugar
2 cups flour	¼ cup oil
2 teaspoons baking powder	

Beat milk and eggs together. Add dry ingredients and mix well. Fry in heated oil until light brown on both sides. Serve with syrup, jam, sour cream, honey, or sugar.

SWEET FRUIT PANCAKES

2 medium apples	½ cup milk
2 tablespoons sugar	⅔ cup applesauce
¼ teaspoon cinnamon	1 cup flour
1 egg, beaten	3 tablespoons margarine

Core and slice the apples. Mix sugar and cinnamon together and sprinkle over apples. Mix eggs, milk and applesauce and beat well. Pour over apples, mix in the flour and beat well. Fry in oil pressing two slices of apple into each pancake. Serve with syrup.

PIZZA

3	cups flour	2	cans seasoned tomato sauce
1	package dry yeast	½	pound munster cheese, grated
1⅓	cups warm water	1	teaspoon oregano
1	teaspoon salt		

Dissolve yeast in ½ cup water, let stand 10 minutes. Sift flour and add yeast mixture, salt and remaining water. Knead and let rise 1½ hours.

Roll out dough and put into greased pans. Spread 1 cup sauce on dough. Sprinkle cheese on sauce, top with oregano. Bake 15-20 minutes at 450°.

POPPY CHEESE LOAF

1	whole loaf French bread	1	tablespoon mustard
⅓	cup butter	2	tablespoons poppy seeds
1	medium onion, minced	½	pound Swiss cheese, sliced

Slice bread about 1″ thick to the crust but not completely through. Mix together butter, onion, mustard, and poppy seeds.

Spread mixture on one side of each slice, then insert pieces of cheese between the slices. Bake at 350° for about 20 minutes or until cheese melts.

CREAMY POTATO SALAD

2	pounds potatoes	1	teaspoon salt
1	celery stalk, chopped	⅛	teaspoon black pepper
½	cup olives, chopped		juice of 1 lemon
1	tablespoon grated American cheese	¼	cup mayonnaise or salad dressing
1	tablespoon minced parsley	8	ounces cottage cheese
¼	teaspoon dill weed	3-4	ounces milk

Boil potatoes in skin. When tender, let cool and peel. Slice thinly and place in a large bowl. Add ingredients and mix well. Cover and place in refrigerator for a few hours, then mix again.

Serve on lettuce leaves or scooped-out tomato cups. Garnish with sprigs of parsley.

Note: For non-dairy potato salad, Potatoes, Section XI.

POTATO VARENIKES

A delicious cooked dough with potato-cheese filling.

Filling:

2 pound potatoes	oil for frying
1 large onion, diced	¾-1 pound cottage cheese

Dough:

1-1½ cups flour	½ glass water
1 egg, beaten	½ teaspoon salt

To make filling, cook unpeeled potatoes. Let cool, then peel and grate. Sauté 1 diced onion in oil until golden brown. Add half the sautéed onion, cottage cheese, and seasoning to potatoes and mix well.

To make dough, combine flour, egg, water and salt. Divide the finished dough into pieces and roll out on a floured surface until very thin. To cut out circles, flour the opening of a glass and press into dough. Dough will yield approximately 25-30 circles.

Place filling in center of circles, then fold in half down the middle. Squeeze ends together. Pricking the outside with a fork helps keep the dough together.

To cook, bring lightly salted water to boil in a 6-quart pot. Drop in 6-8 varenikes and let cook approximately 5 minutes until they begin to rise to the top. Remove and place in rows on a platter, being careful not to stack them one on top of another. Repeat until all are done. Sprinkle with remaining sautéed onion. Yields 25-30.

Serving suggestion: Top with sour cream or yogurt.

RICE PUDDING

½ cup rice, cooked	1 teaspoon vanilla
3 eggs, beaten	rind of orange
½ cup sugar	3 cups milk
¼ cup white raisins	butter

Combine rice, add eggs and sweeteners, mixing well. Add milk and mix again. Grease baking dish with butter. Bake at 350° for one hour.

QUICK RICE PUDDING

1 cup white rice, cooked	cinnamon
1 package instant vanilla pudding	sugar
½ cup raisins	

Prepare pudding according to directions on box. Combine with rice and raisins. Sprinkle with cinnamon and sugar. Refrigerate and serve when stiff.

SPRING SALAD

2-3 tomatoes	3 scallions (optional)
½ cucumber	1 pound cottage cheese
1 green pepper	4 ounce sour cream (optional)
2 sour pickles	salt

Dice all vegetables into a large bowl. Add cottage cheese and sour cream, mixing well. Add salt to taste.

Serve chilled. Yields approximately 4-6 portions.

DIET SQUASH MASH

2-3	small zucchini squash	oregano
½	cup tomato juice	salt
2	slices American cheese	pepper
	garlic powder	

Line a frying pan with slices of zucchini. Cover with tomato juice and American cheese. Add garlic powder, a dash of oregano, salt and pepper. Cover and let simmer until cheese melts and zucchini is soft.

DAIRY VEGETABLE LOAF

1	stick margarine	2	cups hot milk
1	small onion, diced	1	package frozen mixed
2	matzohs, broken (or crackers)		vegetables, cooked and drained
2	eggs	1	16-oz. can tomato and
	dash of salt		mushroom sauce
	dash of pepper		

Sauté onion in margarine until tender. Add broken matzoh, sauté until lightly brown. Combine with eggs, milk, salt and pepper. Add vegetables and place in greased loaf pan. Bake at 350° for fifty minutes. Serve with heated tomato and mushroom sauce. Serves six.

Breakfast Cereals

Getting the family to eat a good breakfast is always a problem. Certainly the breakfast we would prefer the children to eat, especially in the winter, is hot cereal, but getting them to like it is another matter. Perhaps one of the following recipes will help. You can always use these methods to prepare packaged cereals such as wheatena, farina, etc.

INDIAN CORN MEAL

1 cup white corn meal	3 cups water
1 teaspoon salt	1 cup milk

Mix the cornmeal and salt in 1 cup cold water. Bring another 1 cup of water to a boil. Pour in the corn meal, stirring constantly. Lower the flame. Stir until smooth, then add another cup of water. Cook and stir until smooth. Let simmer for 20-30 minutes, checking and stirring occasionally. Then add the milk. Stir well and cook a little while longer. Total cooking time should be at least one hour. Serve hot with maple syrup and/or raisins or chopped nuts. Serves 4-6.

BASIC KASHA

Cook whole kasha according to directions on box. Serve with cold milk. For creamier taste, add a pat of butter to hot kasha, letting it melt before adding milk.

KASHA AND OATMEAL CLUB

½ cup kasha	¼ cup raisins
½ cup oats	3 cups water
¼ cup dry milk powder	honey

In a dry pot mix kasha, oats, milk powder and raisins. In another pot, bring water to a boil. Pour boiling water over the kasha mixture, place over flame and bring to a very low simmer. Cover and cook for 10-15 minutes or until cereal is soft and smooth. Add honey to taste and serve. Serves 3-4.

BROWN RICE CREAM

¼ cup brown rice	2 prunes
3 cups water	½ teaspoon salt
2 figs	

Wash and drain rice. Toast over a medium flame in a heavy skillet until it starts to change color and give off a pleasing smell. Keep stirring rapidly in order to prevent burning. Remove from pan and let cool.

Bring 1 cup of water to a boil. Parboil figs and prunes for 30 seconds, then remove from water and turn off flame. Later on, you may slice them, if desired.

Grind toasted rice in a flour mill or a blender—try to get as even a grind as possible. Mix ground rice in remaining 2 cups water. Add to the water in pot already on stove. Cook over a high flame, stirring constantly until it boils.

Add salt, reduce flame to simmer, stir once more, then cover and let cook 30 minutes. Stir occasionally to prevent burning. Top with figs and prunes. Serves 2 or 3. Make sure the fruit is apportioned equally.

Variation: Instead of figs and prunes, serve each portion with 1 teaspoon hot (toasted) slivered almonds or sunflower seeds or sprinkle with raisins.

Eggs

Eggs are used frequently in Jewish cooking. They are found in gefilte fish, challahs, matzoh balls, kreplach and kugels, and in most cakes and desserts. Eggs also have a special place at our Shabbos afternoon table. Egg salad—plain, or mixed with chopped liver—is often served as an appetizer to the meal. At the Passover Seder, a hard-boiled egg is placed on the Seder plate to remind us of the Passover Holiday sacrifice. And before fasting on Tisha B'Av, hard-boiled eggs are eaten whole, as a sign of mourning.

NOTE: Eggs must be opened into a dish or glass and checked for blood spots before they are cooked (see page 8). If a blood spot is found, the whole egg must be discarded, and the cup or dish should be immediately and carefully washed with cold water. If a blood spot is found in a boiled egg the whole egg must also be discarded.

A Rav must be consulted if the blood spot was found after the egg had been added to a mixture or after it was placed into hot frying pan. (The mixture or the pan must be set aside until the Rabbi states what must be done.)

PERFECT BOILED EGGS

Hard Boiled: Place eggs in pot. Cover generously with water. Add salt and bring to boil. Lower flame and simmer for 15-20 minutes.

Immediately rinse under cold running water and let soak several minutes. Cold water helps eggs peel easily.

Soft Boiled: Bring to boil as for hard-boiled eggs. Lower flame and simmer approximately 3-5 minutes. Rinse in cold water. Make a small hole in top of shell and empty egg into dish.

DEVILED EGGS

6 hard-boiled eggs	dash of pepper
1 tablespoon mayonnaise	1 teaspoon lemon juice
¼ teaspoon salt	dash of paprika

Peel eggs and cut them in half lengthwise. Remove yolks and mash in a bowl. Add mayonnaise, salt, pepper and lemon juice. Mix well and fluff. Fill hollow egg whites with the mixture. Sprinkle tops with paprika.

FRENCH TOAST

6 slices white bread	2 tablespoon milk (optional)
2 eggs	oil for frying
salt	

Beat the eggs well with salt to taste. Heat the oil. Dip each slice of bread into the egg mixture. (Adding milk makes it a bit lighter.) Fry both sides over a medium flame for a minute or two.

Serve warm. Spread with jam or sprinkle lightly with sugar.

Variations: SPICY FRENCH TOAST—Add vanilla with cinnamon to eggs.
FRENCH TOAST WITH CHEESE—Prepare French toast as instructed above. After turning slices over, top with slices of cheese and let melt into the bread.

EXOTIC BREAKFAST OMELETS

4 egg whites	4 egg yolks
2 tablespoon water	½ teaspoon salt
1 tablespoon oil or margarine	¼ teaspoon pepper (optional)

Beat egg whites until frothy. Add water and salt. Beat until stiff peaks form. Add pepper to yolks if desired and beat yolks until lemon-colored and very thick. Fold yolks into whites. Heat oil or margarine in 10″ skillet; leave higher at sides. Reduce heat and cook 7-10 minutes, until omelet is puffy and bottom is golden.

Variations: BAKED—Bake at 325° until knife inserted in center comes out clean.
DAIRY—Add ½ cup skim milk to egg yolks and beat together until foamy. Butter may be used instead of margarine.
GREEN—Cook and drain 1½ cups of spinach or zucchini. Put vegetable in skillet, add egg mixture and cook as above.

GOURMET POACHED EGGS

¼ cup tomato juice	onion flakes
2 eggs	oregano
salt, pepper	paprika
parsley flakes	garlic

Bring tomato juice to a boil. Add eggs, with seasoning to taste; lower flame. Eggs poach quickly.

This is very tasty served over heated vegetables.

SCRAMBLED EGGS AND CHEESE

4 eggs	2 tablespoons oil
½ teaspoon salt	2 slices hard cheese

Heat oil in frying pan. Beat eggs in a bowl and pour into pan. When eggs begin to sizzle at sides, top with cheese and lower flame. When cheese begins to melt, scramble together with the eggs for 1-2 minutes. Serve hot.

SUNNY-SIDE UP

Place 1-2 unbeaten eggs in small amount of hot oil. Egg whites will become white. Yolk should remain whole in middle. When whites are done, turn off the flame. Lift the eggs out of the pan with a spatula.

VEGETABLE OMELET

1	onion	4	eggs
1	large green pepper		salt
1	tomato		garlic
1	can mushrooms		basil
	oil		oregano

Dice vegetables. Cover bottom of frying pan with oil and slowly simmer the vegetables until they are soft.

Put eggs into a bowl and add salt. Mix the eggs well and pour over vegetables. Add spices, if desired. Cook for 2-3 minutes, stirring briskly. Serve hot.

Helpful Hints

Checking Eggs for Blood Spots: Before using eggs, whether raw or boiled, check them thoroughly after opening to make sure there are no blood spots, for that would render the egg unkosher.

Cracking: To prevent eggs from cracking while cooking, let them stand at room temperature. To boil a cracked egg, first wrap it in aluminum foil.

Cutting Eggs: To slice hard-cooked eggs without breaking the yolk, first dip knife into water.

Egg Garnish: Pressing hard-boiled eggs through a sieve makes a perfect garnish for hors d'oeuvres.

Testing Eggs:
   a) if it hardly spins, it's raw.
   b) if it spins a little and slowly, it is soft-boiled.
   c) if it spins very fast, it is hard-boiled.

Peeling Eggs: To easily peel hard-boiled eggs, make sure eggs are always covered with bubbling water while cooking. When they are ready, place them under fast-running cold water for 1-2 minutes. Then let eggs stand in cold water another few minutes.

Separating Eggs: Egg whites and yolks separate best at room temperature. Therefore remove eggs from refrigerator a few hours before baking.

Egg Whites: To beat egg whites to largest volume, first let them stand at room temperature for a few hours.

Egg Yolks: Left-over egg yolks can be made into a garnish over foods by first gently boiling in water for 10 minutes, then pressing through a coarse sieve.

To soothe sore throat, drink raw egg yolks mixed with small amount of sugar until creamy.

Mix 'N' Match Lunches

To avoid last minute panic, and to add variety to your husband's and/or child's lunch and snack pack, here's a list of basic foods to have in your refrigerator and cupboard. Now you are only minutes away from pleasing your family every day.

BREADS
Bagels
Matzoh
Pumpernickel Bread
Rolls
Rye Bread
White Bread
Whole Wheat Bread

Peanut Butter
Peanut Butter & Jam
Peanut Butter & Sliced Banana
Salmon
Sardines & Tomato
Tuna & Lettuce

SANDWICH FILLINGS
Avocado Spread
Butter
Butter & Cucumber Slices
Cheese & Tomato Slices
Cream Cheese
Egg Salad

Jam (Different Flavors)
Lettuce & Tomato (and Green Pepper)
Lox

VEGETABLES
Carrots
Celery
Cucumber
Green Pepper
Lettuce
Pickles
String Beans
Tomato

LUNCH MAIN DISHES
Fish Cakes
Fried Flounder
Kasha Cutlets
Tuna Patties
Vegetable Loaf

FRUIT
Apple
Banana
Fruit Compote
Orange
Peach
Pear
Tangerine

Fresh Fruit
Popcorn
Pudding
Potato Chips
Pretzels

DRINKS
Apple Juice
Chocolate Milk
Milk
Orange Juice

SALADS
Cole Slaw
Egg Salad
Macaroni Salad
Potato Salad
Spring Salad (cottage cheese & vegetables)
Tuna Salad & Green Pepper

DESSERT
Cake
Cookies
Doughnuts

Soup and Accompaniments

SECTION 6

Soup and Accompaniments

PAREVE SOUPS
  Barley Soup
  Hearty Barley-Pea Soup
  Basic Beet Borscht
  Simple Beet Borscht
  Simple and Delicious Cabbage Soup
  Cabbage-Tomato Soup
  Fresh Fruit Soup
  Fruit Soup
  Hungarian Onion Soup
  Easy Onion Vegetable Soup
  Split Pea Soup
  Potato Soup
  Schav
  Tomato Soup
  Tomato and Rice Soup
  Fresh Vegetable Soup
  Vegetable Noodle Soup
  Vegetable Purée Soup

MEAT AND CHICKEN SOUPS
  Sweet and Sour Borscht
  Sour Cabbage Soup
  Spiced Cabbage Soup
Chicken Soup
  Tasty Chicken Soup
  Chicken Soup Supreme
  Chicken-Tomato Soup
  Delicious Chicken-Vegetable Soup
Cholent
  Basic Cholent
  Kasha-Chicken Cholent
  Moroccan Cholent
  Pareven Cholent
  Sweet and Sour Cholent
  White Cholent
  Hungarian Goulash
  Hearty Meat and Vegetable Soup
  Vegetable-Beef Soup

SOUP ACCOMPANIMENTS
  Egg Drop
  Fluffy Potato Drop
Knaidlach
  The Art of Making Knaidlach
  Easy Knaidlach
  Fancy Knaidlach
  Perfect Knaidlach
Kreplach
  The Art of Shaping Kreplach
  Easy Kreplach
  Fancy Kreplach
  Fluffy Kreplach
Kishke
  Cracker Kishke
  Vegetable Kishke
  Challah Cholent Kugel
  Flour Cholent Kugel
  Soup Mandlen

Helpful Hints

Soup and Accompaniments

A soup at the beginning of the meal, or between courses, helps make a meal more complete. There is an endless variety of soups to make, and just about any combination of foods can be mixed in.

The soups in this section are either pareve or meat-based. If you wish to adapt a basic *pareve* soup recipe for a dairy meal, it can be given a creamier texture by substituting 1 cup milk for 1 cup water, and adding a pat of butter. To make a pareve soup meaty, simply cook it with meat bones or a small amount of gravy, or put in a few small pieces of meat.

Pareve Soups

BARLEY SOUP

4 carrots, grated	1 cup pearl barley
3 onions, chopped	2 teaspoons salt
2 parsnips, diced	½ teaspoon pepper
4 tablespoons margarine	2 tablespoons chopped parsley
2 quarts water	

Sauté carrots, onion and parsnips in the margarine for 15 minutes. Add water, bring to a boil and stir in barley, salt and pepper.

Cook over low heat 1½ hours.

Sprinkle with parsley. Serves 6.

Variations: BARLEY-LENTIL, BARLEY-PEA, BARLEY-POTATO or BARLEY-MUSHROOM SOUP—Simply add ½-1 cup of the desired ingredient and 2-3 cups extra water per cup of lentils, peas, potatoes or mushrooms. The taste and texture of each blends very nicely with the barley.

HEARTY BARLEY-PEA SOUP

1 cup barley	1 tablespoon salt
1 cup lentils	¼ teaspoon black pepper
1 cup split peas	1-2 bay leaves (optional)
1 cup chopped onions	8 cups water

This soup tastes best when cooked for a long time. After ingredients come to boil, lower flame and let simmer 2 hours, stirring occasionally.

Variation: DAIRY—Instead of 8 cups water, use 4 cups water and 4 cups milk plus ½ stick (2 ounces) butter.

BASIC BEET BORSCHT

A classic soup made from beets. It is refreshing when eaten cold and is often served that way.

3 pounds beets	juice of one lemon
2 quarts water	pinch of sour salt
2 teaspoons salt	1 tablespoon sugar (optional)
2 garlic cloves	

Scrub beets very well. Do not peel. Put beets in pot, cover generously with water and cook for 1-1½ hours. Remove beets from pot and save the water. When beets are cool, peel and grate them, using the large holes of a grater.

Return grated beets to water. Add seasoning and boil approximately ½ hour. Can be garnished with sliced cucumbers before serving.

Note: When cooked in this way the vitamins are not lost, since beets are cooked in their shells and the nutrient-rich water is saved.

Variations: For a thicker and lighter color beet soup: whip 2 eggs quickly in a bowl. Then add small amount of warm borscht. Beat together and return to liquid in the pot. Stir but do not boil.
DAIRY—Serve cold borscht with 1-2 tablespoons of sour cream added to each serving. Try yogurt instead of sour cream for a tangy, low-fat variation.

SIMPLE BEET BORSCHT

3 pounds small beets	4 tablespoons lemon juice
2 quarts water	or
2 teaspoons salt	juice of 2 lemons
2 tablespoons sugar	

Peel beets and cut into slices. Place into 4-quart pot, cover with water and add salt. Cook until beets are soft (about 2 hours). After it is ready, stir in sugar and lemon juice very well.

Can be served garnished with cucumber slices (or sour cream, for dairy).

SIMPLE AND DELICIOUS CABBAGE SOUP

1 cabbage, grated	salt, to taste
1 onion, diced	¾ stick of margarine
1 can tomato paste	½ cup flour
water	sugar

Grate cabbage, dice onion, and place in 4 to 6-quart pot. Add tomato paste and enough water to cover cabbage. Add salt and margarine.

While soup is coming to a boil, make a thin paste by putting approximately

½ cup of flour in a bowl and very slowly adding water. Mixture should be smooth. Add to boiling soup and put in a small amount of sugar. Lower flame and let simmer 1½-2 hours.

CABBAGE TOMATO SOUP

1 head cabbage	1 4 ounce can tomato sauce
1 onion	or
3 tablespoons oil	18-ounce can tomato juice
water to cover	salt and pepper to taste
	2 tablespoons sugar (optional)

Wash and coarsely chop cabbage. Dice the onion, sauté in oil. Add cabbage with enough water to cover. Add seasoning and tomato sauce or juice. Cook approximately 2-2½ hours.

FRESH FRUIT SOUP

3 apples	sugar
3 peaches	1 tablespoon vanilla extract
3 plums	2 eggs (optional)
water	pinch of salt

Wash fruits well and cut into slices. Place in pot, add sugar to taste and cover generously with water. Cook over medium flame, approximately 20 minutes. Remove pot from fire and let it cool. Add vanilla extract, beaten eggs and salt. Stir in well. Refrigerate and serve cold.

Variation: CANNED FRUIT SOUP—When making larger quantities add to fresh fruits your choice of undrained canned peaches, fruit cocktail, etc.

FRUIT SOUP

1 can cherries	4 plums
4 peaches	water

Cut fruit into small pieces, and place in saucepan with water. The water level should be 3″ above the fruit. Cook ½ hour.

Other fruits may be added in similar quantities, such as nectarines, grapes, etc.

HUNGARIAN ONION SOUP

2 Spanish onions	3 pints soup stock
2 ounces margarine	2 ounces thin noodles
2 tomatoes, cut up	salt
1 teaspoon paprika	pepper

Slice onions thinly and cook gently in margarine until golden brown. Stir in paprika and tomatoes.

Pour into stock. Bring to boil and cook gently for ½ hour. Put through sieve and reboil mixture, adding noodles. Add salt and pepper and simmer for 10-15 minutes.

EASY ONION-VEGETABLE SOUP

1 package onion soup mix	1 package frozen mixed
water	vegetables
1 teaspoon salt	

Prepare onion soup as directed on package. As soon as soup begins to boil add vegetables and salt and stir. Simmer over low flame for 30 minutes.

SPLIT PEA SOUP

1 cup split peas	1 teaspoon garlic powder (optional)
1½ quarts water	1 onion
2 teaspoons salt	1 celery stalk
dash of pepper	1 tablespoon melted margarine

Wash peas, and let stand in cold water for one hour. Drain and cook peas in salted water for 1 hour.

Dice onion and celery. Add them to soup, and cook over a small flame for another ½ hour. Add melted margarine and stir well.

Variations: Instead of raw onion and celery, put in lightly sautéed onion and thin carrot rings. Immediately after washing peas, combine all ingredient and cook slowly. Do not add salt or spices until after peas have softened.

POTATO SOUP

1 small onion	1 parsnip (stem and leaves)
2-3 tablespoons oil	6-8 cups cold water
2 tablespoons cake meal	8 medium redskin potatoes
1 cup cold water	salt
2 small carrots, diced	pepper
1 small stalk celery, diced	½ teaspoon paprika
parsley	

Use a 4-quart pot. Dice onion and brown in oil. Add cake meal. Add one cup cold water and cook for 3-4 minutes.

Dice carrots and celery and (chop parsley fine). Add remaining water and vegetables (parsnip is added whole). Cook until vegetables are tender.

Add potatoes and seasoning last. Cook until potatoes are done. Serve hot.

SCHAV

1 pound schav (sour grass)	1 egg
1½ quarts boiling water	1½ teaspoons salt

Wash leaves well and pick off stems. Place leaves in bowl and chop up in very small pieces. Tie stems together. Add chopped leaves and bundle of stems to boiling water. Cook for 15 minutes. Cool and discard stems.

Beat the egg well, add salt and gradually add salted egg to the schav, stirring well. Serve cold.

Serving suggestions:
1. When serving, cut a hard-boiled egg into the schav.
2. Dairy: Serve with sour cream.

TOMATO SOUP

1 large can tomato juice	2-3 tablespoons flour
2-3 tablespoons oil	1 large green pepper, diced
2 celery stalks, diced	

Blend flour, oil and a bit of juice to form paste. Add the rest of the juice and the vegetables. Cook until the vegetables are tender and the soup is thick—approximately 30 minutes.

TOMATO AND RICE SOUP

8 ounces tomato juice	sugar to taste
12 ounces water	2 tablespoons oil
1 green pepper, diced	2 tablespoons flour
1 onion, diced	1 ounce rice
1 teaspoon salt	

Bring first 6 ingredients to a boil. Meanwhile, lightly sauté flour in heated oil, then add to soup. Rinse rice and add to boiling soup. Simmer 20 minutes, stirring occasionally.

FRESH VEGETABLE SOUP

1 6-ounce package of dried vegetable mix	1 large onion
water	1 carrot
1 tablespoon salt	1 red pepper
2 tablespoons oil	2 carrots, diced
1 tablespoon white flour	1 small tomato
	1-2 tablespoons sugar, optional

Use a 6-quart pot. Fill generously with water, add vegetable mix, salt, and bring to boil.

Meanwhile, grate onion and carrot finely. Heat oil in skillet, stir in flour, then add vegetables and sauté 5-10 minutes.

When slightly cooled, add sautéed vegetables to soup mixture along with pepper, carrots, and tomato. A small amount of sugar helps bring out the flavor of the vegetables. Simmer 1-1½ hours.

Variations: VEGETABLE-POTATO SOUP WITH NOODLES—Instead of red pepper, carrots, and tomato, add 3 large potatoes cut into small slices. Omit sugar. When potatoes are nearly done, stir in 3-4 ounces of fine noodles. Cook additional 10 minutes.

VEGETABLE NOODLE SOUP

6 tablespoons oil	3 carrots, sliced thin
1 cup chopped onion	2 cups shredded cabbage
dash of garlic	1½ tablespoons salt
or	1 bay leaf
1 clove fresh garlic	1 package thin noodles
2½ quarts water	1 cup peas
1 can chopped tomatoes	chopped parsley
or	
2 fresh tomatoes	

Heat oil and brown the onion. Add garlic and cook until tender.

Stir in water, tomatoes, carrots, cabbage, salt and bay leaf. Bring to boil, and simmer for 15 minutes. Add noodles, peas and parsley. Simmer for another 20 minutes, stirring occasionally. Makes about 3 quarts of soup.

VEGETABLE PURÉE SOUP

1	medium zucchini squash	2	quarts water
3	large carrots	½	cup barley
1	large onion		salt
1	medium parsnip		pepper
1	stalk celery		

Peel and cut all the vegetables. Place them in a pot together with the water, barley, and seasoning. Cook for ½-¾ hour, or until the vegetables are tender. The soup may then be served this way—chunky-style. However, for a smooth texture, purée the soup in a blender. If reheating later on, add a little more water.

Meat and Chicken Soups

SWEET AND SOUR BORSCHT

3-4	soup bones	6-8	beets
	water	6	medium potatoes
2	pounds flanken	½	head cabbage
	or	2	tablespoons lemon juice
	chuck for stew		or
1	large can tomato juice		sour salt
	water	2	tablespoons sugar

Place bones in a 6–quart pot with water to cover. Bring to a boil, skim fat, reduce heat and let simmer for 2 hours.

Remove bones, add meat, tomato juice and enough water to fill the pot ⅔ full. Simmer 2 hours or until meat is almost tender.

Peel and thickly slice beets and potatoes and add them to soup. Continue cooking about 30 minutes. Then cut cabbage in small pieces and add to soup.

When the vegetables are soft, stir in lemon juice or sour salt, and sugar to make a sweet and sour taste.

Variation: SAUERKRAUT BORSCHT—To accentuate tangy taste, add a medium can of sauerkraut together with the cabbage.

SOUR CABBAGE SOUP

	meat bones	1½	pounds shredded cabbage
1	pound flanken	3	cans tomato sauce
1	large onion, diced		juice of 2 lemons
	paprika		salt
	water (approximately 3 quarts)		sugar (optional)

Put the bones and meat in a large pot. Cover with water. Add the onion and paprika. Cook over a high flame until boiling.

Meanwhile, wash cabbage well by pouring boiling water over it. Let cool and then shred as for coleslaw. When the soup stock comes to boil, add the shredded cabbage and cook for 1½ hours on a low flame.

Add remaining ingredients. Cook for another ½ hour. The addition of sugar will give it a sweet and sour taste.

SPICED CABBAGE SOUP

3	tablespoons oil	½	teaspoon caraway seeds
2	large onions, sliced	¾	teaspoon pepper
1	large garlic clove, crushed	1	small head cabbage
2-3	meat bones	3	bay leaves (optional)
1½	pounds meat, cut in 1″ cubes	2	teaspoons salt
8	cups water		

Use a 5-quart Dutch oven. Heat oil and sauté sliced onion and garlic in it about 5 minutes over medium fire, until tender. Add bones, meat, pepper, caraway seeds and water. Cook on low heat in covered pot for 1 hour.

Remove bones and add cut cabbage. Bring to a boil, then lower flame. Add bay leaves (optional), and cook covered on a very low flame another 30 minutes. Serves 8-10.

Chicken Soup

This is a classic Jewish favorite. It is popular during the week, on special occasions and especially on Shabbos and the holidays for the evening meal. It may be perfectly enhanced with thin cooked noodles, or *knaidlach* (matzoh balls). It is also excellent with practically any other soup accompaniment.

TASTY CHICKEN SOUP

½	large chicken	
2-3	large carrots, peeled	
1-2	stalks celery	
1	large onion	
1	bunch parsley (leaves only)	

3	stalks dill (optional)
2-3	cloves garlic
1	tablespoon salt
¼	teaspoon pepper
	water

Put all the ingredients into a 4-quart pot, and fill the pot with water. Bring to a boil and then simmer for 1-1½ hours. Serve just the broth, adding to it either noodles or matzoh balls.

Note: Gizzards and/or a meat bone in addition to the chicken makes a tastier soup.

CHICKEN SOUP SUPREME

½	yellow turnip, peeled
6	carrots
1	small onion
	dill
	parsnip
42	chicken gizzards
	water

4-5	stalks celery
1	small tomato, top removed
	parsley
	salt
	pepper
	paprika

Clean and wash vegetables well. Cut the turnip into small cubes. The other vegetables can be used whole or in big pieces. Place vegetables in a heavy pot and cover with chicken gizzards, dill and parsnip. Add salt, pepper and paprika. Cover with water and bring to a boil. Lower flame and let cook about 1½ hours. Check chicken gizzards with a fork to see if they are soft. Serve with vegetables for delicious flavor.

CHICKEN-TOMATO SOUP

1	small chicken
1	medium pepper
1	medium tomato

1	onion
1	tablespoon salt
	water

Cut chicken into quarters and place in a 4 to 6-quart pot. Core pepper and add it whole. Add tomato, peeled onion and salt. Cover with water. Cook for 1 hour.

DELICIOUS CHICKEN-VEGETABLE SOUP

½ chicken	1 large onion peeled
3-4 carrots, peeled and sliced	1 4 ounce can mushrooms
2 stalks celery diced	salt to taste (approximately 1
2 medium potatoes peeled and diced	tablespoon)
	water to cover.

Place all ingredients in a 6-quart pot and cover with water. Bring to boil, then simmer over a medium flame for another 1-1¼ hours. If soup becomes very thick, add more water.

Cholent

Cholent is a tasty stew or thick soup that includes meat and meat bones, potatoes, and often several types of beans in a variety of combinations. It is served on Shabbos day during the noon meal. It is a dish that is eaten by Jews everywhere in the world. Because of its unique manner of preparation, many people place special emphasis on the necessity of eating cholent on Shabbos Day—or at least having a small taste of it.

Its preparation is simple, yet the method by which it is kept warm for the Shabbos meal is unique. According to Jewish law, no cooking may be done on Shabbos. All cooking must be completed before sundown on Friday night. In order to keep the cholent warm, it is partially cooked on Friday—half or at least one-third cooked—and then a short while before Shabbos a metal or asbestos sheet called a *blech* is placed over a medium flame on the gas range. Then, any food (such as cholent) which we want to be warm for the Shabbos meal is kept on the *blech,* until it is ready to be used.

Important Note: Concerning cholent which begins to dry out on the *blech,* some *halachic* authorities permit hot water from another pot on the *blech* to be added to the cholent, while other authorities say that one must instead move the cholent pot to a place on the blech which is further away from the fire. For a final decision it is best to consult a *Rav.* See *Cooking for Shabbos,* page 30.

An interesting story is related in the Talmud about the special taste of cholent. A certain Roman Emperor used to visit frequently with Rabbi Yehuda Hanasi ("The Prince"), the leader of the Jews at that time. The Rabbi and Emperor would converse for long hours on Torah and other important matters.

Occasionally the Emperor would visit on Shabbos Day and would be particularly enamored of the cholent. He begged Rabbi Yehuda Hanasi for the recipe. But when the Rabbi gave it to him, he told him that it wouldn't taste the same since its preparation involved the use of a certain spice that was available only to Jews. The Emperor returned to his palace to give the recipe to his great chefs.

A few days later he returned and admitted that the Rabbi had been right. "What is that special spice you have?" he asked. Rabbi Yehuda Hanasi smiled and answered, "It is called Shabbos."

BASIC CHOLENT

6 small potatoes	½ cup navy beans
1 lb. meat, cubed	water
1 onion	salt
½ cup kidney beans	pepper
½ cup lima beans	garlic powder

Peel potatoes, leaving small ones whole and cutting larger ones in half. Rinse meat and beans and peel onion, and place in a large pot. Add plenty of water, about ¾ full. Add salt, pepper and garlic powder.

Bring to a boil, then reduce heat and let simmer, the longer the better. Keep pot uncovered and keep adding water if and when necessary. Once the beans have expanded they won't absorb the water so rapidly. Before Shabbos make sure you have enough water in the pot, about 1" above ingredients. Add kishka (see page 129) if desired. Cover the pot tightly and place on the *blech*.

Will serve at least 6 for Shabbos lunch.

KASHA-CHICKEN CHOLENT

oil	1 teaspoon salt
1 onion, diced	¼ teaspoon pepper
½ chicken	2½-3 cups water
1 cup kasha	

In 4-quart pot, sauté onion in a small amount of oil. Add chicken and steam in pot for approximately ¾ hour. Then add kasha, seasoning and water. Cook for approximately 20 minutes over a medium flame. A short while before placing cholent on the *blech,* add another ½ cup of hot water, so that kasha doesn't dry out overnight.

MOROCCAN CHOLENT

1½ cups dry chick peas	½ cup brown rice
4-5 potatoes	½ cup wheat berries
1-2 sweet potatoes	olive oil
1 pound flanken	3 dates

Seasoning to taste:

paprika	salt
cinnamon	garlic cloves
tumeric	

Soak chick peas overnight. Mix equal amounts of rice and wheat berries (or use all rice) in bowl with olive oil, salt and paprika. Tie mixture firmly in cheesecloth bag and place in pot with all other ingredients and boil. Cook overnight on *blech*. When serving, remove cheesecloth bag and serve rice separately. It will have absorbed all the delicious flavors of the cholent.

PAREVE CHOLENT

6	potatoes	8	ounces tomato sauce
1	onion	1	tablespoon salt
2-3	stalks of celery		water
4-5	carrots		

Layer bottom of pot with onion rings. Then add celery, carrot and potatoes. Add salt, tomato sauce and enough water to cover. Cook for approximately 1 hour before Shabbos and place on *blech.*

SWEET PAREVE CHOLENT

1-2	sweet potatoes (or in combination with winter squash)	1½	cups pinto or mixed beans
		½	cup brown rice or barley
		3	dates
1	large onion		or
1	turnip	¼	cup raisins
1-2	stalks celery	1	tablespoon corn oil
2	carrots		water
1	potato		

Seasoning to taste:

3	small garlic cloves		salt
	cinnamon		pepper
	good quality soy sauce		

Soak beans overnight. Cut vegetables into large chunks and sauté in corn oil. Add rice and beans and water to cover. Cook until beans are soft. Add dates and seasoning to taste. Cook overnight on *blech.* Cooking alternative: It can be pressure cooked for an hour before Shabbos, then seasoned and placed on *blech.*

WHITE CHOLENT

1	large onion		meat and/or meat bones
5-6	medium potatoes		water
½	cup barley		salt
1½	cups navy beans		

Slice onion thinly and place on bottom of a 3 quart pot. Add potatoes cut in halves or quarters. Add barley, beans, meat and bones. It is not necessary to stir. Add enough water to cover all ingredients. Add salt. Cook over low flame for 2 hours prior to Shabbos. Add water if necessary and bring again to boil. Then place on *blech.*

Variation: RED CHOLENT—For an unusual yet pleasing taste, add approximately 2 ounces ketchup, or replace ¾ cup navy beans with 1 medium can baked beans with sauce.

HUNGARIAN GOULASH

3 tablespoons oil
1½ cups chopped onion
1 small green pepper, finely diced
1 large clove of garlic crushed
6 cups water
2 pounds beef stew meat cut into ¾ inch cubes

2 tablespoons paprika
4 teaspoons salt
¼ teaspoon crushed red pepper
1½ pounds potatoes, peeled and cut into ¾ inch cubes
1 16 ounce can tomatoes sliced

Use 5 quart dutch oven. Heat oil, sauté on small flame onion, green pepper and garlic for 10 minutes or until tender. Add water, meat and seasoning. Bring to boil. Lower flame and simmer covered for 1½ hours. Add potatoes, return lid to pot, and cook 15 minutes (until potatoes are tender). Then stir in tomatoes with juice. Heat for another few minutes. Serves approximately 12.

HEARTY MEAT AND VEGETABLE SOUP

2 pounds meat
2 pounds meat bones
9 cups water
1½ tablespoons salt
2 teapoons parsley
dash of garlic powder
⅓ cup barley

1 package soup mix
1 can puréed tomatoes
1 onion, diced
1 cup string beans, chopped
1 cup carrots, sliced
2-3 stalks celery, chopped

Put in meat, bones, water and seasoning in a large pot. Cook for 1 hour.
Add barley and soup mix, and then cook for another hour. Remove the meat and meat bones from the pot, to be served separately. Add all the vegetables and cook another 45 minutes. Serves 8-10.

VEGETABLE-BEEF SOUP

½ cup split peas
½ cup lima beans
3 meat bones or 1 lb. soup meat
7 cups water
1 tablespoon salt

dash of pepper
½ tablespoon seasoning
1 whole onion
1 large celery stalk
1 large carrot, grated

Place split peas, lima beans, meat bones (or meat) into pot and cover with 7 cups water. Add salt, dash of pepper and seasoning. Cook 1½ hours.
Add whole onion, large stalk of celery, and large grated carrot. Cook an additional 30 minutes. Serves 6.

Soup Accompaniments

When preparing basic chicken or meat soup, alternate soup fillings; it will seem as if you are serving a different soup each time. For a heavier soup, add sliced vegetables or various beans.

HOME-MADE SOUP ADDITIONS (Recipes included in this section)
Egg Drop—Whipped egg added gradually to soup.
Knaidlach (matzoh balls)—Traditional for Friday night and holidays.
Kreplach—Traditional for Erev Yom Kippur, Hoshana Rabbah, and Purim.
Kishke—Dough, matzoh meal, or vegetable stuffing, cooked in cholent.
Mandlen—Baked dough mixture cut into tiny squares.
Potato drop—Whipped mashed potatoes and eggs, cooked like *knaidlach*.

PREPARED SUGGESTIONS
Cook according to instructions on the box, then add to soup.

Brown farfel	Macaroni	Rice, brown or white
Farfel	Noodle bow-ties	
Kasha	Noodles, thin or medium	

EGG DROP

1 egg per 1 quart of clear chicken soup

Begin with a recipe for Chicken Soup. Beat egg(s) well. When soup comes to a boil, add beaten egg, either ½ teaspoonful at a time or drop by drop from the tip of a fork. Stir while soup continues to boil. When ready it should look like clear chicken broth filled with very, very thin noodles. Serve hot.

FLUFFY POTATO DROP

4 large potatoes, boiled	**4-6 eggs**
¼ cup oil	**½ tablespoon salt**

Prepare your favorite chicken soup. In a separate pot, cook peeled potatoes. When potatoes are ready, remove from pot. Let cool slightly. Mash well. Add oil, whipped up eggs, and salt. Mash everything together very well, and set aside until chicken soup is ready.

When soup is done, remove chicken and all vegetables. Then reheat clear soup and keep it boiling.

Uncover pot, and drop in large tablespoonfuls of the potato mixture, one at a time.

The mashed potato mixture will fluff up very nicely when boiling. Occasionally push the potato balls down gently. Let it cook approximately 20 minutes over medium flame, or until potatoes turn a very light yellow.

Knaidlach

These fluffy soup balls, made from matzoh meal, eggs, water, oil and seasoning, are a traditional Jewish food. They are simple to make and very delicious—a great accompaniment to chicken soup and a welcome treat at the Friday night meal.

THE ART OF MAKING KNAIDLACH

1. Beat eggs slightly with fork.
2. Add other ingredients, except matzoh meal, and mix.
3. Add matzoh meal gradually until thick. Stir.
4. Refrigerate for 20 minutes in covered bowl.
5. Form into ball.
6. Drop into bubbling chicken soup or ½ quart boiling water to which 1 tablespoon salt has been added.
7. Cook according to instructions in recipe.
8. Should yield 4 balls per each ¼ cup of matzoh meal.

EASY KNAIDLACH

1 cup matzoh meal	2 eggs, beaten
2 tablespoons oil	½ teaspoon salt
2 tablespooons cold water	

Prepare according to instructions for making matzoh balls. Cook 30-40 minutes.

FANCY KNAIDLACH

4 eggs	1 teaspoon vinegar
½ cup water	1 teaspoon salt
½ cup melted shortening	dash of pepper
1 cup matzoh meal	

Prepare according to instructions for making matzoh balls. Cook 30 minutes.

PERFECT KNAIDLACH

2 eggs, slightly beaten	½ cup matzoh meal
2 tablespoons oil	1 tablespoon salt
2 tablespoons soup stock or water	¼ teaspoon pepper

Prepare according to instructions for making matzoh balls. Cook 30 minutes.

Kreplach

Kreplach is a dough mixture rolled out and then cut in small squares or circles. It is filled with ground meat or chicken and then shaped into triangles. It can then be cooked or fried, and is served in soup or as a side dish.

It is traditionally served on Erev Yom Kippur (see page 41), on Hoshana Rabbah (see page 45), and on Purim (see page 53).

THE ART OF SHAPING KREPLACH

Roll out dough very thin on a floured board. Dough can be cut into approximately—

A. 1. *3" circles,* by cutting into dough with rim of glass. Fill the middle of each circle with ground meat or chicken filling (see Diagram 1a).
   2. Lift up side 1-2 and side 1-3 and let them meet in the middle (over the filling). Pinch ends together (see Diagram 1b).
   3. Fold over the top side, 3-4-2, to the middle and pinch it together to the other open ends, thus forming a triangle (see Diagram 1c).

B. 1. *3" squares* (see Diagram 2). Fill the middle of each square with ground meat or chicken filling.
   2. Lift point 1 over to point 4, forming a triangle. Pinch together all sides.
   3. Now lift point 3 over to point 2 (forming into a smaller triangle, with meat filling well protected inside). Pinch together all sides.

COOKING: Kreplach can be boiled or fried. To boil, place in boiling, salted water. Cook approximately 20 minutes until they begin to float on top.

To fry, heat oil over medium flame and fry until golden brown on both sides.

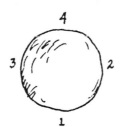

Diagram 1a

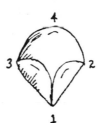

Diagram 1b

Diagram 1c

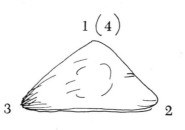

Diagram 2

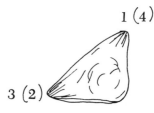

EASY KREPLACH

Dough:

1 cup flour	pinch of salt
1 egg	

Filling:

1 cup ground meat	1 tablespoon grated onion
or	salt and pepper to taste
cooked chicken	

Prepare dough. Knead well and roll out on floured board and cut into square or circles. Then into another bowl grind meat or chicken with onion. Add seasoning, mix well. Put 1 tablespoon of mixture on each dough square or circle. Shape into triangle, and cook or fry.

FANCY KREPLACH

Dough:

2 cups flour	3 tablespoons oil (optional)
2 egg yolks	1½ teaspoons baking powder
½ cup water	or
½ teaspoon salt	1½ teaspoons baking soda.

Filling:

1 cup ground cooked meat	small onion
or	1 teaspoon salt
chicken	¼ teaspoon pepper

Optional:

1 egg	2 tablespoons oil
1 tablespoon matzoh meal	

DOUGH: Combine flour and salt (and oil). In a separate bowl beat egg yolks, water and baking powder (or soda) and add to flour. Knead and roll out on floured surface. Cut into 3″ squares.

FILLING: A simple method is mixing all ingredients in a blender. Sauteeing the onion first before blending improves the taste. If you have an extra 15-20 minutes, try this way: Dice the onion and sauté it until golden brown. Then add chopped meat, and mix well with the onion. Let it heat over a small flame for about 5 minutes. Cool, then combine with remaining ingredients and mix well.

Fill middle of each square or circle with meat mixture, then shape into a triangle.

It is now ready for cooking or frying.

FLUFFY KREPLACH

Dough

1¾	cups flour	½	teaspoon salt
2	eggs	3	tablespoons oil

Filling

1	cup ground beef or cooked chicken	1	teaspoon salt
1	small onion grated	½	teaspoon black pepper

For directions, see Easy Kreplach above.

Kishke

Kishke is a dough or vegetable stuffing. Originally, it was stuffed into the cleaned intestine, or *kishke*, of an animal, after it had been salted. Once stuffed, it was sewn up at the open end, and either cooked together with the cholent or baked separately.

Today, the stuffing is usually placed inside a thin plastic casing, or simply wrapped in aluminum foil, then cooked or baked.

CRACKER KISHKE

1	box crackers	1	medium onion
2	stalks celery		salt
1	stick margarine, melted		pepper
2	raw carrots		

Put all ingredients in blender. Add salt and pepper. Shape into roll, wrap in aluminum foil and place in freezer overnight. Bake at 375° for forty minutes.

VEGETABLE KISHKE

½	cup oil	1½	cups flour
2	stalks celery	1¼	teaspoons salt
2	carrots	1	teaspoon paprika
1	onion		pepper to taste

Blend ½ cup oil and cut-up vegetables in blender until it becomes a thick paste. Empty into bowl, and add salt and seasoning. Mix well. If one long kishke is desired, roll it onto a large piece of greased aluminum foil or greased pan. Cover completely and bake on cookie sheet for 1-1½ hours at 350°. Slice and serve with cholent.

TO PLACE IN CHOLENT: Follow above directions but bake only ½ hour and then place kishke still wrapped in aluminum foil on top of food in cholent pot just before Shabbos and leave it inside until cholent is served.

CHALLAH CHOLENT KUGEL

challah	salt
2-3 eggs	pepper
1 onion, chopped finely	

Soak and drain challah. Mix in other ingredients. Roll in aluminum foil and place in cholent or chicken soup.

Variation: Make a small amount of knaidlach mixture (p. 126). Shape into one large long ball. Add to cholent after it has come to a full boil so that knaidlach won't sink to bottom. Leave in pot until cholent is served.

FLOUR CHOLENT KUGEL

1 medium diced onion	pepper
1 cup oil,	paprika
1 egg	enough flour to form a dough
salt	

Mix all ingredients just until blended. Refrigerate for a few hours. Shape into a loaf and place in cholent that is already boiling.

SOUP MANDLEN

3 eggs	1 tablespoon oil
2 cups flour	1 teaspoon salt

Mix ingredients. Add enough flour to make a soft but firm dough. Roll into long rope and cut in ½" pieces and place on well-greased baking pan. Bake at 375° until golden brown. Shake pan occasionally to brown all sides.

Helpful Hints

Soup Bones: If recipe calls for meat or bones and you don't have any, add 2-3 tablespoons oil to cooked soup.

Cooking: Long, slow cooking is best for soups. To lessen film on soup stock, keep heat low while cooking. Simmer, don't boil.

Fat: If soup is refrigerated after cooking, the fat will rise to the top and congeal. Skim off before re-heating.

Freezing: When freezing soup, remember to leave room on top for expansion.

Salt: Use 2 teaspoons salt for 1 quart of soup. If soup is too salty, add a potato or two. It will absorb the excess salt.

Fish

Fish

Fish

Kashrus and Fish

Fish is an excellent food, high in protein and easy to digest. Since it is pareve, it can be included as a course in either meat or dairy meals. Fish is a traditional Jewish food prepared in many ways. It enhances the mitzvah of enjoying the Shabbos and Holidays to eat fish during their meals. The ever popular gefilte fish has a significant history of its own (see page 138).

Kashrus and Fish

Fish does not have to be slaughtered or "salted" as do meat and fowl. But many fish are not kosher. Only fish which have both *fins* and *scales* are kosher. However, these terms as well as the names of some fish must be defined *halachically* and not according to popular designations. Since some confusion exists, one should be sure to buy fish only from a merchant familiar with the proper types.

When buying fish, it should either be whole—so that one can see the fins and scales—or, if sliced, filleted, or ground, purchased only from a fish store which sells kosher fish exclusively. One is thereby assured that knives or other utensils are not used on non-kosher fish, and that no other mix-up can occur.

If fish is bought packaged or canned, be sure it has a reliable Seal of Kashrus. Smoked fish, too, can only be bought from a reliable dealer to be sure that it was smoked only with other kosher fish, etc.

Some popular kosher fish are:

Cod	Halibut	Pickerel	Trout
Flounder	Herring	Pike	(Most) Tuna
Haddock	Mackerel	Salmon	Whitefish

Some common non-kosher fish and seafood are:

Clam	Lobster	Shark	Swordfish
Crab	Oyster	Shrimp	

Combinations to be avoided are:
a) meat and fish. If the two foods are served at one meal, they should be served on different plates and the fish should be served first. Some juice or other beverage should be taken before the meat is served.
b) fish and milk. These should not be eaten together. However they may be included at the same meal on different plates. (Some people avoid eating fish combined with cheese products as well.)

These combinations may also not be cooked together.

Baked, Broiled and Steamed Fish

BAKED CARP

1 medium carp (5-6 pounds), sliced	1 tablespoon salt paprika
1 small onion	2 teaspoons pickling
4 garlic cloves	spices (optional)

Wash carp slices very well the day before cooking. Do not use slices from large carp as it might be too fatty. After washing carp let it dry, then place on baking pan.

Mince onion and garlic. Rub mixture of salt, onion, and garlic (and spices) into the fish on all sides. (Onion and garlic powder may be sprinkled on instead.) Let stand overnight in refrigerator. (Amounts of seasoning may be increased depending on number of carp slices.)

In the morning, sprinkle paprika on all sides. Bake in 350° oven for approximately 2 hours.

CURRIED COD

2½ pounds fish fillets (cod, haddock, mackerel, etc.)	1 beaten egg
1 teapoon salt	1 tablespoon flour oil for frying
¼ teaspoon pepper	

Sauce

½ cup vinegar	
1 cup water	6 allspice seeds
1 large onion, sliced	1 tablespoon mild curry powder
2 bay leaves	2 tablespoons sugar

134

Cut fish into single portion pieces (about 4″ squares) and sprinkle with half the salt and pepper. Toss in a bowl with egg and flour. Fry in hot oil until golden.

SAUCE: Boil vinegar, ½ cup water, onion, bay leaves, allspice and remaining salt and pepper until onion is soft. Mix curry powder and sugar with remaining water and add to sauce. Boil 10 minutes.

Put fish in a dish and pour the hot sauce over it. Cool and refrigerate. Try to prepare at least one or two days ahead, as the flavor improves with time. Fish will keep at least one week.

WHITE HADDOCK CASSEROLE

3 pounds haddock	1 can mushroom soup
¼ pound margarine	1½ cups non-dairy creamer
4-5 tablespoons flour	5 eggs, separated

Steam haddock and flake. For white sauce, combine margarine, flour, soup and non-dairy creamer. Cook and stir constantly until thickened. Beat egg yolks a little, and add fish to yolks. Add white sauce and mix well. Beat egg whites until stiff and fold into fish mixture. Bake for 1 hour in greased, uncovered pan at 350°.

NEW ENGLAND FISH LOAF

3 pounds fillet of haddock or cod	¼ cup oil
3 large onions	1 tablespoon salt
2 carrots	2 tablespoons sugar
bread crumbs from 1 roll	½ teaspoon black pepper
4 eggs	½ teaspoon paprika (optional)
⅓ cup water	

Grind the fish together with the vegetables and bread crumbs. Add eggs, oil and water and mix well. Add salt, sugar, paprika, and pepper, and mix again. Adjust seasonings to taste. Pour into oiled pan and sprinkle with paprika. Bake at 350° for 1 hour.

Serves 8-10 people.

White Fish

BAKED WHITE FISH IN TOMATO SAUCE

4 pounds white fish, sliced and washed	1 large onion
1 cup flour	oil
salt	dill
pepper	parsley
1 cup green pepper, chopped	3 cups ketchup
1 cup carrots	¼ cup lemon juice
	2 cups water

Roll pieces of fish in flour seasoned with salt and pepper and place in baking dish. Chop all the vegetables. Sauté onion and spoon it along with the oil in which it was fried on top of the fish. Arrange pepper, carrots, dill and parsley around fish.

Cover with ketchup and then add water and lemon juice. Place in 400° oven. When water starts to boil, lower oven to 350° and bake for 45 minutes or until done.

BOILED FISH SAUTÉ

5	pounds white fish, sliced	2	cups ketchup
	salt		water
	pepper		dill
3	large onions, diced	1	parsnip
¼	cup oil	1	lemon, sliced

Sprinkle fish with salt and pepper. Fry onions in oil until golden brown. Arrange fish slices in pan, pouring on ketchup, and enough water to cover. For additional flavor add fresh dill, parsnip, and a few lemon slices. Simmer covered or uncovered for about 45 minutes until done.

BOILED FISH WITH TOMATO SAUCE

3	pounds fish (whole or sliced)		parsley roots, diced
	salt	4	cups water
	pepper	1	ounce margarine
2	large onions, sliced	1	cup tomatoes, strained
2	carrots, diced	2	egg yolks, well-beaten
	celery, diced		parsley

Sprinkle fish well inside and out with salt and pepper. Let stand in refrigerator several hours or overnight. Put onions, carrot, celery and parsley roots in a pot with water. Bring to a boil and let boil gently for a few minutes. Add fish, margarine, tomatoes and more hot water if necessary to cover fish. Let simmer until done.

Sauce: Remove fish and strain liquid. Complete sauce by adding egg yolks to fish liquid. Bring mixture to boiling point but *do not boil.* Stir constantly until smooth. Pour sauce over fish. Garnish with parsley.

DELUXE FISH STEAKS

A delicious dish to serve on special occasions.

4	pounds white fish, sliced	3	large onions
	salt	1	clove garlic
2	carrots		oil
2	celery stalks	1	can tomato sauce
3	green peppers		

Salt fish and then put it into a baking dish and set aside. Mince carrots, celery, peppers, onions, and garlic. Sauté in covered pan for 10 minutes. Add tomato sauce, mix well and sauté for another 3 minutes. Remove vegetables from frying pan and spread evenly on baking dish, under and above fish. Bake for 30 minutes at 375°.

Serves 6-8.

MOROCCAN FISH

1 white fish (2-3 pounds), cleaned and sliced	water
	¾ teaspoon salt
1 large green or red pepper	2 teaspoons saffron
1-2 tomatoes	3 tablespoons spiced oil°
2-3 garlic cloves	

Slice pepper and tomatoes. Peel garlic cloves and cut in half. Line wide pot with pepper, tomatoes, and garlic, and place fish slices on top. Then add water, just enough to cover fish. Bring to a boil, then add salt, saffron and spiced oil.° Lower flame and simmer 40-50 minutes. May be served hot or cold.

°*Spiced oil:* Prepare oil at least 1 week ahead. Place 1 tablespoon hot pepper into a dish or small jar. Cover with 1 cup olive oil. Let it stand in a cool place or in refrigerator. After a few days, red pepper will settle on the bottom, and the oil will absorb the color and taste of pepper. Can be made in larger quantities and stored for several months.

PICKLED FISH

3 pounds white fish, 2″ slices	½ cup white vinegar
1 teaspoon salt	¼ cup sugar
3 cups water	1 tablespoon pickling spices
2 medium onions, sliced	

Place fish in 4-quart saucepan. Add salt, water and one onion. Bring to a boil, then simmer 15 minutes. Discard fish head and carefully remove fish and place in bowl.

Measure 2½ cups of the broth, and add the vinegar, sugar, and pickling spices to it. Bring to boil, then cook 5 minutes. Pour over fish. Chill for 24 hours before serving. Will keep for one week.

Alternate Method: Use a pot with an insert upon which fish can lay.

Note: Fresh salmon is another good fish to prepare in this way.

SWEET AND SOUR FISH

5 pounds white fish or yellow pike or salmon, sliced	1 stalk celery (optional)
	4-5 tablespoons sugar
salt	½ tablespoon salt
pickling spices (bay leaves removed)	12 small black peppercorns
	¼ cup vinegar
2 large onions, sliced	5-6 bay leaves
2-3 carrots, whole or sliced	

Clean, wash, scrape and drain fish. If using salmon, handle it very gently so it won't fall apart. Sprinkle every slice top and bottom with small amount of salt and pickling spices. (Remove bay leaves from spices and set aside.)

Leave in refrigerator overnight and in the morning wash off salt and spices.

Take a large pot and put sliced onions, carrots, celery, salt and sugar on the bottom. Add enough water to cover fish. Place peppercorns in water. Add fish but don't pack too tightly. Cook on medium flame for about 1 hour. Add vinegar and cook another 15 minutes. Place 5 or 6 bay leaves in pot, removing them after fish has cooled.

Gefilte Fish

The Shabbos and Holiday meals always bring to mind *gefilte* fish as the first course—and a tasty dish it is, too! There are several types of jarred or canned gefilte fish available, but they can't compare to the fresh, homemade variety. And it's so very easy to make.

Gefilte fish—literally "stuffed" fish—is a delectable mixture of various ground fishes mixed with egg, matzoh meal, onion, carrots and spices, with the bones removed before grinding. It evolved as a special Shabbos dish because it avoids the need to separate bones from whole fish, which could involve one of the thirty-nine *melochos* (forbidden activities) of Shabbos, unless done properly.

Gefilte fish is often served topped with horseradish, or with a carrot slice from the sauce. It may be served on lettuce leaves, with tomato and cucumber slices or a fresh vegetable salad.

THE ART OF MAKING GEFILTE FISH

PREPARING THE FISH

Fillet the fish. Grind fish and onions. (Note: The fish can be bought ground and the man in the fish store will even grind an onion in with it if you ask him to—only do so if you intend to cook the fish within a day; otherwise the fish will not keep so well with the onion inside.) If recipe calls for specific amount of onion, tell the fishman exactly how many onions to add. Add remaining ingredients according to recipe and mix thoroughly. Feel with hands if fish is thick enough to be shaped into balls. If too stiff, add a little water gradually. When the fish batter is ready, set aside. Prepare the sauce, (see *Basic Fish Sauce*) and don't shape the fish until the sauce is boiling.

SHAPING AND COOKING

Wet hands with cold water. Shape gefilte fish into balls or patties. Keep hands wet constantly as long as you are shaping the fish. Lower the balls gently into the boiling water, one at a time; this way they will remain on top and not sink. Cover and cook over a medium flame for 2-2½ hours (unless specified differently in the recipe). You may taste the sauce after 1½ hours and add some more seasoning, if necessary.

For the special preparation of long fish rolls, or gefilte fish loaves, when it is necessary to prepare large quantities, see Gefilte Fish Hints page 142.

Note: Fish heads can be filled with gefilte fish batter inside and cooked and served like the rest of the fish. This is often done on Rosh Hashana, when it is a tradition to eat a fish head.

Note: The amount of fish stated in the recipes refers to the weight of the fish before it is ground.

1 pound of fish makes approximately 3-4 nice size portions.

BASIC FISH SAUCE

fish bones and heads, washed
2 onions, sliced
3 carrots, whole or sliced
1 potato, peeled and sliced
(optional)

1-3 teaspoons salt
½ teaspoon pepper
1-3 teaspoons sugar (optional)
2 dashes of paprika (optional)
water

Place all ingredients in a large pot and fill approximately one-third to one-half full of water. There should be enough water to cover the fish to be added later. Bring the fish sauce to a boil.

BAKED GEFILTE FISH BALLS

7 pounds fish, ground
4 eggs
3 tablespoons salt
1 package sugar substitute
or
2 teaspoons sugar

1 cup oatmeal
garlic powder
16 ounces tomato sauce
½ cup dry sherry wine

Mix first six ingredients together well. Oil pan. Shape fish into balls and place on pan. Pour tomato sauce liberally over fish, then pour sherry wine on top.

Bake in 11″ x 14″ pan at 400° for 1 hour. Yields approximately 25 balls.
Note: Use only a pareve sugar substitute.

CARP GEFILTE FISH

6 pounds carp, ground
oil
4-5 onions
5 eggs
salt

sugar
pepper
¾-1 cup bread crumbs
½ cup of water
Basic Fish Sauce

Grind carp and put into large bowl. Dice onion and sauté in oil over small flame until soft and golden brown, approximately 20 minutes. Meanwhile, prepare *Basic Fish Sauce*.

Blend together sautéed onion, eggs, and seasoning, to taste. (Mixture is best when whipped in blender because the onion will be ground and the whipped eggs will fluff up the fish balls beautifully when cooked.) Combine fish with egg mixture. Add bread crumbs and water alternately, a little at a time, mixing well after each addition.

Proceed according to *Shaping Gefilte Fish*.

FAVORITE GEFILTE FISH

This may become one of your favorite recipes too.

5	pounds white fish, filleted	3-5	teaspoons sugar
8-10	medium hard onions	5	teaspoons salt
2	pieces hard good celery	1	level teaspoon pepper
½	cup matzoh meal or 2 slices hard challah	3-5	eggs, beaten
			Basic Fish Sauce

Grind fish fillets, onions and celery together, using only the inside, firm part of the celery stalks. Add seasoning and matzoh meal (if you are using hard challah, remove the brown crust and then soak the challah in water and squeeze it out before adding it to the mixture). Mix together. Add the eggs and mix the batter well. Proceed according to *Making Gefilte Fish.*

Variation: Substitute 2 carrots for the celery.

HEIMISH GEFILTE FISH

3	pounds fish (1 pound pike, 1½ pounds white fish, and ½ pound carp)	¼	cup matzoh meal
		1-2	teaspoons salt
		½	teaspoon pepper
2-3	medium onions	¼	cup cold water
2-3	eggs, separated		Basic Fish Sauce

Place ground fish and onion mixture into wooden bowl and chop until smooth. Add egg yolks, matzoh meal, cold water, salt and pepper. Beat the egg whites and add to fish mixture. Proceed according to *Making Gefilte Fish.* Cook uncovered for 1½ hours at slow boil. Liquid will be reduced to one-half. Salt and pepper. Cool fish before removing from pot.

Variation: For a sweeter taste, add 1 tablespoon sugar to fish mixture.

LONG GEFILTE FISH

4	pounds white and pike fish	1	teaspoon salt
1	onion	1	teaspoon black pepper
¾	cup matzoh meal		Basic Fish Sauce
1	tablespoon oil	1	potato, peeled and sliced.

This recipe calls for shaping fish into loaves. Line bottom of pot with vegetables used for *Basic Fish Sauce,* and potato. Add seasoning.

Mix fish batter well, and shape into loaves. Gently place fish loaves over vegetables in pot. Carefully add just enough water to cover fish. Bring to boil, then cook on medium flame for 1 hour.

This batter is also good for standard gefilte fish balls. Bring sauce to boil first, then add fish balls. (See *Making Gefilte Fish.*)

NO MATZOH MEAL GEFILTE FISH

The following two recipes have no matzoh meal. They can be served all year round, but are especially ideal for Passover for those who do not use matzoh meal mixed with liquids. (See Laws of Pesach, page 355.)

CARP GEFILTE FISH WITHOUT MATZOH MEAL

An original gefilte fish mixture.

4 pounds carp, ground	1 medium raw beet, peeled and grated
1 onion, ground	2 tablespoons horseradish
2 eggs	1 teaspoon salt
1 cooked egg, mashed	Basic Fish Sauce

Combine all ingredients and mix very well. Set aside. Prepare standard gefilte fish sauce. Bring to boil and add fish balls one at a time. Prepare according to *Making Gefilte Fish.*

YELLOW AND WHITE GEFILTE FISH WITHOUT MATZOH MEAL

3-4 pounds whole yellow pike and white fish, filleted	2 carrots
	salt
½ pound carp	pepper (optional)
2 eggs	sugar (optional)
1 large onion	Basic Fish Sauce

Salt fish fillets, and refrigerate overnight. In the morning, grind fish. (If you buy fish already ground, add some salt to the mixture.)

Grind the carrots together with the onion and eggs in blender. The carrots will give the gefilte fish a special sweet taste. Combine all ingredients and proceed according to *Making Gefilte Fish.* Cook approximately 2 hours.

Helpful Hints

Using Bread instead of Matzoh Meal

For a fluffier gefilte fish use a few slices of bread instead of matzoh meal. However, remove brown crust of bread so it won't darken color of fish. Then soak bread in small amount of water for a couple of minutes. Squeeze out water well and add soaked bread to mixture.

How to make Gefilte Fish Rolls — Slices

1. COOKED—Take large piece of thin wax paper or aluminum foil. Wet the surface completely. Fill the middle of sheet with gefilte fish mixture down the length of the sheet. Bring over 2 sides to the top and roll together over the middle. Twist together ends of roll. Place in boiling fish sauce and let cook as regular gefilte fish. When it is ready, lift out of pot and slice when cool.
2. BAKED—Prepare gefilte fish mixture. Tear large sheets of aluminum foil, approximately 10-15 inches long. Pile mixture in center of each sheet, roll into loaf, and close off ends. (If you are baking immediately, leave a small opening on top. If you are freezing, close off roll completely, defrost it approximately 4 hours before baking, then open up tops of rolls slightly.) Line 2-3 rolls in a large baking pan and bake at 350°. Open foil completely after 1 hour, then bake for an hour more, or until tops are medium browned. Slice before serving.

Gefilte Fish Loaves

An easy way to make gefilte fish, especially when preparing in advance or for large quantities, is to bake fish batter in loaf pans.

Prepare fish batter as directed in recipe—batter should not feel too stiff. Preheat oven to 350°. Line loaf pans with aluminum foil for easy removal. Add approximately 2 tablespoons oil to each pan, then place in heated oven for about 10 minutes. Remove pans and fill approximately ⅔ full with fish batter. Bake for 1½ hours.

Preparing Gefilte Fish in Advance (Jarring)

This method will enable you to keep large quantities of fish fresh for up to three weeks in the refrigerator.

When fish has finished cooking, remove the lid but keep the pot on a low flame. (This keeps the water boiling so that fish stays on top, making for easier removal.) Take some clean, empty glass jars and fill loosely with gefilte fish balls. Add boiling fish sauce. Close jars very tightly and place them upside down—this vacuum packs the jars. When they cool, place jars of fish in the refrigerator. Not only will they keep well for a few weeks, but the fish tastes delicious when stored in this manner.

Improving the Taste of Jarred and Canned Gefilte Fish

Here are two methods of giving jarred and canned fish a more homemade taste.

1. COOKING: Prepare basic sauce with sliced carrots, onions, water and a very small amount of seasoning. Bring to a boil. Remove fish pieces from original sauce, add to boiling water and cook over low flame for approximately 30-45 minutes. Delicious when served warm.
2. STEAMING: Sauté diced onion in heated oil over medium flame for five minutes. Remove fish pieces from can or jar and place on top of sautéed onion. Oil will sizzle a bit—keep a few steps away from the stove. Top fish with tomato sauce, sprinkle with parsley flakes. Cook over very low flame for about twenty minutes. A slight amount of water may be added, if necessary.

Variation: Add a can of mixed vegetables to fish and steam together.

Flounder and Sole Fillets

BREADED FLOUNDER

4 medium slices fillet of flounder
1 cup matzoh meal
1 teaspoon salt

1 teaspoon onion flakes
1 egg
oil for frying

Season matzoh meal with salt and onion flakes. Beat egg. Dip flounder slices into egg and then into seasoned matzoh meal. Fry both sides in oil on medium high flame until brown. Drain on paper towels and serve hot.

Variation: Instead of thawing flounder completely, leave partially frozen and cut 5-6 slices across the width. Dip in mixture of egg and seasoned matzoh meal.

Note: Paprika in the egg mixture will give fish a nice, crusty color as well as adding flavor.

RUSSIAN DRESSED FLOUNDER

1 pound (frozen) flounder or sole
fillets

½ cup mayonnaise
½ cup ketchup

Defrost fish. Mix mayonnaise with ketchup. Roll fish and fasten with a toothpick. Place in pot. Pour ketchup and mayonnaise mixture over fish. Cook for approximately 30 minutes over low flame.

Variation: Dip fillet slices in mixture of mayonnaise and ketchup. Bake on flat cookie sheet at 350° for 20-30 minutes.

FLOUNDER SALAD

1 pound (frozen) flounder
1 onion
½ pound carrots
3 potatoes
salt

pepper
water
mayonnaise
lettuce leaves
tomatoes

Place flounder, vegetables, and seasoning in pot with enough water to cover. Cook for 1 hour. Drain most of liquid and mash all the vegetables and fish together.

Mix in mayonnaise and add seasoning as desired. Serve on bed of lettuce, and surround with tomatoes.

FLOUNDER AND SALMON FILLING

1 pound (frozen) fillet of flounder	2 teaspoons ketchup
7 ounce can salmon	1 onion, sliced
1 egg	margarine
¼ cup matzoh meal	1 4-ounce can tomato sauce

Defrost flounder. Mix salmon, egg, matzoh meal and ketchup. Fill each fillet with salmon mixture—roll up and secure with toothpicks. Line bottom of baking dish with onion slices and place fillet rolls on top. Dot rolls with margarine. Pour tomato sauce on top. Bake at 350° for 30 minutes.

STEAMED RED FLOUNDER AND VEGETABLES

oil for frying	pepper
1 onion	1 4-ounce can tomato sauce/soup
1 celery	1 package or can, peas and
1 pound flounder fillets	carrots
salt	

Dice or slice onion and celery into fine strips. Heat oil in deep frying pan. Sauté onion and celery over medium flame for 10 minutes until golden brown. In the meantime sprinkle flounder fillets with salt and pepper. Then place flounder on sautéed vegetables. Pour on tomato sauce or soup. Simmer for ½ hour. Add peas and carrots. Cook another 10 minutes.

Serving Suggestion: Serve together with steamed rice mixed with margarine.

GREEN STUFFED FLOUNDER RINGS

6 (frozen) flounder fillets	1 teaspoon salt
paprika	2 tablespoons lemon juice
½ cup olive oil	1 teaspoon garlic powder

Filling:

1 sour pickle	3 sticks celery
½ green pepper	6 green onions (scallions)

Defrost fish. Slice pickle, green pepper and celery into six long strips each. Put one of each and one scallion in center of each fillet. Roll up fillet and fasten with toothpick. In bowl, combine oil, lemon juice, salt and garlic powder. Dip fillets into dressing and place in a row in pan. Pour remaining dressing over fish. Sprinkle with paprika. Bake 20-30 minutes at 350-375°.

MONDAY NIGHT'S STUFFED FILLETS

2 pounds fish fillets	salt
½ pound 3 day old challah	pepper
3 onions	1 large can tomato sauce
2 tablespoons oil	½ teaspoon sugar (optional)
1 egg	

Stuffing: Slice challah and dampen with water to soften. Partially squeeze out the water. Slice the onions and sauté them in oil until transparent. Add the challah and continue to sauté. Add egg, salt and pepper.

Divide stuffing according to number of fillets and place one portion on each fillet. Roll up fillets and place end down in a greased casserole. Heat up the sauce (sugar adds flavor and cuts bitterness) and spoon over fish. Bake at 350° for ½ hour.

TANGY FLOUNDER

2 pounds sole or flounder fillets	1 cup beer
2½ cups flour	4 egg whites, beaten stiff
½ teaspoon salt	oil for frying

Combine flour and salt. Add the beer and mix until smooth. Beat egg whites until stiff and fold in. Let batter stand 6 hours. Dip fish fillets into batter. Deep-fry in oil heated to 375° for 12 minutes. Drain. Serve with salad. Serves 6.

FISH-MISH PATTIES

1 package fish-mish°	1 teaspoon salt
2 eggs	¼ teaspoon garlic powder
3-4 carrots, sliced	¼ teaspoon black pepper
2 onions, diced	oil for frying
¾ cup matzoh meal	

Defrost fish-mish. (Takes approximately four hours.) Place eggs, carrots, onions and seasoning into blender. Blend until very smooth. Combine with fish-mish, add matzoh meal, and mix well.

Heat oil in frying pan. Shape fish into patties and place in frying pan, over medium flame. Fry until crispy brown on both sides—approximately 10 minutes per side.

Variations: FISH LOAF—Pour whole mixture into greased, heated loaf pans and bake 1½ hours at 350°.
TASTY FISH LOAF—When doubling recipe, add a can of salmon and mix very well. Then bake in loaf pans.

°Fish-mish is a package of frozen ground fish weighing around 1 pound.

POTATO FISH CAKES

1 pound fish, ground	salt
1 pound potatoes, cooked and mashed	pepper
	1 egg
¼ cup chopped parsley	bread crumbs
anchovy sauce	oil

Mix fish and potatoes. Add parsley, anchovy sauce, salt and pepper. With lightly floured hands shape fish into small flat cakes. Brush with beaten egg and dip in bread crumbs. Fry until golden brown on both sides.

VEGETABLE FISH CAKES

1 pound frozen fillet of flounder
1 large or 2 medium potatoes
3 stalks celery
2 medium or 1 large carrot
1 medium onion
2 eggs, beaten

½ cup matzoh meal
salt
pepper
paprika
baking powder

Defrost fish. Cook vegetables in moderate amount of water until tender. Add fish for the last 10 minutes. Drain off excess liquid. Mash, grind, or blend entire mixture together. Add remaining ingredients and mix well.

Shape into patties and bake at 350° with a little oil dabbed on top to prevent dryness; or fry in oil over a medium flame until golden brown and crisp on both sides—approximately 10 minutes per side.

More Fish Treats

CHOPPED HERRING

Chopped herring is a very tasty and popular dish often served at *Melava Malkas* (page 303). It also makes an excellent spread on bread or challah.

2 salt herrings
cold water
1 thick slice bread
2 tablespoons vinegar
1 tablespoon onion, chopped

1 large sour apple, chopped
2 teaspoons salad oil
⅛ teaspoon pepper
lettuce leaves
1 egg, hard-boiled

Soak herrings in cold water for 24 hours. Wash well, remove bones and chop finely.

Soak bread in vinegar, break up and mix with herring. Add onion, apple, oil, and pepper. Serve on lettuce leaves, and garnish with hard-boiled egg. Note: try putting the egg through a sieve. The result is a perfect garnish.

TOMATO HERRING-MOCK LIVER

Mock chopped liver can be made using a variety of vegetables (see page 191). This one is made with fish, yet the resemblance to actual liver is uncanny.

1 can tomato herring
2 tablespoons mayonnaise

4 hard boiled eggs

Drain liquid and remove all skin and bone from herring. Chop eggs and herring with mayonnaise until consistency resembles chopped liver.
Note: For *real* chopped liver, see Poultry and Meat Sections (pages 154 and 169).

LOX AND EGGS

½ pound lox
2 large onions, chopped

1 tablespoon margarine
6 eggs, beaten

Soak lox in cold water about 15 minutes. Saute onion in margarine until golden brown. Add lox and fry a few minutes longer. Add eggs and either scramble or serve in pancake form.

Tuna and Salmon

TUNA BURGERS

3 7-ounce cans tuna	½ cup matzoh meal or bread crumbs
1 small onion, diced and sautéed	pinch of salt
2 stalks celery, diced (optional)	oil for frying
2 eggs, beaten	

Drain tuna, then put in bowl. Add onion and celery, then eggs, matzoh meal and salt. Shape into patties and fry in heated oil until golden brown on both sides.

FLUFFY TUNA PATTIES

1 medium onion, sautéed	dash of salt
1 7-ounce can tuna	dash of pepper (optional)
1 potato, boiled and mashed	oil
1 egg, beaten	

Sauté onions in frying pan. Mix tuna, potato, egg and seasoning. Shape into 3 patties. Fry on both sides until golden brown, or broil in toaster oven or in greased pan at 375° for 20 minutes.

PATUNAS

4 potatoes	1 cup mayonnaise
¼ cup green pepper, chopped	¼ cup scallions, chopped
1 can tuna	

Bake the potatoes and cut them lengthwise. Scoop out insides, mash together with remaining ingredients. Spoon mixture back into the potato shells. Heat 10 minutes in oven at 400°.

BASIC TUNA SALAD

1 can tuna	dash of salt
1 scallion, diced fine	2-3 tablespoons mayonnaise
1 stalk celery, diced fine	1 teaspoon lemon juice

Drain can of tuna. Place in bowl and flake well with fork. Add remaining ingredients, and mix together very well.

Serving Suggestions: Ideal to serve in sandwiches as is, or between lettuce leaves in sandwich, with 2-3 tomato slices in the middle.

Also very tasty when served in hollowed out green pepper cups.

Variation: VEGETABLE TUNA SALAD— Combine basic tuna salad with 1 tomato, ½ cucumber, and ½ green pepper, finely diced.

TUNA AND VEGETABLE TOSSED SALAD

½	small head of lettuce	2	cans of tuna
2	tomatoes	4-6	tablespoons mayonnaise
1	cucumber	1	teaspoon salt
1-2	sour pickles		dash of pepper
2	scallions		dash of garlic powder
5	radishes	2	tablespoons lemon juice

Use large mixing bowl. Cut in all vegetables, as for regular salad. Add 2 cans of tuna, flaked well. Mix together. Add mayonnaise and seasoning just before serving to prevent salad from becoming soggy.

SALMON CROQUETTES

1	large can salmon, drained	2	tablespoons matzoh meal
1	onion, grated		oil for frying
3	eggs, beaten		

Mix salmon with onion and eggs and form into patties. Dip into matzoh meal and fry in oil until golden brown. Serves 6.

SALMON LOAF

1	pound canned salmon	⅓	cup matzoh meal or bread crumbs
	salt	½	stick melted margarine
	pepper	4	ounces non-dairy creamer
3	eggs, beaten		

Drain liquid from salmon and remove bones. Flake fish and mash. Add salt, pepper, eggs, bread crumbs and non-dairy creamer. Mix well. Melt margarine in small loaf pan, and add a little fish mixture. Then pour salmon into loaf pan and bake at 350° for 45 minutes.

Poultry and Stuffings

SECTION 8

Poultry and Stuffings

CHICKEN
   American Apricot Chicken
   Breaded Baked Chicken
   Broiled Chicken
   Chicken Dinner Casserole
   Fried Chicken and Vegetables
   G'dempte Chicken
   Gribenes (Schmaltz)
   Honolulu Chicken
   India Chicken Curry
   Ketchup Chicken
Chicken Liver
   Chopped Chicken Liver
   Chicken Liver Pasta
   Juicy Pineapple Chicken
   Stuffed Chicken
   Sweet and Sour Chicken Wings
   Tomato-Potato Chicken
   Topsy Turvy Chicken
Leftover Chicken
   Chicken and Mayonnaise Salad
   Oriental Celery and Chicken
   Chicken and Rice
   Chicken and Vegetable Sauce
   Mock Fish

DUCK and TURKEY
   Baked Duck
   Steamed Turkey
   Turkey and stuffing
STUFFINGS AND SAUCE
   Six Basic Stuffings
   Meat and Poultry, Tomato Sauce

Poultry and Stuffings

Chicken

Chicken has always been a popular dish, frequently served at suppers and at Shabbos and Holiday meals. Chicken contains less fat than red meat and its flesh is lighter and easier to digest. This is probably why chicken is served Friday nights, while meat is usually reserved for the Shabbos daytime meal.

The following pages contain an exciting variety of ways to prepare and serve chicken: bake it, broil it, fry it, steam it and, of course, season it. (For chicken soup recipe, see Soups, Section VI.)

Those fowl which are kosher are listed in the Torah. Knowledge of the types of fowl actually used has been traditionally passed on from generation to generation. Laws concerning the slaughtering and salting process of chicken as well as all other Kosher fowl are nearly identical to those which apply to meat (see pages 163–164 and 335–340) and must be strictly observed.

All kinds of fowl are considered a meat food and may in no way be prepared or eaten together with dairy products. The waiting period between chicken and dairy is 6 hours, as for meat, see page 9.

Margarine which is to be used in meat or chicken dishes, must be pareve, in addition to having a reliable hechsher.

AMERICAN APRICOT CHICKEN

1 chicken	1 tablespoon ketchup
1 tablespoon apricot jam	1 tablespoon mayonnaise
1 tablespoon lemon juice	1 package onion soup

Place chicken skin side up in baking pan. Bring other ingredients to a slow boil, stirring constantly. Remove from heat and pour over chicken.
Bake at 350° for 1¼ hour, uncovered.

BREADED BAKED CHICKEN

1 medium chicken, cut into quarters	1 teaspoon onion powder
1 stick margarine	1 teaspoon garlic powder
½-¾ cup bread crumbs	1 teaspoon salt
	oil

Melt the margarine. Mix bread crumbs and seasonings on a plate. Dip chicken pieces, first into the margarine, then into the bread crumb mixture. Bake in 350° oven for about 1 hour, or fry over a low flame in oil, 25 minutes on a side. or until golden brown.

Variation: Prepare separate bowls of flour, 2 beaten eggs, and matzo meal. Dip moistened chicken into each bowl in order listed, before baking or frying.

BROILED CHICKEN

1 **3-pound chicken quartered**	1 **teaspoon sugar**
3 **potatoes (optional)**	4 **medium tomatoes**
½ **cup margarine**	2 **teaspoons grated lemon peel**
¼ **cup lemon juice**	2 **teaspoons chopped parsley**
1½ **teaspoons salt**	

Place chicken quarters on large broiler pan, skin side down. Add thin strips of potatoes (as for french fries) if you wish. In saucepan heat margarine, lemon juice, salt and sugar until margarine is melted.

Broil chicken for 20 minutes, basting often with margarine mixture. Turn chicken and place tomato quarters on broiling pan. Continue basting chicken and tomatoes often. Broil for another 15-20 minutes. Sprinkle chicken with lemon peel and parsley and serve.

CHICKEN DINNER CASSEROLE

1 **frying chicken, cut up**	2 **cups water**
salt and pepper	¼ **teaspoon pepper**
¼ **cup oil**	1 **teaspoon salt**
½ **cup chopped onions**	1 **cup rice**
2 **8-ounce cans tomato sauce**	1 **10-ounce package frozen peas**

Sprinkle chicken with salt and pepper and brown in oil. Add onions and sauté.

Stir in tomato sauce, water, salt, pepper, and rice. Bring to a boil and simmer 45 minutes. Add peas and continue to cook for another 15 minutes.

FRIED CHICKEN AND VEGETABLES

1 **chicken**	1 **medium can tomato sauce**
oil	1 **cup water**
2 **green peppers, diced**	**salt**
1 **small can mushrooms**	**seasoning to taste**
1 **medium onion, diced**	

Cut chicken into eighths and brown on both sides in oiled skillet over medium flame, approximately 10 minutes on each side.

Add diced onion, pepper and mushrooms into skillet. Pour tomato sauce and water over chicken and vegetables. Add salt and seasoning and cook over small flame for approximately another 30 minutes.

G'DEMPTE CHICKEN

Here is a mild, yet delicious way to prepare chicken.

1½ **medium chickens, quartered**	¾ **cup water**
1 **large onion**	**paprika**
2 **celery stalks**	**garlic and onion powder** (optional)
salt	

Slice onions and cut up celery stalks into quarters. Place them on the bottom of a Dutch oven or skillet. Arrange chicken pieces on top in a single layer. Add 1 teaspoon salt and the water. Sprinkle with salt and cover well with paprika. Other seasonings are optional. Cook on high flame for 15 minutes. Then lower flame and cook an additional hour.

Variations: 1. Add 3-4 sliced potatoes around pot and between chicken quarters. Sprinkle potatoes generously with paprika and seasonings.
2. Use a whole chicken.

GRIBENES (Schmaltz)

Here's how to make the real heimish-style *schmaltz.*

4 cups chicken fat and pieces of skin from neck	1 cup sliced onions

Cut fat and skins from neck into small pieces. Cook over small flame until fat begins to melt. Add sliced onions and continue cooking until onions turn golden brown. The fat should have melted and browned, the skin hardened.

Let it cool, then remove skin and onions. Refrigerate them in a bowl and serve as a meaty appetizer. The melted fat should be strained through a cloth or a fine strainer. Put in refrigerator, and it will gel. Makes an excellent *schmaltz* to use for chopped liver, frying meat products, mashed potatoes, etc.

HONOLULU CHICKEN

1 chicken	½ cup brown sugar
3 tablespoons oil	3 teaspoons lemon juice
flour	1 small can tomato puree
1 medium onion, diced	2 ounces water
1 green pepper, diced	salt
1 small can crushed pineapple	

Heat oil in skillet. Dip chicken in flour and brown on both sides. Remove chicken from skillet and place in dutch oven or covered broiler pan.

Smother chicken with onion, pepper, and pineapple. Add all other ingredients and bake at 300° for over 2 hours until tender. Slow cooking allows chicken to absorb the other flavors.

INDIAN CHICKEN CURRY

3 pounds chicken, cut up	2 teaspoons ground ginger
6 tablespoons margarine	2 teaspoons ground cardamon
2 small onions, chopped	1 teaspoon salt
1 clove garlic, minced	2 medium tomatoes, chopped
2 tablespoons flour	1 cup apple, peeled and chopped
2 tablespoons curry powder	1 cup chicken broth

Wash chicken. Dry and remove skins. Brown chicken until golden brown in half the margarine. Remove chicken from pan.

Add remaining margarine and sauté onion and garlic until tender. Mix flour and seasoning and stir in pan. Add tomato, apple, and broth and simmer 5 minutes. Return chicken to pan and simmer everything for 40 minutes. Serve over rice.

KETCHUP CHICKEN

1 chicken	paprika
salt	ketchup
pepper	onions
garlic powder	

Cut chicken in eighths and sprinkle with salt, pepper, garlic powder and paprika. Then rub each piece with ketchup.

Place in a frying pan over sliced onions, and simmer for about one hour.

Chicken Livers

Here are two interesting recipes with chicken liver which require additional preparation with the liver after it is broiled. It is *important to note* that in order to fry, cook or bake liver it must already have been broiled over an open flame, and this broiling should take place within the 72 hours after the time of slaughtering. (See Koshering Liver, pages 339–340.)

CHOPPED CHICKEN LIVER

½ pound chicken livers	1 medium onion
1 large onion	salt
7 eggs, hard-boiled	pepper

Dice the large onion and fry until golden brown. Add koshered chicken livers. Cover frying pan and lower flame so that mixture will simmer slowly. Steam for ½ hour, mixing once in a while.

Mash or grate livers and onion. Reserve the oil. Mash the eggs and stir into mixture. Add oil. Cool and refrigerate. Before serving, season with salt and pepper, and add a fresh diced onion.

Variation: CHOPPED LIVER

Sauté onions. Grind liver, and eggs. Mix together with onions and seasonings, (see also page 169).

CHICKEN LIVER PASTA

2 pounds small chicken livers	1 3-ounce can sliced mushrooms
1 small onion, chopped	1½ teaspoons sugar
1 small clove garlic, minced	½ teaspoon oregano
4 tablespoons salad oil	1 bay leaf
1 29-ounce can tomatoes, cut up	8 ounce spaghetti or noodles,
1 6-ounce can tomato paste	cooked and drained.

In a large saucepan, saute onion and garlic in 2 tablespoons oil until tender. Drain off fat. Stir in remaining ingredients. Simmer the sauce uncovered for 45 minutes, stirring occasionally.

Meanwhile, cook livers in remaining oil for about 5 minutes, stirring gently. Drain. Add livers to cooked sauce, bringing to a boil. Remove bay leaf. Serve together with boiled spaghetti or noodles.

JUICY PINEAPPLE CHICKEN

This is a colorful chicken presentation that fits right in with a holiday or festive spirit.

1 chicken, quartered	1 medium can of drained
3 tablespoons oil	pineapple chunks
1 large onion, sliced	1 small can mushrooms
1 large can tomatoes	2 scallions
1 green pepper, diced	

Sauce:

1 tablespoon flour	½ cup vinegar
8 ounces pineapple juice	salt
½ cup sugar	

Brown chicken in hot oil. Layer sliced onions in roaster and add browned chicken, all vegetables and drained pineapple chucks. Bake for ½ hour. In the meantime, stir 6-ounces pinapple juice, vinegar, and sugar together over low flame. Make a paste of flour and remaining juice, add all at once to hot mixture, beating briskly. Cook, stirring constantly, until thickened. Pour over chicken and vegetables, and bake another hour.

STUFFED CHICKEN

2 chickens (cut in halves or quarters)

Stuffing:

½ box tea matzoh	½ cup spinach or cabbage, cooked
orange juice	and chopped
2 eggs, beaten	2 stalks celery, finely chopped
salt	2 sprigs parsley, finely chopped
pepper	½ orange, finely cut
2 onions, diced and sautéed	½ cup nuts, coarsely chopped

Soak tea matzohs in orange juice until soggy. Mix together with all other ingredients.

Place separate portions of stuffing on oiled baking pan. Cover each with one portion of chicken, skin side up. Bake at 375° for one hour.

SWEET AND SOUR CHICKEN WINGS

4 chicken wings	2 eggs, whipped
1 cup flour	1 cup matzoh meal
1 teaspoon salt	

Gravy:

1 medium can pineapple chunks,	1 green pepper, diced
undrained	1 small can mushrooms
½ cup ketchup	cooked rice
4 tablespoons brown sugar	
4 tablespoons red wine vinegar or	
red wine	

Remove bones of chicken wings. Cut chicken into small strips. Combine flour and salt in paper bag. Put chicken strips into bag. Shake well until chicken is lightly coated. Remove chicken strips from bag. Dip in eggs and then dip into matzoh meal. Fry until crispy brown.

Gravy: Combine all ingredients of gravy and simmer over low heat for 5 minutes. After chicken is crispy brown, pour gravy sauce into skillet. Mix. Transfer into a baking pan and add peppers, mushrooms and pineapple chunks. Bake at 400° for 20 minutes. Serve over rice.

TOMATO-POTATO CHICKEN

1 medium chicken	1 teaspoon salt
4 potatoes	1 teaspoon garlic powder
1 15-ounce can tomato sauce	1 teaspoon meat seasoning
4 cups water	dash of pepper

Place chicken into baking dish or pot. Peel and slice potatoes and place on top of chicken. In a separate bowl, combine tomato sauce, water, and seasoning. Mix together well. Pour over chicken and potatoes. Cook over medium flame for 1 hour, or bake at 350° F. for 1-1¼ hours.

TOPSY TURVY CHICKEN

3 pounds chicken quartered	1 green pepper, diced
1 tablespoon margarine, melted	2 sprigs parsley, chopped
1½ cups chicken broth	1 cup rice
1 16-ounce can tomatoes	2 teaspoons salt
2 medium onions, diced	¼ teaspoon pepper

Place chicken in shallow greased pan (2½ quart casserole). Brush with margarine. Bake uncovered at 450° for 30 minutes. Meanwhile, heat broth and undrained tomatoes to boiling and set aside.

When chicken has baked for ½ hour, remove from oven and top with chopped vegetables, rice and seasonings. Pour sauce over the casserole and stir. Cover and bake at 400° for about 30 minutes.

Leftover Chicken

Leftover chicken can be cut up for salads, sauces, and side dishes. Here are a few suggestions.

CHICKEN AND MAYONNAISE SALAD

1 pound cooked chicken	1 tablespoon lemon juice
1 cup carrots	salt
¾ cup celery	lettuce
¼ cup onions	tomato
½ cup mayonnaise	parsley

Dice chicken, celery and onion and shred carrots. Combine together with mayonnaise, lemon juice and salt, and mix well. Serve each portion on a bed of lettuce with tomato slices. Garnish with parsley.

ORIENTAL CELERY AND CHICKEN

1 cup cooked chicken, cut into bite-size pieces	3 cups celery
½ cup chicken broth	1 small onion
2 tablespoons soy sauce	2 tablespoons oil
3 teaspoons sugar	¼ cup toasted almonds (optional)

Combine broth, soy sauce and sugar, and set aside. Slice celery and onion thinly and sauté in oil until slightly browned.

Add chicken and sauce mixture to the sautéed ingredients. Cook for 3-5 minutes, stirring constantly. Sprinkle with chopped almonds. Serves four.

CHICKEN AND RICE

1 cup rice	1 4-ounce can tomato sauce
3 cups water	or
2 teaspoons salt	½ cup meat gravy
1 cup cooked chicken, diced	

Bring salted water to boil. Add rice and cook approximately 10 minutes. Stir in diced chicken, and let cook another 5 minutes. Then add tomato sauce or meat gravy. Boil for a minute or two, or until rice is ready.

Variation: CHICKEN AND POTATOES—Mix diced cooked chicken and sauce or gravy with mashed potatoes. Add seasoning.

CHICKEN AND VEGETABLE SAUCE

¼ chicken, cooked	1 cup mushrooms (optional)
1 cup cold soup	salt
2 tablespoons corn starch	pepper
1 can peas, partially drained	

Cut chicken into small pieces. Combine soup and corn starch in saucepan. Cook for five minutes, stirring frequently. Add peas, mushrooms, chicken and season with salt and pepper to taste.

Serve warm over patty shells.

MOCK FISH

Patties:

1 pound chopped chicken (or meat)	½ cup matzoh meal
	salt
1 carrot, grated	sugar
1 onion, grated	pepper

Sauce:

2 carrots, sliced	water
1 large onion, sliced	salt
1 stalk celery	sugar
1 green pepper	

Bring sauce to a boil. Combine ingredients for chicken mixture, and shape into balls. Drop one by one into boiling water. Cook over medium flame for 20-30 minutes.

Duck and Turkey

For the holidays or a memorable occasion try a delicious duck or turkey recipe.

BAKED DUCK

Your guests will certainly remember this one!

Duck:

1 whole duck	paprika
garlic clove or powder	onions

Stuffing:

4 potatoes, grated	pinch of salt and pepper
2 eggs	

Soak duck in water which has just boiled. When cool, scrape yellow from legs. Rub duck with garlic and sprinkle with paprika. Refrigerate overnight.

Next day, prepare the stuffing by combining grated potatoes, eggs and seasoning. Fill duck and sew up.

Line roasting pan with onion slices. Place duck in pan on roasting rack so that the fat can run off. If you don't have a rack, take a pie plate, puncture it with holes, place it upside down in bottom of roasting pan.

Bake covered at 350° for 3 hours until tender.

Note: When buying duck, remember that 1 pound serves 1 person due to large bones and large amount of fat.

STEAMED TURKEY

Place onion and celery slices in the bottom of a large pot. Add salt and 2-3 cups water. Place turkey in pot, and sprinkle generously with salt, garlic powder and paprika. Cook over medium flame for about 2½ hours. Check level of juices occasionally, adding more water if necessary.

TURKEY AND STUFFING

Turkey:

1 turkey, whole	1 cup water
2 large onions	½ teaspoon salt
2 celery stalks	

Stuffing:

1 cup kasha	½ cup carrots, diced
1 egg	½ cup mushrooms
1½ teaspoon salt	2 cups chicken broth
¼ cup oil or margarine	¼ teaspoon parsley
1 large onion, diced	⅛ teaspoon tarragon (optional)
½ cup celery, diced	⅛ teaspoon nutmeg (optional)

Basting:

¾ cup oil or melted margarine	salt and pepper
1 tablespoon paprika	

Slice onions and celery and use to line broiler pan. Add water and salt and then place a rack over the vegetables.

To prepare the stuffing: Beat the egg, mix it into the kasha and add the salt. Set aside.

Chop the vegetables and sauté them lightly in oil in a skillet. Add the kasha mixture and the broth. Cook for 15 minutes. At the end of the cooking time, add the seasoning.

Fill cavity of turkey with stuffing. Use 1 cup stuffing per pound of turkey. Stuff loosely so it will not burst. Wrap any extra stuffing in foil and bake with turkey for 1 hour.

For a nicely browned turkey, baste the skin on all sides with oil or melted margarine, salt and pepper, and paprika. Place turkey breast side down on rack in broiler pan. Bake in a 325° oven for about 30 minutes per pound. Turn it over approximately every 45 minutes, basting each time.

Note: When freezing cooked turkey, always remember to first remove the stuffing from inside. This applies to all other stuffed meats as well.

Stuffings and Sauce

Six delicious stuffings for six different varieties of meat and poultry. With each recipe several different stuffings may be substituted.

Left-over Challah Stuffing—see Stuffed Breast of Veal, page 175.
Mushroom-Cracker Stuffing—See Stuffed Roast, page 172.
Kasha and Vegetable Stuffing—see Turkey and Stuffing, page 159.
Orange Matzoh Stuffing—See Stuffed Chicken, page 155.
Potato Stuffing—See Baked Duck, page 158.
Brown Rice Stuffing—See Crown of Lamb, page 169.

MEAT AND POULTRY TOMATO SAUCE

2 tablespoons oil	1 teaspoon salt
1 small onion, diced	1 4-ounce can tomato sauce
1 green pepper, diced	4 ounces water

Heat oil in skillet. Add diced onion and sauté over low flame until golden brown. Add diced pepper and sauté another minute. Stir in remaining ingredients and bring to a low boil.

Serve over meat or chicken.

Note: For other meat sauces see Apricot Sauce and Mushroom Sauce on page 174.

Meat

Meat

Meat

One of the strongest signs of our Kashrus observance is the meat we eat. The laws cover everything from the type of meat allowed to how it is *slaughtered* and *salted*, and what it may be cooked with and eaten. Jewish law says that under no circumstances may meat be prepared or eaten with dairy dishes and that a six-hour waiting period must be observed before beginning to eat anything dairy.

Meat has often stood as a sign of affluence and royalty. Thus we include it in our Shabbos and Yom Tov meals, as well as at special celebrations. Included in this section are many tasty and unusual meat recipes.

Before the meat recipes, we are including a short section dealing with the basic laws of kosher meat, and a list of kosher meat cuts. *Note:* All Kashrus laws regarding meat apply to chicken as well.

Kashrus and Meat

It has been permissible to eat meat since the days of Noah (after the Flood), but with certain limitations. It is the Will of G-d that we abide by the guidelines He has set for us, and we do so because we wish to bind ourselves to His Will.

In addition we reveal our concern for the spiritual effect of the food we eat. The attitude of reverence for life is revealed in the Torah's repeated commandment not to eat the blood of those animals which are permitted to us. For the Torah states in several places that the essence of the life-source is in the blood. By not eating the blood we also prevent as much as possible the assimilation into ourselves of the animal's life-force and characteristics.

The Ramban (Moshe Nachmanides, 1194–1270), in his commentary on the Torah, explains that the food we eat affects our souls and that since the meat and flesh of an animal absorb the characteristics of that animal, we are especially careful about which types and which parts of the animal we will eat and make part of ourselves. No predatory or scavenger animals are permitted, whether meat, fowl, or fish. In addition, kosher slaughtering, due to its swiftness, protects the animal as much as possible from pain and fear—and thereby also protects us from the harmful toxins that these emotions generate.

By keeping these, and other laws of Kashrus, we affect a physical and spiritual refinement in ourselves, which enables our body to be a more suitable receptacle to the Divine wisdom and laws of the Torah.

In order for meat to be kosher for consumption, it must comply with all the qualifications in each of the following three categories:

1. *Signs of Kashrus:* The signs determining whether an animal is kosher are that it a) chew its cud and b) has split hooves.

    One sign alone is not sufficient. It is interesting to note that the Torah enumerates exactly four animals having only one of these signs: the pig, badger, camel and hare. Despite the vast increase in scientific knowledge and despite man's exploration into the furthest corners of the world—none other than these four have ever been found to have only one of the characteristics of a kosher animal.

In animals that have these two signs of kashrus, only certain parts of the animal are permissible for use after it has been slaughtered (see pages 166–7).

2. *Shechitah:* All kosher type animals and fowl must be ritually slaughtered before they can be used. However, some kinds of exterior blemishes or wounds—e.g. a torn-off limb—renders that animal non-permissible, and it may not even be slaughtered. After the animal is slaughtered, some of the interior organs, such as the lungs, must be examined for defects.

    Shechitah, the act of slaughtering, is done by a *shochet,* a G-d fearing and pious man carefully trained in this profession, who has learned all the laws involved. The act of *shechitah* requires a high degree of skill, precision and speed. The animal is slaughtered in the fastest way possible, causing a minimum amount of pain.

3. *Melicha* (Salting): Once a kosher animal is slaughtered, the animal is sent to a reliable, competent butcher and the following steps are taken:

    a.   All insides are checked to make sure that there are no wounds or blemishes inside which might render the animal non-permissible for use.

    b.   If everything is all right, the butcher must then cut up the animal, and remove all non-permissible veins and fats of the meat. This is known as *treibering.*

    c.   The method of "salting" or *koshering,* which involves 1) rinsing, 2) soaking, 3) salting, and 4) triple-rinsing is then applied to the rest of the animal. This is done to remove the blood from the animal. This process is outlined in detail on pages 335-340.

    d.   The animal must be "salted" within 72 hours after it has been slaughtered.

    e.   If you are on a salt-free diet, consult a *Rav* regarding the manner in which your meat should be prepared.

    f.   For further clarification of these laws, or if you want to salt your own meat or fowl at home, see Section XVII, A Guide to Observance.

Selecting Your Butcher

As in all areas of Kashrus, the integrity of those responsible for the Kashrus of our foods must be of the highest quality.

To be a supervisor, or *mashgiach,* in any area of Kashrus is no light matter. The person must be G-d-fearing, well-versed in all the laws related to that which he is supervising, and very particular over even the slightest deviation from the law.

One of the first prerequisites and signs of a reliable butcher or Kashrus observer is that he observe the Shabbos, both publicly and also in the privacy of his home. This information concerning his observance is not too difficult to acquire. Someone who does not comply with this observance is obviously not too concerned about the laws of Kashrus and should not be entrusted with the great responsibility of adhering to the complex laws involved in supplying our homes with kosher meat.

Here is a short synopsis of many of the laws involving kosher meat. From the many details you will realize that we certainly can't entrust the Kashrus of our meat to a butcher merely because he is located just around the corner.

1. Only meat from an animal which chews its cud *and* has split hooves is kosher.
2. Only fowl which is known by tradition to be kosher may be used. Ex. chicken, duck, goose, pigeon, turkey
3. All kosher animals and fowl to be used for consumption must be ritually slaughtered by a religious and competent *shochet.*
4. Some specific fat and veins must be removed before meat is salted.
5. Only the front part of a kosher animal up to the end of the twelfth rib is considered kosher. The hind part of the animal cannot be used, as it includes in it much forbidden fat which even with great effort cannot always be removed. Therefore, this hind half of the animal is not even brought into a kosher butcher shop, but is sold to a non-kosher butcher. See diagrams on the following pages.
6. Meat must be koshered within 72 hours of slaughtering.
7. All stages and specific times of the salting process must be meticulously observed.
8. A competent butcher always allows a *mashgiach* to inspect his plant to make sure all laws are kept, and the highest standard of Kashrus is maintained.
9. Liver is not koshered in the usual manner—it is broiled separately over an open fire, see page 339.
10. If you plan to kosher the meat or chicken in your home and you order unkoshered meat (not soaked and salted) from the butcher, he should tell you the exact time of the slaughtering so that you will be able to kosher your meat in time.

Unfortunately there are many unreliable butchers in the business. Choose your butcher as carefully as you would select a good doctor. Do not settle for less than the best. Did you know—

1. The simple sign בשר כשר —"Kosher Meat"—is not enough. Sometimes non-kosher meat is also sold in that store. Even if kept separately, mix-ups are bound to happen. Don't take a chance.
2. Even if the store is closed on Shabbos, if your butcher doesn't observe the Shabbos at home he cannot be trusted in the matter of Kashrus.
3. Many non-religious butchers whose shops bear the בשר כשר sign do not kosher (soak and salt) their meat at all; some do so only superficially. Make sure to inquire specifically whether the meat is koshered. If not, switch butcher shops immediately (unless he is a trustworthy butcher and you are willing to kosher the meat at home).
4. *Buying in the supermarket:* Buy only already packaged chicken or meat. Make sure the package has a *reliable* seal of Kashrus and that it has already been koshered, that is, properly rinsed, soaked, salted, and triple-rinsed.

5. Many self-service meat markets are now opening with packaged kosher meat prepared under strict supervision. Make sure the package also states that it has been koshered.
6. Liver included with packaged or other chicken must be removed before chicken is thawed or cooked. The liver must be koshered separately by broiling over an open flame. See page 339.
7. *Restaurants*: All the intricacies involved in selecting your butcher should be kept in mind for choosing a restaurant. A sign indicating the sale of kosher meat is never enough. Check for the best!
8. If you see the word "Kosher" on London broil steak or "spare ribs," inquire carefully. These cuts are not kosher, but we have been informed that some very reliable butchers have begun to use similar names to that of nonkosher parts in order to attract the modern consumer. Make sure the cut of meat comes only from the front part of the animal and has been prepared by a reliable butcher.

Kosher Meat Cuts

The diagrams of beef, veal, and lamb show which parts of these animals are kosher and which are not.

The following list is our basic selection of meat cuts from kosher animals.

BEEF
Breast of Beef
Brisket
Rolled Breast
Chopped Meat
Chuck, single
Deckel or Keilacher
Flanken
Broiled Liver
Top of Rib
Short Ribs

Roast
End Steak
Minute Steak
Rib Steak
Meat Stew
Tongue, if properly *treibered*

VEAL OR LAMB
Lamb Chops
Lamb Stew
Lamb Tongue

Breast of Veal
Veal Cutlets
Shoulder of Veal
Veal Tongue, if properly *treibered*

POULTRY
Chicken
Duck
Goose
Pigeon
Turkey

BEEF

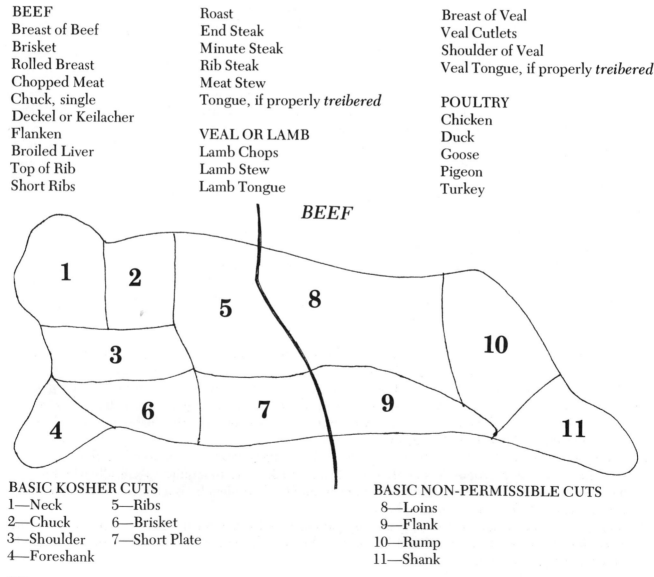

BASIC KOSHER CUTS
1—Neck   5—Ribs
2—Chuck   6—Brisket
3—Shoulder 7—Short Plate
4—Foreshank

BASIC NON-PERMISSIBLE CUTS
8—Loins
9—Flank
10—Rump
11—Shank

166

VEAL

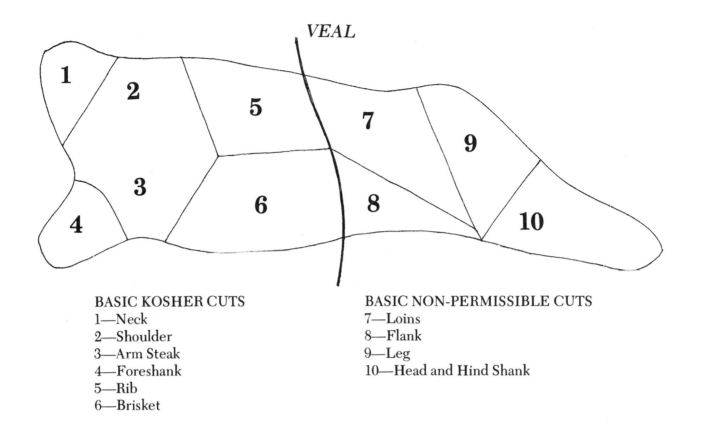

BASIC KOSHER CUTS
1—Neck
2—Shoulder
3—Arm Steak
4—Foreshank
5—Rib
6—Brisket

BASIC NON-PERMISSIBLE CUTS
7—Loins
8—Flank
9—Leg
10—Head and Hind Shank

LAMB

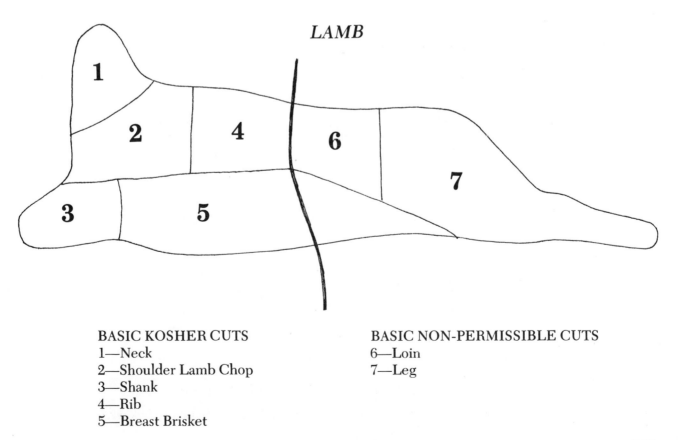

BASIC KOSHER CUTS
1—Neck
2—Shoulder Lamb Chop
3—Shank
4—Rib
5—Breast Brisket

BASIC NON-PERMISSIBLE CUTS
6—Loin
7—Leg

Meat Dishes

BEEF GOULASH

1	pound chuck, cubed		pepper
	flour		garlic
	oil		bay leaf (optional)
1	large onion, diced	1	tablespoon paprika
	salt		

Flour meat and brown in hot oil. Add onion. Cook for 5 minutes.

Add all the spices according to taste and 2 cups of hot water. Simmer for 2 hours, stirring occasionally.

Serve with wide noodles. Serves 4.

HUNGARIAN GOULASH

See Soup, Section VI.

GOURMET BRISKET

3	pounds brisket	4	ounces dry wine
1	envelope onion soup mix		salt
1	clove garlic		pepper

Mix soup mix, garlic, wine, salt and pepper. Marinate brisket in mixture overnight. Be sure to turn it in the sauce mixture a few times.

Place brisket in a pan, pour the sauce over it. Cover tightly with foil and bake at 375° until tender.

BAKED LAMB BRISKET

| 4 | lamb briskets (or shanks) | ½ | cup water |
| 1 | cup marrow or lima beans | | salt and pepper |

Wash and soak beans. Cook with salt and pepper for 1 hour in ½ cup water. Place in casserole.

Add lamb briskets. Cover, and bake at 350° for 50 minutes.

Variation: Add 1 can tomato sauce to casserole before baking.

CROWN OF LAMB STUFFED WITH RICE AND VEGETABLES

1 crown rib of lamb (a row of
attached lamb chops)

Stuffing:

1 cup brown rice	1 green pepper
2 cups water	2 carrots
¼ teaspoon salt	3 tablespoons tamari (soy sauce)
1 tablespoon oil	1 cup mushrooms
2 onions	½ bunch parsley

Stand up crown rib of lamb (attached lamb chops) in a circle. Tie the two ends together or join with skewers. Cover exposed bones(top) with foil so that they do not burn. Cook in 350° oven for 2 hours. Add salt.

To prepare stuffing: Wash rice and drain. Put in water and bring to a boil. Add salt and simmer for 45 minutes.

Chop parsley fine, onions in moons, peppers and carrots in thin slices and mushrooms in halves. Set aside mushrooms and parsley. Heat oil in skillet. Sauté onions, then green peppers and carrots on high flame for 3 minutes. Lower flame, and add ½ cup water and 3 tablespoons tamari (soy sauce) and cook for 5 more minutes. Then add mushrooms and cook for another 5 minutes. When cooked, combine vegetables and their juices with rice and parsley. Add more tamari to taste if necessary.

Place stuffing in center of crown of lamb for last ½ hour of cooking.

Note: For other possible stuffings, see page 160.

Liver

CHOPPED LIVER

A famous Jewish dish, often served on Shabbos afternoon at beginning of meal or as part of main course. Also popularly offered at a Kiddush or other celebration.

1 pound broiled liver	¼ teaspoon pepper
3 eggs, hard-boiled	1 tablespoon lemon juice
1 large onion	(optional)
2 tablespoons oil	½ tablespoon mustard (optional)
½ teaspoon salt	

Grind liver, eggs, and onion. (For added flavor you can sauté onion first.) Mix together well.

Add oil and seasoning and mix again.

Variations: Mix with mayonnaise instead of oil.
LIVER SALAD—Instead of grinding up the main ingredients together, cube liver into ½″ cubes, mash hard-boiled eggs and dice onion. Toss lightly together. Add seasoning and mix well.
CHICKEN LIVER—(See page 154.)

LIVER* BLINTZES AND SAUCE

4 eggs	1 cup water
1 cup flour	1 pound chopped liver (see recipe)
1 teaspoon salt	

Sauce:

1 onion, diced	meat bones
1-2 stalks celery	water
1 8-ounce can mushrooms	oil for frying

Beat eggs and salt, then add flour alternately with water. Heat oil in frying pan. When very hot, add about 2 tablespoons batter, tilting pan to all sides. When surface begins to blister, turn over and fry 30 seconds longer. Take out with spatula and place on paper towel to absorb oil or fat.

Prepare chopped liver according to recipe. Put a tablespoon of liver mixture on each blintze. Then fold the blintze.

To make sauce, sauté diced onion until golden brown, then add in diced celery and sauté another 10 minutes over low flame. Pour in mushrooms, some meat bones and small amount of water. Cook for ½ hour.

Remove bones from pot and spoon out sauce over blintzes. Serve warm. If they were prepared a long time in advance, the blintzes can be rewarmed in oven before adding sauce.

*In order to fry, cook or bake liver it must already have been broiled over an open flame, and this broiling should take place within the 72 hours after the time of slaughtering. (See Koshering Liver, pages 339-340).

MARINATED PEPPER STEAK

2 pounds steak	1 green pepper
1 tablespoon soy sauce	2 stalks celery
2 tablespoons salad oil	1 tablespoon cornstarch
1 teaspoon garlic powder	2 tomatoes
1 onion	

Cut steak into long thin strips. Mix soy sauce, salad oil and garlic powder. Pour over steak and let stand 1 hour. Dice onion, pepper, and celery.

Heat oil in frying pan, add steak mixture and brown thoroughly on all sides. Add vegetables, cover and cook 5-10 minutes.

Add cornstarch dissolved in ¼ cup cold water. Stir until sauce thickens. Add cut up tomatoes. Cover and cook 5-10 minutes longer until meat and vegetables are tender. Serve over boiled rice.

SAUCY PEPPER STEAK

2 pound shoulder steak—¼" strips	¼ teaspoon powdered ginger
¼ cup oil	1 green pepper
1 cup boiling water	1 onion
½ package onion soup mix	1 tomato
1 teaspoon sugar	mushrooms (optional)
1 tablespoon soy sauce	2 tablespoons cornstarch

Brown steak in oil.

Combine soup mix, water, sugar, soy sauce, and ginger. Pour over meat and simmer on low heat until tender, approximately 1 hour.

Cut vegetables. Before serving, add vegetables and cornstarch dissolved in cold water, stirring until sauce thickens. Simmer 5-10 minutes more.

P'TCHAH

An original European delicacy, p'tchah is popular as an entree for meat meals on special occasions. It is a jelled dish, grayish-yellow in color, and garnished with egg slices. The minced garlic adds a sharp taste to it.

1 calf's foot, or 2 dozen chicken feet and necks	salt
water	1-2 cloves of garlic, minced
1 large onion	3-4 hard-boiled eggs

Wash off calf's foot or chicken feet very well. (If you are using chicken feet, soak for a few minutes in very hot water, and peel skin from legs.) Put into large pot, with water to cover. Add a large onion and small amount of salt. Bring to boil, then cook on a very low flame for 3-3½ hours, until meat is very tender. (Calf's foot may take a bit longer.) Pick meat from bones and grind well.

Spread ground meat on the bottom of a 9″ × 13″ pan, and slowly pour on some of the stock. Add minced garlic. For an attractive garnish, use hard-boiled eggs, either sliced or cut fine and placed on top of the stock. When cooled, place in refrigerator. Once it jells, cut into cake-size pieces and serve cold. Serves 16-20.

PLOV

When planning supper, we usually try to include at least one food from each of the following three categories: protein, vegetable and grain. Plov is a tasty dish that combines all three in one easy recipe.

1 pound flanken, cut up	1 green pepper (optional)
oil for frying	salt and pepper
1 large onion, diced	water
2 carrots, sliced	1 cup rice

Heat oil in Dutch oven. Sauté onions until transparent, then add meat and brown over medium flame. Add carrots, ½ cup water, seasoning to taste, and cook for 1 hour. Pour in rice with 2 cups water and cook another 20 minutes.

Variations: BROWN RICE—After carrots have cooked for 40 minutes, add brown rice and water and cook an additional 40-45 minutes.
SWEET PLOV—Add ¼ cup raisins at same time as rice for a juicy, sweet taste.

ROAST BEEF

3 pounds beef	2 stalks celery
½ cup flour	3 carrots
salt	5 potatoes
pepper	½ cup water
2 onions	

Rub beef with seasoned flour and put into floured roasting bag.

Place into roasting pan. Layer bottom of pan with sliced onions and celery, and surround with carrots and potatoes.

Add water. Bake at 400° for approximately 1½ hours.

TASTY GOURMET POT ROAST

3 pounds beef roast	½ teaspoon chili powder
3 tablespoons oil	2 cups boiling water
½ teaspoon meat tenderizer	2 small onions
1½ tablespoons paprika	3-4 bay leaves

Heat oil in Dutch oven and brown meat on all sides over medium flame.

Sprinkle seasoning in the above order over all sides of meat. Important—prick meat on all sides with fork. This enables spices to be absorbed.

Then add boiling water to pot. (Do not use cold water, for this will cause hot oil to sizzle and splatter.) Water should be about 1″ deep. Add sliced onions and bay leaves. Lower flame and simmer for 1½-2 hours depending on size of roast. Check roast periodically, adding more water if necessary.

Slice meat diagonally when cooled, returning to pot to warm.

STUFFED ROAST

4 pounds beef (a large thin slice)

Stuffing:

2 boxes crackers	1 4-ounce can mushrooms
water	matzoh meal
2 eggs	spices

To prepare stuffing, soak crackers and then squeeze out water. Add eggs, mushrooms and matzoh meal. Add spices to taste.

Lay 3 cups of stuffing across the width of the meat, and then roll up the meat along its length. Tie. Cook in 350° oven for 2 hours. Slice and serve.

Serves 6.

VARIETY ROAST

A tasty, all-in-one meat meal.

5 pound roast	⅛ teaspoon pepper
2 tablespoons flour	1 bay leaf
⅓ cup oil	½ teaspoon garlic
1 large onion, diced	3 medium potatoes, sliced
2 celery stalks, cut	6 carrots, sliced
3 cups soup stock	8 ounces string beans
1 can tomato paste	8 ounces green peas
2 teaspoons salt	

Coat meat in flour and brown in heated oil, on all sides, in large Dutch oven. Add onion, celery, soup stock, tomato paste and seasonings. Bring to a boil, then cook on a low flame for 2 hours.

Arrange potatoes and carrots around the meat. Let it cook for another hour. Then add green beans and peas and cook another 20 minutes (less time if using canned or frozen vegetables). Add salt if necessary. Serve the meat on a large platter surrounded with vegetables.

BEEF STEW

1 pound chuck, cubed	1 onion, diced
2 tablespoons oil	seasoning
1 can tomato sauce	peas (optional)
2 medium potatoes, cubed	1 tablespoon flour (optional)
4 carrots, sliced	

Brown meat evenly in oil. Add tomato sauce, vegetables, and enough water to cover. Season to taste. Simmer 1½ hours. Add peas during last 5 minutes. For thicker sauce, add flour dissolved in cold water, stirring until thickened. Serves 4.

ORIENTAL MEAT STEW

3 pounds chuck stew meat	2 green peppers, diced
oil	1 8-ounce can mushrooms
1 cup chicken soup	½ onion, sliced
4 tablespoons soy sauce	cooked rice
½ cup ketchup	

Cut meat into small strips and brown in skillet for 15 minutes.

Prepare gravy by mixing chicken soup, soy sauce and ketchup. Add gravy to skillet. Simmer for 30 minutes.

Add diced pepper, mushrooms and onion. Simmer another ½ hour. Serve hot with rice.

OVEN STEW

2 pounds meat, cubed	4 small carrots, sliced
¼ cup flour	1 cup celery, sliced
2 teaspoons salt	3 small potatoes, cut up
¼ teaspoon paprika	1 cup water
¼ teaspoon pepper	2 8-ounce cans tomato sauce with
2 tablespoons oil	mushrooms
4 small onions, quartered	

Combine flour and spices in bag. Drop in meat and shake until coated. Mix with oil in casserole. Bake uncovered at 400° for 30 minutes. Stir once. Add vegetables and tomato sauce. Simmer at 350° for 1¾ hours. Serves 6.

PICKLED TONGUE IN APRICOT SAUCE

The gourmet cook will certainly want to include this recipe among her favorites. Yet it's simple enough for the novice to prepare as well.

1 tongue (pickled or plain)

Sauce:

1 12-ounce can apricot nectar	1 tablespoon flour
3 ounces red raisins	1 tablespoon lemon juice
2-3 tablespoons white or brown sugar	

To cook tongue: Fill pot with water. Add tongue. When water boils and darkens, change water and cook in fresh water. Repeat the process, changing the water a second time. For the third cooking, bring to a boil on a high flame and then cook over medium flame for 2-3 hours until tender. (With plain tongue only change the water once). After the tongue is cooked and while it is still quite warm, hold it with a fork and peel off the skin. When the tongue cools off, cut it into slices.

Approximately 30 minutes before serving, warm sauce ingredients in a large skillet and bring to boil. Stir in as many slices of tongue as you are going to serve. Shut off flame, and let tongue warm in the sauce for a few minutes.

TONGUE IN MUSHROOM SAUCE

1 tongue, cooked	dash of garlic powder
8 ounces tomato sauce	dash of oregano
16 ounces mushrooms	

Bring tongue to boil as in previous recipe. Peel when still warm and slice it after it cools.

Before serving, mix together all ingredients for sauce in a large skillet. Bring to boil, then stir in tongue slices. Serve warm.

MEAT TZIMMES

1 pound chuck meat	1 cup honey
3 pounds carrots	dash of salt
2 large sweet potatoes	water
½ cup sugar	

Use 4-quart pot. Cube meat, peel and slice carrots and sweet potatoes. Place in pot filled ¾ full of water. Add sugar, honey, and salt. Cook on low flame for 1½-2 hours.

STUFFED BREAST OF VEAL

4-5 pound breast of veal, with pocket

Stuffing:

¾ pound stale challah	celery leaves
water	salt
1 egg	pepper
3 onions	garlic
1 carrot (optional)	½ stick margarine
salt	

Order a breast of veal with a pocket.

To make stuffing, soak challah in water. Dice one onion (and carrot). Sauté until golden brown. Squeeze water from challah, mix with eggs, sautéed onion (and carrot) and seasoning. If mixture is too dry, add a drop of water. Sprinkle salt inside veal pocket, stuff loosely, and sew it up with thread.

Slice onions in rings. In pan, place onions rings, celery leaves from a few stalks, salt, pepper, and garlic. Place veal in pan, and sprinkle all sides with salt, pepper, and garlic. Bake at 400°, preferably in broiler part of oven.

After ½ hour, turn over veal, and let it continue to broil another 1½ hours. Check to see if it is done. If so, cover with aluminum foil. Serve warm.

If prepared in advance, let meat cool off before slicing. Reheat in frying pan prior to serving.

BREADED VEAL CUTLETS

3 veal cutlets	salt
2 eggs, beaten	pepper
1 cup matzoh meal	oil

Beat eggs in bowl. Mix matzoh meal and seasoning on a plate. Heat oil slightly in frying pan. Dip veal cutlets into beaten eggs on both sides and then into seasoned matzoh meal. Fry on low flame about 15 minutes on each side until crispy and golden brown.

Hint: If experiencing difficulty in getting the coating to stick to the veal, try refrigerating for one hour before frying.

Variation: TOMATO SAUCE—Sauté 2 onions in the oil before frying veal. Pour ½ can tomato sauce in baking pan. Add veal, onion, and remainder of sauce. Cover, and bake at 350° for ¾ hour. Goes well with spaghetti.

Chopped Meat

Chopped meat is a popular item in the American diet, especially in the form of hamburgers. There are many other ways of preparing chopped meat, however, including special dishes for special occasions.

Chopped meat recipes are often very tasty. You can buy high quality meat and have your butcher grind it for you or grind it at home. Then be sure to try out some of the recipes included in this section. *NOTE*: All dietary laws regarding kosher meat apply equally to chopped meat. It is koshered *before* grinding.

BASIC HAMBURGERS

2	pounds ground meat	2	teaspoons lemon juice
½-⅔	cup matzoh meal		dash of garlic powder (optional)
3	eggs	1	tablespoon ketchup (optional)
	salt		oil for frying
	pepper		

Mix all ingredients together and form into patties. Heat oil and place individual patties in frying pan. Fry patties over medium flame on each side until nicely browned, approximately 15 minutes on each side.

Variation: BASIC MEATBALLS—Use basic recipe. You may add a small amount of water to it, to make meatballs slightly fluffier. In a 4-quart pot, bring to boil 8 cups water, 4 ounces tomato sauce and 2 teaspoons salt. Lower meatballs gently, one at a time, into boiling water. Cook for 40 minutes.

DIET HAMBURGERS

1	pound lean meat, chopped	1	teaspoon lemon juice
¼	cup club soda		salt
1	small onion, diced		garlic powder

Mix all ingredients together. Do not overhandle because meat may become too tough. Shape into individual patties and place on broiler pan spaced well apart. Broil on both sides until golden brown and slightly crisp.

HAMBURGER ROLL-UP

Meat Mixture:

1¼	pounds ground beef		oil for frying
1	large onion		salt
2	stalks celery		pepper
½	cup green pepper		

Dough:

1¾ cups flour	½ teaspoon salt
⅔ cup water	5 tablespoons margarine
4 teaspoons baking powder	mustard to taste

Cut up onion, celery and green pepper. Fry in oil until soft, but not brown. Add meat and sauté until brown. Add salt and pepper. Remove from heat and cool.

Roll out on floured board in a rectangle. Spread with mustard. Cut margarine into flour, baking powder and salt with two knives, until it reaches consistency of coarse meal. Add water, a few drops at a time, mashing with fork after each addition.

Spread meat mixture on dough. Roll up jelly roll fashion. Put on an ungreased pan, seam side down. Before baking make several vents in dough to allow steam to escape.

Bake at 375° until brown—approximately 45 minutes. Cool slightly, cut into slices and serve.

LASAGNA

1 pound chopped meat, seasoned	1 large can tomato sauce
1 box lasagna noodles	

Brown chopped meat in a skillet.

Par-boil lasagna, place 2-3 tablespoons of meat on each noodle and roll up. Place seam side down in pan and cover with tomato sauce.

Bake at 350° for 30-40 minutes.

SAUCY MEATBALLS

1 pound ground beef	½ teaspoon celery salt
½ cup uncooked rice	⅛ teaspoon garlic powder
1½ cup water	⅛ teaspoon pepper
1 small onion, chopped	1 16-ounce can tomato sauce
1 teaspoon salt	

Preheat oven to 350° degrees. Mix together meat, rice and ½ cup water, onion and spices. Shape into round balls. Place on an ungreased baking dish.

Stir together remaining 1 cup water and tomato sauce and pour over meatballs. Cover with foil and bake 45 minutes. Uncover and bake 15 minutes longer. Makes 4-6 servings.

Uncooked rice in meat mixture gives the meatballs a prickly look.

Variation: PAN FRY—When preparing chopped meat mixture omit water. After forming balls, fry in 2 tablespoons hot oil, turning frequently, until light brown on all sides but not crusty. Be sure balls are small. Add sauce and simmer for about 45 minutes.

MEATBALLS IN SPICY SAUCE

4 pounds spaghetti, cooked and drained

Sauce:

3 large onions	3 cups water
3 small cloves garlic	2 tablespoon oregano
3 tablespoons salad oil	1 tablespoon basil
3 pounds (or 2 24-ounce cans) tomatoes	¼ teaspoon pepper
	3 bay leaves
1 2-ounce can tomato paste	12 ounces sliced mushrooms

Meatballs:

2 pounds ground beef	1 teaspoon salt
3 eggs	2 cups soft bread crumbs
¼ cup water	

To prepare sauce—use a large dutch oven. Chop the onions, crush the garlic, and cut up the tomatoes. Sauté the onions and garlic in oil until tender but not brown. Add the tomatoes, tomato paste, water and spices. Stir. Bring to a boil and turn down the flame. Simmer uncovered for two hours, stirring occasionally. Remove bay leaves and add mushrooms. Simmer further until desired consistency is obtained—about 30 minutes more.

To prepare meatballs—while the sauce is cooking prepare the meatballs. Beat eggs and add in water, salt, and bread crumbs. Mix in chopped meat and shape into 42 medium-sized meatballs. Place them in a shallow pan and bake at 375° until done—approximately 30 minutes. Drain off the fat.

Serve meatballs hot, topped with sauce. Serve together with spaghetti.

SWEET AND SOUR MEAT BALLS

Meatballs:

1 pound ground beef	2½ teaspoons brown sugar
1 egg	1 teaspoon sugar
¼ cup matzoh meal	¼ teaspoon salt

Sauce:

½ cup water	2½ teaspoons lemon juice
1 small can tomato sauce	dash of black pepper

Combine sauce ingredients in Dutch oven and bring to boil. Meanwhile, mix meatball ingredients well. When the sauce comes to boil, begin shaping mixture into individual meatballs and drop in one at a time into sauce. Let cook approximately 25 minutes.

Serve over rice or spaghetti.

EASY MEATLOAF CASSEROLE

8 ounces macaroni shells	1 teaspoon salt
1 cup chopped meat	1 tablespoon bread crumbs
1 4-ounce can tomato sauce	½ teaspoon garlic powder

Parboil macaroni shells and drain. Then combine with meat, tomato sauce and spices, and place into a greased casserole dish. Sprinkle with bread crumbs and bake at 425° for 25 minutes.

POTATO MEAT LOAF PIE

6 medium potatoes, cooked	2 pounds chopped meat,
2 onions, fried	seasoned
2 eggs	paprika

Mash potatoes with 2 eggs and fried onions. Spread half of mixture in greased round pan. Spread meat on top and cover with remaining potatoes. Sprinkle with paprika. Bake in preheated oven at 350° for one hour.

PUNCHIKES

A yeasted knish, filled with ground meat and deep-fried.

Dough:

1½ ounce yeast	¾ cup sugar
½ cup water	1 cup juice
3 eggs	1 teaspoon salt
¼ cup oil	5 cups flour

Filling:

2 cups meat, ground	1 egg, beaten
1 small onion, diced and sautéed	

oil for deep frying

Dissolve yeast in water. Combine remaining ingredients of dough in order given and mix well.

Knead and let rise until double in size. Meanwhile, mix meat mixture and set aside.

When dough is ready, separate into small pieces, flatten them and put filling inside. Close and shape into ball. Let rise a short time and deep fry on medium flame. Brown on all sides. Serve warm.

RAVIOLI

1 kreplach dough (page 127–128)	1½-2 quarts water
1 pound meatball mixture	1½ tablespoons salt
12 ounces tomato paste	½ cup rice (optional)
4-6 bay leaves	

Roll out kreplach dough, and cut into 1″ squares. On half of the squares place ½-1 teaspoon of meatball mixture. Cover with remaining empty squares and pinch sides together.

Meanwhile, bring water, tomato paste, salt and bay leaves to a boil. Drop in ravioli, one by one. If any meat remains make very small meatballs and drop into pot. Cook for 20-30 minutes.

Optional: Cook ½ cup rice in the boiled tomato broth. This makes a delicious rice-tomato soup. The ravioli may be served alone or in the soup.

Stuffed Cabbage

THE ART OF MAKING STUFFED CABBAGE

A favorite Hungarian gourmet dish which is sure to win lots of compliments.

Step 1—Boiling Cabbage

Use a 4-quart pot or larger. Fill it more than halfway with water and bring to a boil. Add whole cabbage, head up. If it seems the cabbage might tip, hold it at the top with a fork. Cook over a small flame for approximately 5 minutes, until leaves soften. Remove from pot, and while cabbage is still hot, cut out inside core and remove outer leaves one by one until you reach leaves which are too small for rolling. (The top layer may have to be thrown out.)

Step 2—Rolling Cabbage, with Meat Filling

While leaves are still hot, place a spoonful of chopped meat mixture on the rib of each leaf. Roll cabbage leaf along its length (a-b). When you are nearly finished rolling it, tuck in both ends (c) and (d) and continue rolling. Cabbage leaves will remain neatly rolled up if they are stuffed while they are still warm.

Step 3—Cooking Stuffed Cabbage:

Line bottom of pot neatly with cabbage rolls. If making a large quantity you can pile up cabbage rolls into a few layers. There should be just enough water or sauce to cover cabbage. Cook on small flame for at least two hours.

Step 4—Preparing Basic Sauce:

Brown flour in oil and add other ingredients. See **Sauce** in *Basic Recipe* below. Mix and simmer for a few minutes. This may be prepared in a separate pot and poured over the cabbage rolls or the cabbage rolls may now be placed in the pot with the sauce. Add more water if necessary. Cook on a low flame for two hours.

Variation: VEGETABLE SAUCE—Instead of flour, sauté diced onion, celery, and carrot. Simmer for 20 minutes until tender, and then add other ingredients.

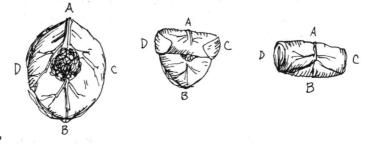

BASIC RECIPE

leaves of 1 medium cabbage

Meat Mixture:

¾ pound ground meat	¼ cup chopped onion
½ cup cooked rice	salt
2 eggs	pepper

Sauce:

3 tablespoons oil	3-4 teaspoons tomato paste
2 tablespoons flour	1-1½ cups water
1 large can tomato juice	2 bay leaves
½ cup sugar	salt

Prepare according to the instructions above.

SWEET AND SOUR STUFFED CABBAGE

2 medium cabbages

Meat Mixture:

1½ pounds ground meat	1½ tablespoons sugar
1 large onion, minced	2 eggs
1 cup raw rice	salt

Broth:

1 large onion, diced	¼ cup raisins
1 large peeled apple	water to cover cabbage rolls
2 meat bones	

Sauce:

4 tablespoons sugar	salt
1½ lemons squeezed	3 medium cans tomato sauce

Prepare meat mixture and set aside. Place cabbage one at a time in boiling water. Separate leaves and fill each leaf with spoonful of meat mixture. Roll up and place in pot.

Add broth ingredients and cook, covered, on a small flame for 1-1½ hours. Add sauce and let cook another hour.

STUFFED GREEN PEPPERS

8 green peppers

Meat Mixture:

¾ pound ground meat	¼ cup chopped onion
½ cup cooked rice	salt and pepper to taste
2 eggs	

Sauce:

1 medium onion, diced	½ cup sugar
1 celery stalk, diced	1½ tablespoons tomato paste
2 medium carrots, diced	salt
oil for frying	1-1½ cup water
1 large can tomato juice	

Prepare meat mixture. Rinse off peppers. Place for a few seconds in boiling water, cut off top of green peppers and cut out inside seeds. Stuff ¾ full with meat mixture. In skillet sauté diced vegetables on low flame until light golden and very tender. Place green peppers in skillet standing up. Add sauce and cook on small flame for 1½ hours.

Variation: RICE FILLING—Fill hollowed peppers ¾ full with one pound cooked rice combined with sautéed onion, carrots and salt. Steam in sauce as above, or bake at 350° for 30 minutes.

Helpful Hints

MEATS

Gravy: Add 2½ cups beef consommé and 1 package dry onion soup mix to roasts or stewing meat (an 8-ounce can tomato sauce and one cup water can be substituted for beef consommé). The gravy will be delicious.

Freezing: Do not freeze meat stuffing or the potatoes in stew as they become very soggy.

Refreezing: Once raw meat is defrosted, do not refreeze. If you do not need it immediately, cook or bake it anyway and then refreeze.

Meat Servings:

  Steak, poultry, lambchops: ¾ pound = 1 serving

  Hamburger, liver, tongue: 1 pound = 3 servings

  Roast with bones: 1 pound = 2 servings

  Boneless roasts: 1 pound = 3 servings

Preventing Meat Shrinkage: a) Rub meat slightly on all sides with oil before cooking or baking. This prevents juices from escaping. b) Cook or bake meat on smaller heat for a longer period of time.

Refrigerator storage: Roast meat, 2-3 days—Ground meat, 1-2 days—Smoked meat, 6-7 days

Cooking tongue: For skin to peel off easily, pour cold water over boiled tongue.

CHOPPED MEATS

Advance Preparation: Mix all ingredients of recipe together, form into individual burgers or balls, place on an aluminum sheet and freeze. After it is completely frozen, remove from sheet, place in a plastic bag and remove from bag as needed.

Easy Defrosting: Put a layer of wax or freezer paper between individual steaks, chops, chicken quarters, and burgers. This makes it easier to separate when you only need a few portions and it defrosts much easier.

Cooking Meat Loaf: Line casserole completely with foil before putting meat in. This enables meat loaf to come out easily.

Vegetables and Salad Dressings

SECTION 10

Vegetables and Salad Dressings

COOKED VEGETABLE DISHES
    All Star Salad
    Bean Salad
    Sunny String Beans
    Beet Salad
    Baked Broccoli
    Broccoli Vinaigrette
Carrot-Tzimmes
    Belgian-Hawaiian Carrots
    Candied Carrots
    Can-Opener Tzimmes
    Carrot Latkes
    Carrot Loaf
    Easy Carrot Tzimmes
    Sweet Carrot Tzimmes
    Coated Cauliflower
    Juicy Cauliflower
    Cauliflower Salad
Chick Peas-Arbis
    Chick Peas
    Erev Shabbos Chick Peas
    Eggplant Parmesan
    Eggplant Relish
    Stewed eggplant
    Red Lima Beans
Mock Chopped Liver
    Lima Liver
    Vegetarian Chopped Liver
    Stuffed Mushrooms
    Baked Winter Squash
    Quick and Sweet Baked Squash
    Vegetable Loaf
    Vegetable Cutlets
    Vegetable Kugel
    Vegetable Kishke
Vinaigrette
    Vinaigrette
    Boiled and Colorful Vinaigrette
    Easy Sweet and Sour Vinaigrette
    Stewed Zucchini
    Diet Squash Mash (Zucchini)

FRESH SALADS
    Avocado Spread
    Blueberry-Radish Salad with Orange-Parsley Dressing
    Basic Coleslaw
    Coleslaw and Tangy Dressing
    Cucumber Salad
    Cucumber-Radish Plate
    Fresh Garden Salad
    Israeli Salad
    Relish Trays
Pickles
    Dill Pickles
    Sour Pickles

Helpful Hints

SALAD DRESSINGS
    Home-made Chraine (Horseradish)
    French Dressing
    Horseradish Dressing
    Italian Dressing
    Lemon Herbal Dressing
    Mayonnaise
    Mayonnaise Dressing
    Homemade Seasoned Mayonnaise
    Russian Dressing
    Basic White Sauce

Vegetables and Salad Dressings

Cooked Vegetable Dishes

Colorful and abundantly rich in nutrients, vegetables can be served at just about any meal, placed in sandwiches, or eaten as a snack.

When using green leafy vegetables, make sure to rinse them out well before using, and to check them over carefully to make sure no tiny insects are crawling on them.

When cooking vegetables, use a small flame and a covered pot. This will prevent many nutrients from being destroyed. Also, in vegetables that have peels, many valuable nutrients are present in the layer just below the peel, so peel your vegetables with care and avoid any excessive waste.

ALL-STAR SALAD

1 cup (or 1 can) sliced carrots	2 cucumbers, sliced
1 cup (or 1 can, French style) cut green beans	mayonnaise
	salt
1 small cauliflower	pepper
3-4 potatoes	garlic powder
1 can green peas	

Cook each vegetable separately. Cook quickly. They should become bright in color, but not too soft. Dice them all. Mix together and add peas, cucumbers, mayonnaise and seasoning. Garnish with stuffed olives and anchovy fillets.

185

BEAN SALAD

1 can chick peas	½ cup oil
1 can kidney beans	½ cup vinegar or lemon juice
1 can green beans	1 tablespoon oregano
1 can wax beans	1 tablespoon garlic
1 can corn	salt
1 onion, chopped	pepper
1 green or red pepper, chopped	

Mix all beans and corn together. Add the onion and pepper. Combine remaining ingredients and toss with salad, gently but thoroughly.

Chill and serve. Keeps up to 2 weeks in closed refrigerator container.

SUNNY STRING BEANS

1 pound fresh string beans	½ cup sunflower seeds
salt	soy sauce

Wash string beans well, and cut off the ends. Cook in very small amount of salted water until beans become bright green (approximately 10-15 minutes). Drain well, and while they are still warm mix with sunflower seeds and a small amount of soy sauce.

Variation: SUNNY CARROTS—Replace half the string beans with ¼ pound carrots that have been cut into thin sticks. Or use carrots only, chopped into thin round slices and steamed.

BEET SALAD

8 medium beets	lemon juice
1 large onion, diced	salt
½ cup oil	pepper

Boil beets in skins until soft. Peel and grate on either of the wider sides of the grater (stringy or slices). Add onion and oil, lemon juice, salt and pepper. Mix well and refrigerate.

BAKED BROCCOLI

1½ cups cooked broccoli	¼-½ teaspoon pepper
3 eggs	2 tablespoons chopped parsley
1 tablespoon flour	¼ teaspoon grated lemon rind
1½ cups liquid (vegetable stock, or non-dairy creamer)	1 teaspoon lemon juice
	⅛ teaspoon nutmeg
1½ teaspoons salt	⅛ teaspoon dill

Cook broccoli. Drain well, chop and set aside. Break eggs into 2-quart bowl with flour. Beat well.

Add all remaining ingredients except broccoli to the eggs. Mix together well, then add broccoli and mix. Place in lightly greased 9″ square or round baking dish. To avoid casserole becoming too dry, place the baking dish into a larger dish filled with 1″ warm water. Bake at 350° for 45 minutes.

BROCCOLI VINAIGRETTE

4 10-ounce packages broccoli spears	⅓ cup snipped parsley
⅔ cup minced green pepper	4 eggs, hard-boiled and diced
⅔ cup dill pickle, chopped	2¼ ounces jarred capers, drained

Dressing:

1 cup salad oil	1½ tablespoons salt
⅓ cup vinegar	1½ tablespoons paprika
⅓ cup lemon juice	1½ tablespoons dried oregano
1 tablespoon sugar	dash cayenne

Cook frozen broccoli spears according to package directions. Drain. Combine in a large bowl with green pepper, pickle, eggs and caper.

In screw-top jar, combine salad oil, vinegar, lemon juice, sugar, salt, paprika, crushed oregano and cayenne. Shake well. Pour over salad mixture.

Carrot Tzimmes

There are a variety of interesting ways to use carrots as a side dish. Sweetened carrots, called *tzimmes,* are also traditionally served the night of Rosh Hashana (page 39). Tzimmes is also often found on the Shabbos table as well.

BELGIAN-HAWAIIAN CARROTS

2 pounds frozen Belgian carrots or	⅓-½ cup honey
2 pounds canned Belgian carrots, drained	2 tablespoons brown sugar
1 16-ounce can unsweetened pineapple chunks with juice	1 teaspoon salt

Use a 4-quart pot. Add all ingredients and mix them together. Bring to boil, then cook on a medium flame for 15-20 minutes. When using frozen carrots, cook an additional 10 minutes.

CANDIED CARROTS

4 carrots	½ stick margarine
½ teaspoon salt	1 orange (optional)
⅓ cup brown sugar	

Cook sliced carrots in small amount of salted water. Drain water. Save ⅓-½ cup of water and set aside in a small pan . To that add the brown sugar and margarine and cook over low heat until margarine melts. Pour syrup over carrots and serve.

Variation: BAKED CANDIED CARROTS—Prepare carrots as above, then place in a 9″ × 9″ baking dish. Leave sides of pan free, and place orange slices along all four sides. Bake at 350° for ½ hour. The taste of oranges will become absorbed in the carrots, but the orange slices themselves become too dry to serve.

CAN-OPENER TZIMMES

1 2-pound can yams	¼ cup honey, sugar, or brown sugar
1 can pineapple chunks, drained	¼ teaspoon of salt
1 can mandarin oranges, drained	lemon juice, if needed

Pour yams with liquid into a large saucepan. Add all other ingredients. Keep tasting for desired amount of sweetness or tartness. Add lemon juice if necessary. Boil until liquid is almost gone and contents are browned and glazed.

CARROT LATKES

For this interesting variation of potato latkes, see Potatoes, Section XI.

CARROT LOAF

2 cups carrots, grated	1½ cups flour
1 cup margarine	1 teaspoon baking power
½ cup brown sugar, packed	½ teaspoon baking soda
1 egg, beaten	1 teaspoon salt
3 tablespoons citrus juice	½ teaspoon cinnamon

Grate the carrots. Cream the margarine and sugar and combine with egg, juice, and dry ingredients. Blend in grated carrots and place into an ungreased mold. Bake for 30 minutes at 350°.

Variation: CARROT CRUNCH—Add ½ cup ground nuts before baking.

EASY CARROT TZIMMES

1 bag carrots	orange juice
2 medium sweet potatoes	dash of salt
½ cup brown sugar	

Peel carrots and sweet potatoes. Cut into small pieces. Top with brown sugar and salt. Pour orange juice over ingredients to cover. Cook over low flame till tender, approximately 1 hour.

SWEET CARROT TZIMMES

1 bunch carrots cut into 1″ pieces	½ cup honey
6 sweet potatoes	½ teaspoon salt
½ cup pitted prunes (optional)	¼ teaspoon cinnamon
1 cup orange juice	margarine or oil

Cook carrots and sweet potatoes in boiling, salted water to cover, until tender but firm. Line a shallow baking dish with silver foil. Drain carrots and sweet potatoes and place in pan with prunes. Stir gently. Mix orange juice, honey, salt, and cinnamon, and pour evenly over casserole. Dot top with margarine or corn oil. Cover with foil and bake in preheated oven at 350° for 30 minutes. Stir gently and bake uncovered another 10 minutes.

COATED CAULIFLOWER

1 head cauliflower	2 teaspoons parsley
or	salt
1 10-ounce package cauliflower	pepper
3 tablespoons margarine	garlic
¼ cup bread crumbs	

Cook cauliflower in small amount of water with 1 teaspoon salt. Cook over medium flame until soft. Drain well.

While cauliflower is still hot, coat with margarine on all sides and cover with bread crumbs, parsley and seasoning. Place lid on pot, and let margarine and seasoning melt into cauliflower. Serve warm.

Note: To reheat, warm in oven for 15 minutes at 350°.

JUICY CAULIFLOWER

1 head cauliflower	thyme
½ teaspoon salt	basil
½ tablespoon lemon juice	oil

Cook cauliflower in a small amount of salted water. A bit of lemon juice added to the water will keep cauliflower white. Cook until tender. When ready, drain well, and season with small amount of oil, thyme, and basil.

Variation: STEAMED CAULIFLOWER—Place cauliflower on a rack above the salted water. Bring to a boil and cook *covered* for 5-10 minutes until tender. Add ¼ teaspoon salt to the other seasonings.

CAULIFLOWER SALAD

1½-2 cups cauliflower, thinly sliced	2 tablespoons oil
½ cup ripe black olives, coarsely chopped	salt
¼ cup pimentos, drained and chopped	pepper
	pinch of marjoram
	pinch of oregano
¼ cup green onions, minced	5 cups torn greens

Put cauliflower, olives, pimentos and green onions in large bowl. Add oil and toss. While tossing, add salt, pepper, marjoram and oregano. Add greens and toss again. Excellent with all meat dishes.

Serves 6.

Chick Peas-Arbis

Chickpeas are traditionally served to the guests the first Friday night after the birth of a new son. (See *Yiddishe Simchas—Sholom Zochor,* page 306.) Chickpeas are also commonly called *arbis* or *nahit.*

CHICKPEAS

4 pounds chickpeas	black or white pepper
2 tablespoons salt	

The day before: check the peas thoroughly to remove any dust or foreign particles. Wash them well and drain. Put them in a large pot with a large quantity of water. Let soak uncovered, for at least six hours. This serves to soften and enlarge the chickpeas.

Then, drain peas in a colander. Put into a pot, filling with water slightly higher than peas. Add salt and cook for approximately 3 hours, or until you notice skin beginning to peel off peas.

While still warm, drain extremely well in a colander. Spread a thick absorbent towel on table and empty drained chickpeas onto it. Spread the peas evenly over the whole towel. Sprinkle lightly with black pepper. Take both ends of towel and bring together so that peas touch one another and pepper becomes distributed and absorbed evenly.

Refrigerate as soon as cooled and *keep in refrigerator* until immediately before serving. Serve in round bowls. There will be enough for approximately 50 people.

EREV SHABBOS CHICKPEAS

When the baby is born on Friday, and there is not time to prepare the chickpeas in the regular fashion, quick measures must be taken. You can use canned chickpeas, for they have already been cooked and you can prepare this easy dish well before Shabbos begins.

5 cans cooked chickpeas	½-1 teaspoon black pepper
3 tablespoons salt	

Drain cans of chickpeas. Place them in large pot and rinse well, then drain in a colander. Spread them out on paper towels or dishtowels on top of a table or counter. Pat them until completely dry. Sprinkle with salt and pepper to taste. Mix well. Refrigerate until serving.

❊❊❊❊

EGGPLANT PARMESAN

A popular eggplant dish baked with cheese. See Dairy, Section V.

EGGPLANT RELISH

2 medium eggplants	water
2 medium zucchini	½ cup ketchup
1 large onion	1 tablespoon sugar
1 green pepper	salt
oil	pepper

Peel eggplant and zucchini and cut into cubes. Dice onion and green pepper. Heat oil in large frying pan or Dutch oven. Sauté the onion until golden brown and then add eggplant, zucchini, and green pepper.

Add small amount of water. Eggplant and zucchini will shrink in size when cooked. Put in ketchup and seasoning and cook another minute or two. Set out in a bowl to be eaten separately, or as a delightful accompaniment to bread.

STEWED EGGPLANT

2 small green peppers	1 6-ounce can of tomatoes
1 small onion	salt
oil	dash of pepper
1 eggplant	

Dice green peppers and onion. Sauté green pepper in oil over a medium flame approximately 5 minutes, then add the onion and sauté until onion becomes golden brown.

Grate or cube peeled eggplant and add to pot. Pour in the juice of a can of tomatoes. Cook over a medium flame for 20-30 minutes. Afterwards, add seasoning and cut up tomatoes from can. Mix all together when warm and refrigerate.

Variations: Dice 1-2 stalks of celery and combine with green pepper, or grate 1-2 carrots and add together with the eggplants.
Instead of canned tomatoes, season with 14-ounce can of tomato sauce or approximately 1 ounce ketchup with 2 ounces water.
SWEET-SPICY EGGPLANT—When nearly ready add ¼ cup of sugar and mix in well. Put in 5 bay leaves for about 10 minutes, then remove them.

RED LIMA BEANS

2 packages frozen lima beans	garlic powder
⅓ stick margarine	8-ounce can tomato sauce

Melt margarine in pan. Add unthawed frozen lima beans. Generously sprinkle garlic powder on beans. Pour tomato sauce on top. Bring to boil, and cook in covered pot for 30 minutes. Serves 5-6.

Mock Chopped Liver

This is an excellent dish for entrées and hors d'oeuvres or as an accompaniment to the main dish. It is often served to guests on occasions when food is served buffet style. You and your guests will be surprised to see how similar in look and taste this vegetable dish is to liver.

LIMA LIVER

10 ounces (1 package frozen) lima beans	¼ bag nuts, ground
3-4 eggs, hard-boiled	2 onions, diced
	salt to taste

Cook beans and eggs separately. Sauté onion in frying pan. Combine all ingredients in blender and mix well until spreading consistency is attained.

VEGETARIAN CHOPPED LIVER

4 eggs	½ pound ground walnuts
⅓ pound kasha	6 onions
5 or 6 stalks celery	2 or 3 cubes boullion broth
1 can string beans	salt
1 can peas	

Cook eggs and kasha. Dice and sauté onions. Grind cooked eggs and kasha together with stringbeans, peas, walnuts and celery. Mix well. Add fried onions, broth and salt. Mix well again. May be served as appetizer or as main vegetable dish.

❈❈❈

STUFFED MUSHROOMS

1 package mushrooms	pepper
1 egg	oregano
salt	matzoh meal

Wash mushrooms and remove stems. Put stems in blender with egg and spices of your choice. Add matzoh meal to obtain desired thickness. Fill mushroom caps. Place in greased pan and bake at 350° for 20 minutes.

BAKED WINTER SQUASH

This is in season in the late fall and winter. It is simple to prepare, tasty, filling and loaded with vitamins.

1 winter squash (acorn, butternut, etc.)	salt
butter or margarine	honey (optional)

Poke a few holes in the squash and bake on a baking pan or sheet in a 375° oven until tender. It should take approximately 1¼-1¾ hours. Cut the squash in half and scoop out the seeds. Cut into portions and serve. Top with butter or margarine, just as with corn on the cob. Some people like to top it with honey.

QUICK AND SWEET BAKED SQUASH

2 butternut squashes	1 tablespoon water
1 tablespoon oil	¼ teaspoon cinnamon
⅛ teaspoon salt	⅛ teaspoon nutmeg
3 tablespoons honey	

Cut squash into halves, quarters, sixths or eighths, depending on size of squash and number of portions desired. Scoop out seeds. Rub oil and salt into squash. Bake in pre-heated 375° oven for 45 minutes-1 hour until tender. Mix honey, water and spices and baste squash, either just before it finishes cooking, or just before serving.

VEGETABLE LOAF

1 cup onions, chopped	2 eggs
1 cup celery, chopped	1 teaspoon salt
1 cup raw carrots, grated	¼ teaspoon mixed seasoning
1 cup walnuts or mixed nuts, ground	1 cup liquid (water, soup stock, or non-dairy creamer)
1 cup bread crumbs, whole wheat or rye	

Heat oil in skillet over medium flame. Sauté onion, then add celery, carrots and nuts. Sauté another 15 minutes.

Add remaining ingredients. Mix everything together well, and pour into greased loaf pan. Bake at 350° for approximately 45 minutes. Delicious when topped with warm tomato sauce or mushroom sauce.

VEGETABLE CUTLETS

1 16-ounce can mixed vegetables	2 eggs, beaten
1 raw potato, grated	matzoh meal
1 medium onion, sauteed	

Drain and mash mixed vegetables. Add potato, onion, eggs and just enough matzoh meal to hold ingredients together—approximately ¼ cup. Do not make a thick batter. It should be a bit watery. Shape into 3 or 4 patties. Fry in vegetable oil on both sides until browned.

VEGETABLE KUGEL

3 carrots	wheat germ
1 10-ounce package frozen string beans	salt
2 eggs	oil

Peel carrots. Cut into pieces and cook for a short time in a pressure cooker. When cooked, drain and mash. Add 1 egg and enough wheat germ to make slightly firm. Add salt.

In a separate pot, cook the string beans. Drain very well and mash. Add 1 egg, wheat germ and salt. Mix well. Grease a 9″ × 9″ baking pan, spread carrot mixture on the bottom, then top with layer of string bean mixture. Bake at 350° for 45 minutes.

VEGETABLE KISHKE

A Shabbos afternoon side dish which is either baked separately or cooked wrapped in aluminum foil in the Shabbos cholent. See Soup Accompaniments, Section VI.

Vinaigrette

A delicious Russian potato and beet salad with a tangy dressing. It is very colorful. An excellent side dish for meat or chicken.

VINAIGRETTE

6-8 medium potatoes, boiled	3 tablespoons oil
2 cans (1 pound) cooked beets	1½ tablespoons vinegar or lemon juice
½ bunch scallions	1 teaspoon salt
3 sour pickles	
6 radishes (optional)	

Cut peeled potatoes and beets into cubes. Dice scallions, pickles and radishes. Mix together. Add dressing ingredients and toss well until potatoes take on a red appearance. Taste for sufficient tartness, adding more seasoning if necessary.

BOILED AND COLORFUL VINAIGRETTE

8 medium beets	½ cup oil
3 medium potatoes	lemon juice
5 carrots	vinegar (optional)
1 cup sour pickles	salt
1 medium onion	pepper
1 cup sauerkraut, drained (optional)	

Peel beets and boil together with unpeeled potatoes and carrots. Cook until soft. Then peel potatoes and carrots.

Dice beets, potatoes, carrots, pickles and onion. Combine all vegetables and toss together for a few minutes.

Add sauerkraut, oil, lemon juice, salt and pepper. Mix again. Refrigerate.

EASY SWEET AND SOUR VINAIGRETTE

5 large potatoes	1 tablespoon salt
5 large beets	½ cup sugar
2 packages carrots	½ cup vinegar
5 large pickles, cut in rounds	½ cup oil
1 onion, diced or 2 scallions	

Rinse potatoes, beets and carrots well, without peeling. Place into large pot and cook for approximately 1½ hours. Drain. Let vegetables cool, then peel and cut into small pieces.

Add pickles, onions, and dressing ingredients. Mix everything together very well, until potatoes take on a reddish color.

❊❈❊

STEWED ZUCCHINI

1 pound small green zucchini or yellow summer squash	1½ teaspoons salt
oil or margarine for frying	⅛ teaspoon pepper
	¼-½ teaspoon oregano
1 onion, chopped	1 tablespoon water
1 green pepper, chopped (optional)	

Wash unpeeled zucchini. Dry and cut into thin, cucumber-like slices. Heat oil in skillet. Add chopped onion and sauté until soft, but not brown. Add sliced zucchini and continue sautéeing another 5 minutes. It is not necessary to add more oil; the zucchini will not burn. Add seasoning and water. Simmer another 15-20 minutes.

Variations: 'ZUCCORNY'—After zucchini sautés, add 1 8-ounce undrained can of corn and 1 4-ounce can of mushrooms. Bring to a boil, add seasoning, and simmer for 15-20 minutes.

RICE 'ZUCCORNY'—Add ½ cup uncooked rice, 1½ cups water and ½ teaspoon salt together with corn and mushrooms and cook until rice is done.

PINK RICE 'ZUCCORNY'—Add 3 tablespoons ketchup or tomato puree with rice. This should turn the liquid from the corn light pink.

DIET SQUASH MASH (Zucchini)

See the Dairy Section V.

Fresh Salads

The fresh vegetables used for salads are abundantly rich in nutrients, colorful and very refreshing. Slice them or dice them—use them by themselves, in combination, or as decoration for food platters.

AVOCADO SPREAD

2-3 small avocados	½ teaspoon coriander seed
6 eggs, hard-boiled	(optional)
1 large onion, chopped	2 tablespoons vinegar or lemon or
2 tablespoons salt	lime juice
½ teaspoon ground chili powder	lettuce leaves
¼ cup minced parsley	

Peel avocado, eggs, and mash well together. Combine with chopped onion. Add all the seasoning and mix well. Serve scoops on bed of lettuce.

BLUEBERRY-RADISH SALAD with Orange-Parsley Dressing

6 cup torn greens	1 cup fresh blue berries
1½ cup shredded radishes	

Dressing:

1 teaspoon grated orange rind	2 tablespoons minced parsley
juice of one orange	salt
6 teaspoon oil	white pepper

Wash greens well and tear by hand. Put them into a bowl. Top with radishes and sprinkle with blueberries.

Make dressing by combining rind, juice, oil and parsley. Season with salt and pepper.

Add dressing. Makes six servings.

Coleslaw

Coleslaw is a seasoned cabbage salad side dish. It is popularly served buffet style at a Shabbos-afternoon kiddush, or on special occasions.

BASIC COLESLAW

4 cups cabbage, finely shredded	⅓ cup green peppers, slivered
⅓ cup celery, chopped	¼ cup radishes, sliced
⅓ cup carrots, grated	1 tablespoon onion, minced

Dressing:

½ cup mayonnaise	¾ teaspoon salt
¼ cup pineapple juice	½ teaspoon sugar
1 tablespoon vinegar or lemon juice	dash of pepper
	paprika

Mix vegetables together. Combine dressing ingredients and toss gently with salad. Refrigerate until ready to serve. Serve 4.

Variations: DAIRY COLESLAW—Coleslaw is tossed in sour cream and seasoning. See Dairy, Section V.

COLESLAW AND TANGY DRESSING

1 cabbage	¼ cup boiled water
1 carrot	mayonnaise to taste
1 green pepper	2 tablespoons sugar
1 medium onion	1 tablespoon salt
¼ cup vinegar or lemon juice	

Finely slice the vegetables and mix together. Then combine dressing ingredients. Pour over vegetables and toss well.

CUCUMBER SALAD

3-4 cucumbers	½ cup water
1 tablespoon salt	½ tablespoon sugar
1 onion	pepper
½ cup vinegar	paprika

Peel cucumbers and slice thinly. Place them with salt in bowl and let stand ½ hour or longer. Squeeze water out of cucumber slices and place in clean bowl. Slice onion rings thinly into bowl. Add vinegar, water, sugar, pepper, and paprika. Refrigerate.

Serve cold with meat or chicken.

CUCUMBER-RADISH PLATE

1 large cucumber, sliced thinly	¾ cup radishes, sliced
2 tablespoons sugar	½ cup vinegar or lemon juice
¼ cup water	2 teaspoons chopped candied
¼ teaspoon salt	ginger

Combine all ingredients in a deep mixing bowl. Cover and refrigerate for 2-4 hours. To serve: drain off the marinade. Arrange vegetables on serving plates. Makes 4 servings.

FRESH GARDEN SALAD

1 lettuce	4 scallions
3 tomatoes	2 pickles
1 green pepper	6-8 radishes
1 cucumber	

Shred lettuce by hand. Cut other vegetables into small pieces. Toss all together. Blend with any type of dressing or pour dressing over vegetables just before serving.

ISRAELI SALAD

1 large tomato	6 radishes
1 large cucumber	lettuce leaves (optional)
1 large green pepper	olives (optional)
3-4 scallions	

Dressing:

1 tablespoon olive oil	pepper or vinegar
2 teaspoons lemon juice or black	½ teaspoon salt

Dice all vegetables into very small pieces. Mix well. Add dressing just before serving.

RELISH TRAYS

4 green peppers	10 sour pickles
8 large carrots	1 pack cherry tomatoes
3 stalks celery	8 ounces green olives

When preparing for a lot of company or a big affair, a colorful relish tray of fresh, crispy vegetables on each table is a nice touch.

Remove top and core of pepper. Cut into slices or rings. Peel carrots, and slice lengthwise, about 4-6 slices per carrot. Wash off celery stalks and remove leaves. Cut into lengthwise strips. Cut pickles lengthwise also.

Divide sliced vegetables into different relish trays. Put a few tomatoes and olives in each tray and arrange attractively.

Pickles

Here are two simple recipes for making your own home-made pickles.

DILL PICKLES

Approximately 5 pounds small cucumbers
1 bunch fresh dill
3-4 garlic cloves, cut in half
½ teaspoon pickling spices (optional)
1 cup salt
4 quarts water
2 1-gallon jar

Wash cucumbers very well. Cut off ends. Place dill and garlic into a gallon jar. Put in cucumbers. Pour 1 cup salt into the other gallon jar. Then fill the jar to the top with water. Mix well. Pour this salted water solution into the jar with the pickles, filling it to the top. (The amount of water needed for a gallon jar will vary depending on size and amount of pickles in jar; the ratio is ¼ cup salt to 1 quart water.)

Cover tightly and keep in a dark room or closet. They will be half sour after one week (and completely sour after 2 weeks).

SOUR PICKLES

5 pounds cucumbers, very tiny and firm
⅓ bunch of dill
⅓ head of garlic
5 tablespoons salt
hot water

Wash cucumbers and dill very well. Put cucumbers into a glass jar until ¾ full. Crush garlic slightly and place in between cucumbers and cover. Pour in salt.

Boil a teakettle of water. Slowly pour boiled water into jar until completely filled. (Hint: Place blade of knife under the jar so that glass won't crack from heat.) Do not handle jar until water has cooled off, as the jar might break.

Close jar lightly and put into a sunny place. After 2-3 days, taste *water* to check if it is sour enough. If not, add a bit more salt. Pickles will be ready within one week.

198

Helpful Hints

Keeping Vegetables Crisp: Clean and peel vegetables. Cut to desired sizes. Put the vegetables in container of cold water and refrigerate overnight. This treatment is ideal for celery stalks, radishes, carrots, etc.

Carrots: Peel under cold water and hands won't become orange.

Carrot Curls: Use potato peeler and slice thin carrot curls down length of carrot. To keep them crisp, see above.

Decorating Cucumbers: Make grooves down length of cucumber on all sides with a fork. Then slice the cucumber.

Green Pepper:

Preparing—Cut tops from green peppers and remove all seeds.

Dips—Use as a container for dips or stuffing. This adds flavor as well as glamor.

Garnish—Cut into rings. Decorate platter or use in salads.

Lettuce:

Keeping Crisp—Wash and clean immediately after buying. Then store in refrigerator.

Cutting—Tear lettuce for salads, don't cut. Cutting makes lettuce shrivel.

Separating leaves—Hold lettuce under hot running water, head up. Leaves will separate easily. Then wash leaves in cold water. Drain and refrigerate.

Peeling Onions: To avoid tears, peel onion next to cold running water, or keep in refrigerator in covered container before using.

Radish Roses: Cut thin, shallow petals around outside of radish. Repeat and cut a few more petals inside. Then make 2 or 3 cuts in center. Crisp in cold water overnight.

Peeling Tomatoes: To skin a tomato easily, spear with fork, plunge into boiling water and then into cold. Peel from top downward.

Stuffed Vegetables: Hollowed out tomatoes and green peppers can be used as containers for salad dips, or stuffed with various spreads such as avocado, eggs, or tuna.

Green pepper and tomato rings can be very decorative when filled with scoops of salads, rice, or mashed potatoes.

Garnishes: Use lettuce leaves, and green pepper and tomato rings, generously as garnishes on your main dish.

Salad Dressings

Give a tangy taste to your salad. Add variety to your meals by alternating dressings with basic vegetable salads. Toss dressing together with salad or spoon on top—unless otherwise specified in recipe.

HOME-MADE CHRAINE (HORSERADISH)

1 pound horseradish root	1 teaspoon sugar
½ pound raw beets	¼ cup vinegar or lemon juice
1 teaspoon salt	

Peel and grate horseradish and beets. (To avoid tearing while peeling horseradish, keep your face turned to the side or cover your nose and mouth with a handkerchief.) Add seasoning and mix thoroughly. Store in refrigerator in a closed glass jar.

FRENCH DRESSING

French dressing usually includes oil, vinegar, mustard, sugar, salt and pepper.

½ cup salad oil	½ teaspoon dry mustard
2 tablespoons lemon juice	½ teaspoon paprika
2 tablespoons vinegar	dash of cayenne
1 teapoon sugar	⅛ teaspoon garlic powder (optional)
½ teaspoon salt	

Combine all ingredients in a screw-top jar, cover and shake well. Keep chilled. Makes about ¾ cup.

HORSERADISH DRESSING

1 cup mayonnaise	¼-½ cup prepared horseradish

Combine ingredients and mix. Refrigerate before serving.

ITALIAN DRESSING

Italian dressing usually includes oil, vinegar, crushed garlic, salt and pepper. Combine in varying amounts, according to taste.

LEMON HERBAL DRESSING

⅔ cup salad oil
⅓ cup freshly squeezed lemon
    juice
2 teaspoons freshly grated lemon
    peel

2 teaspoons parsley
2 teaspoons basil
½ teaspoon paprika
¼ teaspoon salt
½ teaspoon pepper

Combine ingredients in tightly covered container. Shake well and refrigerate.

MAYONNAISE

1 egg yolk (raw)
1 egg yolk (boiled)
½ cup oil

2 teaspoons vinegar or lemon
    juice
salt

Mix the 2 yolks together until smooth. Add oil and vinegar to form paste. Season to taste.

MAYONNAISE DRESSING

1½ tablespoons lemon juice
¼ cup mayonnaise

¼ teaspoon sugar
dash of chili powder (optional)

Add lemon juice to mayonnaise until mayonnaise becomes smooth and liquidy. Add sugar (and chili powder) and mix well.

Note: In addition to salads, this dressing is great for pouring over cooked vegetables such as asparagus, broccoli, brussel sprouts and cauliflower.

HOME-MADE SEASONED MAYONNAISE

1 egg
1 cup oil
3 teaspoons lemon juice
½ teaspoon salt

¼ teaspoon sugar
¼ teaspoon onion powder
⅛ teaspoon garlic powder

Whip the egg in a blender. Then, very slowly, add oil to egg, whipping continuously.

Add all the seasoning. The mixture should thicken. When it is at desired consistency, remove from blender and store in refrigerator.

RUSSIAN DRESSING

Russian dressing contains mayonnaise and ketchup.

½ cup mayonnaise
¼ cup ketchup
3 tablespoons lemon juice

1 tablespoon onion powder
¼ teaspoon celery salt

Mix together all ingredients and chill. Excellent on fresh salads.

Variation: For a strong taste, add 1 tablespoon horseradish.

BASIC WHITE SAUCE

1 tablespoon margarine
salt
1 tablespoon flour

1 cup water, non-dairy creamer, or soup stock

Melt margarine. Stir in flour and salt. Gradually add liquid until mixture thickens to desired consistency. Add mushrooms, herbs, fried onions, etc.
Yields 1 cup. Use to top an omelet or your favorite vegetable.

Grains, Noodles, and Potatoes

Grains, Noodles, and Potatoes

Grains, Noodles, and Potatoes

Kasha

Buckwheat groats, or *kasha* as it has always been known to Jews, is an excellent food. It can be used as a cereal or as a vegetable. High in energy, low in starch, it is easily digestible and exceedingly nourishing.

BASIC KASHA

1 cup kasha	1 teaspoon salt
2 cups water	¼ teaspoon pepper

Boil water in kettle. Meanwhile, heat kasha in pot until grains become dry and separated (about 3 minutes). Add seasoning and hot water. Cover with lid and cook for 20 minutes over a medium flame.

FANCY KASHA

1 onion	oil for frying
½ cup mushrooms (optional)	2 cups soupstock or water
1 cup kasha	1 teaspoon salt
1 egg	¼ teaspoon pepper

Heat oil in 2-quart pan or pot that has a tight-fitting cover. Dice and sauté onions (and mushrooms) until onion is golden brown. Add kasha and then egg. Continue to sauté for another two minutes while mixing with fork or wooden spoon, until grains are no longer sticking.

Simultaneously, bring liquid to a boil. Pour boiling liquid over kasha, add seasoning, and simmer for 20 minutes or until kasha is puffy and dry.

KASHA KNISHES

Knishes are an ever popular, famous Jewish delicacy, and deservedly so. They are a dough mixture filled inside, and then baked in the oven till crispy brown.

Dough:

2 cups flour, sifted	1 tablespoon oil
½ teaspoon salt	2 tablespoons water
1 teaspoon baking powder	2 eggs, well beaten

Filling:

2 cups cooked kasha (1 cup raw)	1 egg
1 onion, diced and sautéed	

Mix dry ingredients. Form a well and add all liquids ingredients. Mix to form a smooth dough. Roll out to ½″ thickness. Then prepare and mix together kasha filling. Fill dough with mixture. Roll up as you would a jelly roll. Moisten edges and fold over. Place in a pan greased with oil. Bake at 350° until brown and crisp. Slice.

Variation: POTATO KNISHES, see page 211.

NUTTY KASHA CUTLETS

½ onion, chopped	2-4 tablespoons sunflower seeds
2 cups cooked kasha	oil for frying
1 egg, slightly beaten	

Sauté onion until golden brown and add to kasha. Then add egg and sunflower seeds. Shape kasha into patties, heat oil in skillet, and fry patties until slightly crisp on both sides.

KASHA VARNISHKES

A popular, classic Jewish dish.

1 cup cooked kasha	2 tablespoons margarine
¾ cup bowtie noodles	

Prepare kasha according to *Basic Kasha* recipe. (For added flavor, cook with sautéed onions.) Cook and drain bowtie noodles (*varnishkes*). Combine cooked kasha with cooked noodles. Mix together with margarine.

Note: Proportion of kasha and varnishkes may be varied for two cups of cooked kasha; anywhere from 1 cup to 2 cups of noodles is common.

Variations: COMPANY KASHA VARNISHKES—prepare kasha according to *Fancy Kasha* recipe. Mix with noodles and margarine, place into a greased casserole, and bake for twenty minutes.
Treat your guests by enhancing this dish with a creamy vegetable sauce. You might try the white sauce on page 202, adding sautéed onions and mushrooms.

BAKED KASHA AND VEGETABLES

1 cup kasha	2 carrots, grated
4 ounces mushrooms	1 small onion, grated
oil	

Prepare kasha according to *Basic Kasha* recipe. Sauté mushrooms in oil. Grate the carrots and onion, mix with mushrooms.

Combine vegetables with kasha, adding seasoning if necessary. Mix well. Put in a greased baking pan and bake at 375° for 20 minutes.

Other Kasha Uses: KASHA & VEGETABLE STUFFING, page 159.
KASHA CEREAL, page 105.
KASHA CHOLENT, page 122.

Noodles

Generally, noodles may be prepared according to the instructions on the box. In addition to the recipes below, many of the Meat Dishes go well with noodles, and are so indicated. Similarly, a number of recipes in the Dairy section feature various combinations of noodles and cheeses.

In this section we are including only *pareve* noodle side dishes.

Noodles are known in Yiddish as *lokshen*. The word immediately evokes a Shabbos afternoon side dish, *lokshen kugel*, which fills the bulk of our Noodle Section. Try out various recipes—sweet or salty, baked or fried. When you get really ambitious and have a little extra time, try to make our Yerushalayim Kugel.

Potato Kugel recipes are included in the Potato Section.

FRIED CABBAGE AND NOODLES

1	head cabbage	1	8-ounce package noodles
1	tablespoon salt		salt
1	ounce oil or margarine		pepper

Cut cabbage fine and sprinkle with 1 tablespoon salt. Let stand 10-15 minutes. Squeeze out the cabbage juice and fry the cabbage in oil until brown.

Cook the noodles and drain. Combine all ingredients. Add salt and pepper to taste.

BROWN FARFEL AND MUSHROOMS

2	tablespoons oil	1-1½ cups water
1	onion, diced	salt
1	4-ounce can mushrooms	pepper
8	ounces uncooked farfel	

Heat oil and sauté in a 2-quart saucepan. When onion is golden brown, add mushrooms and sauté another minute. Then add, in order, farfel, water and seasoning. Cook over a low flame for approximately 20 minutes, mixing occasionally.

MACARONI TUNA SALAD

8	ounces macaroni	1 medium apple
1	7-ounce can tuna fish	mayonnaise
2	sour pickles	salt
2	scallions	cinnamon (optional)
1	stalk celery	

Cook and drain macaroni. Mix with tuna fish. Chop pickles, scallions, celery and apple. Combine all ingredients and mix very well.

MACARONI VEGETABLE SALAD

2 ounces macaroni	1 teaspoon salt
1 cup carrots	½ cup mayonnaise
1 cup cooked peas or beans	¼ teaspoon pepper
⅓-½ cup celery	salad greens and tomatoes
¼ small onion	
½ cup red cabbage, finely shredded (optional)	

Cook and drain macaroni. Dice and cook carrots. Chop celery and onion finely. Add seasoning and mix all ingredients together. Serve on bed of lettuce and garnish with tomatoes for a nice effect.

Noodle Kugels

A Shabbos afternoon side dish (see page 26).

APPLE—LOKSHEN KUGEL (*Sweet*)

1 8-ounce package medium egg noodles
¼ cup melted margarine or oil
4 eggs, beaten
3 medium apples
¼ cup dark seedless raisins (optional)
¼ cup sugar (optional)
1½ teaspoon salt
2 teaspoon cinnamon
½ teaspoon vanilla

Cook and drain noodles and put in large bowl. Stir in margarine and eggs. Peel and chop apples. If using raisins, rinse in hot water and drain. Combine all ingredients together, add seasoning and mix well.

Preheat oven to 350°. Pour kugel mixture into a greased 9″ x 13″ baking pan. Bake for 40 minutes to 1 hour or until lightly browned. Makes 12 pieces. *Note:* For extra softness add another 2 eggs.

FRIED LOKSHEN KUGEL

1 12-ounce package fine noodles	salt
4 tablespoons oil	pepper
4-5 eggs, beaten	oil for frying

Boil noodles until slightly tender. Drain in colander. Put noodles into bowl and add oil. Let cool (approximately 15 minutes). Add beaten eggs and salt and pepper.

Heat oil for ½ minute in 10″ large frying skillet. Pour in noodle mixture and fry on a *medium* flame. After 15 minutes lift kugel with spatula and slide onto a large plate. Add more oil to pan if necessary. Then flip kugel over second side, slide into pan, and fry for another 10-15 minutes.

Variation: Add 2-4 tablespoons matzoh meal to mixture before frying. Instead of frying, this kugel may be baked for one hour at 375°.

LOKSHEN FRUIT KUGEL (Sweet)

1	pound medium-wide noodles	1 cup sugar
4	ounces margarine	2 tablespoons cinnamon
5	eggs, well beaten	vanilla (optional)
1	cup fruit cocktail	
	or	
1	can crushed pineapple	

Add margarine to cooked noodles and mix well. Add all other ingredients and stir. Bake in pre-heated greased 8″ x 12″ pan at 350-375° for 1 hour.

MACARONI KUGEL

8	ounces macaroni, cooked and drained	4 tablespoons oil
4-5	eggs, well beaten	salt
		pepper

Preheat oven to 375°. Grease a 9″ × 9″ pan with a small amount of oil, just enough to cover surface of pan. Place into preheated oven for 5 minutes.

Meanwhile, combine all the ingredients, mix well and taste to adjust seasoning. Pour into heated pan and bake for over an hour until top is lightly browned.

PINEAPPLE SAUCE LOKSHEN KUGEL (Sweet)

8	ounces ¼″ noodles, cooked and drained	1 can applesauce
4-5	eggs	¾ cup sugar
½	cup oil	¼ teaspoon cinnamon
1	can crushed pineapple	½ teaspoon salt

Combine all ingredients. Mix together very well. Pour mixture into a greased 9″ × 13″ pan. Sprinkle with cinnamon and sugar. Bake at 400° for ¾ hour.

YERUSHALAYIM NOODLE KUGEL

This is a popular Israeli kugel. Many Americans make sure to bring this recipe back to the States after a trip to Israel. It takes a little bit of skill and patience to make it come out right. We hope it will be well worth your try.

1	12-ounce package thin vermicelli	salt
	oil	pepper
3	tablespoons sugar	4 tablespoons oil
3-4	eggs	¼ cup water

Boil noodles, drain and set aside.

Put the sugar in a small saucepan, brown it in oil over a low flame for 2-3 minutes, watching it carefully so that it does not burn. As soon as the sugar turns a nice caramel color, add the water. It will get hard immediately. Boil on low flame for a couple of minutes until it gets syrupy. Add this syrup to cooked noodles. Mix well until all noodles are coated.

In separate saucepan heat 4 tablespoons oil. While hot or still warm, add to noodles. Mix in. Then add eggs and seasoning.

Kugel may be prepared either by greasing deep pot and baking in oven at 375° for 1 hour, or by frying well on both sides.

Potatoes

The potato is an extremely versatile side dish: cook it, mash it, fry it. Make it into salads, or bake it whole or halved, peeled or unpeeled, spiced or just glazed, and of course try it out for a potato kugel.

HUNGARIAN BAKED POTATOES

4 baking potatoes	oil for frying
2 large onions	1½-2 tablespoons paprika

Bake potatoes whole at 350°. Dice and fry two large onions. Add the paprika. Fry until golden brown. When potatoes are done, slice with skins on and add the paprika and onion mixture.

Combine well and serve hot. Makes 4 servings.

SOFT BAKED POTATOES

Wash potatoes, pierce with fork and cover with tin foil. Bake at 350° for 45 minutes to 1 hour, or until soft. Cut a slice from the top of each potato. When soft, cut off part of skin to scoop out all of potato. Whip potato with non-dairy creamer or boiling water and lots of margarine. The mixture should have a sticky texture. Fill potato shells and return to oven until lightly browned. Bake for 30 minutes. Can be frozen when done.

SPICY BAKED POTATOES

6 medium potatoes	1 tablespoon salt
3 tablespoons oil	dash of black pepper
1½ tablespoon paprika	

Scrub potatoes well and cut into halves. In small dish, combine oil and seasoning. Line a 9″ × 13″ baking pan with aluminum foil (to avoid a messy clean-up job later). Place potato halves on pan and drizzle tops with oil mixture. Bake at 350° for 1½-2 hours. Serve hot.

BOILED POTATOES

Use medium size smooth potatoes. Scrub potatoes well. Do not peel. Place in pot with salted water to cover and cook until tender—approximately 1-1½ hours, depending on amount. When potatoes can easily be pierced with a fork turn off flame. Let cool a few minutes. Drain water. Peel before using.
Uses: in potato salad; to serve as a side dish plain or with meat gravy, or to rebake in spices, etc.

FRENCH FRIES

4-5 potatoes
oil for frying

salt to taste

Peel potatoes. Rinse off and dry well. Then cut into thin rounds or into long julienne strips.

Heat generous amount of oil in frying pan. Then gently add potatoes to hot oil. Fry on medium flame. With spatula turn potatoes on other side and fry until crisp, another 5-10 minutes. Remove potatoes onto plate covered with paper towel to drain off excess oil. Add salt. Serve warm.

POTATO FRITTERS

2 large potatoes
1 cup cold water
1 teaspoon salt and paprika
2 egg yolks

1¼ cups flour
2 teaspoons curry powder
oil for frying

Peel potatoes and slice thinly. Spread on towel to dry. Mix rest of ingredients together. Batter should be a bit lumpy. Dip potatoes in batter and fry until fritters are puffy and golden. Makes 4 servings.

POTATO KNISHES

2 onions, diced
pastry dough for two 9″ pies (see page 275)
6-7 pounds potatoes
3 eggs
oil for frying
2-3 tablespoons black pepper
salt
beaten eggs for basting

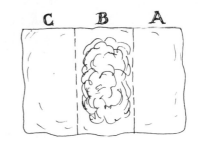

Sauté 2 diced onions and set aside. Peel and slice potatoes. Place in pot with water to cover, add salt, and cook until tender. Prepare your pastry dough and roll out into 2 or 3 very thin layers—each about 9″ square. Work with each piece separately. When potatoes are cooked, drain out most of the water and add the 2 sautéed onions with oil. Add eggs, salt and pepper. Mash well. Add layers of mashed potato on section B of pastry dough. Cover with section A, cover layer A with mashed potato and cover with section C.

Place knish whole on greased baking pan and baste, or cut into slices and baste each slice separately. Bake at 350° until brown and crisp.

Potato Kugels

Another popular Shabbos afternoon Kiddush side dish, page 26.

EASY BLENDER POTATO KUGEL

5-6 medium potatoes, cubed	¼ teaspoon baking powder
1 large onion, diced	¼ teaspoon black pepper
3 eggs	¼ cup melted margarine
1½ teaspoons salt	⅓ cup flour

Blend all ingredients until potatoes are finely ground, or approximately two minutes.

Pour into pre-heated, lightly-oiled pan and bake at 350° F. or until golden brown, about 1½-2 hours.

GOLDEN POTATO KUGEL

1 medium onion	7 tablespoons oil
6 medium potatoes	2 eggs
3 pieces of challah, crumbed (1½ cups)	¾ tablespoon salt
or	
½ cup matzoh meal	

Grate onion and potatoes. Add other ingredients, and mix well. Grease 9" x 13" baking pan. Place in warm oven for 10 minutes. Remove from oven and fill with potato mixture. Bake for 2 hours at 350° or until golden brown.

STANDARD POTATO KUGEL

4 large (or 6 medium) potatoes	1½ teaspoons salt
1 onion	⅛ teaspoon pepper
3 eggs	4 tablespoons oil (or 2 tablespoons chicken fat)
⅓ cup flour	

Peel potatoes and grate. Grate onion. Beat eggs until thick and add to potatoes along with remaining ingredients. Mix well with fork.

Place in greased casserole. Bake at 350° for at lease 1 hour or until light brown and crisp.

POTATO LATKES

Potato latkes are the classic Chanukah treat. Delicious when topped with applesauce.

5 large Idaho potatoes	salt and pepper to taste
1 large onion	oil for frying
4 eggs	pinch of baking powder (optional)
¼ cup matzoh meal or flour	

Grate potatoes and strain through colander. Grate onion. Add grated onion and eggs to potatotes. Mix well. Add matzoh meal and seasoning. Mix well. Heat oil in frying pan. Then add mixture one tablespoon at a time into oil. When golden brown turn over and brown on other side.

Variations: CARROT LATKES—Substitute an equal amount of grated carrots for potatoes.
APPLE LATKES, See Fruit Desserts, Section XIV.
CHEESE LATKES, see Dairy, Section V.

BASIC MASHED POTATOES

2 potatoes per person	salt
water to cover	oil (or margarine or gravy)

Peel and slice potatoes. Place in pot. Add water to cover and salt to taste. Bring to a boil, lower flame and cook until soft. (Approximately ½-1 hour depending on amount). Turn off heat. Let cool 15 minutes. Drain most of the liquid (which can be reserved for adding to sauce). Mash potatoes with remaining liquid until light and fluffy. Add oil, margarine, or gravy. Mash again. Serve warm.

GOLDEN FLUFFY MASHED POTATOES

4-5 potatoes	pepper
4 carrots	1 onion, chopped
1 onion, whole	2 tablespoons oil
water	2 tablespoons soup stock
salt	

Peel potatoes, carrots and onion and cook until soft in seasoned water. Drain. Remove onion and mash vegetables.

Sauté the chopped onion in oil and add it with soup stock to the mashed potatoes and vegetables. Mix together until light and fluffy.

Note: When preparing a dairy meal, milk can be substituted for the soup stock.

Potato Salad

Potato salad is another popular side dish often served buffet style—at a Shabbos afternoon Kiddush, for example, if more than just cake is served.

BASIC POTATO SALAD

2 medium potatoes, cooked and peeled	3 tablespoons mayonnaise
1-2 sour pickles	1 teaspoon vinegar
	½ teaspoon sugar
1 medium onion, or 2 scallions	1 teaspoon salt

Cube potatoes and pickles. Sliver onion. Combine other ingredients, then mix everything together well.

Variations: Use lemon juice instead of vinegar, and season with salt, and dash of garlic powder and white pepper, and a little mustard.

For added color attraction and taste, try adding a small amount of drained peas from can and shredded or thinly sliced raw carrots.

FANCY POTATO SALAD

5 pounds potatoes	½ cup mayonnaise
4 hard-boiled eggs (optional)	1 teaspoon mustard
2 stalks celery	1 teaspoon garlic powder
2 large dill pickles	salt
½ bunch scallions, finely chopped	pepper
¼ cup oil	paprika
3 tablespoons lemon juice	

Cook potatoes with skins and peel when cooled. Dice into bite-size pieces. Chop eggs, celery, pickles, and scallions and add to potatoes. Mix remaining ingredients and add to potato mixture. Mix thoroughly and sprinkle lightly with paprika.

Variation: CREAMY POTATO SALAD—For a very exotic dairy potato salad combined with cheese and olives, see Dairy, Section V.

SWEET POTATO CASSEROLE

2½ cups sweet potatoes	1 small can crushed pineapple
1 teaspoon salt	¼ cup orange juice

Cook sweet potatoes and mash well. Add remaining ingredients. Bake in greased casserole dish at 350° for 15-20 minutes. Serves 4-5.

GLAZED SWEET POTATOES

3 sweet potatoes	1 8-ounce can crushed pineapple,
water to cover	drained
¼ cup brown sugar	½ stick margarine
1 teaspoon salt	

Peel and cut sweet potatoes. Cook in salted water approximately 45 minutes until soft. Drain. Mash sweet potatoes and add brown sugar, pineapple and the margarine. Mix together well until margarine has completely melted.

Rice

Rice is a popular staple dish throughout the world. It goes well with many of the dishes in the meat section, like goulash and stews.

RICE CASSEROLE

3 cups water	1 envelope onion soup mix
½ stick margarine	1 cup rice
4 ounces undrained mushrooms	

Bring first 4 ingredients to boil. Add rice. Cook in oven on very low heat for 20 minutes to ½ hour.

Substitution: Sauté 2 diced onions in heated oil until light golden brown instead of onion soup mix and margarine.

PERFECT RICE

2½ cups water	¾ teaspoon paprika (optional)
1 tablespoon oil	1 cup rice
1 teaspoon salt	

Bring water, oil, and salt to a boil. (Add paprika for a reddish color and added flavor.) Reduce flame, add rice and cook for approximately 20 minutes, stirring occasionally. Turn off flame, letting rice steam in covered pot for another 15 minutes.

RICE PILAF

3 tablespoons oil or margarine	1 cup rice
1 onion, diced	2½ cups water
5 carrots, diced	1 teaspoon salt
1 green pepper, finely chopped	¼ teaspoon pepper
1 4-ounce can of mushrooms	2 garlic cloves, minced

Heat oil in skillet over medium flame. Add diced onions, carrots, green pepper and mushrooms. Sauté until lightly browned and soft, about ten minutes. Add uncooked rice, mix with vegetables and sauté for additional minute or two. Then add water and seasoning. Bring to a boil and let simmer for approximately 20 minutes (45-60 minutes if using brown rice).

Variation: PLAIN SAUTÉED RICE—Lightly sauté one small, diced onion in oil, then add rice, water, and seasonings. (Or add just one of the vegetables mentioned above.) Bring to a boil and simmer for 20 minutes.

SPANISH RICE

1 onion	3 cups boiling water
1 green pepper	1 small can tomatoes
½ cup celery	1 teaspoon salt
2 tablespoons vegetable oil	2 teaspoons saffron (optional)
1 cup rice	

Dice and sauté onions, pepper, celery in oil in a 2-quart pot. When vegetables are slightly browned, add rice and water. Cook over low flame for 20 minutes. Add tomatoes and salt (and saffron). Cook for 3 minutes more.
Note: If using brown rice, cook for 50 minutes before adding tomatoes.

Rice Kugels

These are usually quite sweet and can be used for dessert during the week. Often they are prepared with milk and served as a dairy dish. See Dairy, Section V.

APRICOT RICE KUGEL

1½ cups raw rice	4 eggs, beaten
¾ cup sugar	1⅛ tablespoons melted margarine
¾ cup apricot juice	4 cups water

Cook rice. Add sugar, juice, eggs, and margarine. Mix together well. Bake in oven at 350° for one hour.

CRUNCHY RICE KUGEL

1 cup rice	rind of 1 lemon
4 cups boiling water	3 eggs, well beaten
¼ cup margarine	½ cup raisins
⅞ cup sugar	¼ cup chopped nuts
½ teaspoon cinnamon	

Cook rice in water until tender. Drain and cool.
Cream margarine and sugar. Add cinnamon, lemon rind and eggs. Mix well. Stir in raisins, nuts, and rice. Bake in greased, 1-quart baking dish, uncovered, for one hour, at 350°. Serves 5 or 6.

PINEAPPLE RICE KUGEL

1½	cups raw rice	1	cup sugar
5	cups salted water	5	eggs, well beaten
1	stick margarine	2	tablespoons cinnamon
1	cup crushed pineapple (or fruit cocktail)	1	teaspoon vanilla cherries

Cook the rice and drain. Add margarine to rice while it is still hot. Combine all ingredients except the rice and the cherries and mix well. Place in a shallow pan that has been preheated. Top with rice and bake at 350° for 1 hour. Decorate with cherries.

Brown Rice

Brown rice is much healthier than white rice, and, because it is a whole food, reduces the need for extra calories. Make it right, and your family will really begin to enjoy it.

BASIC BROWN RICE

1	cup brown rice	water (amount depends on method
½	teaspoon salt	of preparation and quality of pot)

Check the rice (for worms and insects) and wash it well. Do this by putting the rice in a pot, covering it with water and mixing the rice around in the water with your hands. Drain through a strainer and repeat.

Then cook according to *Variations* on following page.

BROWN RICE CREAM

A fine breakfast cereal. See Dairy, Section V.

FRIED BROWN RICE DELUXE

2-3	tablespoons oil	¼	cup cabbage, shredded
1	small onion	2	cups boiled rice
1	clove garlic (optional)	2	teaspoons soy sauce
2	scallions	½	teaspoon toasted sesame or
¼	green pepper (or better, a red one if available, for color)		sunflower seeds per person

Use a heavy skillet. Dice all the vegetables into very small pieces. Sauté the onion (and garlic) in oil over a high flame until golden. Add scallions, then peppers, then cabbage, stirring until they become limp.

Add the rice. Break up any lumps with a wooden spoon. (If using leftover rice and it seems very lumpy, steam it slightly first.) Mix and turn rice. Add soy sauce and cook for a few minutes while continuing to stir. Serve immediately. Top each portion with sesame or sunflower seeds.

Variation: SIMPLE FRIED RICE—Instead of the vegetables, use only ½ cup chopped onions or scallions. Use less oil and less soy sauce. The real connoisseurs prefer it this way.

BROWN RICE VARIATIONS

Boiled Brown Rice: Use 2-3 cups water depending on the heaviness of the pot and how tight-fitting the lid is (these two factors control the rate of evaporation). Put rice and water in the pot, cover, bring to a boil. Reduce flame to simmer, add salt and cover and cook for another 45-60 minutes.

Pressure Cooked Brown Rice: Use 1-1½ cups water (the proportion of water goes down slightly if a large quantity of rice is being cooked). Put rice, water and salt in pressure cooker. Pressure cooker should be *no more than half full*. Cook over a high flame until pressure regulator begins to jiggle, then simmer 45 minutes. Then let it stand another 5 minutes or until the pressure goes down.

Leftover Brown Rice: Rice can be re-heated by baking or by sautéeing, but the best way is to steam it in a double boiler. It will taste like fresh rice. (If you don't have a double boiler, make a number of little holes in an aluminum round pie pan, and set it upside down in a pot with a little water and put the rice on top. Cover well, and the rice will steam.)

Sesame Brown Rice: Add 2-3 tablespoons toasted sesame seeds to rice before cooking.

Chick Peas and Brown Rice: Use the water in which chick peas have been cooked. Serve rice with the cooked chick peas. Or cook rice with ¼ cup ready-cooked chick peas.

Helpful Hints

POTATOES

Baked potatoes: To reduce baking time by half, boil potato first for 15 minutes. Always prick skin of potato with a fork to allow steam to escape. To keep skin soft, grease potatoes before baking.
Mashed potatoes: For light, creamy mashed potatoes, add 1 teaspoon baking powder and beat well.
Leftover potatoes: These can be sliced and fried in oil. They make great french fries.

NOODLES

Draining: When draining steamed foods, let cold water run in sink (but not over food). This will reduce heat of the steam.
Storing: Leftover spaghetti or noodles should be stored in airtight plastic containers.
Burned pots: Soak stuck noodles, rice, etc. in cold water. Cover pot. Burned food will lift off easily in approximately ½-1 hour. This works for all burned grains as well.

Cakes and Frostings

Cakes and Frostings

Cakes and Frostings

Baking Equipment and Ingredients

Mixers

Standard-size electric cake mixer with bowls
and/or
Portable electric hand mixer

Common Size Baking Pans

9″ round tube pan (with removable center)
10″ round tube pan
9″ x 12″ pan
8″ x 8″ pan
9″ round pie dish
8″ x 5″ loaf pan
cookie sheets, preferably two
layer cake pans
cupcake pan and papers (also used for muffins)

For best results use correct size pans, as called for in recipe.

Most Commonly Used Utensils

full set of measuring cups—2 cups, 1 cup, ½ cup, ⅓ cup, ¼ cup.
full set of measuring spoons—tablespoon, teaspoon, ½ teaspoon, ¼ teaspoon, ⅛ teaspoon

Use standard measuring cups and spoons. Measure accurately for best results.

egg separater   rolling pin
large mixing bowl   rolling board
small mixing bowl   cookie cutters
spatula   cooling racks
waxed paper   cake tester

Most Common Ingredients Used in Baking

baking powder
baking semi-sweet
   chocolate
baking soda
brown sugar
chocolate morsels
   (or squares)
chopped nuts
cinnamon

cocoa
eggs, preferably large
extracts—vanilla, almond,
   lemon, maple, rum
flour
jam, preserves
juice
lemon juice
margarine

non-dairy creamer
oil
orange juice
salt
shortening
sugar
vanilla sugar
water

Ingredients for Frostings

chocolate for baking
cocoa
confectioners' sugar
eggs

flavoring (extracts)
food coloring
juice
margarine

shortening
water
sugar

Ingredients for Decorating

almonds
candied fruit
chocolate bits
chocolate sprinkles

coconut
confectioners' sugar
food coloring
grated lemon peel

grated orange peel
green cherries
red cherries
walnuts

Baking Equivalents

1 pound almonds in shell	=	¾–1 cup shelled almonds
1 medium apple chopped	=	1 cup
1 ounce chocolate	=	1 square
1 carton non-dairy creamer	=	16 ounces
1 carton (container) pareve dessert whip	=	10 ounces
1 cup egg whites	=	8–10 whites
1 cup egg yolks	=	12–14 yolks
3½–4 cups sifted all purpose flour	=	1 pound
1 grated lemon peel	=	1 teaspoon lemon rind
1 lemon squeezed	=	3 tablespoons lemon juice
1 grated orange peel	=	2 teaspoons orange rind
1 orange squeezed	=	⅓ cup orange juice
2 sticks margarine	=	½ cup shortening
2 cups sugar	=	1 pound
2½ cups packed brown sugar	=	1 pound
3½ cups powdered sugar	=	1 pound
1 package vanilla sugar	=	2 teaspoons vanilla sugar
1 cup shortening	=	½ pound
1 pound walnuts in shell	=	1½–1¾ cup shelled walnuts
1 cup whipping cream	=	2 cups whipped cream

Baking Substitutions

1 square unsweetened chocolate	=	3 tablespoons cocoa plus 1 tablespoon margarine
1 tablespoon cornstarch	=	2 tablespoons flour for thickening
1 cup cake flour	=	1 cup minus 2 tablespoons all-purpose flour
1 cup whole milk	=	½ cup evaporated milk and ½ cup water, or, ½ cup non-dairy creamer and ½ cup water
8 ounces sugar	=	4 ounces honey
1 package vanilla sugar	=	1 teaspoon vanilla extract
1 cake compressed yeast	=	1 package or 2 teaspoons active dry yeast

Cakes

Delicious cakes enhance any good cook's reputation. A tray of various cakes is a good way to lend a festive touch when entertaining, or at a *simcha*. Included in this section is an abundant variety of cakes. Some are easy one-bowl recipes; others are fancy chiffons or filled cakes. Included also are fruit cakes, strudels and yeast cakes. Some are sure to become your favorites.

Important Notes:

The laws regarding the separation of challah when making a dough apply equally to cake batter that fulfills the required flour measurement and liquid content. When cake batter is very loose, or when baking a number of different small recipes at one time, *challah* is often separated after the baking. (See *Laws of Separating Challah*, pages 341-344.)

It is important to check all eggs for blood spots (see page 8). Open each egg separately into a container and examine before combining with other eggs or other ingredients.

The cake recipes included in this section, usually require using liquids other than water because if water constitutes a majority of the liquid ingredients in a cake it may sometimes make the cake *halachically* equivalent to bread, requiring the ritual washing of hands, blessing of *Hamotzi*, etc.

When baking a dairy cake, separate dairy utensils are required, and the use of a separate, portable dairy oven is recommended (see page 329).

Many commercial ingredients are often used in baking. Make sure they all have a *hechsher*, certification of kashrus, and that the product is pareve. Oils and shortenings can only be from a pure vegetable base, and must have a hechsher.

REGAL ALMOND CAKE (Dairy or *Pareve*)*

margarine	3 egg yolks
¾ cup sliced almonds	2½ cups sifted cake flour
1 tablespoon sugar	3 teaspoons baking powder
¾ cup margarine	1 teaspoon salt
1¼ cups sugar	°1 cup milk (or ½ cup non-dairy
¼ teaspoon vanilla	creamer and ½ cup water)
¼ teaspoon almond extract	3 egg whites
1 teaspoon grated lemon peel	

Generously grease bottom and sides of a 10″ tube pan. Press in almonds. Sprinkle with 1 tablespoon sugar. Cream the margarine with sugar. Add vanilla, almond extract and lemon peel. Beat in egg yolks until light and fluffy. Sift together flour, baking powder and salt. Add to creamed mixture alternately with milk, beating after each addition. Beat egg whites until stiff but not dry. Gently fold into batter. Carefully turn into prepared pan. Bake at 325° for approximately 1 hour and 10 minutes. Let cake stand in pan about 10 minutes, then invert onto wire rack to cool.

°Separate dairy utensils are required and a separate, portable dairy oven is recommended for baking dairy foods. (page 329)

EASY APPLE CAKE

2 cups sugar	3 cups flour
8 eggs	½ teaspoon salt
4 teaspoons baking powder	4-5 large apples
1½ teaspoons vanilla	1 tablespoon cinnamon
1 cup oil	3 tablespoons sugar

Mix first 7 ingredients together thoroughly. Peel and slice the apples. Mix with cinnamon and sugar and stir into batter. Bake in greased 9″ x 13″ pan at 350° for 45-55 minutes.

Variations: APPLE TOPPING CAKE or APPLE-FILLED CAKE—For a fancier appearance, place apple mixture on top of cake, or divide batter in half and spread the apple mixture between the halves.

GOLDEN APPLE CAKE

3 cups flour	4 eggs
1¾ cups sugar	1 cup oil
1 teaspoon salt	¼ cup juice
3 teaspoons baking powder	1½ tablespoons vanilla

Filling:

4 large baking apples, peeled and sliced	1 tablespoon cinnamon
	3 tablespoons sugar

Prepare filling and set aside until cake is mixed.

Sift flour, sugar, salt, and baking powder in bowl. Make a well in the center and pour in remaining ingredients. Mix well. Spoon a little over one-half the batter into a baking pan. Cover with apple mixture. Apples should not touch sides of pan. Cover with remaining batter. Bake approximately 1¼ hours at 350°, in a 9″ x 13″ pan.

APPLESAUCE CAKE

½ cup shortening	¼ teaspoon baking soda
2 eggs	½ teaspoon baking powder
1 cup sugar	½ teaspoon salt
½ cup applesauce	1 teaspoon vanilla
2 squares bitter chocolate, melted	½ cup chopped nuts
1 cup flour	1 cup chopped raisins

Cream shortening, add eggs and sugar. Add applesauce, melted chocolate and mix well. Blend in dry ingredients, then vanilla, nuts and raisins. Grease and flour a 9″ x 5″ loaf pan or an 8″ x 8″ square pan. Bake at 350° for 45-60 minutes.

VICTORIAN APPLESAUCE CAKE

2 cups flour
1½ cups sugar
1½ teaspoons baking soda
1½ teaspoons salt
2 tablespoons cocoa
1 teaspoon cinnamon
½ teaspoon ground cloves
½ teaspoon nutmeg

½ teaspoon allspice
1½ cup shortening
1½ cups unsweetened applesauce
2 eggs
¾ cup chopped dates
¾ cup chopped raisins
¾ cup chopped nuts

Sift dry ingredients into mixing bowl. Drop in shortening. Add applesauce and mix with electric mixer. Add eggs and mix again. Stir in fruit and ½ cup of the nuts. Batter will be stiff. Pour into 10″ greased tube pan. Sprinkle remaining nuts on top. Bake at 350° approximately 1½ hours.

Variation: Mix the remaining nuts with 2 tablespoons sugar before sprinkling on top.

BANANA CAKE

2 eggs
1½ cups sugar
½ cup shortening
1 cup mashed bananas
¼ cup orange juice

1 teaspoon vanilla
2 cups flour
¾ teaspoon baking soda
¼ teaspoon baking powder
½ teaspoon salt

Cream eggs, sugar and shortening. Mix well. Blend in mashed bananas, liquid, and vanilla. Add remaining dry ingredients and mix well. Pour into greased and floured 9″ x 9″ pan and bake at 350° for 30-35 minutes. Excellent when frosted with *Basic Jiffy Frosting* (page 250).

FLUFFY BANANA CAKE

3 eggs
2 cups sugar
1 cup oil
2½ teaspoons baking soda
2½ teaspoons hot water

1 teaspoon vanilla
2 bananas
1 cup water
2½ cups flour

Beat eggs and sugar. Add oil and mix well. Mix the baking soda with hot water and add to the egg mixture. Cut up the bananas and mix into batter. Add the remaining ingredients and mix for another minute. Bake in a tube pan for one hour at 350°.

BASIC CAKE

2 sticks margarine	½ teaspoon salt
2 cups sugar	4 teaspoons baking powder
4 eggs	1⅓ cups non-dairy creamer
3½ cups flour	2 packages vanilla sugar

Cream margarine well. Gradually add 2 cups sugar, then the 4 eggs, one at a time. In a separate small bowl, combine flour, salt and baking powder. Add dry ingredients to creamed shortening alternately with the non-dairy creamer, using mixer on low speed or mixing by hand. Add vanilla sugar and mix well. Grease and flour 9″ x 13″ baking pan. Bake at 350° for 45-55 minutes.

Variations: BASIC CAKE—Instead of full amount of non-dairy creamer, use ⅔ cup with ½ cup pineapple juice.

CHOCOLATE CAKE—Melt 2 ounces semi-sweet chocolate with ½ stick margarine, drizzle on top of batter and marble, after the batter is already poured into pan.

APPLE CAKE—Once batter is in pan, arrange thin apple slices on top. Sprinkle with cinnamon and sugar.

PINEAPPLE CAKE—This batter can also be used for Pineapple Upside-Down cake (see page 243 for instructions).

HONEY CAROB CAKE

Carob is similar to chocolate and can be used as a healthier substitute. When converting a chocolate recipe to carob, use equal amount of carob for cocoa, or 3 tablespoons carob powder + 2 tablespoons non-dairy creamer for 1 square of chocolate.

3 cups unbleached white flour	3 eggs
1 teaspoon baking soda	½ cup apple juice (or less
1 teaspoon cinnamon (or ginger	depending on consistency)
or nutmeg)	1 teaspoon vanilla
1 cup chopped nuts	½ cup raisins
½ cup oil	¾ cup carob powder
1 cup honey	

Mix together first four ingredients. In a separate bowl, combine oil and honey, and add eggs, apple juice, and vanilla. Mix well. Add raisins and combine with dry ingredients. Add carob powder. Turn into oiled 9″ x 13″ baking pan. Bake at 350° for 45-60 minutes until done.

EASY CHEESE CAKE (Dairy)*

Crust:

½ pound graham cracker crumbs	½ cup margarine or shortening

Filling:

1 whole egg	1 egg white
1 teaspoon vanilla	4 tablespoons sugar
¾ pound farmer cheese	½ pint sour cream

Topping:

½ pint sour cream	1 package vanilla sugar

In a bowl mix cracker crumbs and margarine and press into a 5″ x 9″ pan. Put all filling ingredients into a bowl and mix with fork until fluffy. Pour into pan and bake at 350° for ½ hour. Cool for 15 minutes. Mix topping and spread on cake. Bake an additional 5 minutes at 450°.

°Separate dairy utensils are required and a separate, portable dairy oven is recommended for baking dairy foods. (page 329)

FANCY CHEESE CAKE (Dairy)°

Crust:
- ½ cup margarine
- ½ pound graham cracker crumbs

or

- 1 unbaked pie shell

Filling:
- ½ pound cream cheese
- ¾ cup sugar
- juice of ½ lemon
- ½ pound farmer cheese
- 2 eggs
- 2 packages vanilla sugar

Topping:
- 1 pint sour cream
- 1 package vanilla sugar
- lemon juice

Line a 9″ x 9″ pan with cracker crumb-margarine mixture or pie shell. Combine ingredients and pour into crust. Bake at 350° for 45 minutes. Combine sour cream, vanilla, sugar and lemon juice and use to frost cake. Bake an additional 15-20 minutes.

°Separate dairy utensils are required and a separate, portable dairy oven is recommended for baking dairy foods. (page 329)

Chocolate Cakes

Nearly everyone that bakes has a favorite chocolate cake recipe. Here are some of ours, all different.

BASIC CHOCOLATE CAKE

- 4-6 eggs
- 1⅓ cups oil
- 3 cups sugar
- 3 cups flour
- 3 teaspoons baking powder
- ½ teaspoon salt
- 1⅓ teaspoons baking soda
- 1½ teaspoons vanilla
- 1 cup cocoa
- 1¾ cups strong, hot coffee

Beat eggs, oil, and sugar until well blended. Add remaining ingredients and beat well. Bake in a greased tube pan or a 9″ x 13″ pan for 1 hour at 350°.

BLACK CHOCOLATE CAKE

1	cup cocoa, dry	4	eggs
2	cups strong hot coffee, made with 1 tablespoon instant coffee	2	sticks margarine
3	cups flour	2¼	cups sugar
2	teaspoons baking soda	2	packages vanilla sugar
½	teaspoon baking powder	½	teaspoon almond extract
	pinch of salt	6-8	maraschino cherries, cut up for decorating

Mix cocoa and coffee in a small bowl until there are no lumps. In a separate bowl, combine dry ingredients. Beat together the eggs, margarine, sugar, vanilla sugar and almond extract. Add flour mixture alternately with the cocoa-coffee mixture, beginning and ending with the dry ingredients. Grease and flour the bottom of a 9″ x 13″ pan. Bake at 325° for 45 minutes to an hour.

CHOCOLATE BROWNIE CAKE

1	cup cocoa	8	eggs
3½	cups sugar	1	cup oil
2	cups flour	2	teaspoons baking powder
2	teaspoons vanilla sugar		pinch of salt

Mix first four ingredients together well. Add eggs and oil and mix on low speed. Then add baking powder and salt. Mix again. Place in a long shallow pan. Bake at 350° for 30-40 minutes.

CHOCOLATE CHIFFON CAKE

7	eggs, separated	½	cup oil
½	teaspoon salt	2	teaspoons vanilla
1¾	cups flour	⅓	cup cocoa
1⅔	cups sugar	1	tablespoon instant coffee
1½	teaspoons baking powder	¾	cup boiling water

Put egg whites into large bowl. Beat together with salt until stiff. Set aside. Mix cocoa, coffee and water together.

Combine flour, sugar, and baking powder in a medium bowl. Form a well and add egg yolks, oil, vanilla and coffee mixture. Beat. Fold in egg whites. Pour into 10″ ungreased tube pan. Bake at 325° for 55-60 minutes. Immediately turn upside down and cool for 3 hours.

CHOCOLATE CHIP CAKE

1	cup shortening	3	cups flour
2	cups sugar	3	teaspoons baking powder
1	teaspoon vanilla	1	cup cold coffee
4	eggs	4-5	ounces chocolate chips or bits

Cream shortening and sugar. Add remaining ingredients and beat well. Mix in chocolate bits and bake in a tube pan or a 9″ x 13″ pan for 50 minutes at 350°.

NO EGG, NO MIXER CHOCOLATE CAKE

1½ cups flour	1 teaspoon vanilla
1 cup sugar	2 teaspoons vinegar
3 tablespoons cocoa	5 tablespoons oil
1 teaspoon cinnamon (optional)	1 cup tea or raisin water
1 teaspoon baking soda	

Pour flour, sugar, cocoa, cinnamon (optional), and baking soda directly into a greased 9″ x 9″ baking pan. Mix with spoon. Now make one large and two small grooves in this mixture. Pour oil into the large groove, vinegar into another groove, and vanilla into the third. Pour liquid over all. Mix with spoon until you don't see any flour. Don't be afraid to scrape the bottom of the pan when mixing. Bake in a preheated oven at 350° for 30 minutes.

Note: To make raisin water, boil ⅓-½ cup raisins in water.

CHOCOLATE-FILLED CAKE

3 cups flour	2 sticks margarine
½ cup sugar	4 egg yolks
⅜ cup juice	2 teaspoons baking powder

Filling:

4 egg whites	½ cup chopped nuts
1 cup sugar	2 ounces bitter chocolate, melted
1 teaspoon vanilla	juice and rind of 1 lemon
2 grated apples	

Mix first set of ingredients and set aside. Beat egg whites and gradually add sugar. Fold into batter and stir in remaining filling ingredients. Place half the dough in a 9″ x 13″ pan. Pour in filling and cover with remaining half of dough. Bake at 350° for 45 minutes. Sprinkle with confectioners' sugar.

CHOCOLATE BROWNIE THREE-LAYER CAKE

Cake:

1 cup cocoa	½ teaspoon baking powder
2 cups boiling water	1 cup margarine
2¾ cups flour	2½ cups sugar
2 teaspoons baking soda	4 eggs
½ teaspoon salt	½ teaspoon vanilla

Filling:

1 cup pareve dessert whip	1 teaspoon vanilla
¼ cup confectioners' sugar	

Frosting:

1 6-ounce package baking chocolate	1 cup margarine
½ cup non-dairy creamer	2½ cups confectioners' sugar

Cake: Mix cocoa and boiling water and allow to cool. In another bowl, sift together flour, baking soda, salt and baking powder and set aside. In large mixing bowl, beat margarine, sugar, eggs and vanilla at high speed for 5 minutes. Then at low speed add the cocoa followed by the flour mixture. Divide evenly into 3 pans — 9″ round by 1½″ deep. Bake at 350° for 25-30 minutes.

Filling: Whip together dessert whip, sugar and vanilla, and place in refrigerator. When cake has cooled, spread in between layers.

Frosting: Put chocolate, non-dairy creamer, and margarine into saucepan and stir over medium flame. Blend in confectioners' sugar. Spread evenly over top and sides of cake.

FIVE-LAYER CHOCOLATE PARTY CAKE

    1 two-crust pastry dough

Cake:

6-8 eggs, separated	1 cup flour, sifted
1 cup sugar	1 teaspoon baking powder
¾ cup juice	2 tablespoons water

Filling:

2 bars bittersweet chocolate, melted	1 egg
1½ cups powdered sugar	3 tablespoons cocoa
½ stick margarine	⅛ teaspoon salt

Dough: Roll out dough into two separate rectangular pieces. Bake in two 9″ x 13″ baking pans until slightly brown.

Cake: Beat egg yolks with sugar and juice until stiff. Mix flour and baking powder and add to the mixture *very slowly.* Continue whipping until completely blended. Whip egg whites together with the water until stiff. Fold in yolk mixture very slowly. Bake in rectangular pan lined with wax paper for 25-35 minutes at 350°.

Filling: Whip chocolate and sugar together. Mix in other ingredients.

Layers: Form cake by layering in the following order: dough, chocolate filling, cake, chocolate filling, dough.

CHOCOLATE LIQUEUR CAKE

4 egg whites	2 tablespoons cocoa
1½ cups sugar	4 egg yolks
1 stick margarine	1 cup flour
5 tablespoons water	1 teaspoon baking powder
1 square baking chocolate	4 tablespoons liqueur

Beat egg whites and 1 cup sugar. Melt margarine with water, chocolate, cocoa and ½ cup sugar. Cool and beat together with remaining ingredients. Bake in a tube pan at 350° for 1 hour.

CHOCOLATE SWIRL MOCHA CAKE

2 cups flour	3 eggs
1 teaspoon baking powder	⅔ cup cold water
1 teaspoon salt	1 teaspoon vanilla
4 teaspoons instant coffee	3 squares semi-sweet chocolate, grated
1¼ cups sugar	
⅔ cup shortening	

Sift together flour, baking powder, salt and coffee. Set aside. Add sugar gradually to shortening, creaming until light and fluffy. Blend in eggs, one at a time, mixing well after each addition. Combine water with vanilla. Add alternately with dry ingredients to creamed mixture — beginning and ending with dry mixture. Mix well. Turn half the batter into a 9″ or 10″ tube pan, well-greased on bottom only. Sprinkle half the grated chocolate on top. Add remaining batter and sprinkle with remaining chocolate. Marble the chocolate into entire batter by folding with a rubber spatula or spoon. Bake at 350°, for 60-70 minutes. Cool and sprinkle with confectioners' sugar or ice with light chocolate icing.

CHOCOLATE-NUT CAKE

Dough:

2 egg yolks	⅛ cup sugar
½ pound margarine	½ teaspoon baking powder
2 cups flour	

Filling:

8 egg whites	1 teaspoon baking powder
1 cup sugar	1 lemon, grated
1 teaspoon vanilla	2 teaspoons cocoa
½ pound chopped nuts	1 tablespoon potato starch
6 egg yolks	

Frosting:

½ box confectioners' sugar	1 tablespoon oil
1 tablespoon lemon juice	1 teaspoon cocoa
maraschino cherry juice, to color	

Dough: Blend all ingredients in mixer. Divide dough in half. Roll into two 9″ x 13″ rectangular pieces. Spread one on a greased cake pan.

Filling: Beat egg whites, gradually add the sugar, then the remaining ingredients. Spread over the dough in pan, then cover with remaining layer of dough. Bake at 350° until lightly browned.

Frosting: Mix together first 4 ingredients. Spread ¾ of the frosting on cake when it is slightly cooled. Add 1 teaspoon cocoa to remaining frosting, mix well, and pour thin strips horizontally and vertically over cake.

FLUFFY COCOA-NUT CAKE

3 sticks margarine, softened	2 teaspoons vanilla sugar
2 cups flour	8 egg whites
3 tablespoons cocoa	2 cups sugar
8 egg yolks	¼ pound medium fine crushed
juice of 1 lemon	nuts
juice of 1 orange	2 ounces chocolate bits (optional)
2 teaspoons baking powder	

Mix first eight ingredients in bowl at highest speed for 10 minutes. Then, in a separate bowl, whip egg whites, adding sugar gradually. Fold this "snow" into batter. Mix well. Place in 9″ x 13″ baking pan or 10″ tube pan. Top with nuts and chocolate bits, if desired. Bake at 300° for 45 minutes.

Coffee Cake

Coffee cake is a fairly dry, not-too-sweet cake that gets its name because it is commonly served for breakfast with a cup of coffee.

When buying coffee cake in a bakery, ask if it is dairy or pareve.

BASIC COFFEE CAKE

1 cup sugar	2 teaspoons baking powder
½ cup shortening	1½ cups flour
3 eggs	½ cup non-dairy creamer
1 teaspoon vanilla	cinnamon and sugar mixture

Cream sugar, shortening and eggs until light and fluffy. Add vanilla. Combine baking powder and flour. Add alternately with non-dairy creamer, mixing after each addition. Pour into greased 9″ x 9″ baking pan. Sprinkle top with cinnamon and sugar. Bake in preheated oven at 350° for 40 minutes or, until done.

CHERRY-ALMOND COFFEE CAKE

Cake:

1½ cups flour	1 egg
¼ cup sugar	2½ teaspoons baking powder
¾ teaspoon salt	¼ cup shortening
¾ cup non-dairy creamer	

Topping:

¼ cup brown sugar	2 tablespoons cinnamon
½ cup sliced almonds	⅔ cup cherry jam

Icing:

1 cup confectioners' sugar	3 tablespoons water
½ teaspoon vanilla	

Grease a 9″ x 9″ pan. Measure all cake ingredients into a large bowl. Blend thoroughly and beat vigorously for one-half minute. Pour into pan. Mix brown sugar, sliced almonds, cinnamon, and sprinkle over cake. Drizzle jam over the topping. Bake for 25-30 minutes in pre-heated oven at 375°.

While cake is baking, prepare icing by mixing all ingredients thoroughly. Ice while still warm.

CHOCOLATE CHIP COFFEE RINGS—(Dairy or Pareve)*

1 envelope active dry yeast	3 tablespoons sugar
1¾ cup sifted flour	½ teaspoon salt
°½ cup milk (or ¼ cup non-dairy creamer mixed with ¼ cup water)	1 egg
	½ cup semi-sweet chocolate pieces
4 tablespoons margarine	

In a large mixing bowl, combine yeast and 1¼ cups flour. Heat milk, margarine, sugar and salt just until margarine is melted, stirring occasionally. Allow to cool. Add to dry mixture and then add egg. Beat in mixer at low speed for 2 minutes. Beat 3 additional minutes at high speed. Add remaining flour and chocolate and mix well by hand. Turn into greased 4½-cup ring mold. Cover. Allow to rise in a warm place until double in bulk, 45 minutes to an hour. Bake at 400° until well done. Remove from pan immediately. Sprinkle with confectioners' sugar while still warm.

°Separate dairy utensils are required and a separate, portable dairy oven is recommended for baking dairy foods. (page 329)

COFFEE CHIFFON CAKE

8 eggs, separated	3 teaspoons baking powder
1½ cups sugar	2 cups flour
½ teaspoon salt	2 teaspoons maple extract
¾ cup hot coffee	½ cup chopped nuts
1½ cups oil	

Beat egg whites until stiff. Mix together the remaining ingredients, except nuts. Fold in egg whites, then the nuts. Bake at 350° for 1 hour, in an ungreased, 10″ tube pan.
Note: If maple extract is unavailable, use an equivalent amount of vanilla.

COFFEE CRUMB CAKE

4 eggs	3 teaspoons baking powder
2 cups sugar	1 cup apricot nectar
1 cup oil	nuts
3 cups flour	cinnamon-sugar mixture

Topping:
½ stick margarine	flour
1 teaspoon vanilla sugar	

Mix first six ingredients. Pour half the batter into greased tube pan. Sprinkle with nuts, cinnamon, sugar. Pour in remaining batter. Prepare crumb topping by combining margarine, sugar and enough flour to make a hand ball. Grate with a grater and add to top of batter. Bake at 350° for 1 hour.

SIMPLE COFFEE CAKE

2 cups flour	2 eggs
3 teaspoons baking powder	1 teaspoon vanilla
1 cup sugar	½ cup apple juice
1 teaspoon salt	¾ cup brown sugar
¾ cup margarine	1 teaspoon cinnamon

Sift flour, baking powder, sugar and salt in bowl. Cut in margarine. Add eggs, vanilla, and apple juice and mix well. Pour half the batter into a greased, 9″ tube pan. Mix brown sugar and cinnamon, and pour half of the sugar mixture over batter. Repeat with remaining batter and sugar mixture. Bake at 350° for 35-40 minutes.

NO-BAKE COOKIE-CAKE

2 heaping teaspoons cocoa
¾ teaspoon instant coffee
1 cup lukewarm water
3 boxes (rectangular or square) biscuits, 2 boxes vanilla and one chocolate

2 eggs, separated
1 teaspoon vanilla sugar
2 sticks margarine
⅔ cup sugar
chocolate sprinkles or grated sweet chocolate

Combine cocoa and coffee with water and mix well. Lightly dip half the vanilla biscuits into mixture. Line them up in tight rows on the bottom of a 9″ x 13″ pan.

To make batter, separate eggs and make a "snow" by whipping egg whites and vanilla sugar. Set aside. In another bowl, cream margarine, sugar and egg yolks, then add snow and mix well. Pour ¼ of this batter over dipped cookies. Top with a layer of chocolate biscuits soaked in the liquid.

Top with another ¼ of the batter. Cover with a layer of vanilla biscuits prepared in the same manner as the others. Top with the rest of batter. Sprinkle with chocolate sprinkles or grated sweet chocolate.

Refrigerate for a few hours until batter becomes firm. Then cut into squares and serve in cupcake holders.

CRUMB CAKE

Dough:

3 cups flour
2 sticks margarine, softened
7 egg yolks

¾ cup sugar
1 package vanilla sugar
1 teaspoon baking powder

Filling:

7 egg whites
1 cup sugar
1 orange rind, grated
1 lemon rind, grated
½ pound chopped walnuts

2 ounces melted chocolate (optional)
1 tablespoon potato starch (optional)
strawberry jam

Mix all dough ingredients together by hand and divide into two parts, one slightly larger than the other.

In a separate bowl whip egg whites, then add sugar, grated orange, lemon, and walnuts, melted chocolate and potato starch.

Fill a 9″ x 13″ pan in the following order: larger piece of dough, a thin layer of jam, and filling. Grate the remaining dough on large holes of a grater. Sprinkle on top of cake.

Bake at 350° for 50 minutes. Cut while hot into diamond-shaped pieces and serve in individual cake liners.

DOUBLE LAYER CRUMB CAKE

Dough:

4 cups flour
juice and rind of one lemon
¾ cup sugar

2 egg yolks
3 sticks margarine (¾ lb.)
2 teaspoons baking powder

Filling:

1	jar apricot jam	1	lemon, juice and rind
6	egg whites	1	teaspoon vanilla
1	cup sugar	2	teaspoons coffee
2½	cups chopped nuts		

Mix all dough ingredients together until well blended. Line a 9″ x 12″ pan with wax paper. Grate or crumble half of the dough into the pan and spread with apricot jam. Beat the egg whites, adding the sugar slowly, until stiff. Add the remaining ingredients. Pour this over the jam-covered dough. Crumble remaining dough over the filling. Bake at 350° until done, approximately 45 minutes.

EASY CRUMB CAKE

½	pound margarine		pinch of salt
1¼	cups sugar		vanilla
2	eggs	1	can cherry pie filling
2⅔	cups flour	1	teaspoon cinnamon
2	teaspoons baking powder		

Topping:

¼	pound margarine	cinnamon and sugar
⅓	cups flour	

Cream margarine and sugar. Add eggs and vanilla and beat well. Add all dry ingredients. Spread half of mixture in pan. Cover with pie filling and top with remaining half. Crumble together margarine, flour, sugar and cinnamon and sprinkle over top. Bake in a 8″ x 8″ greased and floured baking pan at 350° for 1 hour.

DRUM CAKE (Dairy)*

2	cups flour	2	eggs
1	cup sugar	1	cup buttermilk or sour milk
1	teaspoon baking soda	2	teaspoons vanilla
1	teaspoon salt	1	6-ounce package semisweet
½	cup shortening		chocolate, melted and cooled

Mix together flour, sugar, baking soda and salt. Add shortening, eggs, buttermilk and vanilla. Blend on low speed of mixer. Then beat on medium speed for 2 minutes. Combine 1 cup of the batter with melted chocolate. Pour light batter into two greased and floured 8″ round pans. Drop spoonfuls of dark batter on top. Cut through to marble. Bake at 350° until done, 30-35 minutes. Layer with favorite filling and frost.

Variation: For a pareve cake, use 1-cup non-dairy creamer and 1 tablespoon lemon juice.

*Separate dairy utensils are required and a separate, portable dairy oven is recommended for baking dairy foods. (page 329)

BASIC FILLING CAKE

6 eggs
1½ cups oil
1½ cups sugar
1½ teaspoons vanilla

3 cups flour
1½ teaspoons baking powder
1 can pie filling

Cream eggs, oil and sugar. Add vanilla, flour, and baking powder. Spread a little more than half the batter in a 9″ x 13″ pan and cover with pie filling. Cover with remaining batter. Bake at 350° for 1 hour.

FRUIT-NUT CAKE

4 cups flour
¼ teaspoon salt
2 teaspoons cinnamon
2 teaspoons baking powder
2 sticks margarine
1½ cups sugar
4 eggs

1 cup liquid (cherry or orange juice)
1 teaspoon vanilla
½-1 cup maraschino cherries, chopped
1 cup walnuts or pecans, chopped
1 cup raisins

Sift dry ingredients. Cream margarine, sugar and eggs. Add the dry ingredients. Next add liquid, vanilla, cherries, nuts, and raisins. Mix together well. Bake at 350° in a greased and floured 9″ x 13″ pan for approximately 1 hour.

Honey Cake

This sweet cake is a traditional favorite served on Rosh Hashana and the following weeks, symbolizing our prayer for a "good and sweet year." Honey cake is also popular all year round, especially at a Shabbos Kiddush (see *Yiddishe Simchas*, page 302).

In Yiddish, honey cake is called *lekach,* and it recalls a very popular European custom that is still seen today. On Erev Yom Kippur a Rabbi would distribute to each of his congregants or followers a piece of honey cake to symbolize his wish to the person for a sweet year. This custom also symbolizes the wish that this receiving of cake be as a substitute for any charity it may be decreed that the person receive in the coming year.

BASIC HONEY CAKE

3 eggs
1 cup honey
1 cup sugar
1 cup warm coffee
½ cup oil

2 teaspoons baking powder
2 teaspoon baking soda
2 teaspoons vanilla
2¾ cups flour
spices (optional)

Beat eggs and honey together. Add sugar and mix again. Mix baking soda into coffee, then add with oil to egg mixture. Add remaining ingredients and beat together well. Bake in tube pan at 325° for 55 minutes.

Variations: SPICY HONEY CAKE: After mixing together all ingredients add 1 teaspoon cinnamon, 1 teaspoon ginger, and 1 teaspoon ground cloves. Mix again and pour into pan.
Substitution: Use 3 tablespoons margarine and 4 cups flour instead of oil and 3 cups of flour. When using margarine, first cream margarine and sugar, then add remaining ingredients.

HONEY CHIFFON CAKE

4 eggs, separated	½ teaspoon salt
1 cup sugar	1 teaspoon cinnamon
1 cup honey	1 teaspoon nutmeg
1 cup oil	1 teaspoon ground cloves
3½ cups flour	1 cup strong tea
2 teaspoons baking soda	¼-½ cup raisins
2 teapoons baking powder	

Beat egg whites and set aside. In a large mixing bowl, beat egg yolks until fluffy. Gradually add sugar and beat well. Beat in honey, then oil. Mix together all dry ingredients, and add alternately to mixture with tea. Stir in raisins. Fold in egg whites gradually and mix together again. Pour into a 9″ x 13″ greased pan. Bake at 300° for 1 hour.

OLD RELIABLE HONEY-NUT* CAKE

1 cup honey	3½ cups flour
1 cup oil	¼ teaspoon salt
1 cup brown sugar	1 teaspoon cinnamon
3 eggs	1 teaspoon nutmeg
1 cup strong, hot, black coffee	½ teaspoon cloves
2 teaspoons baking powder	¼ teaspoon ginger
1 teaspoon baking soda	¾ cups chopped nuts

Cream honey, oil, and sugar. Add eggs one at a time and beat. Combine coffee, baking powder and soda—mixture will bubble. Combine flour with spices and add alternately to creamed mixture with the coffee. Dust nuts with flour and drop into batter. Bake in greased, wax-papered pan at 325° for one hour.

*Many people have the custom of not eating nuts on Rosh Hashana. If you have this custom, substitute by sprinkling top with ½ cup raisins. Or use this recipe at other times through the year.

Jelly Roll

A jelly roll is made of a thin layer of cake (usually white chiffon) rolled up with jam, whipped cream or ice cream. It is a beautiful addition to any cake platter.

THE ART OF MAKING JELLY ROLLS

Prepare batter according to recipe.
Line cookie pan or cookie sheet with waxed paper.
Pour in batter and bake according to recipe.
Sprinkle clean cloth or dish towel with confectioners' (powdered) sugar.
When cake is baked, immediately remove from oven, peel from waxed paper and place top side down on the sugared cloth. Roll it up starting with one end and let it cool.
Unroll and fill with jam, frosting, or ice cream. Re-roll.

EASY JELLY ROLL

5	eggs	¾	cup flour
½	teaspoon baking powder	¾	cup sugar
	pinch of salt	1	package vanilla sugar

Beat eggs for 5 minutes, until lemon-colored. Add all ingredients and mix well. Bake 12-15 minutes at 425°. Do not overbake.

FLUFFY JELLY ROLL

3	egg yolks		dash of salt
1	cup sugar	1	cup flour
2	tablespoons lemon juice	1	teaspoon baking powder
½	cup water		confectioners' sugar
3	egg whites		

Beat egg yolks until thick. Add ½ cup sugar and the lemon juice. Beat until thick and add water.

In separate bowl beat egg whites, salt and remaining sugar. Fold whites into yolks. Fold flour and baking powder into mixture. Bake at 350° for 15 minutes.

ICE CREAM CAKE CHOCOLATE ROLL

Batter:

3	eggs	1	teaspoon baking powder
1	cup flour	¼	cup cocoa
1	cup sugar	⅓	cup water

Filling:

1	carton pareve dessert whip	3	tablespoons sugar

Topping:

    chocolate bits or sprinkles

Mix batter ingredients together. Bake in a foil-lined cookie sheet for 15-20 minutes. While the cake is hot, lay it on a floured baking cloth and roll. Next, whip the dessert whip and sugar. Unroll the cake when cool, and spread ¾ of the whipped mixture on it. Re-roll. Spread the remaining mixture on top and sprinkle with chocolate bits. Freeze.

Variation: VANILLA CAKE WITH CHOCOLATE "ICE CREAM"— Omit cocoa from the cake batter. Beat the egg whites separately and fold into cake batter. When preparing the "ice cream," use 5 tablespoons sugar and add 3 tablespoons cocoa. For other flavored ice creams see Desserts, Section XIV.

FLUFFY CHIFFON CAKE

2½ cups flour
1½ cups sugar
3 teaspoons baking powder
1 teaspoon salt
½ cup oil
5 egg yolks

7-8 egg whites
¾ cup cold water
2 teaspoons vanilla
2 teaspoons lemon rind

Mix flour, sugar, baking powder and salt in bowl. Add oil, egg yolks, water, vanilla, lemon rind. Beat with spoon until smooth. Beat whites, and beat until stiff, then fold into mixture. Pour into 10″ tube pan. Bake at 325° for 55 minutes and at 350° for 10-15 additional minutes.

ORANGE LEMON CHIFFON CAKE

1¾ cups sugar
8 egg whites
7 egg yolks
¾ cup oil
2 cups sifted flour

3 teaspoons baking powder, sifted
pinch of salt
1 cup orange juice
grated rind of one lemon

Beat ¾ cup sugar and egg whites, making "snow," and set aside. Blend 1 cup sugar, egg yolks, ¾ cup oil, flour, baking powder and salt. Add orange juice and lemon rind and mix. Combine all ingredients. Bake at 375° for one hour in ungreased tube pan. When done, turn over to cool.

Variation: CHOCOLATE CHIFFON CAKE—Use ½ cup less flour and one less egg white. Replace orange juice and lemon rind with ⅓ cup of cocoa, 1 tablespoon instant coffee and ¾ cup boiling water and 2 teaspoons vanilla.

MANDELBROIT

3 eggs
1 cup sugar
½ cup oil
3 cups flour
3 teaspoons baking powder
¼ teaspoon salt

1½ cups nuts
1 teaspoon almond extract
1 teaspoon vanilla
¼ teaspoon cinnamon
2 tablespoons orange juice
rind of one orange, grated

Beat eggs well, and add sugar gradually. Add other ingredients in order given. Blend well and form into five oblong, oval rolls. Bake at 400° for 25 minutes on a lightly greased cookie sheet. While hot, cut into slices, place in pan and return to oven to toast.

Marble Cake

Marble cake looks like a combination of a white and chocolate cake. It is simple to make, and is one of the basic cakes served at a Shabbos afternoon Kiddush (see *Yiddishe Simchas*, page 302).

DRIZZLED MARBLE CAKE

⅔ cup shortening	2⅓ cups flour
1½ cups sugar	3 teaspoons baking powder
1 teaspoon vanilla	¼ teaspoon salt
4 eggs	1 cup water or juice

Marble:

4 tablespoons cocoa	5 tablespoons hot water
3 tablespoons sugar	

Cream shortening with sugar. Add vanilla and eggs one at a time, beating after each addition. Add the liquid and dry ingredients alternately into egg mixture. Pour into 9″ by 13″ pan.

Combine cocoa and sugar and enough water to make paste. Drizzle onto cake and knife through to marble. Bake at 350° until done.

MARBLE CHIFFON CAKE

8 eggs, separated	juice of ½ lemon
1½ cups sugar	pinch of salt
1⅔ cups flour	¼ cup water
3 teaspoons baking powder	¼ cup cocoa
½ cup oil	

Mix egg yolks with sugar. Blend in flour mixed with baking powder. Add oil, lemon juice, salt and mix thoroughly. Fold in egg whites. Put three-quarters of the mixture into ungreased 10″ tube pan.

Mix cocoa and water with remaining batter. Marbelize cake by dropping in one tablespoonful at a time of chocolate mixture, every other inch at the edge of tube pan. Do not stir, will blend nicely on its own during baking process. Bake at 350° for 1 hour. When done turn pan upside down to cool.

QUICK MARBLE CAKE

2 cups sugar	⅛ teaspoon salt
1 cup oil or shortening	3 teaspoons baking powder
4 eggs	2 teaspoons vanilla
1 cup water or juice	3 heaping teaspoons cocoa
3 cups flour	

Cream sugar and oil together. Add eggs one at a time, beating well after each one. Add the liquid alternately with the flour. Add the salt, baking powder and vanilla.

Pour all but ¼ of the batter into greased 9″ x 13″ pan or tube pan. Add cocoa to remaining batter. Then pour it onto white mixture and cut with knife a few times. Do not stir. Preheat oven to 325° and bake for 50 minutes.

Variation: FILLED MARBLE CAKE—Pour only half the batter into the pan. Divide the remaining batter in half. Add cocoa to one half and pour into the pan. Pour the remaining batter over that. Bake.

NAPOLEON CUSTARD CAKE

1 flaky pie crust recipe, page 275	1 cup sugar
2 cartons pareve dessert whip	confectioners' sugar
1 package instant vanilla pudding	

Roll out dough into two pieces and bake as directed. Mix remaining ingredients except confectioner's sugar until stiff. On a cookie sheet, put one baked dough, then filling, then the other baked dough. Sprinkle top with sugar.

Variation: Bake 1 sponge roll and layer on a cookie sheet in the following manner: baked flaky dough, whip, sponge roll, whip, then second half of baked flaky dough.

FLUFFY NUT CAKE

6 eggs, separated	2 cups flour
2 cups sugar	⅓ cup club soda
¼ cup oil	2 teaspoons baking powder
½ teaspoon baking soda	2 teaspoons orange juice
1 teaspoon lemon juice	1 teaspoon vanilla
½-¾ cup nuts	

Beat egg yolks and sugar until creamy and light. Add remaining ingredients except egg whites and mix well. Beat whites until stiff. Fold together. Bake in tube pan at 350° for 1 hour.

Frosting Suggestion: Frost with creamy chocolate frosting.

FROSTED NUT CAKE

7 eggs, separated	⅓ cup hot water
1 cup sugar	1 tablespoon instant coffee
¾ cups flour	pinch of salt
1½ cups ground walnuts	1 teaspoon almond extract
1 teaspoon baking powder	

Frosting:

3 egg yolks	1 tablespoon coffee, mixed in ½
1 cup confectioners' sugar	tablespoon hot water
1 stick margarine	

Cream egg yolks with ¾ cup sugar. Then combine flour, nuts, and baking powder. Dissolve coffee in water and cool. Add the dry mixture alternately with coffee.

In a separate bowl whip egg whites with remaining sugar, pinch of salt and almond extract. Fold into cake mixture. Bake in tube pan at 350° for 50 minutes to 1 hour.

Frosting: Cream ingredients for frosting and frost when cooled.

Variation: FILLED NUT CAKE—Cut cake in half through the middle, and spread frosting on bottom layer as filling.

NUT AND JELLY CAKE

½ pound margarine	2 teaspoons baking soda
2 cups sugar	dash of salt
4 eggs	1 cup orange juice
4 cups flour	2 teaspoons vanilla
2 teaspoons baking powder	1 4 ounce jar jelly

Topping:

4 teaspoons cinnamon	1½ cups chopped nuts
½ cup sugar	

Cream margarine and sugar. Beat in eggs, one at a time. In another bowl, mix together flour, baking soda, salt, juice, and vanilla. Combine both mixtures. Prepare topping.

Grease a 9″ x 12″ pan. Layer ingredients in the following order: half the batter, half the jelly, half the topping, remaining batter, remaining jelly, remaining topping. Bake at 350° for 45 minutes.

ORANGE DRIZZLE CAKE

1 cup shortening	5 eggs
2 cups sugar	3 cups flour
½ teaspoon vanilla	1 tablespoon baking powder
2 tablespoons orange rind, grated	¾ cup orange juice

Glaze:

⅔ cups sugar	⅓ cup orange juice
¼ cup margarine	

Mix shortening, sugar, vanilla, and rind until well-blended. Beat in eggs, one at a time. Add flour, baking powder and juice. Pour into greased 9″ x 13″ pan or tube pan and bake at 350° for 50 minutes. Melt glaze ingredients slowly over low heat and drizzle over cake when slightly cooled.

PINEAPPLE CAKE

4 egg yolks	1 cup pineapple juice
1½ cups sugar	1 cup oil
3 cups flour	4 egg whites
2 teaspoons baking powder	cinnamon and sugar mixture
1 package vanilla sugar	

Mix egg yolks and sugar, then mix in flour, baking powder, vanilla sugar, juice, and oil. Beat egg whites separately and fold into batter. Pour into a 9″ x 13″ greased pan. Sprinkle with cinnamon and sugar. Bake at 350° for 40-45 minutes.

Variation: Add 1 small can crushed pineapple to batter.

PINEAPPLE UPSIDE DOWN CAKE

16 ounces sliced pineapple (8 slices)	¾ cup granulated sugar
¼ cup margarine	1½ teaspoons baking powder
⅔ cup light brown sugar, firmly packed	½ teaspoon salt
	¼ cup shortening
8 maraschino cherries (drained)	½ cup juice
¼ cups pecan halves or walnuts	1 egg
1 cup flour, sifted	whipped cream (optional)

Preheat oven to 350°. Drain pineapple, reserving 2 tablespoons of the syrup. Melt margarine in 10″ skillet over low heat. Add brown sugar, stirring until melted. Remove from heat. Arrange pineapple on sugar mixture in skillet. Fill the center with cherries and put nuts between the slices of pineapple.

In a bowl, sift flour together with granulated sugar, baking powder and salt. Add shortening and juice. Mix with electric beater. Add egg and reserved pineapple syrup, beating for 2 minutes.

Pour cake batter over pineapple in skillet, spreading evenly. Bake for 40-45 minutes or until cake springs back when gently pressed. Let stand on wire rack for 5 minutes. With spatula, loosen cake from edge of skillet. Cover with plate, invert, shake gently, then lift off pan. This cake is best when warm. Serve with whipped cream, if desired.

POUND CAKE

1 cup shortening	2¼ cups flour
1¼ cups sugar	1¼ teaspoons salt
1 teaspoon lemon rind, grated	1 teaspoon baking powder
1 tablespoon lemon juice	3 eggs
⅔ cup liquid	confectioners' sugar

Cream shortening and sugar together until light and fluffy. Mix in lemon rind, lemon juice and add liquid and mix. Add all dry ingredients to juice and mix until smooth. Add eggs one at a time, beating for 1 minute after each one. Scrape sides and bottom of bowl often. Pour into greased loaf pan. Bake at 300° for 1 hour and 20 minutes. When cool, sift confectioners' sugar over top.

Sponge Cake

Another popular cake often served at a Shabbos afternoon Kiddush (see *Yiddishe Simchas,* page 302).

FLUFFY SPONGE CAKE

8 eggs, separated	½ cup orange juice
1½ cups sugar	½ teaspoon baking powder
1 teaspoon vanilla	sugar
pinch of salt	cinnamon
1½ cups flour	

Beat egg whites with ½ cup sugar until stiff and set aside. Cream yolks and remaining sugar with vanilla and salt until lemon-colored. Add flour and orange juice alternately until all ingredients are blended. Add baking powder, then fold in egg whites. Pour half the batter into a tube pan and sprinkle with sugar and cinnamon. Cover with remaining batter. Sprinkle top with sugar and cinnamon. Bake at 350° for 1 hour.

Variation: PINEAPPLE SPONGE CAKE—Replace the orange juice with pineapple juice and 1 tablespoon lemon juice.

NEVER-FAIL SPONGE CAKE

10 eggs, separated	⅛ teaspoon salt
2 cups plus 2 tablespoons sugar	2 cups plus 2 tablespoons flour
juice of 1 lemon	

Preheat oven to 350°. Beat egg whites with sugar until stiff. In another bowl, beat egg yolks with lemon juice and salt. Beat together mixtures on low-speed until well-blended. Add flour gradually and beat lighly until mixed. Bake in tube pan at 350° for 50 minutes. When done, invert pan until cake cools.

Super Strudel

This recipe makes delicious pastry. It can also be used for hamantashen, rugelach, apple pies, etc. Here are three possibilities, any one of which will guarantee your "debut" as a strudel-baker. The quantitites in this dough recipe yield six strudel rolls.

STRUDEL DOUGH

7 cups flour	2 packages vanilla sugar
1 tablespoon baking powder	2 orange rinds
5 eggs	2 lemons, rind and juice
2 cups sugar	1 teaspoon almond extract
1½ cups shortening or margarine	

Mix flour and baking powder. Combine eggs, sugar and shortening and add to flour. Add in remaining ingredients. *Knead by hand* until smooth and resiliant. If dough is too thick, add 1 tablespoon orange juice; if too sticky, add a little more flour.

Divide dough into six equal pieces. Fill with chocolate, fruit or cheese filling.

CHOCOLATE ROLL-UP STRUDEL

2	pieces Super Strudel Dough	3-4	tablespoons cinnamon
⅓	cup sugar		jam
¼	cup cocoa		raisins

Roll out 2 pieces of the dough in long rectangular pieces.

Then mix sugar, cocoa and cinnamon; it should have a semi-sour taste — not too sweet from the sugar, nor too bitter from the cocoa.

Sprinkle sugar-cocoa-cinnamon mixture on rolled out dough. Add thin layer of raisins. Then spread thin layer of jam on top. Roll up each one in jelly roll fashion. Bake ½ hour at 350°.

This recipe is also ideal for making rugelach (page 264).

DIAMOND FRUIT STRUDEL

2	pieces Super Strudel Dough		juice of one lemon
	matzoh meal	¼	cup raisins
10	grated apples	1	tablespoon cinnamon
1	can drained crushed pineapple	2	tablespoons sugar

Roll out each piece of dough into a rectangle to fit a 9″ x 13″ pan. Place one rectangle in bottom of pan. Sprinkle thinly with matzoh meal.

Mix apples and pineapple together with lemon juice, raisins, cinnamon and sugar. Spread filling on dough.

Top with second layer of pastry. Cut a diamond-shaped hole from the center so that dough will not bubble up during baking. Bake at 350° for ½ hour.

CHEESECAKE LATTICE STRUDEL (Dairy)*

2	pieces Super Strudel Dough	1	teaspoon cinnamon
2	large containers cottage cheese, mashed well	1	lemon rind
			matzoh meal
1	small cream cheese		drained crushed pineapple
2	egg yolks	1	tablespoon flour
¼-½	cup sugar		maraschino cherries, cut up
1	package vanilla sugar		

Take one piece of dough and roll out to fit into a 9″ x 13″ (dairy) pan. Grease pan and place dough loosely on the bottom.

Mix together cheeses, eggs, sugars, lemon rind, and cinnamon. If too loose add some flour. Set aside.

Thinly sprinkle dough in the pan with matzoh meal. Add 1 tablespoon flour to drained crushed pineapple and spread over matzoh meal. Then top with maraschino cherries. Finally, spread the cheese mixture over the whole thing.

Roll out the second piece of dough and cut into long, thin 1″-wide strips. Place in criss-cross fashion over cheese. Cut off small pieces of top layer of lattice where it is doubled over lower layer.

Bake at 350° for ½ hour.

*Separate dairy utensils are required and a separate, portable dairy oven is recommended for baking dairy foods. (page 329)

CREAMY WHITE CAKE

⅔ cup margarine	2¾ cups flour
1¾ cups sugar	2½ teaspoons baking powder
2 eggs	1 teaspoon salt
1½ teaspoons vanilla	1¼ cups non-dairy creamer

Beat margarine, sugar and eggs until well-blended and fluffy. Stir in vanilla. Mix flour, baking powder, and salt and add alternately with non-dairy creamer. Mix well.

Pour into a greased 9" x 13" pan. Bake at 350° for 30 minutes.

FLUFFY WHITE CAKE

6 eggs, separated	2 cups flour
1½ cups sugar	½ cup oil
¾ cup liquid	1 teaspoon vanilla
3 teaspoons baking powder	

Beat egg whites with ½ cup sugar until peaks form. Mix remaining ingredients in another bowl and fold in egg whites. Pour into 10" greased tube pan. Bake at 350° for 1 hour.

WHOLE WHEAT CAKE

⅓ cup oil	pinch of salt
¾ cup honey	2 heaping teaspoons baking
or	powder
1½ cups sugar	1 cup unsweetened coconut
5 eggs	or
2 cups whole wheat flour	chopped nuts

Cream oil, honey and eggs. Then slowly add dry ingredients alternately with coconut. Grease pan with oil and a very thin coating of flour. Add batter and bake at 350° for 1 hour.

Note: If using sweetened coconut decrease honey to ½ cup, sugar to 1 cup. If using chopped nuts, increase to ⅞ cup honey or 1¾ cups sugar.

Yeast Cake

BASIC SWEET YEAST DOUGH

2	packages active dry yeast	1½	sticks (¾ cup) margarine
½	cup warm water	½	cup non-dairy creamer, scalded
4	cups flour		and cooled
1	teaspoon salt	2	eggs
½	cup sugar		melted margarine

Sprinkle yeast over water to dissolve. In a separate large bowl, combine flour, salt, and sugar. Mix margarine and dry ingredients on low speed until mixture resembles coarse meal. Combine non-dairy creamer, eggs and dissolved yeast. Add to dry ingredients, mixing thoroughly. Brush with melted margarine. Chill overnight.

HONEY TWIST

1	Basic Sweet Yeast Dough	melted margarine

Icing:

¼	cup margarine	1	egg white
2	tablespoons honey	1	cup powdered sugar

Divide dough in half. Roll each half into a long rope, 1″ in diameter. Coil into two greased 8″ round cake pans, beginning at outer edge of pan. Press down dough to level. Brush with melted margarine. Allow to stand in a warm place until double in volume. Bake in a preheated 350° oven for 30-35 minutes. Remove from pans to cool.

Meanwhile, prepare the icing. In a small mixing bowl, cream margarine. Add honey gradually. Beat in white of egg and powdered sugar. Spread on cakes while still warm. This cake stores well.

APPLE KUCHEN

1	Basic Sweet Yeast Dough	½	cup sugar
4	cooking apples, peeled and	½	teaspoon cinnamon
	sliced	¼	cup margarine, melted

Divide dough in half. Press evenly into two greased 8″ square pans. Press apple slices into dough, rounded edges up. Combine sugar and cinnamon, and sprinkle over the apples. Drizzle margarine over top of each cake.

Allow cakes to stand in a warm place until double in volume. Bake in a preheated 350° oven, 40-50 minutes or until apples are tender and the top well-browned. Remove from pan to cool.

COCOSH YEAST CAKE

Dough:

2 ounces fresh yeast	2 teaspoons baking powder
or	7 cups flour
2¾ packages dry yeast	1 cup oil
1 cup tepid water	or
5 eggs	melted margarine
1 cup sugar	matzoh meal
1 cup oil	

Filling:

2 cups sugar	lemon juice
3 tablespoons cocoa	1 egg yolk

Dissolve yeast in tepid water. Add eggs, sugar, oil, and baking powder and mix. Add the flour gradually. Knead until smooth dough is formed. Place in greased bowl and let rise until double in size (approximately 1½ hours).

Divide dough into 4 pieces. Roll out each piece to about 18″ x 12″. Grease with margarine. Cover with thin layer of matzoh meal. Mix the sugar and cocoa and spread it on the dough. Sprinkle with lemon juice.

Roll up the dough until a long thin strip is formed. Make sure the edge of the dough is face-down in the pan. Close up both ends. Make slits into the roll, about halfway through the cake, 2″ apart. Let dough rise for approximately 1½ hours.

Brush top with egg yolk and bake at 350° for approximately ¾ hour, or until brown. Yields 4 rolls.

Variations: ROUND COCOSH CAKE—Shape filled dough into circle by connecting the ends.
CINNAMON CAKE—Replace cocoa with cinnamon.

Frostings

The simplest cake can look mouth-watering when it is frosted. Use frostings to cover the top and sides of cake. After learning the basics, and with a few pieces of special frosting equipment you can achieve the results of a professional baker. Most of these recipes yield frosting for one 9″ x 13″ cake.

A few drops of food coloring will enhance the look of any basic frosting.

Boiled Frostings

CARAMEL GLAZE

3 tablespoons margarine	¾ cup confectioners' sugar
⅓ cup brown sugar	3-4 tablespoons water
2 tablespoons non-dairy creamer	

Melt margarine in medium saucepan. Stir in brown sugar and non-dairy creamer. Heat until boiling and continue cooking for one minute, stirring constantly. Remove from heat and cool until lukewarm. Stir in confectioners' sugar and enough water to reach proper glaze consistency.

CHOCOLATE FROSTING

3 ounces (squares) baking chocolate	1½ cups confectioners' sugar
	dash of salt
4 tablespoons margarine	1 teaspoon vanilla
3 tablespoons water	3 egg yolks

Melt chocolate and margarine with water over low heat. Remove from heat. Add sugar, salt and vanilla and beat at low speed until blended. Add egg yolks one at a time and mix at high speed until well blended and fluffy. Yields frosting for an 8″ layer cake or 9″ tube cake.

CREAMY ICING

2 tablespoons water	1 teaspoon vanilla
4½ tablespoons sugar	2½ cups confectioners' sugar
⅔ cup shortening	1 egg

Boil water, add sugar and stir until dissolved. Remove from heat. Blend in shortening and vanilla. Add confectioners' sugar and egg. Mix until creamy.

FLUFFY WHITE FROSTING

1 cup sugar	⅓ cup water
dash of salt	2 egg whites
1 teaspoon vanilla	

In a saucepan combine all ingredients except egg whites. Heat very slowly, stirring until sugar melts. Cool until lukewarm. Beat egg whites with mixer, adding sugar gradually. Beat constantly until stiff peaks form, about 2 minutes. Beat in vanilla. Frosts one tube cake.

Frostings – Mixed by Hand

ALMOND FROSTING

4 tablespoons water	½ teaspoon almond extract
1 cup confectioners' sugar	

Combine and mix well. Add water, if necessary to achieve a good spreading consistency.

BASIC JIFFY FROSTING

2 cups confectioners' sugar	2 tablespoons lemon juice

Mix together well. Spread immediately, as frosting hardens rapidly. Place in refrigerator for approximately 1 hour. Frost standard size layer cake.

Variation: Replace lemon juice with any other flavor extract, or a tablespoon of cocoa mixed with water.

COCOA GLAZE

1 cup confectioners' sugar	3 tablespoons oil
3 tablespoons cocoa	4 tablespoons hot boiling water
1 heaping tablespoon coffee	

Mix first four ingredients. Gradually add water and mix by hand until smooth.

Mixer Frostings

CHOCOLATE WHIPPED CREAM FROSTING

3 tablespoons cocoa	1 cup pareve dessert whip
½ cup sugar	pinch of salt

Mix ingredients together. Chill for 2 hours, then whip mixture until stiff. Yields filling and frosting for two 8″ sponge or angel cake layers.

COCOA-MOCHA FROSTING

2 cups confectioners' sugar	1 teaspoon vanilla
¼-½ cup cocoa	1-2 ounces cold water
¼ teaspoon salt	1 teaspoon instant coffee
4 ounces shortening or margarine	

Sift sugar, cocoa and salt. Mix coffee with water. Add to sugar mixture with remaining ingredients and beat until smooth. Yields frosting for two 9″ cake layers.

CREAMY FROSTING

½ stick margarine	1 egg
1½ cups confectioners' sugar	dash of salt
1 teaspoon vanilla	

Blend until creamy and light. Add cocoa if desired. Frosts one 9″ x 12″ cake.

GLAZED FROSTING

1½ tablespoons margarine	¼ teaspoon vanilla
1 cup confectioners' sugar	water
pinch of salt	

Cream margarine and sugar. Add salt and vanilla. Add water until desired consistency is reached.

SNOW FROSTING

2 egg whites	¾ cup corn syrup
¼ teaspoon salt	1½ teaspoons vanilla
¼ cup sugar	

Whip up egg whites with salt. Add sugar gradually, 1 tablespoon at a time, until smooth. Continue beating, then gradually add syrup until peaks begin to form. Add vanilla and mix well.

EASY VANILLA ICING

1 carton pareve dessert whip	1 package vanilla sugar
1 cup sugar	

Mix until stiff. Spread on cake, sprinkle with chocolate crumbs and refrigerate.

Helpful Hints

Baking Cakes: Never open oven door during first 15 minutes of baking.

Melting Chocolate: Grease pan first to prevent chocolate from sticking to the pot, or heat in top of a double-boiler. Or place pieces in aluminum foil and heat in oven for 10-15 minutes.

Cutting Cake: Do not cut more cake than you need, for it will harden fast. When cutting fresh cake, use a wet knife.

Decorating Cakes: First outline design on the frosted cake with a sharp-pointed knife. If you don't have a special cake decorator, cut off one end of a sealed envelope. Fill with frosting, remove tip of corner, and press out frosting.

Eggs: When separating eggs, if an egg yolk falls into the whites, remove it with the egg shell. For a smoother cake, take eggs out of refrigerator a few hours before baking.

Fruit Rinds: Save rinds of grapefruits, oranges and lemons. Wash off well, grate, and store in a tightly covered jar in the refrigerator. Use for flavoring in cakes and frostings.

Greasing Cake Pans: Cake pans may be prepared in various ways for easy removal of cake:

1) Grease bottom of pan very well, using about ½ tablespoon shortening. Dust with flour until bottom is well-coated. Shake out excess flour. (When making chocolate cake, use cocoa instead of flour.)

2) Mix ½ cup shortening and ¼ cup flour into a smooth paste and spread thinly on pan. Keep a supply in a covered container and use when needed.

3) Line with waxed paper.

Never grease the pan when making sponge or chiffon cakes.

Mixing: When adding dry ingredients alternately with liquid, mix just until blended. Overbeating will reduce volume.

Better Whipping: When using whipped cream in cakes, ice cream, desserts and the like, if whipped cream doesn't whip, return it to the refrigerator, chill thoroughly, add a chilled egg white and whip up again.

Raisins: For cooking or baking, rinse and let soak for 5 minutes in warm water.

Salt: Add a pinch of salt to every recipe. It brings out the sweetness of sugar.

Improved Shortening: Add 1 teaspoon lemon juice to margarine and sugar for a lighter cake. Add 2 tablespoons boiling water to margarine and sugar for a finer texture.

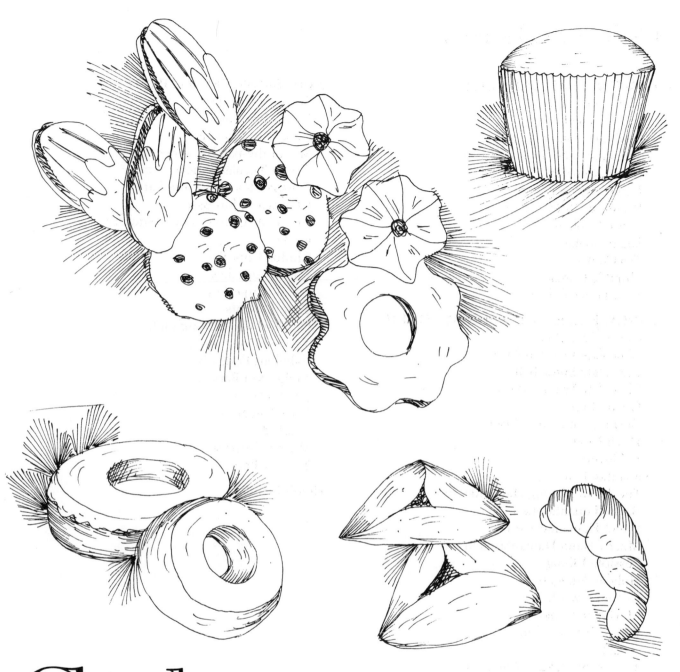

Cookies and Pastries

Cookies and Pastries

Cookies and Pastries

The cookie jar is always a welcome sight to a child, its contents a perfect treat at any time. Cookies come in all shapes, sizes and textures—some very simple to make, others requiring a bit more time to roll out and cut or to shape individually. A set of cookie shapes is a handy kitchen accessory which lends variety to even the simplest recipe. For a special educational treat for children, shape cookies into letters of the Hebrew alphabet.

Cookies can be decorated with frostings, chocolate or colored sprinkles or ground nuts, or lightly sprinkled with sugar.

Note: See beginning of Cake Section for some important laws applying to the baking of cookies as well as cakes, and also for other important baking information.

Variety of Basic Cookies

ALMOND BUBBLES

½ cup soft margarine	⅛ teaspoon salt	
⅔ cup sugar	1 teaspoon grated lemon peel	
½ teaspoon vanilla	1 cup chopped almonds	
⅔ cup flour		

Combine all ingredients in large mixing bowl. Mix in mixer on low speed or by hand until dough forms. Chill until firm.

Preheat oven to 375°. Make 1″ balls and place 2″ apart on ungreased cookie sheet. Bake 8-10 minutes until flat, light brown and bubbly. Cool and remove carefully. While warm drizzle with a confectioners' sugar icing.

BASIC COOKIES

1 cup margarine	1 teaspoon water
1 cup sugar	3 cups flour
1½ teaspoons vanilla	1½ teaspoons baking powder
½ teaspoon almond extract	¼ teaspoon salt
1 egg	

Thoroughly cream margarine, sugar, vanilla, and almond extract. Add egg and water and beat until light and fluffy. Combine flour, baking powder and salt and blend in. Chill for 1 hour.

Roll dough to 1/8" thick and cut to desired shapes and sprinkle with any topping (sugar, nuts, etc). Bake on greased cookie sheet at 375° for 6-8 minutes.

BON-BON COOKIES

1/2 cup shortening	1 egg yolk
1/2 cup margarine	1 teaspoon vanilla
1 cup sugar	2 cups flour

Cream margarine, shortening and sugar. Add egg yolk, vanilla, and flour. Mix well until light and fluffy. Roll into balls and place on ungreased cookie sheet (do not flatten balls). Bake at 350° for 15-20 minutes, until bottom of cookie is light brown.

CINNAMON & SUGAR COOKIES

2½-3 cups flour	1/2 teaspoon baking powder
3/4 cup sugar	3/4 cup orange juice
2 eggs	cinnamon
3/4 cup oil	sugar

Knead all ingredients together to form dough. Roll out and cut into shapes with cookie cutter or small glass. Dip in cinnamon and sugar mixture. Bake on greased cookie sheets at 350° until light brown, approximately 20 minutes.

HONEY COOKIES

3 cups flour	3-4 tablespoons honey
1 cup sugar	1 teaspoon baking powder
3 eggs	1 tablespoon cinnamon
1/2 cup shortening	1 teaspoon baking soda

Combine all ingredients, mixing well by hand. Roll out thin. Cut into desired shapes and bake at 425° for 10 minutes on greased cookie sheet.

LARGE COOKIE DOUGH

6 eggs
8 cups flour
4 sticks margarine

Beat all ingredients together until well-blended. Roll out on floured board. Cut into cookie shapes and bake on a greased pan in 350° oven, until slightly browned. Also makes a good pie crust.

PEANUT BUTTER COOKIES

2 tablespoons shortening	1 egg
3 tablespoons peanut butter	1/2 cup flour
1/3 cup sugar	1/4 teaspoon salt
1/4 teaspoon vanilla	1/4 teaspoon baking powder

Cream shortening, peanut butter, sugar, and vanilla. Add egg, followed by remaining ingredients. Mix well and shape into balls. Flatten with a fork on ungreased cookie sheet. Bake at 400° for 8-10 minutes. Yields 24 cookies.

PECAN COOKIES

½ pound margarine	½ pound ground pecans
4 tablespoons sugar	2 cups sifted flour

Mix all ingredients. Roll into small balls. Place balls in greased baking pan and flatten. Bake at 350° until bottom of cookies are brown. When slightly cooled, roll in powdered or granulated sugar.

SUGAR COOKIES

1 cup shortening	2½ cups flour
1 teaspoon vanilla	1 teaspoon baking soda
1 cup sugar	pinch of salt
2 eggs, well beaten	orange rind

Cream shortening and vanilla. Add sugar gradually. Add eggs alternately with dry ingredients. Grate in orange rind. Chill about 1 hour or more in wax paper. Grease cookie sheets and shape dough into little balls. Dip bottom of glass into water, then into sugar. Flatten each ball with glass. Bake at 350° for 10 minutes or until sides are brown.

TEA COOKIES

5 eggs	½ teaspoon lemon juice
2 sticks margarine	3 cups flour
1½ cups sugar	1 package vanilla sugar
¼ cup oil	1½ teaspoons baking powder

Mix everything together thoroughly, form into balls and bake at 400° on ungreased cookie sheet for 14 minutes.

THIMBLE COOKIES

2 cups shortening	4 cups flour
1⅓ cups sugar	4 teaspoons baking powder
4 eggs	2 teaspoons salt
4 teaspoons vanilla	jam

Cream shortening and sugar. Beat in eggs and vanilla together, then add dry ingredients, mixing well. Shape dough with hands into balls and place on greased cookie sheet. Press centers with thumb and fill with jam. Bake at 350° for 10 minutes, or until golden brown.

YUM YUM COOKIES

1 cup shortening	¾ cup nuts
1 cup powdered sugar	2 cups flour
1 package vanilla sugar	2-3 tablespoons cold water

Cream together shortening and sugar. Add remaining ingredients. Mix well and roll into balls. Press with a fork to flatten. Bake on a greased cookie sheet in pre-heated, 370° oven for 10 minutes, or until golden brown.

Fancy Filled and Holiday Cookies

CHERRY DELIGHTS

1	cup margarine	2½	cups flour
½	cup sugar	2	slightly beaten egg whites
½	cup light corn syrup	2	cups chopped nuts
2	egg yolks		candied cherry halves

Cream margarine and sugar. Stir in corn syrup, egg yolks and flour. Chill the mixture for about 1 hour. Roll into 1-inch balls. Dip in egg whites and then nuts. Press cherry halves on top. Bake on an ungreased cookie sheet at 325° for 20 minutes.

CHOCOLATE LACE COOKIES

½	cup light corn syrup	⅔	cup sugar
½	cup margarine	¼	cup cocoa
1	cup flour		

Bring corn syrup to boil. Stir in margarine. Sift flour, sugar, and cocoa. Blend into liquid. Drop by rounded teaspoons onto well-greased baking sheet. Place 2 inches apart. Bake at 350° for approximately 15 minutes, until golden brown.

CHOCOLATE SNOW BALLS

½	cup shortening	½	teaspoon salt
2	cups sugar	2	cups flour
4	eggs	4	squares melted bittersweet
2	teaspoons baking powder		chocolate
2	teaspoons vanilla		confectioners' sugar

Cream shortening and sugar. Add eggs, baking powder, vanilla, and salt. Mix well. Add flour and chocolate and mix well. Refrigerate dough for 2 hours. Preheat oven to 400°. Pour confectioners' sugar into dish. Roll 1 teaspoon dough at a time into a ball and coat with the sugar. Place on greased cookie sheet. Bake at 400° for 10-12 minutes.

CHOCOLATE WALNUT BALLS

⅔ cup shortening	⅓ cup cocoa
¾ cup sugar	1 teaspoon salt
2 egg yolks	½ teaspoon baking powder
1 teaspoon vanilla	2 tablespoons non-dairy creamer
2 cups flour	¾ cup walnuts

Glaze:

2 egg whites	½ teaspoon vanilla
2 cups confectioners' sugar, sifted	

Chop walnuts medium fine. Cream together shortening, sugar, egg yolks and vanilla. Sift flour together with cocoa, salt and baking powder. Blend into creamed mixture along with non-dairy creamer. Stir in walnuts.

Shape dough into small balls, about 1¼" in diameter. Bake on ungreased cookie sheets in a preheated 375° oven, 8-10 minutes. Remove from oven and cool.

To make glaze: Beat egg whites with a fork just until foamy. Blend in confectioners' sugar and vanilla. Dip each cookie into the glaze and drain on wire racks. When glaze is set, store in airtight containers. Yields about 5 dozen cookies.

CREAM PUFFS

1 cup water	¼ teaspoon salt
½ cup margarine	1½ cups sifted flour
2 teaspoons sugar	4 large eggs

Filling:

1 container pareve dessert whip	confectioners' sugar
1 package instant vanilla pudding	

Bring water, margarine, sugar and salt to a boil in a saucepan. Remove from heat and add flour all at once. Return to medium heat, and stir for about 40 seconds, until dough comes away from sides of saucepan and a film appears. Remove from heat. Add 2 eggs. Beat with wooden spoon, then add 2 more eggs, beating until smooth. Preheat oven to 375°. Grease and lightly flour cookie sheet. Spoon batter onto cookie sheet in big tablespoons. Bake at 375° for 20 minutes.

Lower heat to 350° and bake for 10 minutes more. Let cool. The cookies will be hollow inside. Make a small cut in each and fill, using 1 container pareve whip beaten until thick, mixed with 1 package instant vanilla pudding. Top with confectioners' sugar.

Variation: CHOCOLATE GLAZED ECLAIRS

To make eclairs, drop 1 full tablespoon of batter, 3 inches apart on ungreased cookie sheet. Then, with a spatula, shape them into strips 4" long by 1½" wide.

After it is baked press in filling through a small pierced hole on the side of eclairs.

To *glaze* melt 1 cup semi-sweet chocolate pieces with two tablespoons margarine, in the top of a double boiler. When chocolate melts add two teaspoons honey or corn syrup, 1½ tablespoons non-dairy cream (or orange juice), and 1½ tablespoons water. Stir ingredients together. Keep over flame a couple of minutes and immediately spread glaze over eclairs (or cream puffs). Glaze will harden over eclairs within minutes.

CURRANT-CINNAMON BISCUITS

2 cups sifted flour	4 tablespoons shortening
1 teaspoon salt	⅔-¾ cup juice
3 teaspoons baking powder	

Filling:

½ cup sugar	½ cup currants
1¼ teaspoons cinnamon	

Sift together dry ingredients. Cut in half the shortening with two knives or pastry blender. Add juice, mixing lightly with a fork until a ball forms that separates from sides of bowl. Turn out on lightly floured board. Knead gently for half a minute. Roll or pat out dough ¼" thick. Spread dough with remaining 2 tablespoons of shortening, melted, and mixture of sugar and cinnamon. Sprinkle with currants. Roll lengthwise as tightly as possible, jelly roll fashion. Pinch edges. Cut into one inch slices and place cut side down in greased muffin pan. Bake in hot oven at 400° for 18-20 minutes. Yields 12 biscuits.

Variation: Instead of sugar and cinnamon mixture, use one cup of jam.

DEVIL DOGS

½ cup shortening	½ cup cocoa
1 cup sugar	1 egg
1 cup water	¾ teaspoon baking soda
2 cups flour	½ teaspoon salt

Filling:

½ cup shortening	½ jar kosher marshmallow fluff
1 cup confectioners' sugar	

Preheat pans for 2 minutes at 450°. Mix all ingredients together and drop teaspoonfuls onto preheated pans. Bake 7 minutes at 450°.

To make filling: Mix shortening, confectioners' sugar and kosher marshmallow fluff until creamy. Spread between two cookies, placing bottoms together.

FOLDOVERS

2 cups flour	½ cup orange juice
½ teaspoon baking powder	favorite fruit filling
1 cup soft margarine	powdered sugar
¼ cup sugar	

Combine all ingredients for cookie dough and refrigerate overnight. Roll out to ¼" and cut in squares. Fill with jelly, pie filling, or canned fruit. Fold into triangle. Bake at 350° for 25-30 minutes. Cool and sprinkle with confectioners' sugar.

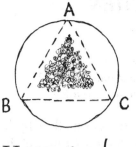

Hamantaschen

A three-cornered pastry filled with all kinds of delicious things. Hamantaschen is a traditional Purim delight.

Since this pastry contains *mohn* (poppy-seed filling), it used to be called *mohn-taschen* (pockets). But gradually the name haman-taschen developed, because of associations with Purim, in which the evil Haman plays a major role. (See pages 52–53).

THE ART OF MAKING HAMANTASCHEN

Roll out dough very thin (approximately ⅛″) on a floured board. Flour the rim of a glass and cut out circles. Spread your favorite filling in the middle of each (see diagram). To shape triangular hamantaschen, pinch together towards the middle segments AB and AC. Then fold upwards toward the middle remaining segment BC and join to other sides.

BAKING

Place onto well-greased cookie sheet. Bake at 350° for approximately 20 minutes until slightly browned.

Following are 3 hamantaschen recipes, and a list of possible fillings. Each recipe should yield about 4 dozen hamantaschen. When rolling out dough, first divide into several sections for easier handling.

BASIC HAMANTASCHEN

¾ cup sugar	4½ cups flour
¾ cup shortening	3 teaspoons baking powder
3 eggs	½ teaspoon salt
¾ cup orange juice	

Cream sugar and shortening. Then add remaining ingredients, and mix together well. Proceed according to directions above.

SWEETER HAMANTASCHEN

1 cup sugar	½ cup orange juice
½ cup oil	4 cups flour
½ cup shortening	1-2 teaspoons baking powder
3 eggs	1 teaspoon salt

Cream sugar, oil, and shortening. Then add eggs, and juice, mixing well. Blend with dry ingredients and proceed according to directions.

MIX BY HAND-HAMANTASCHEN

4 cups flour
4 eggs
¾ cup sugar
2 sticks margarine, softened
1 tablespoon orange juice

4 teaspoons baking powder
1 teaspoon vanilla
pinch of salt
orange rind

Mix all ingredients together by hand. You may add a drop more juice, or flour depending on consistency of dough. Proceed according to directions.

POSSIBLE FILLINGS

Use one or a combination of the following fillings. Place approximately 1 teaspoon of filling in center of each hamantasch after it has been cut into circles.

chopped apricots
chopped dates
honey (combined with chopped apricots or dates)
jams
lekwar (cooked prune concentrate)
poppy seeds

HOLIDAY NUGGETS

2 cups flour, sifted
½ teaspoon salt
1½ cups sifted confectioners' sugar
¾ cup shortening

¼ cup margarine
1 tablespoon almond extract
½ cup chopped nuts

Combine dry ingredients. Cream in margarine, butter, and almond extract. Add nuts and shape into small balls, using about 1 teaspoon of dough for each nugget. Bake at 325° for 20-25 minutes on a greased cookie sheet. Roll warm in confectioners' sugar. Cool and roll a second time.

LEMON-LOVE NOTES

A real treat for special occasions. Will win you compliments whenever served.

Dough:

½ cup margarine   ¼ cup confectioners' sugar
1 cup flour

Filling:

2 tablespoons lemon juice   2 eggs, lightly beaten
1 grated lemon rind   1 cup sugar
2 tablespoons flour   2 teaspoons baking powder

Frosting:

¾ cup confectioners' sugar   1½ teaspoons orange juice
½ teaspoon vanilla   1 tablespoon margarine

Preheat oven to 350°. Cut margarine into flour and ¼ cup of the confectioners' sugar with pastry cutter or two knives. Pat into 9″ square cake pan. Bake for 15 minutes and cool.

Combine lemon juice, rind, eggs, granulated sugar, 2 tablespoons flour and baking powder. Spread over baked crust and return to oven for 25 minutes. Cool.

Prepare frosting by combining remaining confectioners' sugar with vanilla, orange juice and margarine. Spread over the cake and cut into individual bars.

MERINGUE COOKIES

2 egg whites   ⅛ teaspoon salt
¾ cup sugar   ½ cup chopped nuts
½ teaspoon vanilla   1 6-ounce bag chocolate bits

Beat egg whites until stiff. Add sugar, vanilla and salt, beating until peaks are formed. Gently fold in nuts and chocolate chips. Drop by teaspoon on cookie sheet lined with brown paper. Bake at 300° for 20-25 minutes.

POPPY SEED COOKIES

3 eggs   4 cups flour
1 cup sugar   ¼ cup poppy seeds
¾ cup oil   2 teaspoons baking powder
  juice and rind of 1 orange   salt

Beat eggs. Add sugar, oil, orange rind and juice. Stir in dry ingredients. Roll out thin and cut into desired shapes. Bake at 350°. Check after 10 minutes. Remove when browned.

Rugelach

These popular, fancy crescents are usually filled with a cinnamon/sugar, cocoa/sugar, or nut/raisin filling.

THE ART OF MAKING RUGELACH

1. Combine all ingredients for dough, mixing well. Then chill dough for an hour or leave in refrigerator overnight.
2. Roll out dough into large round circles approximately ⅛″ thick and spread filling on top.
3. Cut into 6-12 triangles, depending on how large you want the rugelach to be (Illustration A).
4. Then work with each individual triangle separately (Illustration B), rolling it from the wide outside inwards, forming a crescent (Illustration C).
5. Place on lightly greased cookie sheet and bake at 350° until slightly browned (approximately 30-45 minutes).

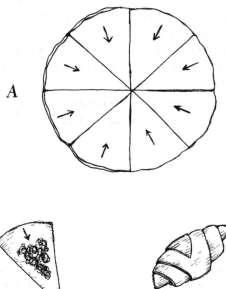

A

B   C

SIMPLE RUGELACH—Mix by hand

Dough:

4 cups flour	½ cup orange juice
2 eggs, beaten	½ pound margarine (2 sticks)
½ cup sugar	2 teaspoons baking powder

Filling:

jam and nuts

or

cinnamon and sugar

Proceed according to directions above.

SWEET RUGELACH

Dough:

5 cups flour	½ cup sugar
4 eggs, beaten	2 teaspoons vanilla
1 cup oil	4 teaspoons baking powder
1 cup orange juice	1 teaspoon baking soda

Filling:

½-¾ cup walnuts, chopped fine	cinnamon
½-¾ cup raisins	2 tablespoons orange or lemon
sugar	juice for moistness

Proceed according to directions above.

SNOW BALLS

1 cup shortening	1 teaspoon almond or vanilla
2 cups flour	extract
½ cups confectioners' sugar	1 cup chopped nuts
1 tablespoon ice water	

Cut shortening into flour and sugar. Sprinkle with water and vanilla and blend well. Mix with nuts. Combine above ingredients and roll into balls. Bake for 10 minutes at 350°. Cool and roll in confectioners' sugar.

WHEAT CRUNCH

2 cups whole wheat flour	½ cup apple jam
2 cups wheat germ	¼ cup raisins
½ cup oil	

Combine all ingredients and form into ball. Divide in half and roll out each piece on a floured surface. Cut into cookie sizes, shaping small squares, triangles or other forms. Bake on a greased cookie sheet at 350° for 30-40 minutes.

Variation: PRUNE CRUNCH—Use chopped, pitted prunes instead of raisins.

Bars, Brownies and Pastries

SPICY BANANA BARS

⅓ cup mashed bananas
¼ cup shortening
1 egg
1 cup flour
¾ cup sugar
½ teaspoon baking powder
¼ teaspoon baking soda

½ teaspoon salt
¾ teaspoon cinnamon
¼ teaspoon ground cloves
¼ teaspoon allspice
⅓ cup nuts (optional)
¼ cup non-dairy creamer

Frosting:
1 tablespoon hot water
1 cup confectioners' sugar

2 tablespoons melted margarine

Combine bananas, shortening and egg. Mix the dry ingredients, and stir into banana mixture alternately with the non-dairy creamer.

Bake at 350° for 20-25 minutes in a 9″ x 13″ greased pan. Cover with frosting while warm. Cut into individual portions when cool.

CARROT BROWNIES

½ cup margarine
1½ cups light brown sugar
2 eggs
2 cups flour

2 teaspoons baking powder
½ teaspoon salt
2 cups finely grated carrots
½ cup chopped walnuts

Preheat oven to 350°. In a saucepan, melt margarine. Add sugar, blend. Remove from heat and allow to cool. Beat in eggs, followed by remaining ingredients, except the nuts. Pour into two 8″ x 8″ x 2″ greased pans. Sprinkle with nuts. Bake at 350° for 30 minutes.

CHOCOLATE BROWNIES

½ cup cocoa
¾ cup oil
2 cups sugar
4 eggs

1½ cups flour
1 teaspoon baking powder
1 teaspoon salt
1 cup nuts, chopped

XIII. Cookies and Pastries

Mix cocoa and oil. When blended, add sugar and eggs, then stir in flour, baking powder, salt and nuts. Pour into greased 9″ x 12″ pan. Bake at 350° for 30-35 minutes. Cut when cool.

MIX-IN-THE-PAN BROWNIES

⅔ cup vegetable shortening	½ teaspoon baking powder
1 cup sugar	½ teaspoon salt
2 eggs	½ cup cocoa
1 teaspoon vanilla	½ cup chopped walnuts
1 cup flour	

Melt shortening in an 8″ x 8″ baking pan over low heat. Stir in sugar. Cool. Break eggs into a small bowl; add vanilla, beat with fork until blended. Stir into sugar mixture. Measure flour, baking powder, salt and cocoa, and add to baking pan. Mix thoroughly with fork. Add walnuts. Smooth top. Bake at 350° for 30 minutes, cut into squares when cool.

CRISP CHOCOLATE STICKS

Cookie layer:

1 square unsweetened chocolate	½ cup sugar
¼ cup margarine	¼ cup flour
1 egg	¼ cup chopped walnuts

Filling:

2 cups confectioners' sugar	1 tablespoon non-dairy creamer
2 tablespoons margarine	¼ teaspoon vanilla

Glaze:

1 tablespoon margarine	1 square unsweetened chocolate

Preheat oven to 350°. Grease 8″ x 8″ inch pan. To make the cookie layer, melt chocolate and margarine in top of double boiler and cool slightly. In medium bowl beat egg until frothy. Stir in chocolate mixture and sugar. Add flour and nuts, blending well. Pour into prepared pan, and bake for 20 minutes. Cool completely.

To make filling, blend all ingredients in a small bowl and spread over cookie layer. Chill at least 10 minutes. Meanwhile melt chocolate and margarine together over hot water. Pour over cake and spread evenly. Refrigerate 15 minutes to harden glaze. Cut into sticks with sharp knife.

BANANA-CHOCOLATE CHIP BARS

⅔ cup shortening	1 cup mashed bananas
⅔ cup sugar	2 cups flour
brown sugar	2 teaspoons baking powder
1 teaspoon vanilla	½ teaspoon salt
1 egg	6 ounces chocolate chips

Cream shortening, sugar, and brown sugar until light and fluffy. Add vanilla, egg and bananas, then combine with dry ingredients. Stir in chocolate chips with spatula. Bake in 10½″ x 15½″ jelly roll pan, greased and floured, at 350° for 20-25 minutes, or until done. Cut into bars.

CHOCOLATE CHIP BARS

4 eggs	3 teaspoons baking powder
3 cups brown sugar	dash of salt
1⅓ cups oil	1 cup chopped nuts
1 teaspoon vanilla	1½ cups chocolate chips
3 cups flour	

Beat eggs and sugar. When light and fluffy add remaining ingredients in order listed. Mix well. Bake in 9″ x 12″ baking pan at 350° for 25 minutes. Cut into bars.

CHOCOLATE CHIP-COCONUT SQUARES

1½ sticks margarine	2 cups flour
½ cup sugar	1 teaspoon baking powder
½ cup brown sugar	¼ teaspoon baking soda
3 egg yolks	¼ teaspoon salt
1 teaspoon vanilla	

Topping:

3 ounces chocolate chips	3 egg whites
½ cup coconut	1 cup brown sugar

Combine first five ingredients in order listed. Blend with dry ingredients and put into greased 9″ x 13″ pan. Sprinkle the chocolate chips and coconut on top. Beat egg whites stiff with brown sugar and spread on top of coconut. Bake at 350° for 40 minutes. Cut into squares while hot.

Cup Cakes

CHIFFON CUPCAKES

1 cup shortening or oil	2 cups orange juice
3 cups sugar	2 tablespoons vanilla
6 eggs, separated	rind of 3 lemons
4 cups flour	¼ teaspoon salt
4 teaspoons baking powder	

Cream shortening, sugar, and egg yolks. Stir in flour and baking powder alternately with juice. Add vanilla, lemon rind, salt and gently fold in stiffly beaten egg whites. Line pan with cup cake liners. Pour batter half full into each cup. Bake at 350° for 30 minutes.

FLUFFY CUPCAKES

2 egg whites	1½ teaspoons baking powder
½ cup shortening	½ cup juice
1 cup sugar	rind of one lemon
2 egg yolks	dash of salt
½ cup flour	

Whip up egg whites with salt and set aside. Then cream shortening, sugar, and egg yolks. Add the flour and baking powder alternately with juice. Then fold in egg whites and lemon rind. Fill cupcake liners one-half full. Bake at 350° for 30 minutes.

YELLOW CUPCAKES

⅓ cup shortening	1 egg
1¾ cups sifted flour	¾ cup non-dairy creamer
¾ cup sugar	or
2½ teaspoons baking powder	orange juice
½ teaspoon salt	½ teaspoon vanilla

Cream shortening, then sift in dry ingredients. Add egg and ½ cup non-dairy creamer or juice. Mix until flour is moist. Beat 2 minutes. Add remaining liquid and vanilla. Mix well. Line muffin tin with paper liners and fill ½-⅔ full. Bake at 375° for 20-25 minutes. Cool and frost.

Variation: CANDY CUPCAKES—Crush peppermint candy until very fine. Use approximately ½ cup crushed candy, and decrease sugar to ½ cup.

Helpful Hints

For easy removal from pan: Line cupcake tin with paper liners in each compartment.

To make cupcakes uniform in size: Use a ¼ cup measuring cup to fill each compartment, filling each liner a little more than one-half full. Do not overfill.

Converting cake recipes to cupcakes: If your cake recipe is basically plain and light, try making it into cupcakes.

Chocolate cupcakes: Use basic cupcake recipe, adding approximately 2 ounces cocoa and 2 tablespoons sugar and mix into batter. Increase oven temperature by 25° and reduce baking time.

Cupcakes always look nice with frosting, and sprinkles on top of frosting makes them even more attractive and colorful.

OLD-FASHIONED DOUGHNUTS

2 eggs	1 teaspoon cinnamon
1 cup sugar	¼ teaspoon nutmeg
1 cup non-dairy creamer	lemon rind
4-5 tablespoons melted shortening	½ teaspoon salt
4 cups flour	oil for frying
4 teaspoons baking powder	

Beat eggs and slowly add the sugar, beating constantly. Stir in non-dairy creamer and shortening. Add flour, baking powder, cinnamon, nutmeg, lemon rind and salt. Chill the dough slightly so it will be firm enough to work with. Roll out to ½″ thick on slightly floured board. Cut with a well-floured doughnut cutter. Let rest for 10 minutes to dry so it will absorb less oil when deep frying. Heat the frying oil to 375°, then add the doughnuts to the oil one at a time. Do not crowd fryer. Let cook for about 3 minutes each. When cooled, dust with confectioners' sugar.

Variation: FRENCH DOUGHNUTS—Instead of deep frying, bake in preheated oven at 350° for 20-25 minutes. Prepare topping by mixing 1½ sticks of melted margarine, 1 cup sugar and 2 cups non-dairy creamer. When doughnuts are done, immediately roll them in the topping mixture. Serve hot.

YEASTED DOUGHNUTS

1 ounce yeast (or 2 packages dry yeast)	1 teaspoon sugar
	½ cup oil
½ cup warm water	3 cups flour
½ cup orange juice	oil for frying

Dissolve yeast in water. Then add other ingredients. Let rise for 1½ hours and then form into small balls. Let rise again until dough doubles in size. Deep fry in hot oil until brown. Slice half open from the side, fill with jelly and sprinkle with powdered sugar, if desired.

FABULOUS FUDGE BARS

½ pound margarine	1 teaspoon vanilla
1 12-ounce package chocolate chips	1 cup flour
	¼ teaspoon salt
1 cup sugar	1 cup kosher marshmallow fluff
4 eggs	1 cup nuts, chopped

Heat margarine and chocolate in top of double boiler until melted. Remove from heat and stir. Let cool. Add vanilla, sugar, eggs and beat. Stir in flour and salt. Add remaining ingredients and mix.

Pour into 9″ x 13″ pan and bake no longer than 25 minutes at 350°. Mixture will look "wet" in texture. Cool until hard. Cut into squares and sprinkle with confectioners' sugar. Keep refrigerated until serving.

FUDGE-NUT BARS

⅓ cup shortening	2 eggs
6 ounces chocolate chips	½ cup flour
½ teaspoon vanilla	1 cup chopped walnuts
½ cup sugar	¼ teaspoon salt

Heat shortening and chocolate in top of double boiler until melted. Remove from heat, stir, and let cool. Add vanilla, sugar, and eggs, beating well. Stir in remaining ingredients. Spread into 8″ x 8″ pan. Bake at 325° for 25 minutes. Cut while warm.

JAM SQUARES

Dough:

¼ cup margarine	sugar
2 egg yolks	1¼ cups flour
½ teaspoon baking soda	salt
½ cup mixed brown and white	

Filling:

1 cup jam	rind of 1 lemon
1 teaspoon lemon juice	1 cup chopped walnuts

Meringue Topping:

2 egg whites	2 tablespoons powdered sugar

Mix dough ingredients in mixer and spread in 9″ x 12″ square pan. Bake at 350° in pan until light brown.

Mix jam, lemon juice, and lemon rind with half of the nuts. Spread on the baked dough. Make meringue by beating egg whites with powdered sugar, until stiff. Sprinkle remaining chopped nuts on meringue. Bake at 350° for 25-30 minutes.

NIFTY NUT BARS

Dough:

½ cup margarine, melted and cooled	½ cup light brown sugar
	1 cup flour

Topping:

2 eggs	1 teaspoon vanilla
1 cup brown sugar	1 tablespoon flour
dash of salt	1 cup chopped nuts

Cream margarine and sugar until fluffy. Blend in flour. Spread on 13″ x 9″ greased pan. Bake for 10 minutes at 350°.

Mix topping ingredients together and spread over crust. Return to oven for 20 minutes. Cool and sprinkle with confectioners' sugar. Cut into bars.

TEIGLACH

Dough:

2½ cups flour, sifted	⅛ teaspoon salt
4 eggs	1 teaspoon baking powder
4 tablespoons oil	

Sweetened nuts:

2 cups chopped nuts (no peanuts)	½-1 teaspoon ginger
1 pound honey	¼-½ teaspoon nutmeg
¾ cup brown sugar	

Dough: Sift dry ingredients. Mix well, then add eggs and oil. Mix again. When dough becomes smooth and thick, roll out into thin long strips about ½″ in diameter. Cut into ½″ nuggets. Place on greased cookie sheet and bake at 350° for 20 minutes until slightly browned.

Sweetened nuts: While dough is baking, combine honey, sugar and spices to taste in large Dutch oven. Cook over medium flame for 15 minutes, then stir in baked dough with a wooden spoon. After a few minutes, add chopped nuts and cook 10 minutes longer.

Shaping the Teiglach: Turn mixture onto moistened bread board. When cool enough to handle, wet hands and form into small balls. Place in individual cupcake holders.

For teiglach squares, flatten mixture on board into rectangle, 1½″ thick. When hard, moisten sharp knife with water and cut into 2″ squares.

Teiglach keeps for several weeks in a closed container.

WALNUT SURPRISES

1 egg	¼ teaspoon salt
1 cup brown sugar, firmly packed	¼ teaspoon baking soda
1 teaspoon vanilla	1 cup walnuts, coarsely chopped
½ cup flour	

Stir together the egg, brown sugar and vanilla. Add flour, salt, baking soda and chopped nuts. Spread into a very well greased 8″ square pan and bake at 350° for 18-20 minutes. Should be soft when removed from oven. Cool and cut into squares.

YUMMY BARS

1⅞ cups flour	1 egg
¾ cup shortening	1 egg yolk
⅜ cup brown sugar	

Topping:

2 eggs	1½ cups coconut
1 egg white	¾ cup chopped nuts
pinch of salt	1 teaspoon vanilla
2¼ cups brown sugar	

Cut flour into shortening and mix with other ingredients by hand until crumbly. Spread in greased 9″ x 12″ pan.

Mix ingredients of topping and spread over dough in pan. Bake at 350° for 45 minutes. When cool, cut into squares.

Helpful Hints

Cookie Utensils: Use bright and shiny cookie sheets. If you don't have enough cookie sheets, turn baking pans upside down, and bake cookies on the bottoms.

Have a supply of different shaped cookie cutters, for a nice variety.

When placing unbaked cookies on cookie sheet, lift them with a spatula.

Have a rack handy to place baked cookies on after taking them out of the oven.

When Making the Dough: For smooth cookies, mix well, but do not overhandle.

Baking Time: Cookies bake quickly. Set a timer to buzz when cookies are ready so that they won't burn. A too-slow oven will cause cookies to be dry.

Storing Cookies: Separate the soft types of cookies from the crisp ones when storing, so that each kind will retain its intended feel. Crisp cookies should be stored in a loosely covered container. Soft cookies should be stored in an airtight container.

Freezing Cookies: When freezing cookies, place them back to back in pairs, and put in even rows in a plastic bag. Unbaked cookie dough can remain frozen for several months.

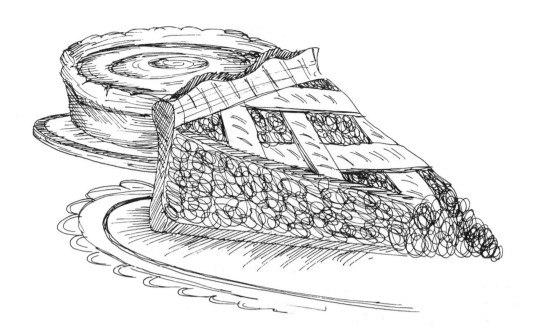

Pies and Desserts

Pies and Desserts

PIES

    Basic Pie Crust
    Perfect Pie Crust
    Five Minute Pie
    Angel Pie
Apple Pies
    Apple Pie
    Crazy Apple Pie
    Quick Apple-Nut Pie
    Swedish Apple Pie
    Cheese Pie (Dairy)
    Pareve Chocolate Pie
    Chocolate Cream Pie
    Chocolate Pudding Pie (Boston Cream Pie)
    Crumb Pie
    Lemon Meringue Pie
    Strawberry Rhubarb Pie
Helpful Hints

FRESH FRUIT DESSERTS

    Apple Cup Salad
    Canteloupe Halves
    Canteloupe Quarters
    Canteloupe Rings
    Orange and Grapefruit Cups
    Fresh Fruit Salad and Cups
    Fresh Fruit Trays
    Watermelon Basket

COOKED AND BAKED FRUIT DESSERTS

    Baked Apples
    Apple Latkes
    Apple Meringue
    Apple Pudding
    Canned Fruit Compote
    Cooked Fruit Compote
    Cranberry-Apple Sauce
    Hot Cranberry-Raisin Sauce
    Fruit Fritters
    Jel Dessert Fruit Cups with Topping
    Crunchy Jel Mousse
    Lemon Jel Mousse

PAREVE ICE CREAM

    Ice Cream Cake Roll
    Cherry Ice Cream Ripple
    Chocolate Almond Ice Cream
    Coffee Ice Cream
    Graham Cracker Lemon Freeze
    Neapolitan Ice Cream
    Ice Cream Pie
    Strawberry Ice Cream
Helpful Hints

Pies and Desserts

Pies

A home-baked pie makes a very special dessert any time, and with a good piecrust the variations are endless. Fresh fruit pies in season are delicious and easy to make.

Note: See beginning of Cake Section for some important laws applying to baking, and for other important baking information.

BASIC PIE CRUST

¼ cup cold water or ice water   1¼ cups sifted flour
½ cup shortening   ½ teaspoon salt

Mix all the ingredients in a blender at low speed for 1 minute. Shape the dough into a firm ball, and flour it. Roll out the dough 1⅛″ thick on a generously floured surface. Shape in a pie plate. Prick bottom and sides well with a fork. Bake at 450° for approximately 10 minutes.

PERFECT PIE CRUST

4 cups flour   1 tablespoon vinegar
1 tablespoon sugar   ½ cup water
2 teaspoon salt   1 large egg
1¾ cups shortening

Mix flour with sugar and salt. Cut in shortening until crumbly. In a small bowl, beat together the water, vinegar and egg. Combine both mixtures. Stir with fork until moistened. Divide into 5 portions, shape into ball and chill for ½ hour. Roll on lightly floured board. Prick when placed in 9″ pie crust pan. Bake at 450° for 12-15 minutes.

FIVE MINUTE PIE

2 cups flour   salt
2 cups oil   filling
¼ cup ice water

Stir lightly all ingredients except for filling until blended. Form into a ball and divide into two parts. Roll out on a floured board or between 2 pieces of waxed paper. Prick pie crust with fork before baking. Fill with desired filling. Bake at 425° for 30-40 minutes. Makes two crusts.

ANGEL PIE

4 egg whites	1 container pareve dessert whip
⅔ cup sugar	1½ teaspoons vanilla
½ cup confectioners' sugar	1½ teaspoons sugar

Beat whites until stiff, adding sugar slowly. Add confectioners' sugar and beat some more. Pour into a greased and floured pie plate and bake at 275° for 45-55 minutes. Cool and break down. Fill with whipped-up dessert whip, vanilla and sugar. Chill 3-4 hours. Serve cold.

Apple Pies

APPLE PIE

4 apples, sliced	1 teaspoon vanilla
¾ cup sugar	1 egg
¼ teaspoon cinnamon	⅔ cup flour
1 tablespoon margarine	½ teaspoon baking powder

Put sliced apples in greased pie pan; sprinkle with ¼ cup sugar and cinnamon. Cover and bake at 400° for 20 minutes. Cream margarine with remaining sugar. Add vanilla and egg and mix well. Stir in the flour and baking powder. It will be a thick mixture. Remove pie tin from oven, spread batter over apples and bake uncovered another 20 minutes.

CRAZY APPLE PIE

1 cup flour	1 egg
2 tablespoons sugar	⅔ cup shortening
1 teaspoon baking powder	¾ cup water
dash of salt	1 can apple pie filling

Combine all ingredients except the pie filling. Mix well and pour into greased pie pan. Cover dough with filling. Do not mix, it will form its own crust. Bake at 425° for 40-45 minutes.

QUICK APPLE-NUT PIE

5 medium apples	1 stick margarine
½ cup flour	¼ cup chopped nuts
½ cup sugar	cinnamon

Place margarine in freezer while preparing apples. Peel and core apples; cut into ½″ slices. Place apples into 2-quart greased baking dish. Mix sugar and flour. Sprinkle over apples. Remove margarine from freezer and place thin slices over apples. Bake in preheated oven at 425° for 20 minutes. Remove from oven and sprinkle with nuts and cinnamon to taste. Bake an additional 10 minutes. Serve warm.

SWEDISH APPLE PIE

Dough:

3¾ cups flour	1½ cups margarine
¼ cup sugar	¼ cup ice water
dash of salt	

Filling:

8 medium apples, peeled and sliced	1 tablespoon cinnamon
1½ cups sugar	1 egg, slightly beaten, for glazing

Combine flour, ¼ cup sugar and salt. Cut in margarine. Sprinkle with ice water, blending well with fork. Gather dough into a ball. Chill. Combine apples with sugar and cinnamon, and toss. Divide dough in 2 equal parts. Roll on lightly floured board to fit jelly roll pan. Place one piece of dough loosely into pan, pour in apple mixture, cover with second pastry. Join edges, flute, slit top, brush with egg, and sprinkle with sugar. Bake at 425° for 25 minutes and 350° for 15 minutes. Serve warm. Yields 12-15 servings.

CHEESE PIE (Dairy)*

18 graham crackers crushed	2 eggs, separated
2 tablespoons butter or margarine	1 tablespoon lemon juice
1 pound farmer cheese	3 tablespoons flour
1 cup sugar	1 cup milk

Combine graham crackers with butter to make crust. Press well onto bottom and sides of baking pan. Cream sugar with cheese until smooth. Add yolks, lemon, flour, and milk and mix thoroughly. Fold in beaten egg whites and pour mixture into crust. Bake in 9″ x 13″ pan for 1 hour at 350°.

°Separate dairy utensils are required and a separate, portable dairy oven is recommended for baking dairy foods. (page 329)

PAREVE CHOCOLATE PIE

1 baked pie shell	¾ cup cocoa
¾ cup margarine	4 eggs
1 cup sugar	1 teaspoon vanilla

Cream margarine, sugar and cocoa. Add eggs one at a time. Stir in vanilla. Pour into baked pie shell and refrigerate. Let set for 2 hours before serving.

CHOCOLATE CREAM PIE

Dough:

1 stick margarine	¼ cup confectioners' sugar
1 cup flour	¼ cup chopped nuts

Filling:

4 egg yolks	6 ounces chocolate bits, melted
3 tablespoons sweet wine	4 egg whites
2 tablespoons sugar	

Combine flour, sugar and nuts. Cut in margarine. Mix well. Roll out to fit 9″ pie pan. Bake 25 minutes at 350°.

Filling: Mix first four ingredients for filling together. Whip whites until stiff and fold it into chocolate mixture. Fill pie shell.

CHOCOLATE PUDDING PIE (BOSTON CREAM PIE)

Dough:

1½ cups flour	½ cup oil or margarine
1 egg	2 teaspoons sugar
½ package vanilla sugar	1 teaspoon baking powder
⅛ teaspoon salt	

Filling:

2 containers non-dairy creamer	2 packages chocolate pudding
1 tablespoon wine	½ package vanilla sugar

Topping:

1 container pareve dessert whip	1 teaspoon vanilla

Mix dough ingredients in mixer. Roll out to fit 9″ pie pan. Prick holes in it and bake for 25 minutes at 350°. Cook pudding with non-dairy creamer and sugar. Add the wine and mix. Place in pie shell. Beat up whip with vanilla for topping. Chill and serve.

CRUMB PIE

2 cups flour	1 egg, beaten
2 teaspoons baking powder	1 teaspoon vanilla
¾ cup sugar	pie filling
pinch salt	confectioners' sugar
1 stick margarine	

Combine dry ingredients. Cut in margarine. Blend with egg and vanilla until crumbly. Grease 9″ pie pan or 8″ square pan. Put half of crumbs on bottom. Fill with pie filling. Cover with crumbs. (Extra crumbs can be refrigerated and used next time.) Bake at 350° for 45-60 minutes. Sprinkle top with confectioners' sugar when serving.

LEMON MERINGUE PIE

1 baked pie crust	1½ cups water
⅓ cup lemon juice	2 egg yolks
1 cup sugar	margarine
⅓ cup flour or cornstarch	⅓ cup lemon juice
¼ teaspoon salt	

Topping:

2 egg whites	¼ cup sugar
salt	

Blend sugar, flour, and salt. Gradually add water. Boil until mixture thickens. Beat yolks in separate bowl and stir in ⅓ cup of hot mixture. Return to pot and blend. Stir in pat of margarine. After 2 minutes, remove from heat, add juice and stir. Pour into baked shell. Cool for 15-20 minutes. Beat egg whites until stiff. Add dash of salt and ¼ cup sugar. Top pie. Bake at 350° for 12 minutes.

STRAWBERRY RHUBARB PIE

1	2-crust pie pastry, unbaked		cinnamon
2	eggs	2	cups rhubarb
1	cup strawberries	1	cup sugar
3	tablespoons flour		salt

Beat eggs with fork, then add remaining ingredients and mix well. Place in unbaked shell. Top with remaining pastry and flute edges together. Bake at 425° for 40 minutes.

Helpful Hints

Proper Texture: Do not overmix flour and shortening; avoid adding too much water; do not overhandle. Pie crusts will be light and flakey.

Equipment: A Pyrex pie pan is ideal for fruit pies and nicely browned crusts.

Fitting in Pie Crust: Roll out half of pastry recipe into a circle about 1½″ larger than outer rim of pie pan, place loosely into pan, and gently press down any air bubbles. Do not stretch dough. 1″ pastry should be left all around the dish. Fold this 1″ piece in half, rolling it slightly under, to make a stand-up edge.

Making a Lattice Top: For a lattice top, roll out second half of pastry dough into a rectangle about 10″ long, 6″ wide and ⅛″ thick. Cut about 10-12 strips along the width making each strip ½″ wide and 10″ long. Place 5-6 strips over one side, spacing them approximately 1″ apart. Then weave through remaining 5-6 strips, by crossing over and under the first strips. A diamond shaped lattice looks very attractive.

Fresh Fruit Desserts

Fresh fruit desserts are refreshing, tasty, colorful and healthy. There's no need to worry about your diet-conscious guests either. Fresh fruit desserts are always "in." Pick out some nice fruits that are in season, and with a little imagination, some time, and a pretty presentation — voilá — you have a wonderful dessert. The following desserts also make excellent appetizers.

APPLE CUP SALAD

4	apples	¼	teaspoon lemon rind
3	tablespoons oil	¼	teaspoon cinnamon
1½	tablespoons vinegar (or lemon juice)	¼	teaspoon sugar
2	small stalks celery	⅛	teaspoon salt

Hollow out apples and moisten the inside with 1 tablespoon oil, and 1 tablespoon vinegar. Shred or dice the celery. Dice apple pulp and mix with celery. Use a salad dressing of your choice or prepare dressing by adding all the seasonings to the remainder of the oil and vinegar. Moisten the apple-celery mixture with dressing and refill apple cups. Sprinkle with chopped nuts and serve on lettuce leaves.

CANTALOUPE HALVES

6-8	cantaloupes	¼	watermelon
1	honeydew	1	box strawberries

Cut cantaloupes in halves and remove seeds. Then, using a watermelon scoop, scoop out large and small balls of cantaloupe and leave them inside.

Next, scoop out balls from honeydew and watermelon. Add strawberries, and mix fruit together.

To decorate cantaloupes, make tops look like a crown by cutting out small v's approximately ½" all around the tops of the cantaloupe halves.

CANTALOUPE QUARTERS

1	cantaloupe	8	honeydew balls
16	watermelon balls		blueberries

Cut cantaloupe into quarters and remove seeds. Then, from each side of a cantaloupe quarter, scoop out 3 balls — one toward each end and one in the middle. Put these balls aside. Fill the holes — the two ends with watermelon balls and the middle one with honeydew. Top with blueberries.

CANTALOUPE RINGS

1	cantaloupe	cherries
	watermelon balls	blueberries
	honeydew balls	

Cut cantaloupe into approximately 5 round rings (excluding the tops). Remove seeds from inside and peel. Place flat on plate. Fill middle of cantaloupe until heaping with watermelon and honeydew balls, a few cherries and blueberries. Refrigerate until serving time.

ORANGE AND GRAPEFRUIT CUPS

2 grapefruits   8 strawberries
4 oranges

Peel, section and pit grapefruit and oranges. Mix together in bowl. Add a drop of lemon juice and sugar. Mix together until a bit syrupy. Divide into 8 individual fruit cups. Top each one with a strawberry.

Place fruit cup on small flat plate lined with doily.

Hint: When using oranges or grapefruits, pour boiling water over them and let them stand for 5 minutes. The white skin will then peel off easily.

FRESH FRUIT SALAD AND CUPS

Fruit of season—apples, pears, grapefruits, oranges, bananas, melons, peaches, plums, strawberries, blueberries, cherries.

Wash or peel fruit, cut into cubes and mix together. Add small amount of sugar (or honey) and lemon juice. Refrigerate until serving time. 10-12 average size fruits yields approximately 8 servings. This mixed fruit salad may also be served as fruit cups.

FRESH FRUIT TRAYS

Practically any fruit will do.

Decide on what fruits you want, and how many servings you have to serve. Cut fruits into different shapes, such as slices, rings or cubes.

Suggestion:

orange slices or quarters (in peel)	watermelon squares
grapefruit slices or eighths (in peel)	grape clusters
apple rings (cored) or sixths	figs and dates
cantaloupe	pineapple squares

Place a cantaloupe half or a whole or peeled pineapple in center of platter. Arrange fruits in decorative manner around platter, piling it quite high.

Decorated toothpicks can be placed in some of the fruit or in holders around the platter.

WATERMELON BASKET

When serving a large crowd in the summer season treat them to fresh fruit from a watermelon basket. It will add beauty to your table as a centerpiece and be very refreshing to eat.

Serves approximately 30-40.

Ingredients:
- 1 medium-large watermelon
- 1 cantaloupe
- ½ honeydew

Optional:
- grapes
- cherries
- blueberries

Equipment:
- pencil
- sharp knife
- watermelon scoop
- large bowl

With a pencil, draw a line around the watermelon as shown, with a loop for handle on top if desired.

Now cut off sections A and B around the whole top.

Cut out all the watermelon from inside and put into a plate. With watermelon scoop make balls from the watermelon. Try to remove as many pits as possible. Put balls into one large bowl.

To decorate basket after the top is cut off, cut tiny ½" triangles into exposed top of rind, forming a crown (see diagram).

Fill the basket with balls of watermelon, cantaloupe and honeydew, and also grapes, cherries and blueberries, if desired.

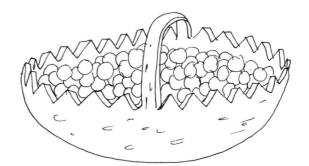

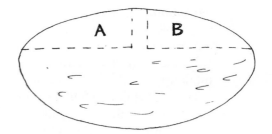

Cooked or Baked Fruit Desserts

BAKED APPLES

6 large baking apples
1 cup apple cider or orange juice

¼ cup sugar or corn syrup (optional)

Fillings: (Choose one of the following:)
cranberries, honey or sugar
pitted dates stuffed with almond
or
pecan halves

seedless raisins

Core apples. Arrange in baking dish. Stuff cavities with favorite filling. Sweetening may be added depending upon the tartness of the apples and individual taste. Use up to 1 tablespoon per large apple.
Bake 45-50 minutes at 350°.

APPLE LATKES

4 apples
½ teaspoon cinnamon
3 tablespoons sugar
1 cup flour
1 teaspoon baking powder
¼ teaspoon salt

2 eggs, separated
3 tablespoons oil
6 ounces beer
oil for frying
confectioners' sugar

Peel whole apples and core. Cut into approximately ¼" rings. Combine cinnamon and sugar and dip apple rings, coating well.
Sift flour and dry ingredients. Separate eggs. Whip whites and set aside. Combine oil and beaten egg yolks with flour mixture. Slowly pour in beer, mixing batter well until it becomes like snow. Then add the whipped egg whites and mix batter well.
Dip apple rings in batter and fry in small amount of oil. When done, sprinkle lightly with confectioners' sugar.

APPLE MERINGUE

1½-2 pounds cooking apples
½-1 cup sugar
water
vanilla

lemon juice
1 tablespoon cinnamon
2 egg whites
confectioners' sugar

Peel, core and slice apples. Stew with sugar and very little water. Add a squirt of lemon juice, vanilla and cinnamon. Cook until soft, then place in dish and cool.
Beat egg whites until stiff. Fold in confectioners' sugar and pour over apples. Refrigerate until serving time.

APPLE PUDDING

2 eggs
1 cup sugar
3 tablespoons flour
1 teaspoon baking powder

1 teaspoon vanilla
nuts
raisins
2 medium apples, chopped

Beat eggs and sugar well. Add remaining ingredients and mix well. Bake in a square baking pan at 350° for 30 minutes.

CANNED FRUIT COMPOTE

1 can pears, diced
1 can peaches, diced

1 can fruit cocktail
1 package frozen strawberries

Mix all ingredients well and chill. Let stand for 24 hours until the juice thickens. Serve well chilled. Cherries or plums can be substituted for strawberries.

COOKED FRUIT COMPOTE

4 apples
½ pound grapes
1 can sour cherries

½ cup sugar
¼ cup brown sugar
water

Cook all together for approximately 30-45 minutes over a low flame, stirring occasionally. Put in a jar to cool and then refrigerate.

CRANBERRY-APPLE SAUCE

1 pound fresh cranberries
3 pounds Macintosh apples

¾ cup sugar
½ cup water

Rinse off cranberries. Peel and slice apples. Add sugar and water, and cook on low flame until cranberry skins burst (30-45 minutes). Cool and then strain. Use as a relish, dessert or side dish.

HOT CRANBERRY-RAISIN SAUCE

1 12-ounce package cranberries
1 cup dark seedless raisins
1 cup water
1 12-ounce jar cherry preserves

¼ cup sugar
1 tablespoon grated orange peel
½ teaspoon salt

In blender, mix cranberries, raisins, and water until cranberries are finely chopped. Do half at a time, pouring mixture into 4-quart saucepan. Then add remaining ingredients to saucepan.

Heat mixture to boiling over a high flame. Reduce heat and simmer 5 minutes, stirring frequently. Serve hot, or cover and refrigerate; sauce will keep for 1 week. Reheat sauce just before serving. Makes about 4 cups.

FRUIT FRITTERS

4 ounces flour
pinch of salt
1 tablespoon oil
¼ pint tepid water

1 egg white
fruit cocktail
oil for frying
confectioners' sugar

Mix flour and salt and form a well in center. Pour in oil and water. Beat until smooth. Let batter stand 1 hour.

Just before using stir in stiffly beaten egg white. Drop fruit cocktail into batter. Fry in 3" of oil, browning both sides. Sprinkle with confectioners' sugar and serve warm.

JEL DESSERT FRUIT CUPS WITH TOPPING

3 packages Kosher imitation-jel dessert	1 can fruit cocktail
4½ cups hot water	1 package pareve dessert whip strawberries

Bring water to boil. In bowl, mix jel dessert with a small amount of hot water until smooth. Gradually add remaining water, and juice of fruit cocktail. Stir well. Let cool and wait until it becomes slightly firm (approximately ½-¾ hour). Stir in fruit cocktail gently and refrigerate until firm. Serve in individual fruit cups. Top with pareve dessert whip and set a strawberry on top.

Variation: LAYERED FRUIT JEL-DESSERT—Prepare each package of jel dessert separately, using 1½ cups water and ½ cup cocktail juice per package. In a 9" x 9" pan, place one package of prepared jel dessert. Let it set approximately ½ hour. Spread ½ of the fruit cocktail over it. Prepare another package. and use it to cover fruit cocktail. Let set approximately ½ hour. Cover with remaining cocktail. Then top with third layer. Let set. Cool in refrigerator until firm.
Note: Using a different flavor for each layer will increase the color attraction.

CRUNCHY JEL MOUSSE

1 package Kosher imitation-jel dessert, cherry flavor	1 container pareve dessert whip chopped nuts
1 cup water	

Cook jello in water and set in dish. Beat dessert whip and add to cooled jel dessert. Dessert should be in small pieces when mixed gently with dessert whip. Sprinkle chopped nuts around entire surface of mold and pour over nuts. Freeze until ready to serve.

LEMON JEL MOUSSE

1 package unflavored kosher imitation-jel dessert	4 eggs, separated
¼ cup cold water	⅔ cups sugar
1½ cups boiling water	1 container pareve dessert whip
	¼ cup lemon juice

Dissolve jel dessert in cold water in pyrex dessert dish. Add to boiling water on a small flame. Beat egg whites until stiff. Beat egg yolks and sugar. Stir jel dessert into the yolks. Add lemon juice and stir in dessert whip. Refrigerate.

Pareve Ice Cream

Ice cream at the end of a meat meal sounds impossible! Yet today we have pareve ice cream whips available to us. Whip it up in your mixer, add eggs and your favorite flavoring, and treat your family and guests to a genuinely refreshing dessert.

All ice creams presented in this section are pareve. They are prepared from a Kosher pareve dessert whip, mixed together with other fruits or flavorings. The standard size of the cartons of pareve dessert whip, referred to in this and other sections of this book, is 10 ounces.

Freeze your ice cream in freezer containers, and scoop out with an ice cream scoop and top with some syrup, or freeze them in cake pans, and cut into squares right before serving. For a very special look, prepare them as pies, cake rolls, or in individual molds.

ICE CREAM CAKE ROLL

1 jelly roll recipe	1 ice cream recipe

For complete jelly roll recipe and instructions, see Section XII.

CHERRY ICE CREAM RIPPLE

1 can cherry pie filling	2 10-ounce cartons pareve
3 eggs, separated	dessert whip

Whip up egg whites until stiff and set aside. Beat the pareve whip until stiff, then add egg yolks. Beat for 2 minutes and add egg whites. Using a spatula, fold in the pie filling. Pour into a bunt pan and freeze.

CHOCOLATE ALMOND ICE CREAM

2 eggs, separated	¼-½ cup chocolate syrup
1 carton pareve dessert whip	1 ounce margarine
⅛ cup sugar	2 tablespoons slivered almonds

Beat egg whites. Beat yolks, and set aside. Add dessert whip and beat until stiff. Add sugar to dessert whip mixture. Blend in syrup. Fold in egg whites. Melt margarine. Roast almonds in the margarine in oven for a few minutes. Drain and add to the ice cream.

COFFEE ICE CREAM

1 carton pareve dessert whip	4 egg whites
4 egg yolks	2 teaspoons instant coffee
1 package vanilla sugar	¼ cup sugar

Beat the pareve whip. Blend egg yolks with vanilla sugar. Beat the egg whites together with coffee and sugar. Fold together and freeze.

GRAHAM CRACKER LEMON FREEZE

1 cup graham cracker crumbs	1 cup sugar
2 tablespoons margarine	⅓ cup lemon juice
cinnamon	4 egg whites
1 carton pareve dessert whip	

Crush graham crackers. Mix with margarine and cinnamon. Press into 11" x 9" pan. Beat dessert whip until stiff. Add sugar and lemon juice and fold in egg whites. Pour mixture onto crust in pan and freeze.

NEAPOLITAN ICE CREAM

Vanilla:

2 eggs, separated	4 tablespoons sugar
1 carton pareve dessert whip	

Whip the 2 egg whites until stiff. Beat pareve whip until stiff, and then add egg yolks and sugar. Beat for 2 minutes and fold in beaten egg whites. Pour the ice cream into a high cake pan and place in freezer.

Chocolate:

2 eggs, separated	6 tablespoons sugar
1 carton pareve dessert whip	3-4 tablespoons cocoa

Prepare in the same manner as the vanilla ice cream, adding cocoa. Spread out on the partially frozen vanilla ice cream and return it to the freezer.

Strawberry:

2 eggs, separated	½-¾ package of strawberry Kosher
1 carton pareve dessert whip	imitation-jel dessert

Prepare as above. Spread out over the partially frozen chocolate ice cream and freeze.
Note: Each flavor can be spread out on a separate foil-lined cookie sheet. When frozen, place one flavor on top of another, removing foil first, or place one flavoring over the other before completely frozen.

ICE CREAM PIE

See *Helpful Hints,* below.

STRAWBERRY ICE CREAM

3 eggs, separated　　　　　　　　1 teaspoon vanilla
1 carton pareve dessert whip　　1 small can frozen strawberries
⅓ cup sugar

Beat egg whites until stiff, set aside. Beat dessert whip until stiff. Beat egg yolks, sugar and vanilla for 2 minutes. Add strawberries. Fold in egg whites. Mix together and freeze.

Helpful Hints

To keep ice cream frozen in freezer, here are two methods:
1. Put a drop of water on all the sides of tray or container before filling with ice cream.
2. Wrap tray or container of ice cream with aluminum foil.

For a delicious ice cream pie, use your favorite pie dough recipe. Bake it, and then top the dough with ice cream and freeze. When serving, cut into squares. One pie dough in a 9″ x 13″ pan is enough for 1 carton pareve dessert whip.

Confectionery and Beverages

Confectionery and Beverages

CONFECTIONERY
Colorful Candy
Chalvah
Chocolate Walnut Bark
Creamy Chocolate Fudge
Peanut Brittle
Polka-Dot Kisses
Rum Balls
Frosted Rum Balls
Sugared Nuts
Sugared Walnuts

BEVERAGES
Cocoa Drink (Dairy)
Egg Milk Shake (Dairy)
Hot Chocolate (Dairy)
Semi-Sweet Chocolate Drink (Dairy)
Fruit Punch
Easy Punch (Pareve)
Tangy Punch (Pareve)
Wine
Equipment and Instructions

Confectionery and Beverages

Confectionery

Sweets have often been used as an incentive for small children in their learning of Torah, and on Holidays, to add to their enjoyment of the occasion. An interesting custom using candy is that a groom on the Shabbos before his wedding is called up to the Torah and afterwards showered with small bags of sweets to symbolize hopes for a sweet future (see page 315).

COLORFUL CANDY

½ stick margarine	¼ cup corn syrup
3½ cups confectioners' sugar	flavoring
⅛ teaspoon salt	food coloring

Cream margarine, sugar and salt. Add corn syrup. Divide dough into sections, according to number of flavors desired. Add flavoring and appropriate coloring. Form into any shape candy desired.

CHALVAH

1 cup tahini (ground sesame seeds)	¼ cup honey
	¼ cup wheat germ (optional)
½ cup shredded or ground coconut (unsweetened)	⅛ teaspoon almond extract
	pinch of salt

Mix all the ingredients together. Either form into small balls immediately or form into a 1″ thick roll (you may have to divide it in two parts first) and cut off pieces. Put in a sealed container and store in refrigerator. Yields 20-24 balls or pieces.

CHOCOLATE WALNUT BARK

2 4-ounce chunks cooking chocolate	2 cups coarsely chopped walnuts

Melt chocolate in the top of a double boiler over hot (not boiling) water. Remove from heat when completely melted. Stir in nuts. Spread in a greased 8″ square cake pan. Cool until firm. Cut into squares. Makes about one pound.

CREAMY CHOCOLATE FUDGE

2 cups sugar
⅔ cup non-dairy creamer
2 tablespoons corn syrup
3 ounces grated baking chocolate
2 tablespoons margarine
1 teaspoon vanilla

Put sugar, non-dairy creamer, corn syrup and chocolate into saucepan. Stir until sugar is dissolved. Cook slowly until a little of the mixture forms a soft ball when dropped into cold water. Remove from heat, and add margarine. When cooled to lukewarm, add vanilla. Beat with a mixer until thick, 1-3 minutes. Pour into greased square pan. Chill, and cut into squares when firm.

PEANUT BRITTLE

2 cups sugar
1 cup chopped peanuts
1 tablespoon margarine
½ teaspoon baking soda
⅛ teaspoon salt

Heat sugar on low flame in saucepan until light brown and syrupy. Remove from heat immediately. Add all remaining ingredients and stir well. Quickly spread out the mixture evenly and thinly onto a well-greased cookie sheet. When cool, break into pieces.

POLKA DOT KISSES

2 egg whites
⅛ teaspoon salt
¾ cup sugar
½ teaspoon vanilla
½ cup chocolate chips

Preheat oven to 300°. Beat egg whites on high speed until frothy. Add the salt, and beat until peaks form. Add sugar gradually, and then add vanilla. Fold in chocolate chips. Drop by teaspoon on paper-lined cookie sheet. Place chocolate chip in center of each. Bake 25-35 minutes at 300°.

RUM BALLS

6 ounces chocolate bits
2 ounces hot water (not boiling)
3 tablespoons light corn syrup
½ cup sugar
½ cup orange juice
3 cups graham crackers, crushed
1 cup nuts, finely chopped
rum flavoring

Melt chocolate bits in hot water. Stir in syrup, sugar and orange juice. Mix in graham crackers, chopped nuts and rum flavoring to taste. Roll into balls and refrigerate for a short while.

FROSTED RUM BALLS

2 cups ground cookie crumbs	½ cup coarse nuts
3 ounces ground sweet chocolate	½ cup candied fruit
1 cup confectioners' sugar	⅓ cup dark rum
3 tablespoons white syrup	

Frosting:

3 tablespoons shortening	½ package chocolate bits, melted
5 tablespoons confectioners' sugar	

Mix ingredients together in order given and form into balls. Mix ingredients for frosting together and spread on balls.

SUGARED NUTS

1 pound shelled nuts	1 cup sugar
2 egg whites, beaten	¼ pound margarine

Toast nuts in pan in oven for five minutes. Beat egg whites and sugar. Add nuts. Melt margarine in cookie pan. Pour nut mixture over margarine. Bake 25 minutes at 325°. Turn batter over after it sets. Don't let it scorch; watch carefully during the last five minutes.

SUGARED WALNUTS

1 cup sugar	¼ cup honey
dash salt	½ teaspoon vanilla
¼ cup water	2 cups walnuts, in pieces

Mix sugar, salt, water and honey in saucepan. Cook until a little of the mixture forms a soft ball when dropped into cold water. Remove from heat. Add vanilla and walnuts. Stir until thick and creamy. Turn out onto waxed paper and separate into individual chunks with 2 forks. Makes about one pound.

Beverages

Here are a couple of suggestions for delicious home-made dairy and pareve drinks.

COCOA DRINK (Dairy)

2 tablespoons sugar	1 cup warm water
2 tablespoons cocoa	3 cups milk
few grains salt	

Combine sugar and cocoa. Add salt and stir in water until blended. Bring to the boiling point over low heat and boil 2 minutes, stirring constantly. Add milk slowly, stirring constantly. Heat but do not boil. Serves 4.

Variations: Add a dash of cinnamon and ¼ teaspoon vanilla extract.

EGG-MILK SHAKE (Dairy)

1 egg	crushed ice to fill glass
1 tablespoon sugar or honey	⅔ glass iced milk

Beat egg with sugar or honey in glass to be used. Add crushed ice and milk. Stir well with a long handled spoon, if a tall glass is used. Serves 1.

Variations: Omit sugar or honey. Beat egg in glass and stir in 3 tablespoons fruit juice. Add crushed ice and milk as in basic recipe.
Beat egg and sugar or honey as in basic recipe. Add extra strong coffee and crushed ice to fill ¾ full. Stir in 2 tablespoons cream and add iced sparkling water to make the mixture foam to the top. Sprinkle a few grains of nutmeg on top.

HOT CHOCOLATE (Dairy)

1½ squares unsweetened chocolate	2½ tablespoons sugar
(1½ ounces)	few grains salt
¾ cup water	2¼ cups milk

Combine chocolate and water in top of double boiler. Cook over boiling water until chocolate is melted. Add sugar and salt. Stir to dissolve and add milk gradually, stirring constantly. Cook 3 or 4 minutes over moderate heat, or 8-10 minutes over boiling water. Before serving beat until frothy. Serves 4.

SEMI-SWEET CHOCOLATE DRINK (Dairy)

4 cups scalded milk
1 cup finely shredded semi-sweet
chocolate

Pour milk over chocolate and stir well. Beat with mixer until well-blended.

Fruit Punch

A large homemade punch is a basic and very refreshing drink when entertaining. The proportions of the following ingredients can vary or you can add your own favorite drinks. Orange slices, strawberries or frozen colored fruit-juice cubes added at the end lend color and taste.

EASY PUNCH

1 package cherry drink mix
1 package lemon drink mix
2 quarts water
14 ounces orange juice

1 lemon, sliced thinly
dash of marjoram or cinnamon
(optional)

Blend 2 flavors of drink mix with 2 quarts of water. Add orange juice and mix well. Slice lemon and use as garnish.

TANGY PUNCH

1 large can fruit punch
1 6 ounce can frozen orange juice
mixed with
3 cups water

1 lemon soda
1 ginger ale
ice cubes

Combine all ingredients and stir gently. Add ice cubes last.

Variations: Use 1 can apricot nectar instead of fruit punch or,
1 can pineapple juice instead of frozen orange juice mixed with
water.

Wine

Wine has always been used for very special occasions: for Kiddush on the Shabbos and Holidays, for the "four cups" at the Pesach *seder,* at *simchas*—and when a *L'chayim* is called for. Wine is also mentioned in the Torah, as an important part of the offerings brought to the Sanctuary in the desert and in the Holy Temple.

Wine thus has a special and sacred place in Jewish life. Because in the past wine was commonly used in the service of worshipping idols, our Sages prohibited the use of non-Jewish wine lest the wine of idolatry become mixed or confused with Jewish wine. This prohibition remains in effect and a further reason for it is that it prevents social situations that lead to assimilation and to the formation of attachments leading to intermarriage. Therefore even previously kosher wine handled by a non-Jew when unsealed becomes forbidden.

Several brands of kosher wine are available; make sure the bottle has its seal intact. If you are really ambitious and somewhat of a connoisseur of wine, try making your own. With enough space, some simple equipment and a lot of patience you can achieve results that will impress everyone.

EQUIPMENT:

	Approx. Price
1 40-pound case of wine grapes (yields 2-3½ gallons)	$9-10.
1 grape cutter (optional)	$15.
1 food or wine press or cleaned burlap potato sack	$12.
2 large wood, copper or porcelain pots (no chips)	
Oak wine barrel, or large empty wine bottles, preferably dark and gallon sizes.	$20 (barrel)
Barrel tap or plastic syphons for bottles.	

About the Wine Grapes—Buy *only* wine grapes. They are cheaper, packed differently and carry more sugar content than other grapes.

The best time for buying wine grapes is early fall. There are generally 3 kinds of wine grapes:
a. muscatels (white wine)
b. zinfandels (light red wine)
c. concords (very deep red) — has very little sugar content

When using muscatels or zinfandels it is not necessary to add more sugar. Therefore when making your own wine we recommend you use either one of these and not the concord grapes.

Where to buy Grapes and Equipment—Grapes can be ordered in the right season through your local grocer. Better yet, buy straight from a wine grape dealer in the wholesale food terminals.

In the right season you can probably also buy from them most of the equipment you will need. If you intend to buy used equipment, check before buying with a Rav as to which necessary equipment may be 'koshered' and how to do so.

Another place where you can buy most of your equipment is in a local hobby shop.

Once you have everything, you are ready to start.

Step I—Crushing the Grapes

Wash grapes out very well, then crush grapes into a large wood, copper or porcelain container — crush very well as this will ultimately determine the amount of wine your grapes will yield.

Crush by hand or with a wine crusher.

Step II—Initial Fermentation

Let the wine stand open for 1 week in a cool room (a cool basement is ideal). During this week the juice from the grapes separates from pulps, and the initial fermentation takes place.

Step III—Pressing Wine

After one week you should separate juice from pulp. To do so use a food or wine press or a burlap potato sack. If using the latter, first wash it out very well in a washing machine and then dry.

If you are going to use a barrel for your storage container, buy a barrel tap and *drill* into barrel about 2″ from the bottom (Diagram A).

(Diagram A)

If you are using glass bottles, make sure you have enough wine locks or fitted corks with plastic tubing for each bottle (the importance of this will be explained below).

Do not try to press wine directly into the storage containers. This is difficult since the openings of these containers are very small, namely one-two inches in diameter and the initial flow of wine through the press is very fast and even with a funnel cannot be controlled. Also, a full barrel of wine is very heavy — the empty ones weight at least 15-20 pounds each, and no liquid weighs less than 7 pounds to the gallon — so even a 5 gallon keg of wine weighs at least 50 pounds. Therefore the storage container (wooden keg or barrel) is placed where it will stay, and the wine is gathered from the press in two pails (one full, and one to be filled) and poured from the pails into the barrels.

To separate juice from pulp, pour wine through press or sack. Juice will flow through into your set containers and pulp will remain inside press or sack.

Step IV—Sealing and Storing Wine Containers

Fill storage containers to the top and *secure tightly.* How well you secure the bottle is probably the most crucial step in the wine-making process.

Understanding the Physiology of the Making of Wine

During the next 2-3 months the wine will sit untouched and the sugar in the grapes will break down. As this happens it lets off carbon dioxide (gas). As the gas is in a closed container and under pressure, it must have a way to escape. At the same time, no air may be allowed to enter into the wine. Therefore barrels and bottles must be secured extremely tightly, while the solution to having a means by which carbon dioxide can escape is a small gadget called a wine lock. It is made in different sizes to fit various bottles, and has a small tube in it which empties into a small amount of water. The gas escapes through this tube, enters the water and evaporates. (Diagram B).

If you don't have wine locks, buy corks to fit bottles and use plastic tubing drilled in the middle of the corks. The other ends of the tubes are placed in a large container of water.

When barrels have a bung hold, the bung is the stopper. Drill hole in stopper (bung) and put in wine-lock (air-lock). Drill hole and put in one end of tubing. Put other end of tubing in container of water.

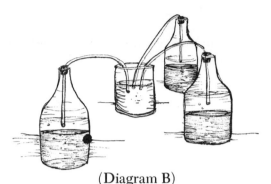

(Diagram B)

Step V—Fermentation Stage

Once they are tightly closed, place barrels or containers in a dark room. If the room is light, cover glass containers. Leave wine alone for at least 2-3 months.

As it ferments a certain amount of sediment, which we don't want to use, will remain on the bottom. When the wine is ready it will have to be decanted into other containers where it can remain stored permanently.

If the wine is fermenting in a barrel, it is preferable to place the barrel a few feet above ground level, and on its side, with the "bung" of barrel on the top. This provides for easy decanting. A barrel need not be decanted all at once, but wine may be drawn from the barrel in the barrel tap as needed. That is why the tap is placed 2″ from the bottom — so that the sediment will not be disturbed.

Step VI—Decanting

Have cleaned bottles on hand. If decanting from wine barrel, use barrel tap. If decanting from glass containers, use rubber or plastic syphons. Put one end into wine container and other end into the empty container.

The tubing should be inserted only about ¾ of the way down the wine container and not more, since you want to control the tubing to see that it does not disturb the sediment at the bottom (approximately 2″).

Step VII—Drinking

Cover bottles tightly and use.

L'chayim!

Yiddishe Simchas

SECTION 16

Yiddishe Simchas

L'Chayim! - To Life!
Kiddush - Shabbos Afternoon
Melava Malka - Escorting the Shabbos Queen
Naming of a Child
Birth of a Daughter
Sholom Zochar - Birth of a Son
Bris Milah - Covenant of Circumcision
Pidyon Haben - Redemption of the Firstborn
Upsherenish - Haircutting Ceremony
 A Candlestick for our Daughter
 The Beginning of a Child's Formal Education
Bas-Mitzvah - A Girl Comes of Age
Bar-Mitzvah - A Boy Comes of Age
Vort or T'nayim - Engaged
Ufrauf - The Chosson is Called Up
Forshpiel - Rejoicing with the Kallah
Chassanah - The Wedding
 Kabbalas Panim - Reception
 The Chupah - Marriage Canopy
 The Meal
Sheva Brochos - A Royal Week
Chanukas Habayis - A New Jewish Home
Life by Life - A New Cycle

Suggested Menus and Serving Style for Each Simcha

Yiddishe Simchas

L'chayim-To Life

"To life" . . . The toast that is on our lips has a special meaning in our minds. We celebrate life because it is purposeful, inherently good, a gift from the A-mighty. The birth of a new child is an occasion for great *simcha*—which means both "joy" and, in our context, the celebration of this joy with a special party and meal.

Jews have affirmed life in all situations, even the most dire. When Pharaoh instituted his form of population control by ordering the death by drowning of all Jewish males born in Egypt, the Jewish men and women at first were afraid to continue having children. Why bring children into the world, and to such a fate? Then Miriam, the sister of Moses, came and said to her parents: "Pharaoh wants to kill the boys but you are killing the girls as well!" The people recognized their error and resumed having children—and, as we know, Moses was born and lived to lead the Jewish people to freedom.

When a Jew says *L'Chayim!* to celebrate a moment of simcha it is with a deep-rooted knowledge of life's many faces. After all, the *neshomah,* the spark of G-dliness which we call the soul, comes into this world to fulfill a mission and to face challenges. To live as a Jew—this itself is a triumph and a cause for simcha! To bring another Jewish *neshomah* into the world, another boy or girl who will grow up to "Torah, *Chupah,* and Good Deeds" is indeed a privilege. Proudly a mother and father face the important task ahead of raising and educating a new child.

Each step along the way will represent an elevation of the person to a new stage, a new level of responsibility and commitment. That is why Jewish life accords each of life's milestones such recognition and marks it with such ceremony.

A *simcha* may be celebrated in a variety of ways. Different occasions traditionally call for either a formal or informal approach. Sometimes special foods are associated for symbolic reasons with a particular event, like chickpeas at a *Sholom-Zochor.* Some occasions call for a *Seudas-Mitzvah* (Mitzvah Meal) at which at least a *minyan* (10 men over Bar-Mitzvah age) eat a meal with bread and afterwards say the Blessings-After-A-Meal together over a cup of wine. In the following pages we will discuss each of the special occasions in Jewish life in turn, mentioning major customs and their significance, and providing a guide to menu preparation.

The beginning of life is the beginning of life's celebration—reflecting our joy in fulfilling our mission in this world—which grows from day to day and year to year.

L'Chayim!

Kiddush

Shabbos Afternoon

One of the most common ways of celebrating a simcha is by giving a *Kiddush* in shul after the morning prayers. A Kiddush usually takes place after the Shabbos Morning Services, when everyone is in shul at the same time. This mini-affair takes its name from the "Kiddush" prayer said over the wine on Friday evening and Shabbos day, for it is with this prayer that the Kiddush begins (see page 24).

A Kiddush will usually take place when Jewish Law does not prescribe another form of celebration as, for example, in celebrating the birth of a daughter. And even when there are other ways to mark an occasion, it is always nice to make a Kiddush! There are times when it seems that almost every week at shul someone is giving a Kiddush to celebrate something—a baby girl, an engagement, a new home, a Bar Mitzvah . . .

The suggested menu for a Kiddush, below, provides a wide variety of serving possibilities. Your selections will depend on how formal or informal the Kiddush will be and the number of people expected. A buffet-style Kiddush is a common practice. In fulfilling the requirement of hearing "Kiddush" recited on Shabbos, one says *Amen* to the blessing over wine and eats at least an ounce of cake or similar food (unless a formal meal is served).

If a formal meal is served, whether at home or in the synagogue hall, the "Kiddush" is recited and then all participants receive a small challah, over which they must wash their hands in the ritual manner. The Kiddush may be an elaborate party taking the place of a catered affair. Then steaming hot cholent and kugel are often served. The cholent should be kept warm on the *blech.*

302

Suggested Serving Style and Foods

Light Buffet: Wine; assortment of cakes (sponge, marble, chocolate etc.), cookies (optional); gefilte fish balls or slices, herring; soda, liquor for *l'chayim*.

Complete Buffet: All the above; and an assortment of side dishes such as noodle and/or potato kugel, coleslaw, potato salad, sliced vegetables.

Dinner: Wine; large challah, challah rolls; gefilte fish and vegetables or salad; cholent, sliced meat or coldcuts; kugel, coleslaw, potato salad; soda, liquor for *l'chayim*; and assorted cakes.

Melava Malka

Escorting the Queen—Saturday Night

Melava Malka, the Saturday night, post-Shabbos meal is another traditional time to celebrate such important events, as an engagement or Bar Mitzvah. It is also a wonderful time for a plain, *heimish,* relaxed get-together with friends and relatives. This meal, which represents the farewell to the Shabbos Queen, can range from very simple to very elegant, depending on the nature of the special occasion. For a fuller understanding of the importance of Melava Malka (see page 29).

Traditional foods as part of the meal are herring or smoked fish, whole cooked potatoes, and something hot to drink. The choice of food is up to you, but keep in mind that most people probably have had a meat meal towards the end of Shabbos and therefore may not have any dairy dishes until six hours afterwards.

Suggested Serving Style and Foods

The following foods can be served in a casual buffet style or in a formal dinner style.

Buffet or Dinner: Challah rolls; chopped herring and/or smoked fish; boiled or baked, whole or sliced potatoes; vegetable side dishes; soda; assorted cakes and tea.

Naming of a Child

Every Jewish parent experiences a little bit of *Ruach Hakodesh* or "Divine inspiration" when it comes to the naming of a child, say our Sages. A Jewish name is closely linked to the life of the child for whom that name is chosen.

The Torah and Holy Writings contain many instances in which the name of a person is an indication of that person's personality, character or goal in life. Foremost is the change in Abraham's name when he was given a higher purpose in life: G-d added a letter to his name, changing it from Abram to Abraham. Each Hebrew letter of the name is a "channel" for the flow of life-force which will reach that person. The additional letter in Abraham's name changed its meaning and gave him an additional power in his service of G-d.

It is customary to give a name which perpetuates the memory of a close relative or friend, or to name a child after a great person, outstanding in virtue and piety, in the hope that in growing up the child will be closely linked with the ways of this righteous person.

One's full Jewish name is used in the *kesubah* (marriage contract), when one is called up to the Torah, when prayers are offered on behalf of a person, and at other important moments in life. Using one's Jewish name in everyday life is an expression of Jewish pride and identity. Our sages teach us that one of the reasons the Jews merited to be redeemed from bondage in Egypt was their tenacious clinging to Jewish identity despite the pressure of Egyptian culture—they kept their Jewish names, language and mode of dress. Proud names, ancient names, preserved throughout many generations of dispersal, remained part of our collective identity.

A Jewish name is thus a precious heritage. We approach the ceremony at which the boy or girl is named with a feeling of dignity. It is an important moment. And whatever the name, it will be the "right one"—for the parents' *Ruach Hakodesh* cannot be wrong!

Birth of a Daughter

A girl is born. A strong link is added in the proud chain which began with Sarah, Rivka, Rachel and Leah. A child who will grow to be a woman responsible for insuring the continuity of the very essence of Judaism. For Jewishness is determined by the mother; a child is Jewish according to *halacha* (Torah law) when the mother is Jewish. The Torah recognizes the woman as the prime influence in her child's development, especially in the crucial early years. Although a baby girl enters the world subtly and quietly, she may before long be exerting a powerful influence on her sisters and brothers, a foreshadowing of the influence she will have later in life as the "pillar" of her family.

A girl is named at the reading of the Torah after her birth on a Monday, Thursday, or Shabbos, whichever comes first. After services come *l'chayims* and refreshments. Some people make a point of waiting for the Shabbos following the birth to give the name and herald the little girl's arrival in full style, and make a big Kiddush then. When a boy is born, he is not named until the eighth day, at the circumcision ceremony.

Why is there no ceremony for a girl corresponding to the Bris Milah of a boy? There are two general ideas which must be understood before we jump to any conclusions about the way Torah views women.

One effect of doing mitzvohs is the purification and refinement of the individual who performs them. A larger number of mitzvohs to be performed thus indicates a greater need for purification. Since a woman is not obligated to keep many of the positive mitzvohs, namely, those which must be done within a fixed time period, such as *tefillin,* it can be understood that a woman is less in need of purification than is a man.

One of the underlying purposes of Bris Milah is to bring about a corresponding *milah* (purification) of the heart. A woman, for whom no *milah* is required, does not need a concrete sign for a reminder of her higher purpose.

The second reason that celebrating the birth of a daughter is done in a more quiet manner is an indication to the modest way in which she will be raised. This modesty and "innerness" will eventually become the strength that the woman brings to the man-woman partnership (see *Bas-Mitzvah,* page 312).

Suggested Serving Style and Foods

Buffet: Light refreshments; soda and liquor for *l'chayim* after services during the week, or buffet-style Kiddush on Shabbos.

Dinner: No official ceremony is prescribed, yet certainly the parents may want to celebrate this occasion with relatives and friends in the form of a festive dinner. If this is the case, it is usually done within the first few weeks of the baby's birth.

Sholom Zochar

Birth of a Son

A baby boy is born, a son who will soon enter into the covenant of the Jewish people with G-d. Two celebrations will be given by the family within the next eight days to honor their new son: the *Sholom Zochor* and then the *Bris Milah.*

The Sholom Zochor always takes place the first Friday night after the birth of the son. It is commonly translated as "Welcome Male," but actually gets its name from the fact that it is on Shabbos (which is known as *sholom,* peace) that we gather to greet the newborn boy (*zochor*). Guests are invited to come in the evening, after the Friday night meal. This always comes before the Bris Milah (circumcision ceremony) on the eighth day, so the boy is still unnamed.

It is customary to serve light refreshments at the Sholom Zochor. Chickpeas, also known as *arbis* or *nahit,* are traditionally served because they are symbolic of mourning and we "mourn" the fact that at birth the child has forgotten the Torah which he had been taught when yet unborn. This initial learning of the entire Torah will later give him the strength to acquire the knowledge of Torah on his own, for it is an obligation for him to study as well as to keep the Torah throughout his life. (A girl is also taught the Torah and is obligated to *know* its laws, but the obligation of constant study is not upon her.)

On preparing *arbis* see *Chickpeas,* Section X.

Amidst song and a table of refreshments and drinks, the guests rejoice as yet another member is added to the Jewish people.

Suggested Serving Style and Foods

Buffet: Assorted cakes and cookies; fruit bowls; arbis (chickpeas); soda, beer, liquor for *l'chayim.*

306

Bris Milah

Covenant of Circumcision

The time has come to initiate the son into the Jew's special relationship with G-d. Now after eight days of being called "the baby" or "him," the boy will be given a Hebrew name.

Before the Bris Milah, it is customary for the father to stay awake the whole evening, often with some relatives and friends taking turns remaining with him throughout the evening. The prayer *Shema Yisroel* is said for the child and the entire night is dedicated to Torah study. Light refreshments are served throughout the evening. The Bris Milah is usually planned for early in the morning, a sign of our eagerness to do G-d's will.

Ever since Abraham, the very first Jew, each Jewish male has affirmed his side of the eternal covenant with G-d, and made himself fit for that covenant through circumcision, as commanded in the Torah. As soon as the actual Bris Milah is completed, all present shout together, "Mazel Tov!" Just as he has entered into the covenant, so may he enter into a life of "learning Torah, marriage, and doing good deeds."

The *mohel* chosen to perform circumcision on the child should be a G-d fearing and Torah-observant man, and a person of great skill. A couple (*kvater*) is honored with bringing the child in from his mother to the *sandek*, the man who has been honored to sit and hold the child in his lap on a pillow during the *milah*. Various blessings are recited by the *mohel* and the father. Afterwards, the baby is quieted by the taste of his very first drop of wine and returned to his mother. The whole procedure happens very quickly.

If the child is premature or ill, G-d forbid, or weak for some other reason, it is necessary to consult with both the *mohel* and the doctor as to whether the *bris* should be postponed, and if so, for how long. Otherwise, the *bris* usually takes place early in the morning of the eighth day, amidst much rejoicing among family and friends. If the eighth day is Shabbos the *bris* is usually performed around noon-time after the Shabbos morning service, after which relatives and friends join the celebrating family for a full Kiddush meal.

The Bris Milah is always followed by a complete meal, known as a *Seudas Mitzvah,* a meal in honor of a mitzvah. At such a meal, all participating guests start the meal with the ritual washing of the hands and blessing over the challah or bread. Several special verses are added to the Blessings-After-A-Meal, and are recited by the honored guests. Usually a meat meal is served, but if one prefers, a pareve fish meal, or even a dairy meal may be served instead.

People are not invited to a *bris,* since it would not be fitting for them to refuse such an honor. Therefore to avoid possible refusals, our relatives and friends are simply informed of the time the *bris* is to take place. The prophet Elijah himself is said to come to each ceremony of circumcision, and so a beautiful chair called, for this occasion, the chair of Elijah is always set out for him. No one sits on this chair during the Bris Milah.

Suggested Serving Style and Foods

Dinner I (Fish and Dairy)*: Large challah, challah rolls; appetizer; smoked fish, or other fish; variety of cheeses; side dishes such as macaroni cheese salad, egg salad, potato salad and/or cole slaw, sliced fresh vegetables; soda, liquor for *l'chayim;* fruit dessert and assorted cakes.

Dinner II (Fish and Meat)**: Challah rolls; appetizer; fish and vegetables; sliced meat or cold-cuts or baked chicken; side dishes such as sweet kugel, potato salad, cole slaw, fresh vegetables; soda, liquor for *l'chayim;* dessert and assorted cakes.

*Fish and dairy foods are served on different plates.
**Fish and meat are served on different plates.

Pidyon Haben
Redemption of the First Born—One Month Old

If the boy is the firstborn of his mother, born in the normal manner and not through Cesarian birth, still another ceremony takes place in these early days of his life—the *Pidyon Haben* (redemption of the first-born son).

Originally, all firstborn males of the twelve tribes of Israel were to have been consecrated as *Kohanim* (Priests) in the service of G-d. This function, however, was relegated to Aaron and his descendants, all of whom are of the tribe of Levi. Therefore, a firstborn male of any of the other tribes—i.e. whose father is not a *Kohain* or a *Levi,* nor his mother the daughter of a *Kohain* or a *Levi,* must be redeemed from his obligation to the priestly service. This redemption takes place when the first-born son is one full month of age.

The Pidyon Haben takes place a little over 29½ days after the baby's birth. If this date should coincide with Shabbos or a Festival, it is postponed until the following day. The father gives the *Kohain* five silver coins of a specified value as the price of redemption. (The value in modern currency will vary.)

As at the Bris Milah, all attending guests are invited to partake of a complete *Seudas Mitzvah.* Serve a full course, sit-down meal, beginning with the ritual washing before challah. Your menu can vary depending on the time of day (morning until late afternoon) you have the Pidyon Haben.

Suggested Serving Style and Foods

Dinner: Large challah, challah rolls; appetizer, fish° and vegetables; chicken or meat, side dishes; dessert; soda, liquor for *l'chayim.*

°Fish and meat are served on different plates, with separate utensils.

Upsherenish
Third Birthday—Haircutting Ceremony

Until the age of three, a little boy is allowed to grow an uncut mane of hair. The Torah states, "Behold man is like a tree of the field" (Deut. 20, verse 19). Man is compared to a tree, as he and the tree both grow from a small seed, reach maturity, bear fruit and extend branches (see *Tu B'Shvat*, page 51). In light of this, many Jewish communities have the custom of symbolically applying the laws of a tree to a man. During the first three years of a tree's life, its fruits are not to be cut. Likewise, we let the hair of a boy grow for his first three years.

The age of three also represents the beginning of a child's education in the area of Torah and mitzvohs—although his parents, and particularly his mother, begin teaching him *Shema Yisroel* (Hear O Israel), the Hebrew alphabet, the blessings over foods, and other short prayers as soon as he is able to talk. It is at this impressionable age that a child develops a love for G-d, for the Torah, for saying Prayers, giving charity, and doing mitzvohs in general.

Accordingly, at three the boy has an *Upsherenish*. His hair is cut, leaving the *peyos* (traditional side-locks), and officially starting him off on the Torah path. Father invites friends and prominent members of the community to each cut off a snip of hair, but leaves the main job for a barber. Now that those long locks are gone, the youngster will have to wear his *yarmulke* (skull cap) all the time. He is proud of himself as he shows off his new set of *tallis katan* and *tzitzis* (undergarment with ritual fringes) which he has put on, usually for the first time. The guests give him the admiring attention he deserves while enjoying the offered refreshments.

Often the hair is cut in shul after morning prayers, and there it is enough to serve a small *l'chayim* (cake and whiskey). If the Upsherenish takes place at home, you may wish to serve a meal.

In Israel, *Sephardic* (Eastern) Jews perform the ceremony for all the eligible three-year-olds together at the holy resting place of Rabbi Shimon Bar Yochai on the day of *Lag B'Omer*, the *yahrzeit* of Rabbi Shimon Bar Yochai and a day of celebration (see pages 62-63).

A Candlestick for our Daughter

Many people have the custom to initiate the daughter, too, in a special mitzvah at this age. The first Shabbos after her third birthday she will proudly stand next to her mother and light her very own Shabbos candle in her own Shabbos candlestick. Before lighting her own candles, her mother will help her in kindling the flame and saying the *brocha* (blessing), with which she is already familiar. Another light added to the glow of the Shabbos table—certainly a time of great rejoicing for the family and especially for a little Jewish girl.

✿   ✿   ✿

The Beginning of a Child's Formal Education

It will soon be time for our young boy or girl to begin formal learning in school. Now influences outside the home will begin to have a strong effect on the child's mind and character development; we should remember this when choosing the school—and type of school—in which we plan to enroll our children. A school which provides a sound Torah as well as secular education imparts values and a sense of true Jewish identity which will never leave the child as he continues to grow and learn.

A European custom worth remembering was the common practice of giving a party for a child as he entered school, an experience which might be a little awesome. Bringing the child's friends together for a celebration sweetens the occasion with extra joy.

✿   ✿   ✿

Suggested Serving Style and Foods (Upsherenish)

Buffet: Light refreshments served in shul. Assorted cakes, soda, liquor for *l'chayim.*
Dinner: Complete dinner meal served at home. Challah rolls; entree; fish and vegetables (optional); meat or chicken with assorted side dishes; soda and liquor for *l'chayim;* assorted cakes and dessert.

Bas Mitzvah

Twelve years—a girl comes of age

The days have flown by and turned into weeks, months and years. The first stage of education is complete—an important milestone has been reached. Now begins the era of obligation; no longer will a mitzvah be merely a nice thing to do; now it is a responsibility.

A girl is considered mature at twelve, and now is responsible for keeping the Torah and Mitzvohs. Her "coming of age," a quiet event for the most part, is treated in the same manner as that in which she is taught to live her life, with discretion and subtle reserve, which should not be mistaken for passivity or weakness. We hope that she will grow into a strikingly refined, superior woman, one in whom feminine strength and inner beauty emanates. This is reflected in her speech, her clothing, and in her actions. Her education in this area begins at the earliest age, but it is at the age of twelve that she takes on the full obligation to dress modestly, in accordance with the Torah.

While it is expected that she will powerfully affect the lives of all with whom she comes in contact, she will accomplish this with modesty, gentleness, refinement, concern, and generosity. These are the qualities which Torah values in a woman, and indeed, these are the qualities for which Jewish women have always been known, down through the centuries. Although it may seem that the men receive all the outer attention, it is known and acknowledged that the Jewish woman is a strong hidden light . . . as the Torah says, "a woman of valor is the *crown* (highest level) of her husband."

Suggested Serving Styles and Foods.

Jewish law does not prescribe an official form of celebrating this event. Often the Bas-Mitzvah girl celebrates this occasion in the form of a happy get-together with her friends on Shabbos afternoon or during the week of her birthday. Refreshments or a buffet or dinner meal can be served.

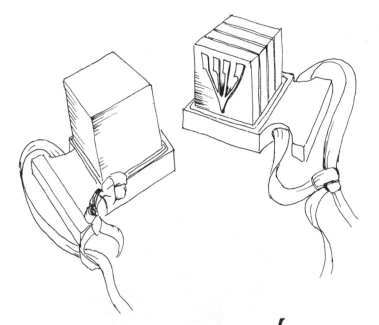

Bar Mitzvah

Thirteen years—a boy comes of age

Our once young boy, now at age thirteen, has become fully responsible for the keeping of the many mitzvohs. *Bar-Mitzvah* means "son of the commandments." Friends and relatives are invited to come to the synagogue to look on proudly as the Bar-Mitzvah boy is called up to the Torah to recite the blessings over it. It is an auspicious and awe-inspiring moment for parents and son, as the Torah community recognizes another full-fledged member.

The special mitzvah he now begins to perform every weekday is that of *Tefillin*, as the Torah states: "And you shall bind them upon your hand, and they shall be for frontlets between your eyes." (Deut. 6:8) *Tefillin* consist of two small leather boxes in which are contained four sections of the Torah inscribed on parchment. One of the boxes is bound to the left arm so as to rest against the heart and the other is placed on the head, above the forehead, so as to rest upon the cerebrum. Attention is thus directed to head, heart and hand, teaching us to dedicate ourselves to the service of G-d in all that we think, feel and do. If one is left-handed a Rav should be consulted as to which hand the tefillin should be placed on; this will not necessarily be the right hand.

The Bar-Mitzvah boy is well-prepared for this great day of his life. For months he has excitedly practiced how to put on *Tefillin*, how to conduct the various prayers in the shul and how to read from the Torah. Now the great moment has arrived. From now on he can "complete a *minyan*" and can conduct services on behalf of the congregation.

A Bar-Mitzvah is accompanied by a *Seudas-Mitzvah*. It may take the form of a Kiddush following Shabbos services or a Melava Malka after Shabbos is over. Others celebrate the event with a more elaborate catered affair in the week following the Bar-Mitzvah.

The highlight of the Kiddush and/or dinner meal is of course the Bar-Mitzvah boy. Proudly he walks up to the podium as he is called to give his Bar-Mitzvah speech. This won't be any ordinary speech. For months his Hebrew teacher and his father have prepared and taught him his special Torah discourse. The guests are spell-bound as they listen intently to the young scholar.

Kiddush: Buffet or dinner Kiddush in Shul. (See page 302). If Bar-Mitzvah is on Monday or Thursday, then assorted cakes and cookies; soda, and liquor for *l'chayim* are served.

Dinner: If a Shabbos dinner Kiddush was given, it is optional to have another special dinner in honor of the Bar-Mitzvah. The Bar-Mitzvah dinner can be given in the form of a Melava Malka dinner (see page 303) or as a regular dinner during the week following the Bar-Mitzvah. An elaborate meat or chicken dinner is appropriate. Serve: A large challah, challah rolls; appetizer; fish and salad; meat or chicken and side dishes; soda, liquor for *l'chayim*; dessert.

Vort or T'nayim
Engaged

Mother is joyous, Father is beaming. Their child has brought a new member to the family. Now, not only have they forged new links onto the chain of the Jewish people, but their offspring will do so as well. Surely a celebration is in order as the agreement is made to arrange the wedding.

Traditions may vary in the celebration of the engagement. Some will sign a written agreement (*T'nayim*) right then, while for others who leave the written part until the wedding day itself, an oral pledge (*Vort*) suffices to bind the *Chosson* (groom) and *Kallah* (bride).

A meaningful explanation for why this form of engagement is called a Vort is that vort means verbal agreement. On this special occasion Chosson and Kallah give their word to each other to dedicate their lives to one another in honesty, trust and devotion. What greater way of building one's life together is there than to begin with trust—trust in each other's word of commitment.

The Vort is usually celebrated either the day the engagement is announced, or within a few weeks of the announcement. Usually the Chosson will say a short Torah discourse at the Vort or T'nayim, for Torah must be the foundation of every Jewish home. The Vort or T'nayim can range from an informal gathering at home to a formal dinner, either home-made or catered in a hall.

An earthenware plate is broken at the T'nayim, and customarily at the Vort as well, as a reminder of the destruction of the Holy Temple. The Kallah may distribute pieces of the broken plate to her unmarried friends as a token of wishing them similar good fortune in finding their ideal mate in the near future.

After the engagement is the opportune time for the Chosson and Kallah to begin to learn the important laws pertaining to Jewish marriage. They should each choose a teacher thoroughly versed in these laws.

The new couple should also be guided and advised by their parents or a Rav in choosing a wedding date which is suitable according to Jewish Law.

Suggested Serving Style and Foods

Dinner: An elaborate dinner meal is usually served. A large challah, challah rolls; fruit or fish; entree; a favorite gourmet meat or chicken recipe; vegetable side dishes of your choice; soda and liquor for *l'chayim*; dessert and assorted cakes.

Ufrauf

The Chosson is "Called Up"

It is the Shabbos before the big event, but the young couple will not face the world unprepared, as they seek to build a world of their own. Just as when G-d wished to create the world, He looked into the Torah, the blueprint of creation, now the Chosson must also take a peek at that blueprint before he begins laying the foundation. As he ends the final blessing on the Torah, bags of sweets are thrown in his direction, to symbolize our wishes that the couple have a sweet life. This event is called in Yiddish the Ufrauf.

Following the Ufrauf, a Kiddush is given. Besides being attended by relatives and friends of the family, the Chosson's pals from bachelor days come to bid him a jolly farewell.

Suggested Serving Style and Foods

Kiddush: A buffet Kiddush is served in shul after services. This is often followed by a complete, sit-down Kiddush meal at home for close family and friends. (See page 302.)

Candy Bags: Small bags containing an assortment of candies, peanuts and raisins. (The children in shul are always thrilled to collect these bags after services.)

The Forshpiel

A Rejoicing with the Kallah

The Kallah is not left alone either. Many of her friends and relatives will gather at her home for refreshments after the regular Shabbos meal. Their good wishes for her happiness are expressed in joyful singing and lively talk. The cheerful atmosphere brings everyone into a mood of anticipation for the great *simcha* which is to take place, and on wishing the couple a good and happy life, a home based on Torah and Mitzvohs, and a partnership which will grow from strength to strength as the years go by.

Suggested Serving Style and Foods

Buffet: Complete assortment of refreshments which includes: platters of plain and fancy cakes and cookies; *nasherie* such as potato chips, pretzels, popcorn, peanuts, raisins, candy; fresh fruit platters and/or individual servings of pareve ice cream; soda.

מזל טוב

Chassanah

The Wedding

A traditional Jewish wedding is guaranteed to captivate the heart of anyone who witnesses it. Chassidic weddings are known to be particularly joyous; those who attend such a wedding for the first time are left spell-bound by the high spirit of rejoicing and happiness that envelops them.

Jewish weddings are special for several reasons. One is that everyone who attends is conscious of the obligation to make the Chosson and Kallah happy—and is determined to fulfill that obligation. After all, it is taught that a Chosson is a "king" and a Kallah is a "queen." The Talmud tells of many great, scholarly rabbis and teachers who would halt their important affairs for the privilege of dancing and singing and in other ways rejoicing before a bride and groom.

With this motivation to please the Chosson and Kallah pervading every movement, coupled with the realization of the sanctity of the occasion (see *Chupah*, below), the excitement and merriment continues for long hours into the night.

An outline of a traditional Jewish wedding follows, with explanations of many details.

The Kabbalas Panim—Reception

At the *Kabbalas Panim* (receiving of guests), amidst the enthusiastic handshakes and *l'chayims*, the Chosson may say a short Torah discourse on an appropriate subject. Light refreshments, like assorted cakes and drinks, are generally served. While the Kallah greets her guests and prepares to go to the Chupah, the women guests entertain her with lively or graceful circle dances. Hors d'oeuvres are usually served now.

The *Kesubah* (wedding contract) is witnessed and signed here, preceded by the witnessing and signing of the *T'nayim* (see Engaged, page 314) if this was not done during the period of the engagement. The signing of the *Kesubah* emphasizes that for the Chosson and Kallah, the marriage is to be a legal and moral commitment to each other, and not only a physical and emotional union.

Note: At all times throughout the marriage, the *Kesubah* must be preserved and kept in a secure place within the couple's home. If one notices that it is missing, a Rav must be consulted.

The Chupah—Marriage Canopy

The Badeken—At last, it is time. A dramatic hush falls upon the crowd in the room where the Kallah awaits her Chosson, who now enters escorted by the fathers of the couple and followed by a procession of men. Slowly, the Chosson approaches the Kallah to lower her veils over her face. This custom was instituted by our forefathers and mothers Isaac and Rebecca, and Jacob, Leah and Rachel. This is known as the *Badeken* (covering).

Next, having donned his *kittel* (white garment symbolizing purity, worn only on the most sacred occasions), he proceeds to the Chupah, accompanied by his parents or both fathers. The Chupah is a canopy held over the wedding party and suspended on four poles. Shortly afterwards, the Kallah arrives at the Chupah, escorted by her parents or the two mothers. Before standing next to the Chosson, she walks around him seven times. This symbolizes her new role as a protector of her family and home. She may be accompanied in this circling by her mother, mother-in-law, father and father-in-law, according to custom. As they walk around under the Chupah, each carries a lit candle, a reminder of the giving of the Torah when G-d "betrothed" the Jews amidst much light.

The ceremony is customarily held outdoors so that the Chupah is exposed directly to the sky, or it may be inside a synagogue in which part of the ceiling can be lifted up and the Chupah set directly below, so that the sky can be seen.

The ceremony begins. It is a solemn moment, and an intense and awesome one for the young couple. The day is a "Yom Kippur" for them, a day of cleansing and purification, for our Sages teach us that a bride and groom are forgiven all their sins when the day of their marriage arrives. It is for this reason that they both fast on this day.

The old gate closes and the new gate opens; this is a moment they have been anticipating all of their lives ("Forty days before the formation of a child, a voice from Heaven announces, 'This child is to marry the daughter of So-and-So'"—Talmud Sota 2A). The moment when one stands under the Chupah is holy and blessed with the Divine Presence. It is a special time for prayers on behalf of oneself and others.

The encircling is completed and she stands at his right. The mood of awe and expectancy grows. The Rabbi performing the ceremony says two blessings while holding a full cup of wine. The bride and groom each get a sip. The ring is taken out and two witnesses come forward to confirm its validity. They watch carefully as it is placed on the right forefinger of the Kallah while the Chosson says the Hebrew words meaning "Behold! You are consecrated to me with this ring according to the laws of Moses and Israel." Then, the *Kesubah* (marriage contract) is read aloud by an honored guest, and presented to the Kallah to be guarded by her forever. The Seven Blessings are said over the cup of wine, either by the Rabbi in charge or by other attending Rabbis or honored guests. Finally, the Chosson and Kallah take a sip of the wine. The glass which was used at the ceremony is put under the right foot of the Chosson, and with the tinkling of shattering glass (in memory of the destruction of the Temple and a reminder of something missing from our happiness) comes an outburst of "Mazel Tov! Mazel Tov!" from all the guests, and a round of joyous music.

No speeches, no sermons, no additional flourishes are necessary, for how can anyone add to the sanctity of a Chupah. As the guests resume dancing and singing, the Chosson and Kallah go off to the Yichud (Unity or Oneness) Room, where a short period of privacy will make their marriage official and also provide them with their first opportunity of the day to relax, and to break their fast which began at sunrise. Shortly the newlyweds will emerge and join their guests, whereupon they will promptly be lifted aloft on shoulders and chairs and triumphantly borne about until at last they are permitted to descend and participate in the dancing and feasting, and also to be fussed over and entertained by their eager guests, as is proper for a king and queen.

(It should be mentioned that all of these details contain many levels of significance, and should be explored more thoroughly by anyone planning a wedding, for they are part of every Jew's heritage.)

The Meal

Now comes the *Seudas Mitzvah*, which will be a multi-course banquet of the most elegant foods. Of course the food is not the main attraction for most guests. The music continues throughout and the dance floor, with a division between men and women, is always crowded between courses. Nowhere is there such enthusiastic dancing as at a real Jewish wedding.

"Blessed art Thou, O G-d, Who brings about the rejoicing of groom and bride."

Separate Seating

To the guests attending a traditional wedding for the first time, the separation between men and women, begun at the *Kabbalas Panim* and maintained throughout, may seem strange at first. But many such guests come away feeling that such a wedding has been one of the most memorable and truly joyous they have ever attended. Perhaps it is the awareness all have of the unique, spiritual glow surrounding the event. Perhaps it is because the separation allows for the most uninhibited and enthusiastic dancing, free from social tensions or distractions.

At any rate, the separation between men and women seems all the more appropriate at a wedding where the bride and groom have been "separated" for each other. The Hebrew word *Kiddushin* refers to the "sanctification" which, in marriage, indicates both holiness and separateness.

In this spirit, the guests join in starting the young couple on their new life—not with random socializing, but with a keen sensitivity to the words they have just heard expressed at the Chupah:

"Behold you are consecrated to me according to the Laws of Moses and Israel."

319

Sheva Brochos—Seven Blessings

The meal concludes with the Blessings-After-A-Meal (see page 349) said over a cup of wine, followed by *Sheva Brochos* (seven special blessings), which are said by seven honored guests over another cup of wine. The wine remaining in the two cups is mixed together and then the Chosson and Kallah each sip from one of the cups and pass it around to the men and women guests, respectively. Before they leave, all the guests make sure to bless the Chosson and Kallah for a long life of happiness, health, and genuine *"Yiddishe Nachas,"* and a beautiful Jewish home based on a foundation of Torah and Mitzvohs.

Suggested Serving Style and Foods

Dinner: A complete and elaborate dinner meal is prepared for all guests. Your caterer will have a large variety of menus to choose from. Choose a menu according to your taste and within your financial means. Also, plan what to serve for the reception (Kabbalas Panim).

Sheva Brochos
A Royal Week

The newlyweds' faces shine. Their appearance suits the royal treatment they are to receive for the next seven days, for in the week of their wedding, Chosson and Kallah are considered a "king" and "queen." They are not permitted to do any work, neither at jobs nor in their new home. Dinners called *Sheva Brochos* are usually given by close friends and relatives or the parents of the couple on each of the seven days following the wedding. Each is a *Seudas Mitzvah*, at which the same seven blessings that were recited under the Chupah are said after the Blessings-After-A-Meal. At each Sheva Brochos, in addition to the regular guests, there is one man who is invited as a "new face" (not having been at the wedding or to any of the previous Sheva Brochos in honor of this couple), except on Shabbos, for the Shabbos itself is a "new face."

If you are making a Sheva Brochos, plan your menu as you would when inviting special guests for dinner. The type of menus to serve are manifold. Sometimes the meals can be quite elaborate, which is appropriate when you are preparing the royal meal for a newly coronated king and queen!

Suggested Serving Style and Foods

Dinner: A festive chicken or meat meal is usually served. The hostess will usually select from her fancy favorite recipes to serve for this occasion. A complete dinner is served from challah to dessert.

Friday Night: The Friday-night Sheva Brochos are usually given by the parents of the bride or groom. The immediate family will join together for the complete Friday-night meal, whereas friends are invited to come join the celebration after the meal, and are served assorted fancy cakes, dessert and tea.

Chanukas Habayis

A New Jewish Home

Binyan Adei Ad—An Everlasting Edifice

A new Jewish home—another strong fortress, built on the fundaments of Torah and Mitzvohs. A home whose very foundations and walls will be steeped with Torah. How beautiful is the custom of bringing children into the house to fill its rooms with the song of Torah learning, even before the new couple moves in.

An official house-warming party, called *Chanukas Habayis,* or "dedication of the home," may be in the plans of the young couple in the form of a Kiddush or Melava Malka, and sometimes may coincide nicely with the fulfillment of the commandment of *Mezuzah,* which takes place within thirty days of moving into a new house.

A Mezuzah is a small scroll of parchment with two *parshios* (paragraphs) of the Torah inscribed on it by hand. The scroll may or may not be enclosed in a case. It is with the hand-inscribed parchment scroll that the mitzvah is fulfilled. The case, which may come in a variety of materials, shapes, colors, and decorations, is just an added touch.

The mitzvah of Mezuzah is obligatory for all Jews. At least twice every seven years, but preferably every year in the month of Elul, it is necessary to bring the scroll to an authoritative scribe to be examined.

All doorways that enter into the house, and all doorposts inside the house (including garage and basement and excluding the bathroom) must have Mezuzos attached to them—consult a Rav as to the correct procedure. The Mezuzos must be put up within the thirty days after moving into a new dwelling. No blessing is said when putting a Mezuzah up within the thirty days, but it is said after the thirtieth day.

Right from the beginning, the house takes on a Jewish identity as the Mezuzos are posted and holy books like the *Siddur*, (prayer book), *Chumash* and *Tanach* (Bible), *Tehillim* (Psalms), *Shulchan Aruch* (Laws), and other books of Jewish laws, customs, and wisdom get a prominent place. They contribute an aura of sanctity, noticeable to anyone who enters the house.

Of course, the *Kashrus* of the kitchen has been well planned by the bride right down to the appropriate color scheme of her separate meat and dairy dishes, pots, and other accessories. She now excitedly bears her new title—*balabusta* (lady of the house).

Jewish homes have always been noted for their hospitality, and this one will be no exception. A Jew gets a special gratification in being able to share his home and his food with those who might be in need of temporary lodging. These include relatives coming to visit, visitors from out-of-town, and other guests for a Shabbos or Yom Tov. The den or family room soon becomes called the "guest room," so frequently is it used as such in the Jewish home.

The charity boxes for *Tzedokah* are also sure to get a conspicuous place, as a constant encouragement to all the members of the house to put in a coin or more each day. Continually helping other Jews less fortunate than we are financially is yet another way of manifesting our constant *Ahavas Yisroel* (love and concern for our fellow Jews).

The Shabbos and Holiday Glow

As our newlywed couple begins to set up their home, they are proud of their many new responsibilities. The bride eagerly looks forward to the end of the week when she will prepare her first Shabbos and many, many more to come. Her favorite recipes for gefilte fish, chicken, kugels, and cholent (see *Shabbos*) all require busy shopping and cooking . . . and if she is very ambitious she may even make her own home-baked challah.

Sunset approaches Friday evening; everything is prepared. The house is immaculate and looks fit to receive the most royal guests. The bride ushers in the Holy Shabbos with awe and with lighting of the Shabbos candles; she knows that the moment will be a spiritual and emotional highlight each week for all the years to come. She knows how Shabbos brings each week to a happy culmination, and how from Shabbos we draw strength and blessing for the ensuing week to come. She knows that the observance of Shabbos will bring into the house each week a fresh spirit of faith and commitment to G-d and the Torah.

Soon a Jewish holiday is approaching. Our young couple sit down together to review all the laws and customs of the holidays to make sure that they are aware of all details. They want their home to have the same joyful holiday mood they experienced in their parents' homes. The bride also has in mind all the special holiday recipes which she is anxious to try.

A Strong Spiritual Bond

While the Jewish atmosphere of the family home is greatly strengthened when husband and wife observe the law and customs already mentioned, it becomes solidly established when they strictly observe those mitzvohs of the Torah that are directly concerned with a Jewish marriage. These laws, known as *Taharas Hamishpochah* (Family Purity) are the laws that govern the physical union between husband and wife, and are based around the women's monthly immersion in the *mikvah,* a gathering of natural waters used for spiritual purification (not physical cleansing). This immersion is an experience of renewal after which physical contact, suspended for a time governed by the woman's monthly cycle, is resumed. In addition to ensuring a constant newness and freshness for their relationship, there are many other benefits which the husband and wife reap—both physical and psychological—as a result of the observance of this Mitzvah of Family Purity. Nevertheless, the basic reason we keep these laws of Family Purity—as well as all the other laws—is because they are the Will of G-d, as expressed in the Torah.

These laws have been carefully studied by both bride an groom before the wedding. There is an abundance of literature available in English now, drawing on both our *halachic* and mystical traditions to explain the observance of these marriage laws and their benefits. It is necessary, of course, to obtain more detailed information from a competent teacher or Rav.

Behind all the observances mentioned above, which do so much to form the atmosphere of the true Jewish home, is a certain underlying mood of softness and peace. This feeling, which seems to quietly and subtly set the tone of the house, is known as *Shalom Bayis*—Peace of the Home. This which is such a strong ingredient of the Jewish home, can come about only when the husband and wife both live in the spirit of the Torah, and thus are united in their goals and ambitions.

Shalom Bayis has been stressed by the Torah ever since the first Jewish home of Abraham and Sarah, who, with tremendous unity, spread the truth of One G-d by continually opening their hospitable home to everyone.

The Talmud also speaks highly of *Shalom Bayis,* as in the teaching of Rabbi Akiba: "When man and woman live peacefully together, then G-d's presence dwells in their home."

When *Shalom Bayis* is based on and combined with a strong attachment to the Torah, the two together comprise the deepest and most solid foundation for a Jewish home. It is a home which will stand out as an everlasting edifice to be emulated by all those who admire its beauty.

Life by Life

A New Cycle

The celebrations are over; the excitement has quieted down. . . . A new couple has established a home, and soon, G-d willing, a new cycle will begin, a new generation will inherit and in turn pass on the riches of a heritage that has guided and strengthened them in all aspects of life.

So it is with the Jewish people. Every day we are thankful to G-d Who gives us life and Who directs us in life by means of the Torah. And so we look forward to celebrating all the special landmarks on the path of life with joy and genuine inner involvement; each Simcha, representing a Jew's constant growth, physically and spiritually.

A Guide to Observance

SECTION 17

A Guide to Observance

We have referred throughout this book to various mitzvohs, the careful observance of which requires more detailed explanation. Discussion of many basic laws, particularly in the field of Kashrus, have been placed together in this section, called *A GUIDE TO OBSERVANCE*. The following topics are included:

Setting Up the Kosher Kitchen
    Separation of Meat and Dairy
    Kashering Utensils
    Food Products Brought into Your Home
Eating Out
Laws of Koshering Meat, Fowl and Liver
Laws of Separating Challah
Blessings Over Food
    The Different Brochos and When to Say Them
    Laws Concerning Saying Brochos
Pesach Preparation and Laws
    The Prohibitions Concerning Chometz on Pesach
    Laws and Customs Concerning Foods Eaten on Pesach
Glossary of Terms; for the Kosher Kitchen, Shabbos and Holidays
Mitzvohs - An Everlasting Link

For further clarification of these laws or any topic in Jewish law consult a Rav.

A Guide to Observance

Setting up the Kosher Kitchen

Setting up a kosher kitchen is something we can rightfully be proud to do. In observing G-d's Law, we are establishing a link to Jews all over the world and throughout the ages who have kept Judaism alive by following the Torah. We are also safeguarding the Jewish feeling and identification of our whole family. It is an important job we have ahead of us, and one that will be richly rewarded.

Where do we begin?

Before beginning to shop for new dishes and utensils, be very familiar with all different kosher food types; know where to buy your meat, baked goods, and dairy products. Become familiar with those grocery stores or supermarkets in your neighborhood which carry a large selection of processed kosher products.

And, of course, above all, make contact with a *Rav*, his wife, or a friend or neighbor already observing kashrus, so that they can give you practical guidance and assurance all along. A *Rav* is a Rabbi qualified to judge questions of Jewish Law and should be consulted whenever such questions arise.

Many of your food utensils will probably have to be replaced. However, some utensils may be *kashered* (see page 330) in a special way, and after being *kashered* may be used once again as part of your newly set up kosher kitchen.

When shopping for new utensils, keep in mind that you will need to purchase two completely different sets of cooking and serving ware and accessories, (besides additional utensils for Pesach).

Toiveling: Before using most types of dishes, pots and other utensils, the Torah requires them to be *toiveled,* ritually immersed in a *mikvah* (ritualarium). Consult a Rav concerning procedure of toiveling, which vessels are toiveled with or without a brocha, and other laws.

Once this is done, you are ready to set up your new kitchen and begin using all your new utensils. In a very short time, you will feel as if keeping kosher has always been part of your life.

Separation of Meat and Dairy in the Kosher Kitchen

FOODS

Meat, Dairy, and Pareve: Definitions and Laws

Complete definitions of what constitutes "meat" and "dairy" products are given on pages 6–8. Examples of such foods and some laws concerning these foods follow the definitions. Important information concerning kosher meat cuts, etc. are on pages 163–7.

The term "pareve" is explained on page 7. Many examples of pareve foods are listed with various laws concerning these foods.

Separation of Meat and Dairy

Meat and dairy foods may not be cooked or eaten together, nor may one benefit from a combination of these foods. Therefore a complete separation of *fleishig* (meat) and *milchig* (dairy) utensils, accessories, and appliances is maintained in the kitchen. (See page 9)

It is also necessary to wait a specified amount of time between eating meat and dairy foods and between dairy and meat (see page 9).

UTENSILS and APPLIANCES

A total separation of meat and dairy must be maintained throughout the entire kitchen.

A very practical and widespread practice in Jewish homes is to plan the different sets of meat and dairy utensils around a color scheme, for example: *fleishig* (meat)—red, *milchig* (dairy)—yellow. You may choose you own color scheme depending on the color of your dishes, your kitchen or whatever pleases you.

The different sets should be kept in different cupboards of the kitchen, preferably on separate sides. The differentiation of silverware and pots should be marked by separate patterns.

Food Utensils

Completely separate sets of dishes, pots, silverware, serving dishes, bread trays and salt shakers are necessary. If wooden-handled kitchen knives are used the difference between the meat and dairy knives should be noticeable through either of the following ways: the wood handles should be different colors, different designs, or the letter M (meat) or D (dairy) should be scratched into the wood, or, a line on the tops of the handles should be painted according to the color scheme.

Kitchen Accessories

Have completely separate sets of draining boards, draining racks, dish sponges, dish towels, tablecloths. (Dish soap, cleanser, and scouring pads used for dishes and pots must have a *hechsher.*)

The Sink

Separate sinks for washing dishes and preparing foods is highly advisable and recommended. If the two sinks are one right next to the other, there should be an effective separation between the two so that no water or food splashes from one sink to the other.

If there is only one sink, it may be used, but the inside of the sink should be regarded as *trefah*, unkosher. No food or any dishes should be put directly into it. There should be separate dish pans and slightly elevated racks under the dishpans for both meat and dairy.

Refrigerators and Freezers

These may be used for all food types. However, separate places should be designated for meat and dairy foods.

Often a shelf or the door of the refrigerator or freezer is kept for dairy to keep it completely separate.

If dairy is kept on a shelf inside the refrigerator, the shelf should be lined with aluminum foil or a tin sheet, so that no milk or other dairy product can drip down from containers to another shelf. If the milk does drip on the foil, the foil must be carefully removed and replaced.

The Stove

The laws concerning the accidental mixture of meat and dairy foods become much more complex where heat is involved. Therefore, strict precautions are taken concerning the use of the stove and oven for meat and dairy products.

Separate burners designated for meat and dairy on the gas or electric stove are preferable. Otherwise, extra care must be taken to keep the burners very clean.

Some kitchens have two separate stoves. This is of course an ideal set-up in the kosher kitchen. (A practical alternative is to use the full-size range for meat, and a portable gas or electric range for dairy.)

When using only one stove, even when separate burners are kept, it is best to avoid cooking foods in meat and dairy pots at the same time, since the steam or food of one pot might splatter on another, and could present a serious problem regarding the food and pots involved.

(If one is pressed for time and it becomes necessary to cook both meat and dairy foods in separate pots at the same time, utmost care should be taken that the lids are secured tightly at all times and an upright sheet of tin or asbestos should separate the pots. If the lids must be lifted in order to check the food or to add any ingredients, care should be taken:
- never to lift lids of opposite pots at the same time;
- to raise a lid only slightly off the pots so that no steam or liquid should drip down or splash.

The Oven

Since the oven is closed on all sides, and all heat vapor remains inside, meat and dairy foods should never be baked or broiled at the same time, even in separate bakeware.

It is best to use the oven for only one type of food; meat, pareve or dairy. The use of portable broilers or ovens for the other food types is advisable.

To keep the oven strictly pareve (that is, if one wishes to use it for both meat and dairy at separate times), then meat and dairy foods cooked in that oven must be tightly covered on all sides and the pot may be opened for testing only when it is removed completely from the oven.

If the oven is basically meaty, then pareve foods baked in it should not be served on dairy dishes, and vice versa if the oven is basically dairy. However, regarding pareve foods baked in such an oven, the full waiting period between meat and dairy foods (see page 9) does not apply *if* the oven is kept clean.

If a pareve cake was baked in a clean, meaty oven at least twenty-four hours *after* the oven had been used for meat, then this cake may be served with milk or on dairy dishes, and similarly with pareve cake baked in a clean dairy oven.

Small appliances

A mixmaster, blender, or grinder does not require a separate motor in order to be used for meat and dairy. However, one must buy separate attachments if the appliance is to be used for more than one food type (meat, dairy, or pareve). Even when using separate attachments, the machine should be cleaned well, on all sides, after each use.

Electric portable broilers

These should be used for either meat or dairy exclusively.

Dishwashers

These should preferably be designated for the exclusive use of either meat or dairy. If you have further questions, consult a Rav as there are many factors involved.

Kashering

Kashering is a way of making some kind of utensils that have become trefah *(by meat and dairy mix-ups, etc.) permissible again for use.*

Children playing around with kitchen utensils or adults accidentally using the wrong pot or spoon can create *halachic* problems in the kitchen. If there has been a mix-up with the food, pots, dishes, cutlery, etc., where some dairy item came into contact with meat items or vice versa, or non-kosher food was accidentally placed on, or cooked in a kosher vessel, set aside the item(s) in question and consult a Rav.

If the item(s) can be separated before being set aside, this should be done. For example, if a dairy knife was used in cutting meat, remove the knife from the meat and wipe off all traces of meat from the knife, then set aside both the piece of meat which was cut and the knife which was used. Never rinse utensils with hot water when there is a question; use only cold water.

Where a question on a utensil or food has arisen, the Rav should be consulted as soon as possible. One should keep in mind the circumstances and details involved in the mix-up, for this will help the Rav determine the nature of the question, and its respective laws.

Some of the criteria to keep in mind and to tell the Rav are:
- type(s) of food involved.
- type(s) of utensils involved.
- whether mix-up occurred in dishes or in cooking ware; and before or after cooking process.
- if it occurred while in cooking ware—manner in which food was prepared is important; (cooking, frying, broiling, etc).
- temperature of food or utensils: whether hot, cold, or room temperature.
- if you can possibly remember when the utensil was last used prior to the mix-up, and for which foods it was used.
- the amount of milk or meat involved.

There are several different methods of *kashering*. The appropriate method will depend upon the answers to some of the above questions. Only utensils made of certan materials, however, may be *kashered*.

Another type of question that can arise is when a pareve utensil comes in contact with hot meat or dairy foods, in which case it may become *fleishig* or *milchig*, respectively, and a Rav should be consulted.

With each situation that arises, a new question should be asked of the Rav for the answer to every case is determined on its own. One should not draw one's own conclusion based on an answer to a previous question (*sha'alah*).

Food Products Brought into Your Home

Any processed food which comes into your home must have a hechsher or certification of kashrus. Read the label carefully for ingredients and to see whether the food is meat, dairy or pareve.

However, relying merely on reading the food ingredients which are printed on the label or package, without a certification of *kashrus* is not sufficient since:
- Not always are all ingredients that are put into a product listed, especially, if that ingredient is of minimal quantity.
- A food can be processed in a factory where other non-kosher products are prepared, and therefore it is possible that by using the same utensil for the kosher ones, the product will become non-kosher.
- One would have to be familiar with the many factors involved in determining the kashrus of certain foods.
- One would have to be familiar with the process by which many foods are made, and with the many additives included in them for flavor, texture and/or color. These also require Rabbinic supervision.

Trumah, Ma'aser and Shmittah

In the case of food products from Israel, it is necessary to be aware of the law of *trumah-and-ma'aser* and of *shmittah*.

Trumah and *ma'aser* are two types of separations required by the Torah in relation to food grown in the Land of Israel. Before such food may be eaten, certain portions of the produce must first be separated. Before eating any Israeli products, it must be known that *trumah* and *ma'aser* were separated properly. If this is not known, one should separate *trumah* and *ma'aser* before eating the product. Consult a Rav to find out how this is done.

Shmittah is the law that the land of Israel must be left "free" every seventh year. No food may be grown or attended to at this time, and all poor or needy people are welcome to collect any crop remaining in the field. It is forbidden to eat food grown by a Jew in Israel during a *shmittah* year. Israeli products which may have been grown during the *shmittah* year may not be eaten even if exported outside the Land of Israel. A reliable hechsher will insure that the product is not made from ingredients grown during the *shmittah* year.

Eating Out

Restaurants, Snack Bars, Caterers, and other Food Institutions

Eating out in kosher-advertised restaurants and snack bars, often presents a problem for a kashrus-observant person, since the signs *Kosher* or *Dairy* or *Vegetarian* can be very misleading. After reading through the preceding chapters on kashrus, you have probably come to appreciate how intricate and involved are the laws governing a kosher kitchen, especially when meat is involved.

Therefore, before eating in a restaurant or any other eating establishment, take the following precautions:

Hashgacha (Supervision)

Find out who is responsible for the kashrus of the premises. When food is prepared in large quantities and a number of people are working in the kitchen, mix-ups and all kinds of problems and questions are bound to occur. A *mashgiach*—kashrus supervisor—is essential and may be required to be on the premises at all times.

Shabbos Observance

One should eat in a restaurant only when one trusts those who manage it. As was mentioned earlier in the discussion of butcher shops, *Shabbos* observance is a criterion which is often used to determine a person's commitment to the Torah and its laws. Therefore, before eating out, make sure the establishment is closed on Shabbos and Holidays.

Meat Restaurants and Caterers

All laws pertaining to kosher type meats, kosher meat cuts, salting, treibering, separation from dairy, etc. must be strictly upheld by any restaurant or caterer. (See pages 6, 163–67, 335–340.)

Vegetarian and Dairy Restaurants

These are not automatically kosher simply because they do not serve meat. Below are just a few of the reasons why vegetarian and dairy restaurants must also have a *mashgiach*, be closed on Shabbos and Holidays, and maintain a high standard of kashrus.
- All **fish** served in the restaurant, must be kosher. Otherwise all the pots, dishes, dishwashers, etc. become non-kosher, and no foods prepared in such utensils may be eaten.
- All **dairy** ingredients must also be kosher, in order to maintain the kashrus of utensils and all other foods.
- Certain **vegetables and grains** must be washed and checked (see *Pareve,* page 8) to ascertain that they have no insects or worms. Eggs must also be inspected for blood spots.
- All **oil** or shortening used must be made of **pure** vegetable products and must be Rabbinically approved.
- Food which is usually not eaten raw, and which was prepared for consumption entirely by a non-Jew is not permissible for use, even if cooked in kosher utensils. Such food is called *bishul akum.* (See Glossary) If a Jew assists, even if only lighting the flame, the food is not *bishul akum.*

Bakeries

All Jewish bakeries must have reliable kashrus supervision and comply with the laws of Shabbos observance. A discussion of some of the kashrus laws are found in *Cakes,* Section XII.

Bread or cake which was completely and exclusively baked by a non-Jew in most cases may not be used. Such bread is called *pas akum.* However, in places where it is too difficult to get baked goods baked by a Jew (and only in such places) it is permissible to eat the bread of a non-Jewish *bakery* (not an individual), if certain specific conditions are fulfilled. Such bread is called *pas palter.* The conditions for using *pas palter* are:
- The ingredients must be absolutely kosher.
- The bread must not have been prepared in vessels used for other baked goods which may not be kosher.
- The pans are not smeared with non-kosher shortening.

Concerning the cakes of a non-Jewish bakery, these almost always contain non-kosher ingredients. They should not be used unless all the above conditions have been met.

If a Jew has supervised and *assisted* in the baking of the bread, even if just by lighting the fire of the oven, such bread is not considered as *pas akum*, or even as *pas palter* (provided all the above conditions have been met). Such bread is permissible in all cases.

Airlines

Most airlines today will readily arrange for strictly kosher meals at no extra cost, upon request. When making your reservation, make sure the kosher meal has a reliable hechsher. The food must be brought to you, complete with its wrappers still sealed. It may not be warmed in the airline oven once the original wrappers are removed, and may not be handled with non-kosher utensils.

Hospitals

Many hospitals have a separate kosher kitchen for the benefit of their Jewish patients. If a stay in the hospital is necessary, find out if the hospital has a kosher kitchen and under whose supervision it is. Even without a special kosher kitchen, hospitals frequently have a supply of pre-cooked and pre-packaged kosher meals available. If warming is necessary it must be warmed while still sealed in its original wrappers.

If this service is not available, arrange with the head nurse for your family to bring you food from home. Often the nurses will be helpful; they may even allow you to keep some food in the refrigerator. The food, of course, should be clearly marked and sealed.

Wine

For wine to be kosher it must be produced only by Jews, in addition to having, of course, only kosher ingredients. Due to its sacramental use—as in the times of the Temple and for Shabbos, Holidays and at a Simcha—the laws regarding wine are extra-strict. We are not allowed to drink any wine (or grape juice) or any drinks containing wine (or grape juice) which has been touched by a non-Jew after the seal of the bottle has been opened, unless the wine has been previously boiled (*yayin mevushil*).

Boiling the wine rendered it unfit to be brought upon the altar in the time of the Holy Temple; therefore it is not included in this prohibition.

This law has its roots in the historic use of wine for libations to idols, and the need to safeguard the purity of kosher wine for our religious purposes. It also discourages social drinking with non-Jews which can and does lead to involvement in a non-Jewish way of life.

These laws apply to all products containing wine and grape juice, which includes many liqueurs, brandies and blended whiskies as well as herring in wine sauce and grape-flavored sodas and jellies.

334

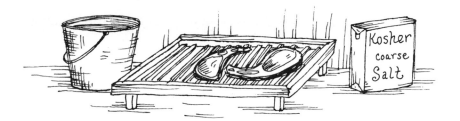

Laws of Koshering Meat, Fowl and Liver

Introduction to Koshering Meat

Koshering is the process by which the blood of meat and fowl is drawn out before we may use the meat or fowl. Of course, only meat from kosher-type animals, properly slaughtered and with the forbidden parts already removed, may be koshered. This mitzvah underscores the value Torah places on life (see page 163).

If you are koshering meat for the first time, it is advisable first to watch the whole process done by someone who is experienced and well-versed in it. Also, rather than rely exclusively on the guidelines provided below, it would be best to consult a Rav for further clarification and personal direction.

The koshering process basically entails the following steps: washing or rinsing off the meat; soaking it; salting it; and then rinsing it off very well three times. All the steps are explained on the following pages. An outline is also included of additional information concerning the koshering process for chickens, how to kosher liver, and situations concerning the koshering of meat or chicken which require your consulting a Rav.

Various factors are also involved *before* the meat is koshered. These are explained in the following paragraphs. A list of utensils and equipment needed for the koshering process is also given.

Note: Anyone on a salt-free diet should consult a Rav as to how to kosher and salt their meat.

Before Koshering Meat

Once a kosher animal has been slaughtered according to *halacha* and the forbidden hindquarters removed, it is brought to the butcher who must then prepare it for the salting process.

In addition to cutting the meat, the butcher *triebers* the meat. This is the process in which some forbidden veins and fats are cut out. This requires special skill, as one must be able to recognize the different parts and know which are allowed to be eaten and which are not. This must be done before the meat is salted. If the meat is to be ground, the koshering must take place first.

The complete koshering process should take place *within 72 hours* after the meat was ritually slaughtered. At least the soaking of the meat (see below) should have begun in this time. It is therefore very important to find out the exact time of the *shechita* (slaughtering).

If 72 hours elapses and the soaking process for the meat was not started, then the only way to kosher it is by roasting it on an open fire (see *Koshering Liver*). It may *not* be recooked, fried in oil or made into a pot roast afterwards.

If the 72 hours ends on Shabbos, and the meat was not soaked before Shabbos, consult a Rav before proceeding further.

If the soaking was done within the 72 hours, but it was not possible to continue the next process, salting, until a later time, then the koshering process must be done again in its entirety, beginning with the soaking. This must be started within 72 hours of the completion of the first soaking.

After receiving the meat from the butcher, one may put it into the refrigerator before koshering it; just be sure it is covered. It should be removed from the refrigerator and the koshering process started within 72 hours after the *shechita*.

Meat which is very cold should be allowed to stand at room temperature to warm up, but it should not be put too close to a fire or immersed in hot water, for then the blood will be cooked in and the salt will not be effective in drawing it out. Just let it stand at room temperature.

Utensils and Equipment Needed for the Koshering Process

These utensils should be used exclusively for UNKOSHERED meat.

A. *A Pail*: to hold the meat.

B. *A Board with a lot of Holes in it*: to place salted meat on. Holes are necessary so that the blood can flow out. (If the board doesn't have holes in it, it should be placed on a slant to enable the blood to flow down.)

C. *A Knife*: to cut out blood clots or to cut larger pieces of meat into smaller pieces. (The pieces of meat should be small enough to handle easily).

D. *Coarse Salt*: to draw out the blood. Thin table salt is not good as it melts into the meat and does not draw the blood out. Salt which is too large is not good either, for it can easily roll off the meat.

E. *A Basin*: for the board to be placed on. The space underneath the board should be hollow, so that the blood can drip into it.

F. *A Sink with Running Water*: to soak, rinse and wash off the meat. Water used in the koshering process should always be at *room temperature.*

Important Note: Lighting—During the complete koshering process make sure the room is well lit with electric and/or a large amount of natural sunlight, to make sure that all stages of the koshering process are done properly.

Steps in the Koshering Process

A. *Rinsing:*
The meat must be rinsed off very well to remove all visible blood, and all blood clots should be cut out.

B. *Soaking:*
The meat should then be soaked in a pail of water for at least ½ hour. If it accidentally remained in the pail for 24 consecutive hours, the meat becomes forbidden.

336

After the meat has been soaked one may cut it into smaller pieces if desired, but must rinse each cut piece very well, especially the newly cut ends. The meat does not have to be soaked for the half hour again.

C. *Salting:*
1. Immediately *before* the actual salting it is necessary to:
   a) wash it again—use either the same water in which it was soaked or fresh water.
   b) inspect the meat to make certain that no visible blood is left on the meat.
   c) Shake off excess water, so that the salt does not dissolve too easily. The meat should however remain damp enough for the salt to stick to it.
2. Salting the meat
   a) The meat must be salted thoroughly on all sides, but not too thickly, for the blood would then be prevented from flowing out.
   b) The salted meat should remain on the board for a minimum of 1 hour and a maximum of a little under 12 hours. If it should remain in salt for 12 hours or more a Rav should be consulted.
   c) If a piece of meat should fall off the board while the salt was still on, it should be returned immediately, preferably to a separate board. It must be kept apart throughout the remaining process, and a Rav should be consulted as soon as possible.

D. *Triple-Rinsing:*
After the meat has lain in salt the required period of time, it must then be rinsed off well, and all the salt rubbed off and removed on all sides. This is done three separate times.
First the meat should be rinsed under running water. It should be rubbed while under the water, and constantly turned so that all sides come into contact with the water.
The second and third times the meat may either:
1. be rinsed again under running water as before, or
2. be soaked in a *clean* pail of *fresh* water. The pail must be rinsed out separately for each time, and fresh water used for both the second and the third rinsing.
   Note: In the latter method, care should be taken so that the water is poured into the pail before the meat is placed into it.

Koshering Other Parts of the Animal

Special care must be taken concerning the koshering of the head, heart and lungs of an animal. If you wish to use these parts, a Rav should be consulted. The head must be removed from the animal before one begins to kosher it.

Meaty bones are koshered just like meat and together with the rest of the meat. However, if the bones have no meat on them, they should be koshered like chicken eggs: they should be kept on top or on the side of the board so that no blood from the other pieces of meat reaches them.

Special Care to be Taken in the Koshering of Chickens *

* *Note:* All laws pertaining to the koshering of chicken apply to all Kosher fowl.

Once a reliable butcher has removed all the insides from the chicken and has checked it for any possible irregularities which would render it unfit, the koshering process for chickens is the same as for meat: rinsing, soaking, salting, and triple-rinsing. However, there are certain additional points to be aware of regarding the preparation of the chicken for koshering, removing certain parts from it before koshering it, and how to handle it during the koshering process.

A. *Removal of Certain Parts:*

Just as in koshering an animal, certain parts of the chicken must be removed *before* the salting process can begin. Since many people who kosher meat and chicken at home often buy their chicken whole, it is important to know and be able to recognize the parts of the chicken which must be cut off or removed.

The chicken should preferably be cut into two halves for the koshering process. If it is desired that the chicken remain whole for broiling on a rotisserie, the opening at the neck where the head is cut off should be wide enough to remove all the insides.

The following steps must be taken before koshering the chicken:

1. *From the Head and the Neck—*

    a. The complete head is removed.
    b. The gullet (foodpipe) and windpipe of the neck are be removed.

2. *From the legs—*

    a. The ends of the wings, the nails from the toes of the fowl are removed.
    b. The lower leg is cut into, at the joint which joins the lower to the upper leg.

3. *From Inside—*

    a. The lung is removed (it may be possible to kosher it later on).
    b. The stomach must be opened, all waste products removed, then the stomach wall checked to make sure it has not been punctured by a stone or nail which would create a *sha'alah* (question for a Rav).
    c. The intestines are removed. If they are to be used, they should be placed separately on the salting board.
    d. The heart is removed, and the auricles and ventricles cut open to remove all the blood collected inside. (The tip of the heart should also be cut off.)
    e. The liver should be removed and set aside for roasting (see *Koshering Liver*).
    f. The spleen should be removed.
    g. Some veins: There are four veins that should be removed—two are thin white veins inside the neck which can be exposed by cutting at bottom of neck or down the length of neck. One other vein is in the skin of the neck on the left side and the fourth is under the food pipe.

        All four veins should be removed. If it is too difficult to remove them at least cut several slits into the neck and the other veins so that the blood will flow out.

4. *The Feathers—*

The feathers are removed from the chicken before the koshering process. The chicken may not be soaked in warm water to soften the feathers, nor held over a large fire. However, one may pass the chicken lightly above a small flame, moving it continuously so that the chicken will not become heated.

B. *The Handling of the Chicken During the Koshering Process*

The koshering process for chicken is the same as for meat, but additional attention must be given to the following factors. It is preferable, and easier, to kosher the chicken if it has been cut in half.

1. *Rinsing It:*

   The chicken must be rinsed off very well, especially in the following places:
   a. the hole of the neck (the head and skin of the neck must have already been removed as well as the skin of the neck)
   b. all the flaps, e.g. by the wings
   c. between the skin and meat
   d. all around the fat

2. *Salting It:*

   a. The chicken should be salted all over very well, and especially in all the crevices mentioned above (I a, b, c, d).
   b. If the chicken is still whole, make sure to salt the inside very well.

3. *Placing it on the Board:*

   When the chicken is to be placed on the board after it is salted, it should be placed so that the blood can flow out.
   a. If it has been cut in half, then the cavity should be placed facing downward.
   b. If the chicken is whole, it should be placed with the larger hole downward.

Note About Chicken Eggs:

Eggs which are found in the chicken, whether they are with or without a shell, should be koshered according to the regular koshering process and are considered *fleishig*. However, they should be placed on the top of the board so that no blood from the other pieces of meat can flow on them. The skin of the eggs must be removed before soaking. These eggs should be prepared in meat utensils. (They are very delicious cooked in chicken soup.)

Koshering Liver

A. *A different koshering process and why:*

Since liver has too much blood in it for salt alone to do an effective job, it is not salted in the regular way. It is salted on all sides and also must be broiled over an *open fire* (not an electric fire). The pieces of liver should not be too large for the heat to penetrate. If roasting a whole beef liver, cut into it across its length and width before roasting.

B. *The procedure for the koshering of liver is as follows:*

1. *Washing*

Thoroughly wash off all outside blood and remove all visible blood clots.

2. *Salting*

Salt the liver on all sides with coarse salt immediately before the roasting.

3. *Roasting*

Roast over an open fire with nothing between the fire and liver so that the blood can flow out freely. A thin wire net with large holes may be used to hold the liver over the fire. The liver should be rotated over the fire a few times, so that all sides will have been exposed to the fire and become roasted.

When broiling livers over an open fire from a gas range, cover all sides around the open fire very well with aluminum foil, so that no blood can splash on the stove and render it unkosher.

For the same reason, the liver should not come into contact with any kosher utensils such as plates, bowls, and knives etc. until it is completely koshered.

Note: If liver is wrapped in a packaged chicken it must be removed before cooking the chicken or placing the chicken under hot water. The liver can then be koshered separately.

When to Ask a Sha'alah (*Question of Torah Law*)

When koshering meat or chicken, a *sha'alah* should be asked as soon as any irregularity in the meat or chicken is noticed and anytime there is some deviation from the normal pattern during the koshering process.

Never hesitate to ask a *sha'alah* even if somewhat similar situations have occurred previously, for every case is judged according to its own circumstances. A *sha'alah* should be asked as soon as possible after first noticing the problem. If possible, bring the piece of meat or chicken to the Rav. If one notices a *sha'alah* on the chicken while it is whole, then preferably the whole chicken should be brought to the Rav.

If something appears questionable even after the meat or chicken is koshered, whether by the butcher or at home, do not hesitate to ask a *sha'alah*. An oversight may have occurred. If the question arises after the koshering, consult a Rav before cooking the meat or chicken, in order to prevent further complications.

As a general rule, consult a Rav on any apparent abnormality in the meat or chicken. Some particular abnormalities which might be noticed are:

1. An unusual growth in the animal, or an extra, missing or deformed organ.
2. Any broken bones, or an unusual collection of blood in any organ, which may indicate some damage to the animal.
3. Any unusual coloring of any organ.
4. Unusual softness of the tissues of any organ.
5. Any foreign material (eg. stone or pin) found inside the animal.

Laws of Separating Challah

The separation of *challah,* removing a small amount of dough from the main dough, is one of the three mitzvohs given by the Torah especially to women. In doing this seemingly small act, the woman proclaims to herself and her family her firm belief in G-d as the provider of all sustenance.

A special *brocha* (blessing) is usually said when separating the *challah,* but some circumstances require it being separated without a brocha. When explaining the requirements for separating *challah,* we have indicated whether the *challah* is to be separated with or without a brocha. (see also pages 76–7).

Note: Throughout the following pages, the word *challah* refers to the small piece of dough removed from the larger dough rather than, in its usual sense, to the special loaves of breads made for *Shabbos, Yom Tov,* or *Simchas.*

I. Conditions Under Which Dough Requires the Separation of Challah

Challah must be separated from any dough that fills the requirements of *all* four of the following categories: type of grain used, amount of flour used, liquid content, and consistency of dough.

A. *Grain*

The grain must be either one or a combination of the following five types—wheat, rye, barley, oat, spelt.

B. *Amount of flour*[1]

1. In order to separate, or take, *challah* with a brocha, the minimum amount of flour required is 1666.6 grams (approximately 3 lbs. 11 oz.).

2. From flour weighing 1250 grams (approximately 2 lbs. 12 oz.) to 1666.6 grams (3 lbs. 11 oz.), *challah* is taken without a brocha.

3. Less than this amount does not require the taking of *challah.*

4. One may not intentionally evade the mitzvah of taking *challah* by avoiding using the above-mentioned quantity of flour. On Erev Shabbos, it is especially significant to take *challah.* However, if only a small amount is available, or the recipe calls for only a small amount of batter, it is not necessary to increase the amount in order to take *challah.*

5. There are other *minhagim* (customs) concerning the required amount of flour. If you already have such a *minhag*, it is proper to follow it.

Suggestion: Because a standard cup-measure of flour contains less than 8 ounces of flour by weight, accurately weigh each of the significant measurements of flour for taking *challah* and mark them on a container. The flour should not be compressed or especially loose. Be sure to shake the flour a bit; this prevents air pockets which could lead to inaccurate measurement. The container can then be used for the measuring the correct amount of flour for taking *challah* whenever one is baking.

C. *Liquid*

In order to say a brocha when taking *challah*, even with the required amount of flour, the liquid in the dough must include a certain amount of one of the following liquids: water, milk, honey, wine, or olive oil.

1. If water is included, even one drop is enough to require that *challah* be taken from it with a brocha. The drop of water should be added before the dough is well mixed.

2. If water is not included, but one (or more) of the mentioned liquids is, then it (or they) must constitute more than 50% of the liquid contents in the dough in order that the *challah* be taken from it with a brocha.

3. If the amount of the other liquids (milk, honey, wine or olive oil) is less than 50% of the liquid contents of the dough, then *challah* is taken without a brocha.

Therefore, whenever preparing two doughs at the same time, of which only one would require that *challah* be taken from it with a brocha, (and provided of course that this *challah* had not yet been taken), then it is preferable to combine both doughs together (see also II-G-3) and take *challah* with a brocha from the dough which contains the required amount. The brocha thus applies also to the other dough or doughs as well.

Other authorities recommend taking one or more small doughs having less than the required proportion of one of the five liquids, and combine these with a dough which does not have the required proportion of liquid. Then take *challah* without a brocha from the small doughs.

4. If the recipe doesn't call for any of the above five liquids, (e.g. only eggs, or pure fruit juice), a small amount of one of the five liquids, preferably water, should be added (due to involved *halachic* reasons) unless one is sure that the grains were washed (bleached) in water. The drop of liquid should be added *before* the flour and liquid are well mixed together.

D. *Consistency*

1. The dough should be of a thick enough consistency to enable someone to handle it and remove the piece of *challah* by hand.

2. If due to its loose texture one cannot separate challah prior to the baking, then *challah* is separated with a brocha, after the dough is baked. This occurs in the preparation of many cake doughs.

3. If one kneads a dough with the intention of cooking or frying it (e.g. for noodles or *kreplach*), *challah* should be separated, but without a brocha.

If this dough is kneaded with the intention of baking just part of it, and part of it is in fact baked (even a small amount), then *challah* is taken with a brocha (providing that the liquid content and amount of flour meet the above-mentioned requirements).

II. THE MANNER OF TAKING CHALLAH

A. *Who takes challah?*
1. The woman, since:
   a. she is the one who usually does the baking.
   b. this is one of the three special mitzvohs for a woman to keep.
2. If necessary, anyone over Bas Mitzvah or Bar Mitzvah age may also take *challah.*

B. *What is the quantity of dough taken off?*
1. A small piece, the size of a *k'zayis,* "like the volume of an olive." This is approximately 1 ounce of dough.

C. *What is the brocha said on the separation of challah?*
Brocha—Transliteration: Bo-ruch A-toh A-do-noi,* E-lo-hai-nu* Me-lech Ha-o-lam Asher Kid-sho-nu B'mitz-vo-sav V'tzi-vo-nu L'ha-frish Challah.

Translation: Blessed are You, O G-d, our G-d, King of the Universe, Who has commanded us with His Mitzvohs, and commanded us to separate *challah.*

Note: The real name of G-d has been used in this text. When practicing the blessing, say *Ha-Shem Elo-kai-nu* instead of the third and fourth words, so as not to say G-d's name in vain. One may say the actual Name, however, when teaching a child under *Bar* or *Bas Mitzvah* age how to say a brocha.

D. *When is the brocha said?*
The brocha is said just before separating the dough. Then, while actually separating the dough, a verbal declaration is made:

"Harai zeh challah," (This is challah).

E. *What is done with the piece of challah?*
Today, since we cannot give it to the *Kohanim* (priests) and since we may not use it ourselves (see page 76), the prevailing custom is to burn this piece separately (e.g. in a piece of aluminum foil). It should be burned in the oven (preferably, in the broiler part). However, if one burns the *challah* inside the oven, it should not be burned at the same time as the loaves or cakes are being baked, or for that matter, when any other food is being cooked in that oven.

F. *What is the law if one forgot to take challah before the dough is baked?*
All the baked loaves should be put into one container to combine the baked doughs. Then cover it on top to make it appear as "one dough," making certain that the sides are covered by either the container or the covering. *Challah* is then taken with a brocha from one of the loaves.

G. *When else may one use the above procedure to take* challah *from already baked loaves?*
1. When the consistency was too wet prior to the baking (see I D, 2), provided it had the required amount of flour and liquid.
2. When several doughs made of the same grain and with similar ingredients are baked and each contains less than the required amount of flour, they may be combined and *challah* taken with a brocha from one of the loaves, provided that collectively they at least meet the minimum amount of flour (see I B 1-3).

3. If several doughs were baked, only one requiring *challah* to be taken from it with a brocho, the doughs can be combined and *challah* taken with a brocha from the dough which has the required amount. This then applies to and absolves the other doughs as well (see I C, 3 above).

H) *What if one forgot to take* challah *and becomes aware of the mistake on Shabbos or Yom Tov?*[2]

1. One may not take *challah* on Shabbos or Yom Tov (Exception, see #3 below). However, there is a difference regarding the use of the loaves or cakes on Shabbos and/or Yom Tov depending on whether they are from inside or outside the Land of Israel.

2. In the Land of Israel one may not use the baked loaves at all until after Shabbos or Yom Tov, when *challah* can be separated, and then the rest of the loaf can be used.

3. Outside the Land of Israel however, the baked loaves may be used on Shabbos or Yom Tov in the following way: First, a small amount should be left over from each loaf, then, after Shabbos or Yom Tov, a small piece is removed from each leftover slice, thereby fulfilling the precept of taking *challah*. Upon removing *challah* in this manner, a brocha is still said.

Note: If the actual kneading rather than only the baking is done on Yom Tov, *challah* may be taken on Yom Tov in the regular manner. This applies both in the Land of Israel and outside of Israel.

FOOTNOTES

[1]These measurements are based on the amounts given in **Shiurei Torah,** written by Horav Hagaon Rabbi Avroham Chaim Noeh, of blessed memory.

[2]Jewish Holidays on which some cooking for that day only is allowed: both days of Shavuos, both days of Rosh Hashana, first 2 days of Succos and the last 2 days of Succos, namely Shemini Atzeres and Simchas Torah. (On Pesach, of course, there is no bread at all, and on Yom Kippur there is no cooking.)

Blessings Over Food

Reciting blessings on food is an expression of gratitude to G-d, the Creator of all foods. It also serves to elevate the physical substance of the food to fulfill a higher purpose. (See also page 11.)

There are two categories of blessings said over foods—those that are said **before** and those that are said **after** eating foods.

Brocha Rishona (A Preceding Blessing):

A *brocha rishona* is a very short blessing said before partaking of any nourishment, acknowledging that G-d, the Creator of the universe, is the One Who provides us with all food.

There are six main brochos that come under this category, depending on the type of food eaten.

Brocha Achrona (An After Blessing):

A *brocha achrona* is said after the food is eaten, thanking G-d for the sustenance it provides. A *brocha achrona* is a little longer than a *brocha rishona*.

There are several blessings in this category, also depending on the type of food eaten.

Most brochos in general, and all brochos related to food, begin with these six words:
Boruch A-toh A-do-noi* E-lo-hai-nu* Me-lech Ho-o-lom
Blessed are You O G-d, our G-d, King of the Universe
With these words at the beginning of a brocha we acknowledge G-d as our G-d and as the source of all life and the ever-present Master of the Universe and all that is in it.

*Note: When practicing these brochos, say the words *Ha-Shem Elo-kai-nu* instead of the third and fourth words, so as not to say the name of G-d in vain. However, when teaching a child under *Bar* or *Bas Mitzvah* age how to say a brocha it is permissible to say the name of G-d.

I. The Different Brochos and When to Say Them

A. Brochos Rishonos: (Preceding Blessings)

Each brocha which precedes the eating of food begins with the above six words and concludes with a few words related to the particular type of food over which it is being made.

Below is a list of the conclusions of these brochos, each with its transliteration and examples of foods which require that brocha. Make sure to begin each brocha with the six first words cited above.

Brocha	Translation	Examples
1. *Ha-motzi Le-chem Min Ha-oretz*	Who brings forth bread from the earth	bread, challah, matzoh, rolls
2. *Bo-rai Mi-nay Mizonos*	Who created different kinds of sustenance	cakes, cereal—from wheat, barley, rye oat, spelt; cookies, macaroni, noodles, oatmeal
3. *Bo-rai P'ri Ha-go-fen*	Who created the fruits of the vine	wine, grape juice
4. *Bo-rai P'ri Ha-aitz*	Who created the fruits of the tree	All fruits from permanent trees as apples, oranges, pears, peaches, grapes, dried fruits
5. *Bo-rai P'ri Ha-adama*	Who created the fruits of the ground	All vegetables and greens; and some fruits such as bananas, honeydew, pineapple, watermelon
6. *She-hakol Ni-h'yoh Bi-D'voro*	That all came into being through His word	Candy, dairy, eggs, fish, liquids, meat, mushrooms, and anything else not covered by the five specific blessings above

There are two other brochos connected with foods which are said before eating. Begin the brochos with the first six words

7. *Asher Kid-shonu B'mitz-vo-sov V'tzi-vo-nu Al N'ti-las Yo-doy-im*	Who has sanctified us with His commandments and commanded us on the washing of the hands	

When it is said: Before eating bread it is necessary to wash one's hands ritually with a vessel, two or three times consecutively on each hand (depending on one's custom). If 2 ounces or more of bread will be eaten, this brocha is said. The hands are rubbed together before drying. As soon as this is completed, the blessing *Ha-motzi* over the bread should be made immediately, without any interruption. The two activities should be done in immediate sequence.

This is also the first of the early-morning brochos said each day for washing the hands as required immediately upon arising. This is done six times alternately beginning with the right hand (as opposed to 2-3 consecutively on each hand as when washing for bread). See a *Siddur* for the text of the other Morning Brochos.

8. **She-hech-i-yo-nu**   That He has kept us
   V'ki-mo-nu V'hi-   alive and sustained us and
   gi-o-nu, Lē-zman   enabled us to reach this time
   Ha-zeh

When it is said: Before eating a new fruit in the season (peaches, cantaloupe, etc.). This brocha is said preferably before the regular brocha for eating fruit is said, although some say it after.

B. Brochos Achronos (After Blessings)

There are three different *brochos achronos* which are said depending on the type of food eaten and whether a specific minimum amount was eaten (1 oz. food; 3-1/2 oz. liquid). The text of these brochos can be found in any *Siddur* (prayer book).

1. Birchas Hamozon (Blessing-After-A-Meal)

This is said after concluding a meal in which at least 1 ounce of bread was eaten, or after eating a sandwich, or bread in any form. It contains several paragraphs originally instituted by some of our great leaders in history, thanking G-d for giving us food.

Birchas Ma'ain Sholosh (Special After-Blessing for specific grains, wine, and specific fruits)
This is a shorter paragraph which is said after eating certain foods (see below). A few words at the beginning and end of the paragraph change to indicate the type of food eaten. The brocha contains the main themes of the first three blessings of the Blessings-After-A-Meal, and is usually printed in the *Siddur* right after the Blessings-After-A-Meal.
Al Hamichyo V'Al Hakalkolo (over sustenance) This refers to food (cakes, noodles, oatmeal, and most cereals, etc.) which have been prepared from at least one of the following grains—wheat, rye, oat, barley and spelt.
Al Hagefen V'Al Pri Hagefen (over wine)
Al Ho-aitz V'Al Pri Ho-aitz (over certain fruits) This refers to those fruits for which the Torah says that the Land of Israel is especially praised—olives, dates, grapes, figs and pomegranates.

3. Borai N'foshos (A short after-blessing)

This is a short sentence said after eating all types of food except those singled out for the special brochos listed above.

II. Laws Concerning Saying Brochos

A. Brochos Rishonos (Preceding Blessings)

1. A brocha is made even on the smallest amount of food.
2. One should know the correct brocha to say before beginning to say it over any food.
3. The food over which the blessing is being said should be in front of the person—preferably held in the right hand if the person is right-handed—when saying the blessing.
4. As the name of G-d is mentioned in each **brocha**, and we are not allowed to say G-d's name in vain, we should never say a **brocha** unnecessarily. (When practicing brochos, one should pronounce G-d's name as Ha-Shem Elokainu in place of the third and fourth words of the blessing.)
5. One should not talk from the moment of beginning a brocha over food, until the first mouthful of food has been swallowed.
6. When hearing a brocha being said by another person, one should answer *Amen* immediately after the conclusion of the blessing. (One should not say *Amen* after one's own brocha).
7. When bread is part of a meal, after washing the hands with a brocha, and saying the brocha *Ha-Motzi* over the bread, no other brochos need be said over food during the meal, with the following exceptions:
   a. If dessert is eaten, separate from bread, the appropriate brocha for that food is made.
   b. If wine is taken and *Kiddush* was not said before the meal, the brocha *Ha-gofen* (I A,3) must be said.
8. When bread is not eaten and when various foods which all require the same brochos are to be eaten at one sitting, the brocha is made over the preferred one of them, with the intention that this brocha applies to all the food of that kind.
9. When eating different kinds of food, each requiring a different brocha, there is a basic order in which the brochos are made. This is the order in which they are listed on the previous page (I A,1-6).

   Two exceptions are:

   a. We say *Kiddush* over wine before the **brocha** over bread or cake on Shabbos and Yom Tov.

   b. When eating foods belonging to the categories of both *Ha-aitz* and *Ha-adama* (see I A 4-5), one says the brocha over the preferred food first.   *Ex.*: fruit salad containing apples and bananas.
10. When a main dish contains different kinds of food mixed together which, if separate would each require a different blessing, the laws are determined by the following criteria:

   a. If one food is clearly the main food, then even though many different foods are mixed together, a blessing is made over the main food only.

   Ex. 1: Tuna salad in which vegetable bits are added. The brocha is made over the tuna which is considered the main food.

   Ex. 2: In a baked or cooked item (e.g., pie) containing dough from one of the five species of grain requiring the blessing *Mizonos* (see above), the dough is considered the prime ingredient and the preceding brocha *Mizonos* is said over the entire item and includes the other ingredients.

      b. If the different foods are equally important then the one in the majority is the criteria unless it is a mixture of solid and liquid which were not cooked together. Then, if the two foods belong to different categories, separate brochos are said: first on the solid and then on the liquid.

11. Concerning juices and mashed foods: most juices and totally strained foods require the brocha *She-hakol* (I-A-6). However, if the food is only mashed and is easily recognizable as being apples, pears, etc., the brocha which would be made over the food in its raw form is said.

12. When in doubt as to which brocha to say, one may:

a. wash hands ritually and eat bread, making the appropriate brocha on the bread. Then the food in question may be eaten during the course of the meal. If the food over which there is a question is a fruit, then at least the first bite should be eaten together with bread.

b. If in doubt as to which of two brochos should be said over a particular food, first eat a bite of two different foods, one for each brocha, having in mind also the food that is the subject of doubt. Then that food may be eaten.

c. If one said the brocha *She-hakol* over any food instead of its more specific brocha, then the food is absolved of further brochos. However, this alternative may only be used if there is a dispute among halachic authorities as to the proper brocha for this food. One should make an effort to be well-versed in the laws of brochos in order to know what to say when.

13. Before partaking of a new fruit in season, one says an additional brocha—*She-he-chiyono* (see I-A-8)

14. If one says the brocha *Ha-gefen* over wine, additional brochos over other liquids one drinks are not necessary.

B. Brochos Achronos (After-Blessings)

1. After-brochos should be said as soon as possible after finishing eating, and in the case of the special after-brochos (I-B-2) just as with the Blessings-After-A-Meal, it should be said in the same place where the food was eaten.

The Blessings-After-A-Meal

2. When bread is eaten, the entire Blessings-After-A-Meal is said.

3. The Blessings-After-A-Meal should be recited seated at the same place where one ate unless there was the intention at the time of the original brocha over the bread to complete the meal elsewhere.

4. Before saying the Blessings-After-A-Meal, it is necessary to slightly rinse the tips of the fingers and the lips. If this is done at the table, the water brought for this purpose is removed before the Blessings-After-A-Meal is begun. This water is called *Mayim Achronim* (the final water of the meal).

5. When 3 or more men (over age 13) recite the Blessings-After-A-Meal at one time, a short introductory paragraph is recited. This is known as a *Mezuman*.

6. On Shabbos, Yom Tov, Chanukah, Purim and Rosh Chodesh, there are special inserts to be said in the Blessings-After-A-Meal.

The Shorter After-Blessings

7. If more than one of the categories of food requiring a special after-brocho (see I B 2)—wine, grains or special fruits are eaten at one sitting, one says the appropriate after-brocho only once, but all categories over which it is said are specified in the beginning and end of the brocha.

8. On Shabbos, Yom Tov or Rosh Chodesh, an added sentence is said in the middle of this after-brocha.

9. When bread is not eaten and two different kinds of foods are eaten which require two different after-brochos (e.g. cookies and milk), then the special after-brochos for grains is said **first and is immediately followed by the short after-brocha.**

Exceptions: a) wine exempts all other liquids; b) the specified five fruits of the land exempt all other fruit. So, in both cases, only the special after-brocha need be said.

10. If one eats, at the same sitting, different foods requiring the same after-brocha (e.g. cheese and apples; or cake and doughnut), then only one after-brocha is said.

Pesach Preparation and Laws

As soon as Purim ends, the rush to prepare for Pesach starts, even though Pesach is still thirty days away. Why? This is due to the additional *Kashrus* laws of Pesach. (See pages 10 and 54–60.) Assuring ourselves of a "Kosher Pesach" involves the removal from one's possession and the non-use of any *chometz,* and the fulfilling of all the commandments concerning Pesach observance.

Only a brief outline is presented here. It is essential to consult a Rav well-versed in all the laws of Pesach, for further clarification and guidance in all these laws. To eat, own, or have any benefit from *chometz* constitutes a grave transgression.

Laws Concerning Chometz

What is *Chometz?*

Chometz is any wheat, barley, rye, oats or spelt, or any form of these grains such as flour, to which a leavening agent has been added, or which has come into contact with water or other liquids, and is left alone for eighteen minutes or longer. Such a mixture becomes forbidden since it has started to ferment, causing the flour to rise. Even where we do not know for sure that the grain has come in contact with water, unless we have proof to the contrary—meaning that the grain was guarded so that it didn't come into contact with water we always suspect that it is chometz.

In addition, various grains (rice, kasha, etc.) and beans (peas, lentils, beans, etc.) and corn are not eaten due to their similarity to actual chometz. However, Sephardic Jews have the *minhag* of allowing beans on Pesach.

The Prohibition Concerning Chometz on Pesach

The prohibition concerning *even the minutest particle* of chometz falls into the following general categories:

Not to Eat Any Chometz

All processed foods which are brought into the house must have a proper *hechsher* for Pesach. It is necessary that the *Kosher L'Pesach* label be written together with the name of a prominent Rabbi who has supervised its production.

Dishes Used for Chometz

All dishes, cutlery, etc. used for food on Pesach must be especially set aside from year to year for use on Pesach only, unless dishes and utensils are properly *kashered* for Pesach. Only some types of utensils may be *kashered* and the manner of *kashering* varies depending on the type of utensil (see page 330).

Not to Derive Any Pleasure From Chometz

This refers to using chometz in situations other than eating it, and this, too, is strictly forbidden. Examples:
1. not to feed chometz to an animal: dogs, cats, birds, fish
2. not to make paste from it
3. not to engage in any business with chometz
4. not to give chometz as a gift to a non-Jew

Not to Own Any Chometz

The Torah tells us that "no chometz may be seen or found" in our possession on Pesach. (Exodus 12:19; Exodus 13:7; Deut. 16:4) Therefore, any chometz left in one's house, store, or car or in any of one's possession must be disowned before Pesach by selling it to a non-Jew through the agency of a Rav.

Ridding the House of Chometz

To be sure that no chometz is left in our possession over Pesach, we must do an extremely thorough cleaning during the weeks preceding Pesach.

Every room and all things in one's house or office must be cleaned very well before Pesach. Extreme care should be taken when cleaning places in which it is known for sure that chometz has been during the past year. The car must be cleaned thoroughly.

Of course, the greatest care must be taken when cleaning the KITCHEN for Pesach—as this is where all chometz was kept and eaten during the entire year, and is also the main place where the Pesach food will be prepared. Therefore, all traces of chometz must be scrubbed out, and then all surfaces covered with aluminum foil, formica, or other covering.

The stove is thoroughly cleaned out. If possible, it is preferable that all parts that come in direct contact with the pots be special for Pesach, and kept aside from year to year. Such parts of a gas stove can usually be purchased in duplicate. In order to be able to bake on Pesach, one should also clean out the oven extremely well, and get a special oven insert for Pesach.

If it is not possible to get duplicates for the stove or an insert for the oven then the entire stove and oven and all removable parts must be *kashered* with a blow torch and made red hot. Consult with a Rav as to exactly how this is done.

It is also advisable that heavy aluminum foil be used to cover the area all around the stove thoroughout Pesach.

As soon as possible, clean out thoroughly one small room or area and set it aside for storage of packages for Pesach. Nothing is put in the kitchen until it is completely ready for Pesach, or *Pesachdig*, which usually does not occur until the eve of Erev Pesach.

The Selling of Chometz

When a non-Jew buys the chometz before Pesach, he is told the value of the chometz and the place where it is being held. He places a small deposit on it and the balance is considered as a loan to him. From the moment the non-Jew puts down a deposit on the chometz, he becomes the full owner of it. The balance should be paid within the following 9-10 days (depending upon which day before Pesach it is sold), but the option of paying out the balance is totally up to the purchaser. If he wishes to return it to the original owner instead and to get back his deposit, he may do so. (This is normally his choice.) The selling of chometz is legal and binding and *must* be done.

In order to avoid halachic doubts as to the validity of the sale, some authorities require a text of sale in which the procedure includes a guarantor who takes on the entire liability for paying the Jewish seller. In this way the original owner of the chometz has no further dealings with the non-Jewish purchaser and the guarantor—who never owned any of this chometz—anticipates payment from the purchaser. The purchaser has the option after Pesach to pay the amount due or return the merchandise, and so also if the seller is willing can do the same with the guarantor.

The selling of chometz sounds complicated but can usually be accomplished using a simple contract available through most Rabbis. Speak to a Rabbi in your area about this crucial aspect of Pesach preparations.

The Time in Which the Prohibition of Chometz Takes Effect

No Chometz may be eaten after ⅓ of the day before Pesach. The time varies slightly from year to year but usually comes out approximately to 9:30 A.M. in New York City—check Hebrew calendar for precise local time. The sale of the chometz and the burning of the chometz (see below) must be completed no later than one hour after this time.

All chometz utensils must be brought together in a room or closet(s). These designated places are then sealed off with tape or locked with a key. These areas are included in the sale of chometz as described above and may not be opened or entered.

Erev Pesach: The Search and the Burning

All cleaning and scrubbing must be completely finished by the night before Pesach. On that night, once we are confident that the house is thoroughly clean, and all chometz put away, we are obligated to formally search the house (and office and car) for chometz in all the rooms, in the closets, on all shelves, behind furniture, and so forth. The searching for chometz is customarily done by the head of the household, but may be done by a woman in the absence of the head of the household. The blessing (see *Hagadah* or *Siddur*) is recited in front of all the members of the household who intend to help. They should answer *Amen* in order to be included in the blessing.

Ten pieces of bread are placed throughout the house to be "found" during the search. They should be wrapped in paper or other wrapping to prevent crumbs. It is wise to write down all the hiding places of the chometz so that one cannot forget where they are! The search is traditionally conducted using a candle, with the use of a feather, wooden spoon and paper bag for collecting any chometz found. The search for chometz represents the culmination of a huge effort and a highlight of the year for the whole family.

After the search is completed, the head of the household says aloud the paragraph *Kol Chamirah* (see *Hagadah* or *Siddur*)—verbally disowning any chometz that might have been overlooked and is in the house. It is important that one understand clearly this paragraph when saying it. If one does not understand the original Aramaic, one must recite it in a language one knows.

All the chometz that was found during the search and any chometz left over from the morning breakfast must be burned before approximately 5 hours into the morning, usually around 10:30 A.M. (for the exact time from year to year in each location, consult your Rabbi or Jewish calendar) and another declaration annulling all chometz similar to the one said the night before is said again. By this time all chometz that we know of in the house has already been sold to a non-Jew. If, G-d forbid, any chometz is found in the house after Pesach begins, it must be burned immediately, unless the day is Yom Tov (1st, 2nd, 7th or 8th day) or Shabbos, in which case it is covered during those days and should be burned at the first possible moment, on *Chol Hamoed* or after Pesach. If one finds an ounce or more of chometz, one should burn this chometz and say the appropriate brocha.

When Pesach Begins Saturday Night

When the first night of Pesach occurs on Saturday night, many complications arise. One must know the latest possible time of searching for, selling, and burning the chometz—for these are obviously not done within the usual twenty-four hour period before Pesach, as this comes on Shabbos when such activities are prohibited. A Rav will be glad to provide this information, as well as answers to all *halachic* questions that arise concerning the observance of Shabbos on the day before Pesach (e.g. eating chalah and getting rid of crumbs, what utensils to use, the latest time permissible to eat chometz, etc.).

Laws and Customs Concerning Foods Eaten on Pesach

Categories of Foods to be Eaten on Pesach.

Once the house is free of all chometz, we might wonder what there is left to eat on Pesach. The fact is that a large selection of foods is available for use; e.g. meat, chicken, eggs, dairy, fish, fresh fruit and vegetables, and some processed foods (see paragraphs below).

When using these foods make sure that none of them come into any contact with chometz or *chometzdig* utensils. Therefore when ordering fish or meat, be sure to tell the butcher or fishman that you are making your Pesach order, and that he should prepare the order for you in his special Pesach equipment.

Fruits and Vegetables

There is a widespread custom to peel fruits and vegetables wherever possible to avoid any part of the food that may have come in contact with chometz or been greased or sprayed.

Dried fruits used on Pesach must have a Kosher for Pesach insignia because their processing often involves actual chometz. Canned fruit and vegetables which are permissable must also have a Kosher for Pesach certification in order to be used on Pesach.

You might be surprised to see that, although the foods available for use on Pesach are limited, a varied menu is still possible. You might try different types of soup (a popular Passover soup is hot or cold beet soup known as borscht). There is a variety of ways to prepare meat, chicken, and fish. Vegetables and fruit can be served raw, in salads, or cooked. Fruit compote is popular as a Pesach dessert.

Packaged Goods

Any processed food that is brought into our homes on Pesach must bear the certification that this food is Kosher for Pesach. Such a *hechsher* should be accompanied by the name of the Rabbi who supervised its processing or be an accepted hechsher. The certification should be an integral part of the product's label rather than being stuck on after the product is packaged. There are some people who avoid the use of practically all processed foods.

We would like to bring the following to the attention of our readers. We are all familiar with the "new look" many supermarkets and groceries get the month before Pesach. All these tempting and delicious foods suddenly fill the special shelves reserved for Pesach products. It seems there is hardly a food not available with a kashrus certification for Pesach. Packages of cakes, cookies, candies, and all other processed foods are stacked on the shelves.

With the most stringent precautions taken by each individual in one's own home, it seems somewhat out-of-line with the atmosphere of Pesach, to allow ourselves to indulge in so many types of processed goods. It is difficult to assume that the strict measures necessary for Pesach are always totally enforced and upheld in factories which might employ hundreds of workers. Certainly this is not to undermine the kashrus quality of many reputable food manufacturing companies known for observing the highest standards of kashrus laws for Pesach. Nor do we mean to infer that no processed goods are brought into the home. Such basics as coffee, tea, salt, etc., with a reliable hechsher for Pesach are used by most people.

Yet some people habitually stock up on packaged foods as if they were afraid of a coming food shortage. Pesach lasts only eight days and with a bit of care and special effort you'll be able to prepare an appetizing variety of foods at every meal. Your family will certainly appreciate the special fresh, home-made taste of all these things, and the extra attention that goes into them.

Medicines and Cosmetics

Drugstore items very often contain chometz-based ingredients. Many brands of commonly used products are available however with a hechsher for use on Pesach. A Rav usually works together with a pharmacist in determining which products may be used and should be consulted before Pesach about items that it may be necessary to use during Pesach. Many detailed laws are involved, especially concerning the use of medicine for ill persons and a Rav should be consulted for individual cases.

Matzoh

Matzoh is, of course, a classic Pesach food; especially since there is a special mitzvah attached to eating it on Pesach at the Seder. Not all matzohs are Kosher for Pesach, however. The label on the box will always indicate whether it may be used on Pesach or not.

Strictest measures are taken in the baking of matzohs, with the dough being constantly worked on to avoid any lapse of time which would cause the dough to rise (even without a leavening agent). Matzoh carefully guarded throughout the complete process of its preparation is called *Shmura Matzoh* (guarded matzoh).

There are different degrees of *Shmura Matzoh*. Some people use only such matzoh which is made of flour which was watched from the moment the wheat was reaped from the field to make sure it never came in contact with water or other liquids from the time it was reaped. Such matzoh is called *Shmura M'sha'as K'tzera*, guarded from the time of harvest.

Another type of *Shmura Matzoh* is made from flour which is watched from the time it is ground. This is known as *Shmura Ma'sha'as T'china* (guarded from the time of grinding).

If one cannot obtain *Shmura Matzoh* for eating during all of Pesach, one should at least use it at the Seder, and particularly in fulfilling the mitzvah of eating matzoh on the Seder night. Shmura Matzoh is expensive as it is hand-baked and requires so much careful attention, but it is the only matzoh with which one completely fulfills the mitzvoh of eating matzoh. Further, it is said to nourish our power of faith; this matzoh, eaten by our ancestors before their dough could rise, testified to their faith in G-d's ability to provide for them in the wilderness. Shmura Matzoh, so lovingly and carefully baked, also has a delicious taste and texture unduplicated by factory matzohs.

Customs Concerning G'broks

Many people have the strong custom of keeping matzoh from coming into contact with any water or liquid even *after* it is baked, although already-baked flour cannot continue to rise. The reason for this precaution is that if even a minute amount of flour was not completely baked, and remains somewhat raw, it can rise as soon as it comes in contact with water or any liquid. People who observe this extra precautionary measure do so to avoid the slightest possibility of, G-d forbid, eating even a tiny amount of leavened dough.

Other customs allow the mixing of already-baked matzoh, (or matzoh-meal) with liquids. This custom is known as eating *g'broks*, matzoh dipped into liquid. This is why some people cook and eat matzoh-balls on Pesach and others do not. On the eighth day of Pesach, however, nearly everyone eats *g'broks*, as the eighth day is a Rabbinical injunction (see Calendar, page 71).

Cakes

No flour whatsoever may be used in even the smallest quantity to make cakes and pastries on Pesach. All Pesach cakes and pastries are made from one or a combination of the following staples: matzoh-meal, potato starch, and ground nuts.

Those who have the custom not to eat *g'broks* do not eat any mixture of matzoh-meal and liquids. Some avoid eating any type of cake mixture altogether.

Praiseworthy are Those Who are Extra-Cautious

Our Sages tell us concerning the preparations made for insuring a "Kosher Pesach" that the stricter one's precautions, the more praiseworthy it is. For, to eat even the smallest amount of chometz constitutes a very serious violation of the Torah.

Therefore, because of all precautionary measures taken, many people have taken upon themselves the custom of not eating outside their homes at all on Pesach, not even in the homes of relatives or friends in whose homes they eat during the rest of the year. One who has an appreciation of religious values can understand such a custom, and will not be offended when someone refuses to accept an invitation to eat in his house on Pesach.

The Recipes in this Book

Because of all the above precautions, and the many different customs concerning foods eaten on Pesach, we have not included a special Pesach recipe section in this book. We hope that the above guide will help you in deciding what foods to prepare for your family during the days of Pesach.

Important Note: Consult a Rav—the above pages contain only a short review of some Pesach laws. For further clarification and more details, it is of utmost importance that you consult and be guided by a Rav who is thoroughly versed in these laws.

Details on how to prepare the Seder Plate and more about Pesach are included in the Yom Tov section (pages 57-59).

Glossary of Hebrew Terms
for the Kosher Kitchen, the Sabbath, and Holidays

The terms in this glossary are often explained at greater length in their appropriate sections. Some terms are used very often and cannot be translated and explained in all sections. Names of the holidays, Simchas, traditional foods, and other individual words which are translated and/or explained in the text are not included.

The majority of the following terms are related to Kashrus, Shabbos, Yom Tov, and Jewish Law in general.

AMEN: It is true. These words are said by one who hears a brocha (blessing), thereby acknowledging the truth of the blessing.

ASUR: (See Mutar-Asur)

BENTCHING: Blessings-After-A-Meal. Said upon concluding a meal in which bread was eaten. (A shorter blessing is said after eating foods without bread.)

BENTCHING LICHT: (See Licht Bentching).

BISHUL AKUM or BISHUL NOCHRI: Cooking by a non-Jew. A Jew is not allowed to eat certain types of food which are cooked entirely by a non-Jew even if they were cooked in kosher utensils.

BLECH: An aluminum or asbestos sheet which is put over a gas or electric fire before Shabbos and remains there until the end of Shabbos. Food may be eaten warm on Shabbos if it was already cooked and placed on the blech BEFORE Shabbos.

BLOOD SPOT: A blood spot in an egg, whether it is raw, cooked or fried, renders that egg unkosher.

BODEK: To inspect and examine. This refers to the inspection of green vegetables and certain grains and fruits before using them to be sure there are no worms or insects.

BROCHA: A blessing made before and after partaking of foods or drink. Brochos are also said when observing certain precepts of the Torah.

CHALLAH: 1—Special loaves of bread, used on Shabbos and Yom Tov. These loaves are often braided or formed into different shapes. 2—A small piece of dough removed from the complete dough before baking and burned.

CHOL HAMOED: The non-Yom Tov days of the holidays of Succos and Pesach. On these days (unless one day is Shabbos), a limited amount of necessary work may be done. Nevertheless, the day is still celebrated in a festive manner, and special prayers are added to the services.

CHOLOV YISROEL: Milk supervised by a Jew from the beginning of the milking process onwards. This term also refers to dairy products made from such milk.

CHOMETZ: Leavening, or any food containing leavening, or any mixture of grains or flour with water which is left to stand for a minimum of 18 minutes. Even a minute quantity may not be used on Pesach or be found in the possession of a Jew at that time.

CHUMRAH: A stringent measure taken in the observance of a mitzvah—going beyond the call of duty.

DIN: (See Halacha)

ERETZ YISROEL: The Land of Israel. Many laws apply only in the Land of Israel, and sometimes there is also a halachic difference on the observance of some laws whether in the Land of Israel or Chutz L'Oretz (outside Israel). For example, an extra day of Yom Tov is observed Chutz L'Oretz.

EREV: The day preceding the onset of Shabbos

or Yom Tov. For example: Friday is Erev Shabbos. If a Yom Tov starts on Tuesday evening, then Monday night and Tuesday are Erev of that Yom Tov.

ERUV: An enclosure meeting specified requirements, enabling one to carry outdoors on Shabbos. There are several types of eruvim for different circumstances.

ERUV TAVSHILIN: When Shabbos is the second day of the holiday or the day after the second day of the holiday, it becomes necessary to cook on Yom Tov for Shabbos. This can be done only when a special preparation of foods is set aside before Yom Tov. This preparation, the Eruv Tavshilin, consists of one cooked and one baked food, over which a blessing is said. Under regular circumstance one my not cook on one day of Yom Tov for the second day Yom Tov.

FLEISHIG: Any food containing meat or fowl or their derivatives. It is necessary to wait six hours and rinse the mouth after eating such foods before eating milk products. See *milchig*.

GLATT KOSHER: 1—Meat which comes from a kosher, properly slaughtered animal, that upon its examination after the slaughtering has been found completely free of any imperfections whatsoever. Simply "kosher" is when some of these imperfections are found, yet declared permissible. 2—The term "glatt kosher" is also commonly used to declare certain foods, restaurants, etc. completely kosher with strict supervision.

HALACHA: A law of the Torah. (synonym: Din)

HAMOTZI: The identifying word in the blessing over bread. Must be preceded by the washing of hands.

HAVDALAH: Separation. A prayer and ceremony at the conclusion of the Shabbos and/or Yom Tov proclaiming the separation between days and things which are holy, and those that are mundane. During the Havdalah, we also pray that the rest of the week be blessed.

HASHGACHA: (See Mashgiach)

HECHSHER: A certification by a Rav that a food has been supervised throughout its processing, verifying that the food does not contain any non-kosher ingredients and was processed according to laws of kashrus.

KASHERING: (Different from Koshering) The process by which a non-kosher utensil is made kosher. This also applies to a vessel which was originally kosher, but which has become non-kosher.

KIDDUSH: Sanctification. At the beginning of a Shabbos or Yom Tov meal we proclaim the holiness of the day by saying a special blessing. This is usually done over a cup of wine, or over the two loaves of challah.

KOSHER: Food which is permissible for consumption according to the Jewish Dietary Laws.

KOSHERING: The process of salting a kosher and ritually slaughtered animal according to dietary laws, thus making it fit and permissible for use.

K'ZAYIS: "Like the size of an olive," approximately one ounce. The minimal amount of food which makes it necessary to say a blessing after eating. This is a common size referred to in many *laws* concerning food.

LICHT BENTCHING: Lighting of the Candles. It is the obligation of every married woman and customary for a single girl from approximately the age of three to light candles in honor of Shabbos and Yom Tov.

MARIS AYIN: To the appearance of the eye. This usually refers to being careful not to eat or do something which, although it may be permissible, might look like a forbidden act to an on-looker. For example, non-dairy creamer and margarine should be served in their wrappers at a meat meal.

MASHGIACH: A person in charge of supervising for kashrus the preparation of food at all levels of production, whether by a factory, caterer, butcher shop, etc. The Mashgiach should be a G-d fearing, knowledgeable, person. HASHGACHA is the noun, meaning "supervision."

MAYIM ACHRONIM: Last waters. Before saying the blessings at the conclusion of a meal, one should wash off the fingertips and the lips.

MELOCHA: Creative work. This refers to the thirty-nine catagories of work forbidden on Shabbos. Most melochos are also forbidden on Yom Tov.

MEZUMAN: When three or more men over Bar-Mitzvah age partake of a meal together one of them leads the rest of the people in a few introductory sentences to the Bentching, as an added honor to G-d.

MIKVAH: Ritualarium. A gathering of natural waters of specified dimensions, used for spiritual purification.

MILCHIG: Dairy. Any food containing milk or milk derivatives. It is necessary to wait at least half an hour (some wait a full hour) before eating meat products. See *Fleishig.*

MINHAG: A Jewish custom. Minhagim exist in all areas of Jewish law. Those hallowed by tradition are precious and should be preserved. Some customs related to the Kosher Kitchen are: (1) number of times the hands are ritually washed before the eating of bread, and (2) various food served at various occasions, e.g. chickpeas at a Sholom Zochor.

MINYAN: A group of ten or more males over the age of 13. A minyan is needed before certain prayers can be said, such as Kaddish and the Seven Blessings during the first week of marriage.

MITZVAH: A commandment of the Torah. This refers to all the *dos* as well as *don'ts* found in the Torah, amounting to 613 in all.

MUTAR-ASUR: These two terms mean Allowed and Forbidden, respectively, and are common halachic terms, used especially in areas of Kashrus.

N'TILAS YODAYIM: Washing the hands. It is necessary to wash one's hands ritually and to say the appropriate blessing: (1) when awakening in the morning, one pours water from a cup three times alternately on each hand, (2) before eating bread, one pours water 2 or 3 times consecutively (depending on the custom) over each hand.

PAS AKUM-PAS PALTER: Bread or cake which was completely and exculsively baked by a non-Jew. This as a rule may not be used. However, in places where it is very difficult to get baked goods baked by a Jew, it is permissible to eat kosher bread from a non-Jewish bakery (not an individual) if certain specific conditions are fulfilled. Such bread is called *pas palter.*

PAREVE: Food containing neither meat nor milk derivatives and which may be used at either meat or milk meals, e.g., fish, eggs, juices, fruit and vegetables.

RAV: A Rabbi qualified to make fine judgments in problems and questions of Jewish law. A *sha'alah* should be brought only to a Rav.

SAGES: The term Sages refers to the great Rabbis who lived in the time of the Second Holy Temple, and several hundred years afterwards. The sayings of these Sages are often recorded in the Mishnah and Talmud.

SHA'ALAH: A question in Jewish Law. For example, to find out if a certain food is kosher or not, a sha'alah should be asked of a Rav. It is better to ask rather than risk making an error.

SHABBOS: The seventh day of the week which commences with sundown on Friday evening, and ends after 3 stars appear on Saturday night. It is observed as a holy day and as a day of rest, in which no work may be done. It is also a day of great celebration and joy.

SHECHITAH: The manner of slaughtering kosher animals or fowls as prescribed in the Torah. The man skillfully trained to perform shechitah is called a *shochet.*

SHEHECHIYONU: Blessing of thanks to G-d for bringing us to a new season; said on Holidays and when eating a new fruit of the season.

SHOLOSH REGOLIM: The three pilgrimages when Jews inhabited the Land of Israel, before the current Exile. All Jewish males over thirteen were commanded to come to celebrate the three holidays of Pesach, Shavuos, and Succos, in the place first of the *Mishkan* (Portable Sanctuary) and later in Jerusalem at the Holy Temple.

SEDER: Order. Often used to refer to the ritual gathering and meal which takes place on the first two nights of Pesach.

SEUDA: Meal. Refers to the Shabbos and Yom Tov meals and also to the festive-like meals which accompany mitzvohs such as weddings and circumcisions; such meals are known as *Seudas Mitzvah.*

SHMITTAH: Unattended. This refers to the laws for the land in Israel, which must be left free every seventh year. We may not eat any food processed by a Jew in Israel during a *shmittah* year.

SHULCHAN ARUCH: The Code of Jewish Law. It contains a lengthier description of all the laws, explaining in exact detail how the laws are to be observed, and various situations related to these laws.

SIMCHA: Rejoicing. Often used to refer to the celebration of a special event.

SIDDUR: A Prayer Book. A prayer book contains all the prayers to be said during the week, on Shabbos and Holidays, and other occasions. A list of brochos and the bentching can also be found in the Siddur.

STAM YAYIN: See YAYIN NESACH.

TOIVELING: The process of totally immersing food utensils made of glass or metal into a mikvah (ritualarium) before they are used. Other utensils, such as enamel and china must also be toiveled, without a brocha.

TORAH: The Written and Oral Law. Also used more specifically to refer to the Five Holy Books given by G-d to Moses, which contain in them the happenings of the world from the beginning of Creation until the Jews were about to enter Israel. Every word and even every letter contains many teachings for us as explained by our Rabbis. It also contains the seeds of all the laws by which we live.

TREFAH: Literally means torn. This refers (1) to an animal which has a torn limb and is not to be used, and (2) (commonly) to non-kosher food or utensils.

TREIBERING: The removing of certain forbidden veins and fats from an animal.

TRUMAH U'MA'ASER: Before any food grown in Eretz Yisroel may be eaten, a certain small portion (t'rumah) of the product must be separated and given to the Kohanim and then another small portion to the Tribe of Levi (ma'aser).

YAYIN NESACH: This refers to wine, grape juice, or drinks containing wine or grapes which has been touched by a non-Jew, once the seal of the wine has been opened. It is technically known as STAM YAYIN. Such wine is not permitted.

YOM TOV: A Jewish Holiday. A chart of all the holidays can be found on p. 72.

Z'MIROS: Songs. At the Shabbos and Yom Tov meals, it is customary for the members at the table to sing songs from the Siddur about the Shabbos and Holidays. *Nigunim* are tunes without words.

Mitzvohs : An Everlasting Link

Throughout history, the Jews have drawn strength and inspiraton—indeed, their very existence—from Torah and observance of its mitzvohs. The word *Torah* is derived from the word *hora'ah*—guidance or teaching. The Torah has been our cherished guide to every aspect of life. It has also been the strong unifying force among all Jews in all places.

The word *mitzvah* has several meanings. It is a *commandment* given to us by G-d in the Torah. It is also related to the word *tzavta*—attachment. There are six hundred and thirteen mitzvohs in the Torah, each one a means of binding ourselves closer to G-d.

When each Jew fulfills all the mitzvohs which apply to him, the result is that all Jews everywhere benefit and share in the positive spiritual and physical effects created by the fulfillment of each mitzvah.

Of the six hundred and thirteen mitzvohs, 248 are "positive" mitzvohs requiring a specific act in deed, speech or thought, and 365 are "negative" mitzvohs involving prohibitions against specific actions. Together they comprise a totality corresponding to all the different parts of the human body. Performance of the mitzvohs thus binds our very limbs and sinews to the Creator.

All of the negative and most of the positive mitzvohs are obligatory for both men and women, while most positive precepts which must be fulfilled within a specified time limit are obligatory only for men. This does not represent a lesser opportunity for the Jewish woman to attach herself to G-d or express her Jewishness, but indicates that the ability to fulfill one's purpose in the realm of *time* is for the man dependent upon the external acts and discipline of the mitzvohs of set time, while the woman is not in need of these additional reminders of G-d's presence in the world. Putting on *tefillin*, wearing *tzitzis*, and eating in the Succah are examples of mitzvohs of set time.

Those mitzvohs which we do not fulfill in deed are nevertheless constantly relevant. The idea of serving G-d with one's heart and mind, for example, is embodied in the wearing of tefillin but is applicable to all Jews—just as the idea of bringing the first-fruits of one's crop to the altar, or offering one's best to G-d, is relevant today just as it was in the times of the Holy Temple.

Further, the Torah which commmands the man to put on tefillin entrusts the woman with the mission of raising Jewish children in the ways of the Torah. In creating an environment for this and imbuing her children with the very lofty values of Judaism she is on call by the Torah literally throughout the day. The unqualified obligation to fulfill certain mitzvohs within a limited period of time would interfere at times with her higher, and also most unrelenting responsibility towards her family. The Torah therefore exempts her from these mitzvohs.

In addition, the Torah gives to the woman three special mitzvohs which are uniquely hers to fulfill.

1. Candlelighting in honor of the Shabbos and Yom Tov
2. The Separation of Challah
3. The Laws of Family Purity

(Men share in these mitzvohs to the extent that candlelighting and the separation of *challah* are done by the husband or another member of the family in the women's absence, and in that the Laws of Family Purity are also the responsibility of the husband although the prime responsibility rests with the woman.)

The special connection women have with these mitzvohs has been discussed in their respective chapters. These three mitzvohs are not only a means by which women attain a high level of holiness; they are in a sense the focal points of three of the most basic observances of Judaism: the observance of Shabbos and Yom Tov, kashrus, and the Laws of Family Purity. These are keys to the spiritual survival of the Jewish home and thus the entire Jewish nation.

Through lighting the Shabbos and Yom Tov candles and making all the household preparations beforehand, the woman ushers into her home the spirit of the Shabbos and Yom Tov. Jews have drawn spiritual strength and sustenance from the Shabbos every week, and inspiration from the Yomim Tovim throughout the year.

By separating *challah,* the woman openly demonstrates her belief that G-d provides all physical sustenance. She separates a portion of the dough, according to G-d's Will, as commanded in the Torah. Only then does she use the remaining dough for her personal needs— that which is offered for holiness comes first. Through this small but significant act the woman elevates the complete dough, showing that her use of food is in accordance with the Will of G-d.

So it is with all the laws of kashrus. By observing these laws we express our belief that G-d is the Creator of all things including food, and that we may use only those foods allowed to us by G-d, and only in the manner prescribed by G-d. As explained several times throughout this book, by observing the laws of kashrus we also affect an elevation in the physical world.

By observing the Laws of Family Purity, by regulating her married life in accordance with the Divine Will, the woman brings spiritual strength into her home. Every month the woman strengthens her personal connection to G-d as she faithfully carries out all the laws with which G-d has entrusted her, and an added spiritual quality enters the home.

In the Torah G-d did not state the reason for observing laws such as those of Family Purity. They are to be fulfilled simply because they are His Will. Yet many benefits have been observed among those who follow them. To name just a few: increased harmony between husband and wife, a stronger famly unit, refined qualities in children, a highly moral, ethical and strong nation, and also a low incidence of certain diseases.

We hope that *The Spice and Spirit of Kosher Jewish Cooking* has enhanced the reader's appreciation of Jewish life in general. We sincerely hope that in reading the book through, and in experiencing some of the beauty of the Jewish life brought into the home, the reader will be imbued with a desire to increase her knowledge of Torah and all its mitzvohs.

Index